CW00696801

Nitrous Oxide
Performance Handbook

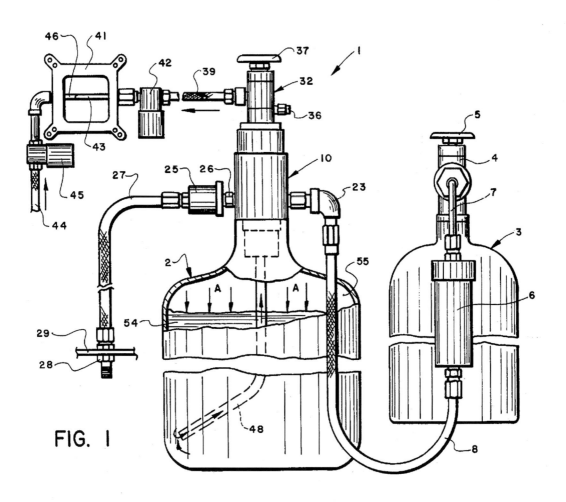

FIG. I

By Jeff Hartman

motorbooks

Dedication

This book is dedicated to my big brother,
Andy, who always treated me well and instilled in me
a love of reading, knowledge, and "what makes it tick."

First published in 2009 by Motorbooks, an imprint of MBI Publishing Company, 400 First Avenue North, Suite 300, Minneapolis, MN 55401 USA

Copyright © 2009 by Jeff Hartman

All rights reserved. With the exception of quoting brief passages for the purposes of review, no part of this publication may be reproduced without prior written permission from the Publisher.

The information in this book is true and complete to the best of our knowledge. All recommendations are made without any guarantee on the part of the author or Publisher, who also disclaim any liability incurred in connection with the use of this data or specific details.

We recognize, further, that some words, model names, and designations mentioned herein are the property of the trademark holder. We use them for identification purposes only. This is not an official publication.

Motorbooks titles are also available at discounts in bulk quantity for industrial or sales-promotional use. For details write to Special Sales Manager at MBI Publishing Company, 400 First Avenue North, Suite 300, Minneapolis, MN 55401 USA.

To find out more about our books, join us online at www.motorbooks.com.

Library of Congress Cataloging-in-Publication Data

Hartman, Jeff, 1952-
  Nitrous oxide performance handbook.
     p. cm.
  ISBN 978-0-7603-2624-4 (pbk. : alk. paper)
  1. Nitrous oxide injection systems (Fuel systems) 2. Automobiles--Motors--Fuel injection systems. 3. Motor fuels--Additives.
  I. Title.
  TL214.F78H373 2009
  629.25'3--dc22

2009007918

ISBN-13: 978-0-7603-2624-4

Editor: Kris Palmer
Designer: Danielle Smith
Illustrators: Wren Bentley, Whitney Stofflet

Printed in Singapore

On the cover: What's better than a bottle of nitrous? Two bottles of nitrous. And a high-tech, wet, multi-port injection system to go with them.

On the back cover: The telltale plume of a nitrous oxide purge system. This is the car whose engine and nitrous bottles are seen on this book's front cover.

About the author
Jeff Hartman is the author of *How to Tune and Modify Engine Management Systems*; *Fuel Injection: Installation, Performance, Tuning, Modification*; and the *Turbocharging Performance Handbook*, all from Motorbooks. Hartman lives in Austin, Texas.

Contents

Chapter 1
War Birds, Air Enrichment, and the Origins of Nitrous Oxide Injection

Piston engines have been starving for oxygen ever since Nikolaus Otto's progenitor four-stroke cycle engine first chugged to life back in 1876. Later, when gasoline-fueled internal-combustion engines were installed in aircraft in the years after 1903, it became clear that the thinner air of higher altitude only made matters worse: Piston engine military aircraft clawing for an altitude advantage in air combat were down to 50 percent power by 18,000 feet.

Fighter air combat effectiveness has always been a function of an aircraft's ability to operate at very high speeds and high altitude, which requires as much power as possible. The twin engines of a fully loaded modern F-4 fighter jet achieve an amazing 36,620 horsepower running on afterburner at 55,000 feet at mach 1.8, which is a testament to the awesome power available from hydrocarbon fuels. Just the *vapor* left behind in an emptied 1-gallon gasoline canister contains the power of two sticks of dynamite. A single gallon of gasoline contains the energy equivalent of 2,700 horsepower for one minute or 162,000 horsepower for one second. Fuel is not typically the constraint when it comes to making power.

The trouble is, it takes air to burn fuel, and air is scarce. Or at least it's scarce inside an internal combustion engine. By weight, you need at least 10 to 15 times as much air as gasoline to optimize combustion pressures in an ordinary piston engine. Burning a single gallon of gasoline requires nearly 10,000 gallons of air at standard pressure! Unfortunately, throwing more fuel in an engine starving for air is worse than useless because burning a hydrocarbon such as gasoline involves a precise chemical reaction that ultimately transpires in fixed proportions of fuel and oxygen, meaning that pouring in large amounts of additional fuel will not make more power. What it will make is black smoke and pollution, not to mention diminished power as surplus fuel molecules get in the way of efficient, complete combustion. As mixtures approach rich flammability limits, flame fronts from a spark plug cannot be sustained and the engine will gasp and die.

One reason that combustion requires so much air is that only the *oxygen* in air will actually burn anything, and air is only 23.2 percent oxygen by weight (20.9 percent by volume). Air, in fact, is a well-mixed stew of oxygen and what might

German BF109 Fighter, some of which were equipped with nitrous oxide injection by the end of World War II. All belligerents were desperately looking for ways to increase the performance of combat aircraft.

Early piston engines had terrible specific power, and the first air-supercharged engine applications arrived in the first decade of the twentieth century.

Sir Humphrey Davy invented the first practical use for nitrous oxide in 1815, the Davy miner's lamp, which used nitrous as an oxidizer in a lamp less likely to trigger underground methane explosions. Davy became addicted to inhaling nitrous oxide, "laughing gas," and died young.

be called "inactive ingredients"—78 percent nitrogen gas and tiny amounts of argon, water vapor, and trace amounts of the greenhouse gases carbon dioxide, carbon monoxide, methane, oxides of nitrogen, and so forth. Because nitrogen gas (N_2) is virtually impossible to burn (and when it does, it's an endothermic reaction that *absorbs* heat!), the presence of nitrogen in air serves mainly to slow down combustion by getting in the way of oxygen reacting with fuel (though nitrogen gas heated by surrounding combustion does expand and contribute to cylinder pressure).

EARLY ENGINE BOOSTING

A hundred years ago at the dawn of the automotive age, piston engines universally had very poor specific power. The peak output of an early 2.9-liter Model T Ford, for example, was a miserable 20 horsepower at 1,600 rpm! Engineers, inventors, and early racers looking for ways to augment horsepower confronted a fact of life that is still true today: Even the most efficient normal-charged piston engines running on air eventually experience air famine at full throttle. One obvious approach to delivering more power where required was increasing engine displacement to enormous levels. Early John Deere Model A tractors were equipped with huge *two-cylinder* engines displacing 5.26 liters that were capable of 19 to 34 horsepower, depending on fuel. But large-displacement

engines tend to be big and heavy, which is impractical for many vehicular applications, particularly aircraft.

It soon became clear that the trick to increasing horsepower in a piston engine was to charge the cylinders with more *oxygen* than was available in air at ordinary atmospheric pressure—at which point it would be simple to richen up the charge mixture with additional gasoline. An obvious way to increase charge oxygen was to force-feed the powerplant with pressurized air. Shortly after the turn of the nineteenth century, a number of inventors realized that air pump designs previously used to supply air for mines, forges, and foundries could potentially be modified to pressurize the intake systems of internal combustion engines. As is so often the case, the cutting edge of the new air-supercharging technology would be racing and warfare.

In 1901, Sir Dugald Clark's experiments proved conclusively that regardless of the native volumetric efficiency (VE) of an engine induction system, increasing the pressure of air entering the throttle would improve VE, pack more charge in the cylinders and increase power. In 1908, American Lee Chadwick entered a supercharged car in the Wilkes-Barre, Pennsylvania, hillclimb—and won!—making this not only the first supercharged car in competition, but the first to win. Chadwick campaigned the car extensively over the next two years with great success, and it was the first car to officially exceed 100 miles per hour. At this point, despite his success, Chadwick lost interest in automobile research and development (R&D) and moved on to other pursuits, and it would be another 12 years before anyone in the United States continued with further development of the supercharger. In Europe, Georges Sizaire and Marc Birkigt were experimenting with centrifugal and piston-type supercharging for auto racing in 1911 and 1912—and then World War I ended all car racing in Europe in 1914 for at least five years.

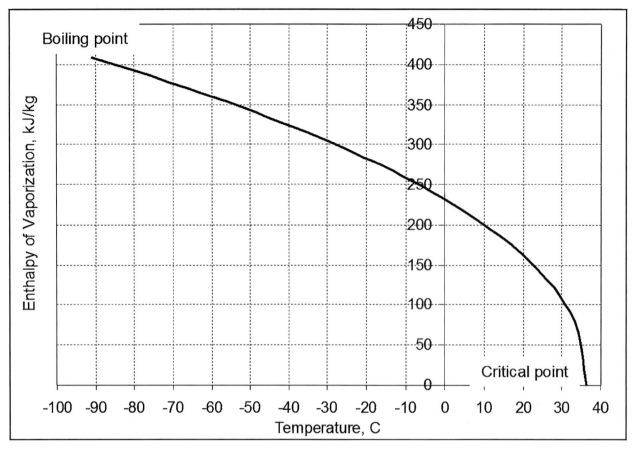

Vaporization heat as a function of temperature

American scientists investigating nitrous oxide for chemical supercharging confronted the fact that compressed nitrous oxide liquefied at room temperature when compressed above 750 psi, but when liquid nitrous is boiled, it had a vastly powerful refrigeration effect from the "heat of vaporization." Chilled intake air increases engine volumetric efficiency and horsepower, but a boiling refrigerant like nitrous can be difficult to control during the chemical supercharging process.

To capitalize on the deadly promise of early tactical military aircraft, the nations involved in the Great War invested heavily in R&D efforts to improve the specific power of aviation piston engines and to formulate high-octane aviation gasolines. Piston engine development with forced induction for motor racing resumed when the war ended in 1918. Throughout the following inter-war period, high-altitude military aviation applications continued to drive piston-engine R&D. Development of tremendous, high-performance piston engines escalated to a crescendo with war fears in the 1930s and continued with the highest emergency priority throughout the World War II until turbojets abruptly rendered them obsolete in the immediate post World War II period.

OXYGEN INJECTION

Scientists dreamed up the idea of injecting nitrous oxide into high-performance combat aircraft engines during World War II in order to enrich the oxygen content of the charge mixture and increase horsepower. English scientist Joseph Priestly (1733–1804) had discovered nitrous oxide, also known as dinitrogen oxide

or dinitrogen monoxide, in 1772 when he was systematically searching for chemical elements and compounds with practical value for medical or other scientific applications. Priestly separated and identified gaseous nitrous oxide but saw no obvious application for small amounts of the substance, lost interest, and moved on. Because no equipment existed at Priestly's time to achieve the low temperature or high pressure needed to liquefy nitrous oxide (-126 degrees F at atmospheric pressure, 776 psi at room temperature), there was no way nitrous oxide could be stored in quantities sufficient to be useful. For almost 43 years the lack of any obvious utility discouraged further study of nitrous oxide.

Sir Humphrey Davy (1778–1829) developed the first practical use for nitrous oxide in 1815 when he invented the Davy miner's lamp, a sealed oil lamp with a self-contained oxidizer using nitrous oxide in place of ambient air. Although room-temperature nitrous is useless for burning anything, Davy discovered that when heated to 566 degrees F, nitrous oxide (N_2O) molecules dissociate, releasing heat and recombining into nitrogen gas (N_2) and gaseous oxygen (O_2)—which, of course, *will* support combustion. Because nitrous oxide is 36 percent oxygen by mass, cooking nitrous oxide to produce nitrogen and oxygen results in a brew containing 36 percent oxygen, which can burn much more fuel than air.

The first mass-produced oxygen for industrial use arrived in 1895, when German scientists developed a commercially viable method of producing liquid oxygen. Pure liquid oxygen would eventually be used in bulk as an oxidizer for liquid-fueled rocket engines, but as an oxidizer for internal combustion engines, pure oxygen burns much too hot (up to 6,290 degrees F!). Even if used as an oxygen source diluted with other gases, liquid oxygen poses troublesome handling issues because it's so cold. Compressed oxygen gas may sound like a better approach but it also has its limits. At 3,000 pounds per square inch—a common pressure limit for oxygen tanks—a gallon of the gas contains only 2.4 pounds of oxygen at standard temperature. By contrast, a gallon of liquefied nitrous oxide under standard conditions contains 3.8 pounds of oxygen. Thus, *liquid nitrous oxide actually contains more oxygen per gallon than high-pressure oxygen gas* yet requires no cryogenic handling measures because it remains a liquid to nearly 100 degrees F in a closed storage tank as long as there's enough left to maintain high internal vapor pressure.

WORLD WAR II AIRCRAFT HOT RODDING

The earliest tentative secret military experiments with nitrous oxide as an engine-boosting oxidizer seem to have occurred in the inter-war years between 1919 and 1939, but the priority of aviation engine power-boosting increased radically after the Nazi blitzkrieg into Poland in September 1939, and the subsequent swift invasions that successively defeated Norway, Belgium, Holland, and then France, each in a matter of weeks.

British scientists worked frantically to determine whether nitrous oxide would be feasible as a reliable secondary power-adder on supercharged powerplants for spy planes sent to extreme altitudes and airspeeds. American scientists eventually conducted similar research.

In June 1945, the National Advisory Committee for Aeronautics (NACA) reported on efforts to use nitrous oxide for "additional supercharging" of an aircraft engine without any reduction in the knock limit. The relatively constant-speed nature of an aviation piston engine making power on a prop-driven aircraft meant that NACA scientists had zero interest in acceleration (exactly the opposite of the situation in modern times where the value of nitrous is related

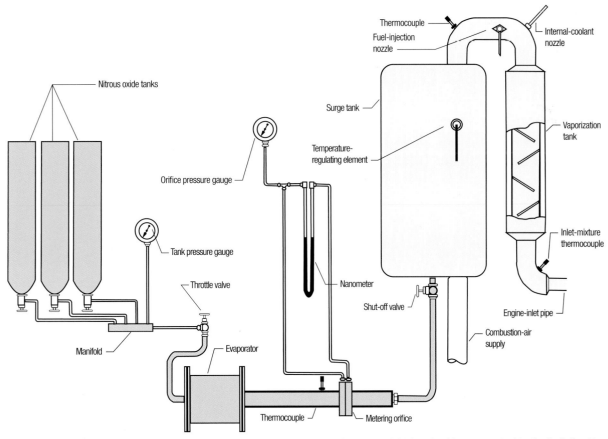

The National Advisory Committee for Aeronautics (NACA), the predecessor of NASA, experimented with nitrous injection using this test apparatus intentionally designed to provide very predictable results by mixing nitrous oxide gas warmed to a control temperature a precise mass of warmed air to deliver a precise mass of oxygen-enriched charge air to the single-cylinder test engine. *NACA*

almost exclusively to its ability to *improve* acceleration). In marked contrast to the meager benefits of oxygen injection, the NACA Wartime Report on nitrous found that replacing 10 or 20 percent of charge air with nitrous oxide gas permitted power gains of 14 or 25 percent, respectively, with optimal spark timing and detonation controlled by rich fuel-oxygen ratios and/or alcohol-water injection (to limit heat). Applying mathematical modeling techniques to liquid nitrous injection, NACA scientists estimated that replacing nitrous oxide gas injection with liquid and adding supplemental fuel would approximately double power for a given level of manifold pressure exclusively by improving the contribution of charge air to combustion oxygen mass using the tremendous cooling effect of boiling nitrous liquid to dramatically increase the mass of air that fit in a given space as the nitrous-air blend raced through the intake system. Nitrous was the real deal.

Although nitrous oxide was never widely deployed in operational combat aircraft, nitrous-boosted aircraft engines were capable of dazzling performance, with 30 percent power increases demonstrated in flight from supercharged aero engines breathing a charge enriched with nitrous from 23.2 to 26.7 percent oxygen. This increased the service ceiling of some planes to altitudes in excess of 50,000 feet, a stunning achievement for piston-engine aircraft of the World War II era.

Nitrous-based engine boosting was a closely guarded Allied military secret every bit as clandestine in its time as the advanced technologies of more recent times, like the supersonic turbojet-ramjet Pratt & Whitney J58-P4 turbines developed for the 2,500-mile-per-hour SR-71 Blackbird spy plane. Axis aviators were openly mystified by the high-altitude abilities of supercharged, nitrous-boosted Allied aircraft late in the war, though German scientists were actually a year or

so ahead of the Allies in the sophistication of aircraft engine technology. In the final year of the war, Germany deployed the first operational turbojet-powered aircraft in the world. The ME-262 entered service equipped with twin jet engines packing a combined equivalent of 6,500 horsepower, giving it more than triple the power of a supercharged Merlin V-12. Though it arrived too late to have any significant impact on the outcome of the conflict, the ME-262 had such enormous air-superiority when finally sorted out that it eventually delivered an Axis-Allied kill ratio of nearly 5:1 in the final months of the war. The Allies, however, had nitrous: One of the Allied countermeasures against the German fighter's 100-mile-per-hour speed advantage was to equip the more maneuverable American P-51 Mustang with nitrous oxide injection, enabling the pilot of a P-51 chasing an ME-262 to hit a button that dumped massive amounts of nitrous and fuel into the engine to deliver a critical burst of speed at the right moment.

Actually, German scientists had secretly developed their own nitrous oxide injection system for boosting the

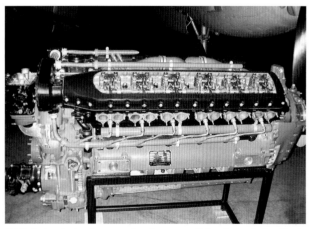

NACA's test engine for nitrous experiments was essentially a single cylinder robbed from the normal-charged four-valve Allison 1725 CID V-12 and equipped with an add-on centrifugal supercharger to approximate the configuration of the Merlin, which was not immediately available in time for the emergency test program. *NACA*

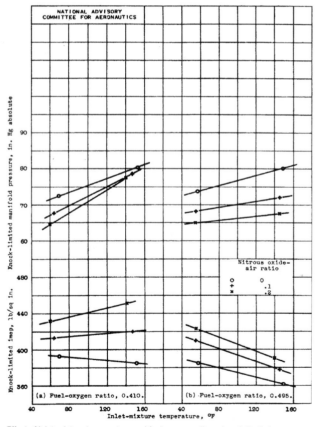

Effect of inlet-mixture temperature and fuel-oxygen ratio on knock-limited performance of single-cylinder engine with nitrous oxide supercharging. Engine speed, 3,000 rpm; compression ratio, 6.0; inlet oil temperature, 185F; outlet coolant temperature, 250F; fuel 33-R high-octane avgas. NACA scientists tested nitrous oxide–air ratios with 0 nitrous, 10 percent nitrous, and 20 percent nitrous. They tested the effect of fuel enrichment using fuel-oxygen ratios of .401 and .495. *NACA*

Increase in Engine Power with Nitrous Oxide Injection at Constant Manifold Pressure

Nitrous oxide–air ratio	Nitrous oxide injected as gas at 210F		Nitrous oxide injected as liquid at -128F (a)	
	Indicated mean effective pressure	Percentage increase	Indicated mean effective pressure	Percentage increase
.00	237	-	237	-
.05	255	8	275	16
.10	271	14	311	31
.15	285	20	338	42
.20	297	25	369	56
.25	307	30	406	71

(a) Calculated values

NACA testing found that injecting nitrous oxide vapor at 10 and 25 percent of intake air increased power 14 and 30 percent. There were no actual experiments with liquid nitrous injection, but mathematical models predicated -128F liquid nitrous in the same percentages would increase power 31 and 71 percent—which is why modern racers and hot rodders always strive to make sure a nitrous system is injecting liquid nitrous. *NACA*

Knock-limited Performance with Nitrous Oxide Injection

Fuel 33-R; fuel-oxygen ratio, 0.410

Nitrous oxide air ratio	Nitrous oxide injected as a gas at 210F			Nitrous oxide injected as a liquid at -128F		
	Knock-limited manifold pressure (in. Hg absolute)	Knock-limited indicated mean effective pressure (lb/in²)	Percentage increase in indicated mean effective pressure	Knock-limited manifold pressure (in. Hg absolute)	Knock-limited indicated mean effective pressure (lb/in²)	Percentage increase in indicated mean effective pressure
.00	80.5	385	-	80.5	385	-
.05	79.6	405	5	75.0	404	5
.10	78.8	420	9	69.1	415	8
.15	78.0	436	13	64.5	422	10
.20	77.0	452	17	-	-	-

NACA testing of nitrous injection under knock-limited conditions at .410 fuel-air ratio (versus the .293 fuel-oxygen ratio equivalent to a 14.7 stoichiometric air-fuel ratio). At this relatively lean ratio, knock was a serious limitation on power, particularly at higher levels of oxygen enrichment. Note that liquid nitrous injection actually made less power because of required excessive ignition timing retard, and the test engine could not be run at .20 liquid nitrous injection due to excessive spark knock. *NACA*

Daimler-Benz DB600 inverted V-12 aircraft powerplant, and even deployed nitrous-DB600s equipped with a 22.5-gallon (85-liter) nitrous oxide tank in Luftwaffe Focke-Wulf Ta 152C/H high-altitude interceptors. The German system nitrous supposedly injected 12 pounds per minute of nitrous oxide directly into a special gear-driven supercharger fitted to a modified DB600 driving a special prop, resulting in a 350-horsepower boost (I know, that's theoretically not enough nitrous for 350 horsepower!) and the capability to operate at extremely high altitudes with full rated power. The system was reportedly efficient enough in its use of nitrous oxide that boost was available continuously for as long as 20 to 30 minutes, during which time the engine gobbled at least 250 pounds of nitrous! Other reports indicate that the German system could deliver a 50 percent nitrous power boost for five minutes during emergency dog-fighting without overheating, with a teardown and engine rebuild required after only 25 to 30 minutes of total nitrous boosting time, versus a total non-boosted time between overhauls (TBO) of only 40 hours (about 1 to 2 percent of the TBO of modern piston aircraft engines). Many German aero engines used 87 octane

After World War II, the U.S. military abandoned piston engines for high-performance combat aircraft, and nitrous research was declassified. Jet-powered aircraft like this NASA SR-71 Blackbird became the focus of aeronautical engineers who had once labored to advance the performance of piston-engine fighter aircraft with nitrous oxide injection. *NASA*

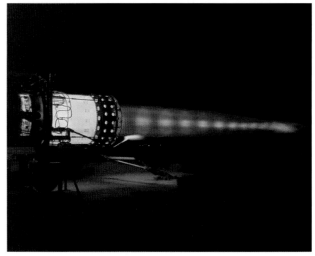

Modern jet afterburners are exactly similar in concept to the nitrous supercharging systems used in World War II to temporarily improve climb performance and service ceiling. Jet afterburners dump raw fuel into the jet exhaust to burn the oxygen surplus as it exits the engine such that the extreme heat cannot melt delicate internal combustion chambers, axial compressor fans, and exhaust turbines. *NASA*

fuel, but this type of high-performance fighter required the equivalent of American 100/130 (lean/rich) octane, which the Germans had a hard time producing as the war turned against them.

Nitrous injection is one of many cumulative emergency wartime developments that dramatically boosted the performance of large, high-performance aviation piston engines over the course of the conflict. Its value as a secret military hot-rodding trick disappeared almost instantly with the end of the war and the subsequent across-the-board abandonment of piston engines for combat aircraft in favor of jet propulsion.

POST-WAR NITROUS INJECTION: WHOOP-ASS FOR THE MASSES

After the war, nitrous oxide injection dropped out of sight for a decade or two, during which time it appeared sporadically as a hidden power-adder on the race cars of a few techno-savvy nitrous mavens—say in a drag race, or to take the lead in a critical sprint during a road race. In the world of terrestrial racing (other than land speed record trials), acceleration was everything, and nitrous injection had to work in an environment that was tremendously dynamic.

Starting in the late 1950s, automotive writer Colin Campbell discussed nitrous oxide injection on a number of occasions in limited-circulation racing publications, but most people who understood the massive engine-boosting potential of nitrous injection definitely did not want anyone else to know the secret. The few people who really understood the dramatic nature of what nitrous could do as a power-adder guarded the secret with the same kind of zealotry wartime adversaries used in seeking an aviation advantage in combat.

Hidden nitrous injection kicked ass and won races, and the early legacy of nitrous lives on to this day in the names of modern systems from companies like Nitrous Oxide Systems where "Cheater" brand nitrous kits are designed to appeal to something . . . *interesting* in the human soul: the desire to win at most any cost.

It wasn't until the early 1970s that nitrous oxide injection was out of the closet as an automotive power-adder and the subject of widespread discussion, controversy, and articles on the pages of *Hot Rod Magazine*—it is almost ridiculously easy to construct and camouflage a minimalist nitrous-injection system capable of providing a momentary power surge at a critical time. A 25-horsepower shot of 1,000-psi liquid nitrous need only pressurize an orifice the size of a carburetor main jet at the right time to give a driver the win, and enrichment fuel can be provided from the primary carburetor or fuel injectors. This small, race-winning shot requires limited plumbing and nitrous storage.

Nitrous boost was dramatically effective, affordable for almost anyone, dirt-cheap to install compared to any other method of adding significant horsepower to an engine, and had zero effect on an engine except at full throttle when the nitrous system was armed. The fact that it could blow up your engine if you didn't know what you were doing only added to the chemical's allure as powerful, semi-dangerous magic requiring competency and maybe a pinch of wizardry to avert disaster and kick serious ass with the big dogs. Nitrous oxide injection might've seemed almost too good to be true, but it really was affordable, it really was easy to install, and it really gave an engine super powers: 50, 100, 200, *300, or more* additional horsepower! The only downside was that you only had a few minutes or seconds of full-throttle superpowers before the stagecoach turned back into a pumpkin. Well, that and the fact that in the early days most people—including most kit builders!—were playing with evil spirits they didn't fully understand that really could torch an engine, given half a chance. Well, that and the recurring cost of nitrous oxide refills (current price $3.50 to $4.00 a pound, making a 15-pound nitrous refill cost $50 to $60).

The first commercially available bolt-on nitrous kits arrived in this era from entrepreneurs eager to make a buck. Unfortunately, these guys were rarely automotive engineers fully equipped with the knowledge and resources to understand, develop, and test their products adequately. Early kit designers and their customers ran head-on into the reality that although dumping a fixed blast of additional fuel and nitrous oxide into an engine regardless of rpm sounds easy, in reality it is *much* more complicated than it looks, and there are plenty of ways to get it disastrously wrong. Along with early crude prefabricated nitrous-injection kits came rumors and reports of mysterious, unexplained engine explosions and fires. The truth of the matter is that nitrous combustion is hotter, faster, and more difficult to control than air combustion, and is thus not very forgiving, so it requires "fail safe" systems and components at every level— the simplest example being that if a nitrous powerplant shuts down or stalls, the system better *instantly* stop injecting fuel and nitrous to keep from turning the intake system into a pipe bomb when the engine restarts. Typically, forensic analysis of early kits following nitrous explosions and fires revealed insufficient engineering or components incompatible with the pressure and temperature of liquid nitrous oxide.

In the end, even though performance automotive magazines almost never report any bad news about commercial products (especially those of advertisers!), and even with no Internet to spread performance gossip about what's hot and what's not, the word still got around, and manufacturers of unreliable nitrous kits had to clean up their act or die.

In 1978, two automotive technicians who raced with some success on weekends saw the potential of turning nitrous oxide into a successful consumer product. According to the history page of the Nitrous Oxide Systems (NOS) web site, these aspiring entrepreneurs, Mike Thermos and Dale Vaznaian, focused on making nitrous-injection systems as foolproof, fail-safe, and reliable as possible with the technology of the time. In any case, NOS thrived as a company, capturing and then maintaining a dominant position as a provider of nitrous oxide injection kits and components to the extent that NOS (originally pronounced as the initials N-O-S) has been glamorized as "Noss" (rhymes with "hoss") in movies such as *The Fast and the Furious*, essentially transmogrifying the word into a generic term for *any* automotive nitrous oxide. NOS, now part of the performance automotive conglomerate Holley Performance, credits the National Hot Rod Association's (NHRA) sanctioning of nitrous oxide injection for Pro Mod drag racing with singlehandedly providing the greatest boost to the popularity of nitrous oxide. Early nitrous pioneers Charles Carpenter, Bill Kuhlmann and Robby Vandergriff deployed nitrous to kick ass and take names in huge 1950s and 1960s stock-bodied cars, capturing the imagination of race fans with their stunning performances. Vehicles sporting NOS decals on the side dominated a record-breaking series of performance benchmarks in stock-bodied vehicles or racers with stock-appearing bodies and functional doors ("Doorslammers"), including the first 200-mile-per-hour speed run, the first 6-second drag run, and other landmarks.

The focus of modern piston engine development shifted from military aviation to automotive engineers and racers. In modern times nitrous oxide injection is almost exclusively used to temporarily improve acceleration in drag-type conditions.

One exception to the common application of nitrous for improving acceleration is Land Speed Record vehicles, which race for 7 or 15 miles in a quest to achieve the highest speed over a measured mile.

As factory-stock automotive engines modernized with fuel injection, digital computer engine management, turbochargers, gasoline direct injection, complex emissions controls, and vehicle management strategies, nitrous-injection technology has evolved over the years from the relatively simple early system designed to deliver a brutal sledgehammer hit of torque to carbureted V-8s. Automotive nitrous oxide injection was originally a self-contained "wet" power-adder that delivered both nitrous oxidizer and matching supplemental enrichment fuel into carbureted automotive intake manifolds purpose-built to distribute a wet charge mixture of liquid gasoline and air to the various cylinders with acceptably good distribution. EFI presented both problems and opportunities.

The mass "injectionization" of the automotive world in the period between 1977 and 1987 was a mixed blessing when it came to nitrous injection. Multi-port electronic fuel injection provided precise fuel delivery and distribution under computer control, and it provided automotive engineers the freedom to optimize intake manifolds exclusively for handling dry air with high volumetric efficiency since no compromises were required to simultaneously deal with liquid gasoline. But tuning fuel delivery and spark timing was suddenly much more esoteric than changing jets and adjustment screws in carburetors and clocking a distributor or changing centrifugal advance springs in a points ignition.

There were more complex electronic emissions controls as well. Port EFI forced nitrous kit-makers to design single-point and direct-port nitrous-injection systems capable of achieving equal distribution of supplemental enrichment fuel to all cylinders in the more difficult environment of multi-port EFI engines with air-tuned "dry" intake manifolds, and in some cases reverse-engineer the electronic control units that now provided engine management for all modern street cars.

One solution for port-EFI engines was to search very carefully for a specific location in the manifold plenum or throttle body where it just so happened that a precisely calibrated single-point fuel spray bar or injection nozzle could deliver supplemental nitrous fuel at full throttle with acceptable distribution. Another tactic was to inject enrichment fuel (and sometimes nitrous) directly into the individual ports. Yet another strategy was to deliver supplemental fuel through the electronic injectors by (1) transiently increasing fuel rail pressure during nitrous injection or intercepting and tweaking the MAF sensor signal, (2) modifying nitrous-injection pulsewidth with piggyback computers or replacement standalone programmable engine management systems, or (3) by upgrading to higher capacity electronic injectors (with commensurate changes to stock injection pulsewidth).

The most sophisticated modern nitrous-injection kits typically abandon continuous nitrous injection under at least some circumstances in favor of a series of intermittent pulses of variable frequency similar in concept to electronic fuel injectors or up to a half-dozen or so stages of nitrous mass flow, such systems are controlled using powerful standalone programmable engine management systems that tightly integrate nitrous oxide injection with the other engine management tasks. Modern systems designed to be street legal may in some cases deploy sophisticated "piggyback" microcomputers to integrate nitrous injection

The traditional wet plate nitrous system injects nitrous oxide and gasoline in a constant flow from a "spraybar" located under a four-barrel carburetor fueling a performance V-8 engine. Electromagnetic solenoid valves operate as on-off switches for fuel and oxidizer, delivering low-pressure (5-50 psi) fuel and high-pressure (self-pressurized) 950 psi nitrous oxide liquid. *Nitrous Works*

Nitrous is commonly used to boost the performance of motorcycles, watercraft, snowmobiles, ATVs, and other relatively small-displacement engines. This wet NOS V-twin nitrous kit "fogs" a spray of nitrous and fuel into twin-cylinder carbureted or EFI motorcycles like the V-twin Harley. *NOS*

Nitrous injection is commonly used to boost drag boats, but is also fully compatible with air-supercharging to provide a race-winning burst of performance in endurance boat racing—an application much closer to the original warbird nitrous systems than most drag-oriented modern nitrous systems.

with other engine management events by intercepting and modifying data to or from the stock engine management onboard computer so as to modify fuel delivery and ignition timing while simultaneously implementing and controlling electronic nitrous injection. In other cases, one or more dedicated electronic "black boxes" may be installed specifically to modify a particular aspect of stock engine management, such as lengthening fuel-injection pulse or retarding ignition during nitrous injection to fight spark knock. In general, nitrous oxide has proven that it can be compatible with increasingly stringent federal emissions standards (which have typically not required full-throttle emissions testing) and increasingly sophisticated full-authority closed-loop factory engine management systems. Meanwhile, nitrous suppliers have successfully adapted modern nitrous-injection technology to smaller engines on motorcycles, ATVs, boats, and snowmobiles, which have finally almost universally adopted fuel injection and electronic engine management. Diesel performance vendors have adapted nitrous injection to hot rod diesel engines with or without propane injection.

In the early days, the most sophisticated nitrous injection deployed two- and then three-stage nitrous and fuel delivery systems to bring on the power boost more gradually in order to maintain traction and prevent shock engine and powertrain damage from the huge onslaught of power on big-ass nitrous systems. In more recent times there has been a trend toward moderating the onset of the nitrous hit using single-stage pulsewidth-modulated "progressive" nitrous delivery that turns the nitrous solenoid into a metering device by fluttering the valve rapidly open and shut like an electronic fuel injector to provide almost continuously variable nitrous delivery ranging from 5 to 95 percent. (More commonly, the range is from 30 to 60 percent before the system goes static on either end).

Nitrous oxide injection adapted especially well to engines with forced induction, as it had on World War II combat aircraft. Nitrous proved especially compatible with the increasing number of turbocharged cars and trucks that arrived in the final decades of the twentieth century, either as (1) a secondary contribution to peak power or (2) a highly effective countermeasure against turbo lag that delivered instantaneous nitrous torque and a blast of high-energy exhaust well below the non-nitrous boost threshold of the turbocharger.

Nitrous injection has penetrated extreme-performance applications light years beyond street hot rodding. Nitrous injection has been used in competition with much success in drag racing, land-speed record trials, hydroplane racing, snowmobile racing, drag boats, tractor pulls, and unlimited-class air racing where Rare Bear, a heavily modified Grumman Bearcat warbird with a transplanted 3,350 CID Wright radial engine, dominated the series for decades and managed to achieve 540 mph in straight and level flight at 5,000 MSL.

Bob Norwood's Integra dragger used nitrous oxide injection to wake up the spooling capability of the large turbochargers on this 325-CID *four-cylinder* designed to make nearly 4,000 horsepower on methanol and nitromethane.

a self-pressurizing monopropellant for lightweight satellites using the heat of dissociation as nitrous is catalyzed into its component parts with a specific impulse of about 170 seconds. In many cases, the fluid and refrigeration dynamics of nitrous oxide are so complex that its behavior cannot be modeled but must be simulated with digital computers.

Fortunately for most people, this is the whack-job zone of extreme performance, where high levels of oxygen enrichment have pushed the fire chemistry of combustion to the ragged edge of detonation and meltdown, where exhaust gas temperatures constantly flirt with danger, where perfect fuel combustion cooling is all that stands in the way of burning exotic internal engine components, where extreme cylinder pressures constantly threaten to stretch high-strength head studs and lift the heads off the block, and where races are won by hundredths of a second. In other words, where it's not just important how much power you can make, but exactly when you make it.

For less extreme applications, nitrous oxide is a mature technology that is well understood and very well suited to hot-rodding sophisticated modern vehicles with complex

The author's 4.2L Jaguar I-6 was equipped with NOS sequential progressive nitrous injection integrated into the NOS/EFI Technology engine management system, providing supplemental nitrous fuel enrichment through the two-injectors-per-cylinder electronic fuel injection system.

Nearly 70 years after nitrous injection appeared for the first time in heavy aircraft engines, the complex behavior and interactions of liquid and gaseous nitrous oxide, enrichment fuel, oxygen-rich combustion fire chemistry, and engine management systems are still not widely understood in extreme applications. As nitrous and fuel move from the storage tank through plumbing and control valves to the charging and combustion chambers of an engine, they often change phase between liquid and gas with concomitant changes in temperature and density that are notoriously difficult to predict but may have a significant impact on power, torque, combustion temperature, and flame speed. Nitrous is once again being tested as the oxidizer of choice for many hybrid rocket designs and has been used frequently in amateur high-powered rocketry. It has also been tested as electronic engine management and emissions controls. Some nitrous systems are still rather simple. That said, the availability of affordable electronic controls has also resulted in bolt-on nitrous-injection systems that are complex and sophisticated, and tightly integrated into complex engine management and vehicle systems.

All of which is why nitrous kits and components are still selling well after all these years, and why we are now approaching a dozen or so important players in the prefabricated nitrous-injection game. Installing nitrous injection remains the best performance deal on earth for people with engines that occasionally need super powers.

This book is designed to tell the dramatic story of a great power-adder, providing a complete understanding of the theory, practice, and evolution of going wild with nitrous oxide injection.

Nitrous injection is most common as a hot rodding trick for street hot rods like this one-of-a-kind Alamo Autosports BMW Cabriolet with transplanted M3 engine with turbo conversion.

John Carmack's Armadillo Aerospace quest for the X-prize for 100-kilometer altitude manned spaceflight used pulsewidth-modulated nitrous solenoids to deliver fuel to the pulsed rocket platform. Nitrous oxide has been used as a rocket fuel oxidizer, and its ability to self-pressurize and to give up the heat of formation when oxygen and nitrogen are catalyzed from the nitrous oxide molecules has made it attractive for satellite propulsion. *Courtesy Armadillo Aerospace*

Back to the future. As of this writing, the fastest piston engine aircraft on earth was still *Rare Bear*, a modified Grumman Bearcat with Wright 3350-CID radial engine, which dominated the Reno Air Races for decades and has achieved a level flight of 528.33 mph using tons of nitrous oxide injection.

Chapter 2
The Physics, Chemistry, and Combustion Properties of Nitrous Oxide

The powerful chemical energy in nitrogen, which makes up two-thirds of nitrous oxide, is the basis of most high explosives: Exotic, unstable nitrogen-based designer molecules more or less dying to break apart with high velocity, release thermal and kinetic energy, gain volume tremendously, and rearrange with great rapidity into a much more stable mixture of low-energy molecules including good old nitrogen gas. On the other hand, elemental nitrogen bonds to itself extremely strongly, to the extent that ordinary atmospheric nitrogen gas (N_2) in charge air is essentially *inert* during combustion despite peak temperature and pressure that can approach 2,000 degrees F and 2,500 psi in high-output boosted engines. In fact, diatomic (two-atom) nitrogen gas is so stable, and the triple chemical bond so strong, that creating more complex molecules out of nitrogen and almost anything else requires a considerable infusion of energy to trigger the endothermic reaction. This *heat of formation* is recovered later when high-energy nitrogen-based compounds with inferior stability break apart, sometimes violently so. Liquid nitroglycerin is probably the best example—a contact explosive that dissociates with incredible violence from mild physical shock.

Nitrogen is very flexible in the ways it can bond with other atoms, because its outer atomic shell can form up to three ordinary chemical bonds either by receiving or sharing up to three electrons, or by donating up to five electrons to other atoms as *coordinate* (ionic) bonds, which are just as strong but have special electrical properties. Nitrogen gas will not burn, but there are a variety of ways nitrogen can be *forced* to combine with oxygen, one of which is nitrous oxide—the subject of this book.

There are four types of nitrogen oxides, and they have widely varying properties.

Hot, high-pressure combustion in piston engines produces trace amounts of exhaust gas **nitric oxide** (NO) and **nitrogen dioxide** (NO_2)—brownish-tinged air pollutants typically referred to as NOx. NOx is good for nothing, and one purpose of three-way catalytic converters is to transform NOx gases back into diatomic oxygen and nitrogen gas.

Dinitrogen pentoxide (N_2O_5) and **dinitrogen trioxide** (N_2O_3) are unstable and mildly explosive chemicals of no current commercial value.

Catalytic oxidation of ammonia moderated with steam produces the powerful, corrosive, and unstable oxidizer

DEFINITIONS

Gas: A substance such as air: a substance that is neither a solid nor a liquid at ordinary temperatures and has the ability to expand infinitely, e.g., air. A gas is a state of matter, consisting of a collection of particles (molecules, atoms, ions, electrons, and so on) without a definite shape or volume that is in more or less random motion.

Liquid: A fluid that has the particles loose and can freely form a distinct surface at the boundaries of its bulk material. The surface is a free surface where the liquid is not constrained by a container. One of the principal states of matter, liquid is a flowing substance that is a fluid at room temperature and atmospheric pressure, and whose shape, but not volume, can be changed.

Thermal expansion: The tendency of matter to change in volume in response to a change in temperature. When a substance is heated, its constituent particles move around more vigorously and by doing so generally maintain a greater average separation. Materials that contract with an increase in temperature are uncommon; this effect is limited in size, and only occurs within limited temperature ranges. The degree of expansion divided by the change in temperature is called the material's coefficient of thermal expansion and generally varies with temperature.

Density: Physics relative mass: a measure of a quantity such as mass or electric charge per unit volume. Symbol p. In physics the density (p) of a body is the ratio of its mass (m) to its volume (V), a measure of how tightly the matter within it is packed together. Units are kilograms per cubic meter (kg/m^3) or grams per cubic centimeter (g/cm^3). Density is defined by $p = m/V$. Various substances have different densities and it is this quantity that can determine how they interact when mixed together. In SI units the density of lead is 11.35×103, water is 1×103, and cork's density is 0.24×103. Lead has a greater density than water so it sinks; cork has a lesser density, so it floats. In some cases the density is expressed as a specific gravity or relative density, in which case it is expressed in multiples of the density of some other standard material, usually water or air.

Boosted by dinitrogen tetroxide (nitrous oxide on steroids) and mono-methyl hydrazine, Ulysses blasts toward Jupiter. *NASA*

systems on earth!—is a colorless gas at ambient pressure and temperature, with a slightly sweet taste and smell in higher concentrations (industrial automotive nitrous oxide is denatured with sulfur to make it a stinking irritant that cannot be abused as an inhalant). The most common applications for nitrous oxide—dental anesthetic and aerosol whipped cream propellant—have nothing to do with oxidation but derive from nitrous oxide's affinity for *fat*. Nitrous oxide works as a low-grade inhalation anesthetic because high enough concentrations in the blood will cause nitrous oxide to dissolve in synaptic lipid *fatty cell membranes* (but *not* be metabolized), thus temporarily interfering with neurotransmission to produce an analgesic effect as well as the mild euphoria, hysteria, and giggling that caused nitrous to be nicknamed "laughing gas."

Nitrous oxide is not particularly effective as a pure anesthetic—and must therefore be inhaled in fairly high concentrations with oxygen—but since nitrous cannot be metabolized biologically into its component parts, pure nitrous oxide will cause suffocation and death if inhaled continuously without oxygen. Not coincidentally, nitrous oxide works well as a whipped cream propellant and foaming agent precisely because it temporarily dissolves in *fatty cream* but is nonreactive with anything in the recipe. Nitrous oxide itself cannot burn anything, but heated above 565 degrees it

dinitrogen tetroxide (N_2O_4), a liquid that is used as a robust oxidizer in high-powered liquid-fuel rockets. The Space Shuttle orbiter uses dinitrogen tetroxide as a kind of "super-nitrous" to combust high-energy mono-methyl hydrazine with godlike power.

And then there's **nitrous oxide** (N_2O) itself—anesthetic, aerosol propellant, and oxidizer: The subject of this book.

Direct production of nitrous oxide from nitrogen and oxygen gases occurs in the following endothermic reaction:

$$2N_2 + O_2 + 18,500 \text{ calories of energy per mole of } N_2 \rightarrow 2N_2O$$

In this reaction, two molecules of diatomic nitrogen and one molecule of diatomic oxygen combine to form two molecules of nitrous oxide, each consisting of two atoms of nitrogen and a single atom of oxygen. However, nitrous oxide is usually manufactured another way, by carefully heating ammonium nitrate fertilizer to produce nitrous oxide and water vapor.

Pure nitrous oxide—oxidizer, engine intake refrigerant, source of the most cost-effective engine horsepower-boosting

NASA Shuttle main engine test firing. Oxides of nitrogen have commonly been used as a rocket-fuel oxidizer. *NASA*

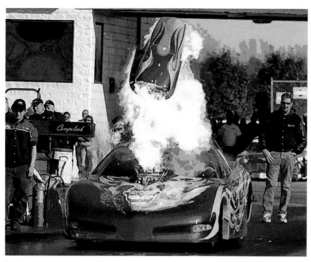

With much more oxygen than air, nitrous oxide becomes a powerful oxidizer once the molecules break apart at 565 degrees F into oxygen and nitrogen. Nitrous backfires can be serious.

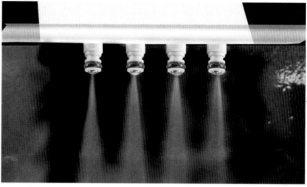

It's the fuel that burns to make the horsepower, but getting fuel into an engine is much easier than air as seen in this photo of the spray pattern of four electronic fuel injectors, which normally deliver fuel according to engine demand in variable-length pulses at a fixed increment above manifold pressure. Supplying plenty of fuel is easy compared to supplying air mainly because an engine requires more than 12 times more air mass than fuel to make maximum power (and much more air volume than that). Most engines depend on atmospheric pressure to deliver air (whereas fuel can be supplied at any required pressure up to about 25,000 psi in some diesel engines). *Bosch*

dissociates powerfully in an exothermic reaction that produces 36 percent oxygen, 64 percent nitrogen, and heat—a gaseous blend that supports combustion significantly better than air. Liquid nitrous is much more dense at colder temperatures.

THE PHYSICS OF NITROUS OXIDE

Nitrous oxide was used in small quantities as an oxidizer as far back as 1815 to lengthen the time between refills of the Davy miner's lamp. As the industrial revolution proceeded, liquefied nitrous oxide arrived for the first time in the late nineteenth century after engineers devised efficient compressors and compression-expansion refrigerant methods of cooling gases and liquids to extreme low temperatures to liquefy air, oxygen, and nitrogen. Liquid nitrous at any temperature turned out to be many times as dense as gaseous nitrous at standard temperature and pressure—meaning that a vastly larger mass of nitrous oxide could be stored in a particular space in liquid form.

Nitrous oxide's utility as an engine-boosting agent was originally seen exclusively as a substitute for oxygen in air-enrichment without some of the nastier aspects of pure oxygen. An engine breathing nitrous-enriched air could burn more fuel and make more power, a form of chemical supercharging. However, *liquid* nitrous oxide turned out to have additional benefits. Not only does liquid nitrous fit in a smaller space than compressed oxygen gas—a gallon has more oxygen than compressed oxygen does!—but liquid nitrous oxide is a powerful refrigerant when it expands and boils into a gas, absorbing tremendous amounts of heat that enable it to drastically chill an expansion chamber like the intake tract of a piston-engine powerplant. In fact, evaporating liquefied nitrous has such a powerful chilling effect that total-loss liquid nitrous is sometimes sprayed on the *exterior* of racing

air-air intercoolers to enhance charge-cooler effectiveness for air-supercharging without nitrous even entering the powerplant. Whether liquid nitrous evaporates in the charge air stream or against the convoluted surfaces of a heat exchanger, the effect is an intake air density increase and significantly more air mass per cubic foot of inducted air. This produces a second-order air-supercharging effect that can, under some circumstances, jack up engine volumetric efficiency by up to 10 percent even after the negative effect of nitrous-displaced intake air. The powerful chilling effect of boiling nitrous liquid has the added benefit of reducing the starting temperature of combustion, which helps to lower peak combustion temperatures and suppress detonation as long as correct oxygen-fuel ratios can be maintained.

As we shall see, due to the complex interaction of temperature and pressure on the nitrous boiling point, nitrous-injection systems for chemical supercharging are inevitably forced to deal with nitrous oxide in both liquid and gaseous phases.

NITROUS PHASE

At normal atmospheric pressure, nitrous oxide gas must be extremely cold before the molecules lose enough energy to rearrange phase and condense into liquid. The boiling point of nitrous at standard atmospheric pressure is -128 degrees Fahrenheit, ensuring that liquid nitrous oxide does not exist in nature on earth. (OK, a few times in recorded history the coldest temperature on earth has reached -129 degrees F at Vostok Station, Antarctica—which would liquefy nitrous oxide, were any present.)

But nitrous oxide gas can be transformed into a liquid another way—by using *pressure* to *raise* the boiling point, exactly the way an extra atmosphere of steam pressure in a pressure cooker raises the boiling point of water from 212 to 248 degrees F, thereby keeping water in the cooker liquid to higher temperatures in order to cook food faster. Like water, once nitrous oxide liquefies, it cannot be further compressed no matter what the pressure, though its density can change with temperature due to thermal contraction or expansion.

How much pressure does it take to force nitrous oxide gas into liquid form (or hold it there)? At 0 degrees F, 315 psi will liquefy nitrous oxide, but at 70 degrees F it will take 760 psi. If temperature continues to increase, a tank of liquid nitrous will eventually reach its *critical* temperature at 97.7 degrees F and 1,069 psi—the highest temperature at which nitrous will remain a liquid, no matter what the pressure. At temperatures over 97.7 degrees F the physical properties of gaseous and liquid nitrous oxide merge and 100 percent of the contents in a nitrous tank exists as a *supercritical fluid*, which will dissolve some chemicals like a liquid but has mainly gas-like properties. Above 97.7 degrees F, no amount of gas pressure in the universe can hold nitrous oxide in liquid form, though pressures above 1.74 *million psi* will force supercritical nitrous oxide into *solid* form!

Nitrous oxide is nonflammable, and it is quite stable at ambient temperatures. But when heated by combustion or compression above 565 degrees F, it becomes unstable and the molecules dissociate, breaking apart to release thermal and kinetic energy and rearranging into a mixture of oxygen (O_2) and nitrogen (N_2) gases—with almost 60 percent more oxidizing power than air. The heat and pressure increase of dissociating nitrous has been improved via a catalyst and investigated for use in self-pressurized light satellite propulsion systems as a monopropellant.

When stored in a strong, closed containment vessel, liquid nitrous oxide will self-pressurize at ambient temperatures. To picture why this is so, imagine that -128F liquid nitrous oxide is pumped into a sealed tank and the tank is allowed to warm. As the nitrous inside warms up, it begins to evaporate or *boil* into vapor, creating pressure above the noncompressible liquid. Warming liquid nitrous continues boiling until the environmental pressure of the bubble of nitrous oxide gas forming above the liquid reaches equilibrium with the *vapor pressure* from liquid nitrous trying to evaporate at the current temperature—at which point the rate of condensing gas and evaporating liquid are equal, and boiling stops with no additional net conversion into gas. At 0 degrees F, the vapor

Turbos and superchargers inevitably heat air during the compression process, which is why this triple-turbo 4.2L Jaguar engine is equipped with a large air-air intercooler. On the other hand, the engine is also equipped with nitrous oxide injection, which is a perfect match with turbocharging precisely because liquid nitrous injection *cools* intake air as the nitrous boils, and because turbochargers make tons of high-end torque, and nitrous makes tons of low-end torque.

Thermodynamic Properties of Nitrous Oxide (NACA MR No. E5F26)

Property	Conditions	Value
Heat of formation, Btu/lb, 14.7 psia	64.4°F gas	691
Latent heat of vaporization, Btu/lb	-130°F	172.3
	-40°F	139.1
	5°F	121.4
	50°F	95.8
Specific heat of liquid, Btu/lb °F	-125°F	0.422
Specific heat of gas at constant pressure, Btu/lb	5-86°F	0.212
Ratio of specific heats of gas	5-86°F	1.280
Density of liquid, lb/ft3	130°F	81.2
	86°F	39.1
Fusion temperature, °F	-	-152.3

Thermodynamic properties of nitrous oxide. In addition to supplying oxygen-enrichment to charge air, nitrous oxide produces a powerful cooling effect when room-temperature liquid boils into vapor. Nitrous contributes heat to the combustion process when nitrous molecules break apart into nitrogen and oxygen. *NACA*

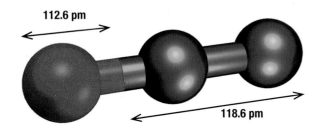

Nitrous oxide molecular schematic showing the presence of two nitrogen molecules and one oxygen molecule. Nitrous oxide is about 36 percent oxygen mass, whereas air is only 23 percent oxygen mass.

pressure of the nitrous tank will be 315 psi, and by 70 degrees F it will have increased to 760 psi, as mentioned above. At 97.7 degrees F, just before the liquid disappears and the entire tank becomes a gas-like supercritical fluid, vapor pressure is 1,069 psi. If the temperature continues to rise above 97.7 degrees F, the nitrous fluid will acquire more energy and pressure will continue to increase, but there is no longer any liquid in the tank. A nitrous-injected C6 Corvette with a full nitrous tank mounted in the cargo area sitting outside on a warm Los Angeles January day with sunlight blazing through the rear hatch and the interior a toasty 120 degrees F has 1,500 psi nitrous tank pressure and no liquid nitrous oxide whatsoever in the tank. On the other hand, at the 20 degrees F Mammoth Mountain ski area parking lot at zero-dark-thirty in the morning, the nitrous tank has mostly liquefied and the gauge reads 400 psi (assuming you didn't give in and use any nitrous blowing past Hummers with ski racks on the five-hour trip into the mountains from L.A.).

What is really interesting is that, once the temperature of a tank containing liquid nitrous is stabile anywhere between -128 and 97.7 degrees F, releasing nitrous from the tank cannot, per se, permanently change the pressure *as long as there is any liquid in the tank*, because nitrous liquid will boil and expand on a continuing basis to the extent required to restore equilibrium pressure between the liquid and gas phases. Of course, for reasons we'll see shortly, a tank spewing nitrous will tend to *cool* itself, which—in the absence of countermeasures like tank heaters or external nitrogen pressurization—will lower tank pressure temporarily until the tank warms back up to ambient temperature. Depending on the rate of outflow, tank pressure can also fall temporarily if the mass of nitrous liquid in the tank cannot boil fast enough to maintain vapor pressure (or if the temperature of liquid, or gas and liquid, in the tank is not uniform—picture the cylinders of an old steam locomotive gobbling steam faster than the boiler can boil water to replace it). When a high-output nitrous engine is "on the juice," with liquid nitrous blasting out of the tank at, say, 950 psi into the engine intake, liquid nitrous in the tank is boiling furiously and the interface between liquid and

gas is a boiling, steaming foam—much like the surface of water at a rolling boil or a shaken soda bottle.

Assuming a tank of nitrous oxide is below the critical temperature of 97.7 degrees F and above -128 degrees F, it is possible to dispense nitrous in either liquid or gaseous form—depending on the orientation of the tank. If a tank filled with nitrous is mounted vertically with the valve at the top, then denser, heavier nitrous liquid will be at the bottom and vapor pressure in the gas bubble floating on top will push *gaseous nitrous* out the open valve. On the other hand, if the tank is mounted upside-down with the valve at the bottom, then vapor pressure in the nitrous gas bubble at the top will force *liquid nitrous* out the valve until the tank is empty of liquid, at which point the tank will deliver gas until pressure is totally exhausted. Because actuating a nitrous valve can be awkward when the tank is upside-down and it may be inconvenient to mount the tank vertically, automotive nitrous tanks are typically equipped with the valve connected to an internal pickup tube that runs to the lowest point of the tank. When the valve is open, pressure from the gas bubble floating on top forces heavier liquid nitrous into the pickup tube and out of the valve. To ensure liquid nitrous delivery in a moving vehicle, automotive nitrous tanks must be mounted with the nitrous pickup located toward the *rear* of the vehicle so that strong vehicle acceleration does not slosh liquid nitrous away from the pickup and cause the tank to intermittently dispense nitrous gas when the tank is partially empty of liquid nitrous.

When dispensing nitrous gas, all boiling and heat of vaporization goes on inside the tank, with tremendously robust cooling effects. (In one experiment, dispensing gas at a constant mass rate for as long as possible slowly lowered tank temperature to -120 degrees F!)

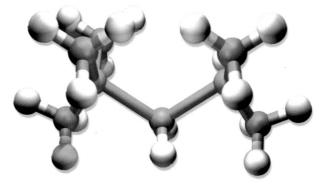

Isooctane (C_6H_{18}) is one of the two reference fuels used to measure the resistance of various fuels to auto-ignition, the other being n-heptane (which detonates very easily). If a given gasoline or fuel has the same detonation characteristics as 90 percent isooctane (which is very resistant to spark knock and 10 percent n-heptane), then the fuel is said to have an octane of 90. Hydrocarbon fuels like toluene that are even more resistant to detonation than isooctane are rated relative to the knock-resistance of isooctane. Isooctane is often used as a representative hydrocarbon of gasoline, which has similar weight and average number of carbon molecules, but is actually a stew of various hydrocarbons in the 6-9 carbon range.

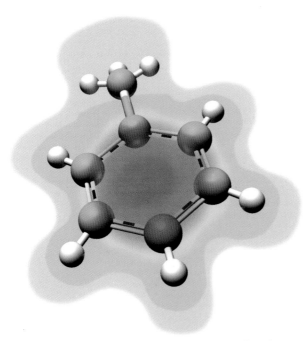

Toluene (C_7H_8 or $C_6H_5CH_3$), an aromatic hydrocarbon like benzene with a robust ring structure which is sometimes used as a component of racing gasoline, is as good as it gets when it comes to octane, with a research octane of 121 and motor octane of 107, giving it an (R+M)/2 pump-type octane rating of 114. Nitrous oxide fire chemistry is very hot and requires the highest practical octane fuel for safe combustion and maximum knock-limited power.

Nitrous tank orientation is important because the gas-versus-liquid *phase* of injected nitrous will have a critical effect on nitrous mass flow rate, engine volumetric efficiency, nitrous combustion temperature, and engine octane number requirement (ONR). As a firewall against catastrophic lean oxygen-fuel ratios, nitrous system supplemental fuel subsystems are *virtually always* calibrated assuming liquid nitrous delivery (i.e., the maximum oxygen boost)—though there are some tricks that can be used to vary the amount of fuel injected along with variations in nitrous pressure or mass flow, such as pulse-width modulation (PWM) solenoid pulsing, variable-orifice injectors, and so forth. This being the case, it is essential that the nitrous subsystem actually inject liquid rather than gaseous nitrous in order to:

1. Deliver enough oxygen to burn the bulk of injected supplemental fuel.
2. Avoid grotesquely rich fuel-oxygen mixtures that significantly degrade the flame speed and thermal efficiency of the engine—in order to run as close as possible to rich best torque (RBT) without detonation or overheating—and could cause severe wear or even engine seizure if fuel washes lubrication off the cylinder walls.
3. Intercool intake charge air to the greatest possible density so that charge air contributes as much oxygen as

possible to the combustion mixture for highest possible horsepower.
4. Minimize intake mass airflow reductions by keeping as much nitrous in liquid droplets, and at smallest volume, for as long as possible on the way into the cylinders—thereby maximizing the amount of oxygen-rich cold air that accompanies it in the intake tract. (When liquid nitrous is very cold, the volume of a given mass of nitrous liquid can be as little as 1 percent that of gaseous nitrous of the same mass.)
5. Achieve the target maximum horsepower "shot"/addition/offset to ordinary, nitrous-off power.

NITROUS AS A REFRIGERANT

Having discussed some properties of nitrous oxide's liquid and gas phases, let's look at the implications of nitrous phase *change*.

The boiling point of any liquid represents the temperature and pressure at which individual molecules possess enough thermal energy to overcome the various intermolecular attractions and forces holding them together and escape the pool of liquid. In order for liquid molecules to evaporate or boil, they need energy. This is usually accomplished when

NOS nitrous refilling station. Onboard nitrous tanks typically contain enough liquid nitrous for two minutes of boosting, after which they must be refilled. It is often possible to transfer nitrous liquid using gravity without a pump, in some cases by chilling the recipient tank in a freezer overnight to lower the pressure, but electrical pumps make the job easier and quicker. Nitrous liquid typically has vastly greater density than nitrous vapor, but this difference disappears at the critical point. At room temperature, nitrous oxide self-pressurizes to at least 750 psi, meaning that nitrous tanks expel nitrous liquid from a pickup tube without requiring a pump. *NOS*

nearby molecules donate heat (which is why sweat feels cool on the surface of your skin in a light breeze), but not always. Microwave ovens boil water by directly energizing the polar water molecules in a process called dielectric heating. In any case, a liquid's *enthalpy*, or *heat of vaporization*, is the energy required to transform a given quantity of a liquid substance into a gas. As individual liquid molecules approach the threshold energy required to evaporate, they steal heat from anything nearby—including *other nearby liquid molecules* (which is one reason the entire mass of liquid doesn't normally flash off into a vapor instantly just because *some* of the molecules have gained enough energy to boil and why the pool of liquid can become *very* cold). Nitrous oxide has a high heat of vaporization, so boiling or evaporating nitrous requires a lot of heat, which produces a strong chilling effect on anything nearby. Obviously, the colder the starting temperature, the more thermal energy liquid nitrous requires to evaporate—which is an argument for keeping the supply of liquid in the tank cooler.

When nitrous liquid blasts into the air from a 950-psi injector nozzle, it shears into a high-speed mist of tiny droplets hurtling through an environment where pressure is suddenly only 14.7 psi and the boiling point of nitrous is down almost 200 degrees. Nitrous droplets are immediately swept into a vortex of full-throttle, high-speed charge air in which the droplets are constantly losing mass as the surface vaporizes furiously and peels away in waves, stealing heat from anything nearby. The chilling effect from evaporating

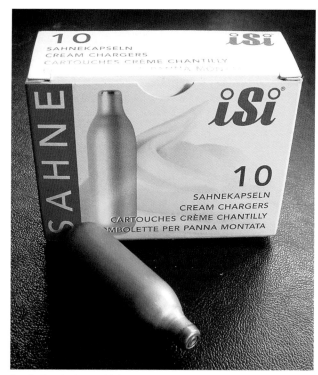

Pure food-grade nitrous oxide is commonly used as a whipped-cream propellant. Medical-grade nitrous oxide is a mild anesthetic that is still commonly used in dentistry. Both applications are dependent on the affinity of nitrous oxide for dissolving in the fatty molecules of cream and the fatty lipids of nerve cells.

nitrous in an enclosed space is so extreme that the temperature drop *decelerates the rate at which droplets can continue to gasify*. Water vapor in the air condenses into a visible cloud of frozen ice-nitrous crystals that coat the injection nozzles and anything else reasonably cool with frost. The cooling effect of evaporating nitrous is so powerful that charge air in the vicinity literally *shrinks*. Meanwhile, of course, the tremendous expansion that makes nitrous such a great refrigerant (volume can increase by a factor of *679* in the liquid-to-gas phase change!) robs more and more space in the intake tract as nitrous continues to evaporate. Up to a point, however, intake air volume lost to gasified or liquid nitrous may be outweighed by gains in *air density* from the intercooling effect, resulting in mass air flow gains of up to 10 percent. On well-engineered street nitrous-injection kits, where the nitrous-to-air mass ratio is less than about 25 percent, the net effect of liquid nitrous injection is predictably that more, rather than less, *air mass* enters an engine during nitrous boost.

MEANWHILE, BACK AT THE NITROUS TANK . . .

When an engine is on the juice, nitrous oxide liquid is boiling furiously in the tank to maintain the gas-liquid pressure equilibrium. In the absence of pressure-maintenance

Carbon-fiber nitrous tanks in a Z06 Corvette. Note the electrically controlled bottle valves and pressure gauges. On self-pressurized nitrous tanks, the pressure is purely a function of temperature. Most people would suggest that nitrous tanks in the passenger compartment of a vehicle like this should be equipped with external venting systems so that over-pressure that blows out the pressure-relief to prevent the possibility of tank explosions will not flood the car with nitrous oxide, an anesthetic.

countermeasures such as very powerful electric tank heaters or nitrogen-assisted pressure normalization, this boiling will chill the tank and lower its vapor pressure. Pressure drop is partially a function of the percentage of gaseous nitrous in the tank. (If there is a lot of gas, there is more immediate propellant to push liquid nitrous out of the tank, resulting in less pressure drop, but reduced pressure drop also slows the rate of boiling that's required to produce more pressurized vapor in a hurry to maintain pressure.) This is one reason some people talk about the percentage of "sweet" nitrous in a tank: A large, full tank containing more nitrous mass has greater thermal momentum and won't lose heat (and, therefore, pressure) as fast as a smaller, emptier tank. Temperature-based pressure drop is one important reason people have invented and patented ingenious devices to maintain nitrous pressure (NANO's system normalizes nitrous pressure and conserves heat by feeding nitrogen from a small, high-pressure auxiliary tank at a regulated pressure into the nitrous tank to keep pressure constant at, say, 1,000 psi; nitrogen gas, of course, floats on top of the nitrous liquid exactly as air floats on water, although nitrogen may aerate nitrous liquid near the critical point).

When the nitrous system is inactive, the opposite problem—tank overheating—can be a problem, and people have engineered solutions for this as well. Nitrous tanks have actually been rigged to self-cool by periodically bleeding nitrous through an expansion valve to keep the tank refrigerated below 97.7 degrees F—though this approach does waste expensive nitrous oxide, which is also a virulent greenhouse gas. Bleeding nitrous gas produces a far more powerful cooling effect inside the tank than bleeding liquid.

Bottle Temperature and Nitrous Self-Pressurization

Bottle Temp. °F	Vapor Pressure (psi)
-30	167
-20	203
-10	240
0	283
10	335
20	387
32	460
40	520
50	590
60	675
70	760
80	865
85	950
97	1,069

Most nitrous systems feed the engine nitrous oxide under pressure of self-generated vapor pressure in the tank. Vapor pressure increases from zero at -128F (the boiling point of nitrous at atmospheric pressure) to 1,070 psi at 97.7 degrees. Pressure will continue to increase at higher temperatures, but 100 percent of the nitrous will be a gaslike "super-critical" fluid, which will have far less cooling effect when the nitrous is released into the engine intake system. *Tsinghua University*

Nitrous injection system for radio-controlled mini-vehicles uses whipped-cream nitrous "whippets." *Nitrous Express*

BOTTOM LINE

Here are the reasons hot rodders and racers should care about the physics of phase change in nitrous oxide:

1. Liquid nitrous oxide is typically much more dense than gaseous nitrous, so there is a significant difference in the mass of each that will flow through an injection orifice per time at a given pressure: Dispensing liquid from the bottom of a nitrous tank usually delivers a much greater mass of oxidizer than bleeding vapor from the top of the same tank.

2. When liquid nitrous boils into gas—for example, during the sudden tremendous expansion that takes place when high-pressure *liquid* nitrous blasts through an injection nozzle jet into low-pressure charge air—there is a powerful cooling effect that greatly increases the density of charge air and nitrous per cubic inch of intake volume. Gas expansion from injected *gaseous* nitrous produces a similar, but much less powerful, cooling effect.

3. It is important to know whether you have a tank of liquid nitrous at 90 degrees F, or a tank of gaseous (supercritical) nitrous at 100 degrees F, because as long as a tank of liquid nitrous oxide remains at a fixed temperature, the pressure is stabilized by the self-regulating mechanism of vapor pressure until all liquid is gone. The pressure of a tank containing only nitrous gas, on the other hand, declines when the system discharges gas, progressively affecting how much nitrous will flow through injection jets.

THE FIRE CHEMISTRY OF NITROUS COMBUSTION

When something burns, it is combining with oxygen, i.e., oxidizing. It's the oxygen content of the intake charge that's critical in supporting internal combustion in an engine, because only the oxygen actually reacts with fuel. The more oxygen there is available for combustion, the more fuel the engine can burn, thus the more horsepower the engine can produce. Any substance able to contribute oxygen to the combustion process is known as an "oxidizer." Air is an oxidizer. Nitrous oxide is a more powerful oxidizer than air.

As we've already discussed, nitrous injection can have a supercharging effect by refrigerating or intercooling charge gases, increasing air density and therefore the oxygen content of inducted charge air. More significantly, nitrous injection functions as a type of "chemical supercharger" by enriching the percentage of oxygen available for combustion in the inducted charge gases.

The percentage of oxygen in nitrous is easy to calculate. We start with the atomic weight of the oxygen atom, which is approximately 16 (8 protons, 8 neutrons), and the atomic

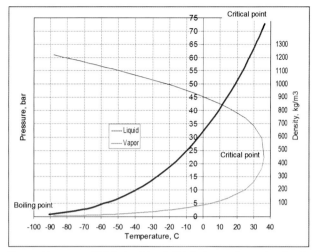

Nitrous oxide pressure (thick line) and density (thin line) versus temperature. Density and pressure changes tend to offset each other, greatly reducing the effect of temperature on liquid nitrous mass flow from a tank.

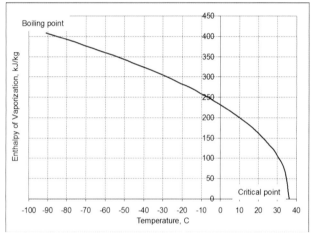

Heat required to vaporize nitrous oxide at various temperatures.

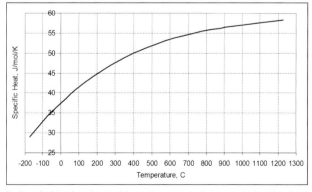

Heat required to raise nitrous oxide one degree versus temperature when there's no phase change.

weight of a nitrogen atom, which is roughly 14 (7 protons, 7 neutrons). The combined atomic weight of a nitrous oxide molecule, which contains two nitrogen atoms and one oxygen atom, is thus:

2 × 14 [two nitrogen atoms] + **16** [one oxygen atom] = **44** [total atomic weight of 44]

Oxygen constitutes 16/44, or 36.36 percent, of the weight of nitrous oxide, making it a significantly more powerful oxidizer than air, which is only 23.2 percent oxygen. Nitrous oxide thus contains almost 60 percent more oxygen molecular weight than air (and nitrous is denser as well).

The flip side is that, because nitrogen tends to moderate and slow combustion (a bit like the control rods in a nuclear reactor), nitrous oxide's reduced 63.64 percentage of nitrogen makes it a *harsher* oxidizer than air, which has 75.47 percent nitrogen mass.

So, how much oxygen does it take to burn fuel in a nitrous-equipped internal combustion powerplant?

STOICHIOMETRIC COMBUSTION

In theory, required oxygen should be determined according to the chemically ideal, or *stoichiometric*, ratio of oxidizer to fuel. Stoichiometric combustion is the ratio of the weights of the oxidizer and fuel at which 100 percent of both are consumed in the burn. Ratios with a greater percentage of oxygen than stoichiometric—in which some of the oxygen cannot be used—are referred to as *lean* mixtures and occur as higher numbers. Mixtures with an excess of fuel that cannot be completely burned are called *rich* mixtures and are represented by lower numbers.

As you'd expect, the *stoichiometric* ratio of combustion varies for various fuels and oxidizers according to the chemical composition of the fuel and the oxygen content of the oxidizer. In the case of gasoline burning in air, it is not actually possible to compute a rigorously *perfect* stoichiometric air-fuel ratio because gasoline is not typically one homogeneous molecule but a stew of a dozen or so

The ability of nitrous liquid to generate extremely high vapor pressure that can reach tank-bursting pressure requires the installation of a safety disk that blows off to relieve pressure well below the bursting threshold of an aluminum tank. There have apparently only been two automotive nitrous tank explosions in history, though it is fairly common for the blow-out disk to burst if solar or engine heating raises tank temperature much above 120F. *Nitrous Outlet*

hydrocarbons in the 6 to 12 carbon atom range. However, we can compute the precise stoichiometric ratio using the stand-in representative hydrocarbon *isooctane* (C_8H_{18}), also known as 2,2,4-Trimethylpentane, a fuel with properties similar to gasoline that can be seamlessly used to fuel spark-ignition engines designed to run on gasoline. Isooctane and air react to produce carbon dioxide, water, nitrogen exhaust gas, and heat as follows:

$$C_8H_{18} + 12.5O_2 + 47N_2 \rightarrow 8CO_2 + 9H_2O + 47N_2 + \text{heat}$$

Looking up the precise atomic weights of carbon (12.0107) and hydrogen (1.00794) in a periodic table, we find the atomic weight of **isooctane** (C_8H_{18}) is exactly:

$$(8 \times 12.0107) + (18 \times 1.00794) = 96.0856 + 18.14292 = 114.22852$$

Looking up the atomic weights of oxygen (15.9994) and nitrogen (14.0067), we calculate the atomic weight of the **air** required to burn a single atom of isooctane as follows:

$$(12.5 \times 15.9994 \times 2) + (47 \times 14.0067 \times 2) = 399.985 + 1316.6298 = 1716.6148$$

The stoichiometric **air-fuel ratio for isooctane** is thus exactly **1716.6148/114.22852 = 15.0279** or roughly **15.0:1**.

Because typical gasoline is not isooctane but a stew of hydrocarbons that usually average out to weigh slightly more than isooctane, the stoichiometric **air-fuel ratio of gasoline** is usually understood to be **14.7**. That said, the specs of gasoline often vary according to the season, altitude, and local smog laws of the market into which it is sold. Racing fuels, in particular, can sometimes be atypical, as competitors forced to use "event fuel" in competitions like the Land Speed Record Trials have sometimes discovered to their misfortune when their perfectly tuned engines were suddenly too rich, too lean, or down on power.

Because only the oxygen in air can actually burn anything, and only 23.2 percent of the weight of air is oxygen, you actually need only about 3 1/2 pounds of pure oxygen to burn a pound gasoline, as follows (once again using isooctane):

$$399.985/114.22852 = 3.5016, \text{ or roughly } 3.5:1$$

Using **pure nitrous oxide as an oxidizer to burn gasoline**, stoichiometric combustion occurs as follows, with nitrous oxide dissociating into oxygen and nitrogen in the intermediate step (in the process producing additional heat):

$$C_8H_{18} + 25N_2O \rightarrow C_8H_{18} + 25N_2 + 12.5O_2 \rightarrow 8CO_2 + 9H_2O + 25N_2 + \text{heat}$$

Before

After

One of the two historic nitrous tank explosions took place in this Nissan Maxima weekend club racer, which was reduced to junk when the tank exploded for reasons that were not available at the time of this writing. Fortunately, the car was in the garage and unoccupied when the tank let go. *Never* tamper with the safety blow-out disk in a misguided attempt to make more power.

As we've already seen, the true atomic weight of nitrous oxide is

$$(14.0067 \times 2) + 15.9994 = 44.0128$$

The stoichiometric ratio of nitrous to isooctane is therefore

$$(25 \times 44.0128) \text{ [weight nitrous]}/114.22852 \text{ [weight isooctane]} = 1100.32/114.2285 = 9.6326$$

Burning a pound of gasoline in stoichiometric combustion thus requires only 9.6 pounds of pure nitrous versus 14.7 pounds of air, meaning a given mass of nitrous oxide can burn at least 50 percent more fuel than air—which is the main point of injecting nitrous. What's more, because nitrous oxide gas has greater density than air, a particular *volume* of nitrous actually has even more of an advantage as an oxidizer, with 2.3 times the oxygen of air.

Whether the oxidizer is air, oxygen, nitrous oxide, or something else, stoichiometric ratios vary as well according to the *fuel*. For combustion with air, stoichiometric ratios range from a low of 1.7 with nitromethane (the main virtue of which is that it requires so little oxygen to burn), 6.45 burning methanol, 9.0 with ethanol, 14.7 for gasoline, and 15.6 for propane (using LP or natural gas, the stoichiometric ratio falls between 15.5 and 16.5, depending on the mix of propane/butane or methane/ethane in the fuel). For nitrous combustion, the numbers range from 4.13 burning methanol to 5.74 for ethanol, 9.6 for gasoline, and 10.0 for propane. Many people would say it's dangerous and crazy trying to burn nitromethane with nitrous oxide because the risk of engine damage is so extreme, but it *can* be made to work if you know what you're doing (see the sidebar "Quest for Power").

The tidy concept of chemically ideal stoichiometric combustion is *useful as a reference point,* but, unfortunately when it comes to combusting fuel in high-performance automotive engines with nitrous oxide injection, the stoichiometric nitrous-fuel ratio is essentially academic.

Why so?

1. Stoichiometric combustion makes suboptimal power and raises the octane number requirement of an engine. Stoichiometric combustion works fine at idle or light cruise to deliver good fuel economy and low emissions on low-performance street cars, but it is dangerous to almost any high-compression, high-performance, spark-ignition engine under heavy load, particularly when there is a power-adder involved. Stoichiometric combustion will destroy a nitrous engine in a hurry due to the lack of evaporative fuel cooling, the higher heat of lean combustion, and the reduced percentage of nitrogen available to act as a combustion moderator for oxygen-enriched combustion (see the sidebar "Stoichiometric Combustion and Fuel Enrichment" on page 29).

2. It would be impractical to replace air completely with nitrous as the sole oxidizer for a performance engine during nitrous boost because so much nitrous would be required.

3. Even if you could carry enough nitrous, it would be virtually impossible to support high-power combustion using pure nitrous oxide without overheating or detonation due to the high oxygen content and low nitrogen content of a pure nitrous-fuel charge mixture. During World War II, scientists tried very hard to get a single-cylinder aircraft test engine boosted with oxygen injection to run reliably on air enriched to 38 percent oxygen in high-power wartime testing by pouring

QUEST FOR POWER

Power is the great aphrodisiac.
—Henry Kissinger

"Keith Black's shop was 20 miles away, so we called him," says Dallas supercar-builder Bob Norwood, thinking back on the days in the late 1960s when he worked full time on a competition nitrous research project in southern California. "I said, 'We're gonna dyno us a Top Fuel drag motor on nitro and laughing gas; you're close, why don't you come on down?' There's this silence, and then he says, 'I'm already too close.'"

You mention testing a Top Fuel drag motor on a horsepower dyno to people who know, their eyes get wide: How do you test the power of a Keith Black Race Hemi drag engine making the power of a railway locomotive from 500 cubic inches on rocket fuel with a full-power life span of maybe 60 seconds? With computer simulations, generally. But not always: Bob Norwood is surely one of the few people on earth who had a Fueler engine on a real dyno—with nothing in the way of that time-bomb engine a few feet away but the plate-glass window of the control room.

"We had this humongous Clayton dyno we called Tugboat Annie," says Norwood, "built to test the horsepower on World War II heavy bomber engines and tugboat clutches and stuff. Dale Armstrong and I were racing blown fuel Funny Cars at the time, and we had this all-steel blown 426 Hemi that was winning races at 250 miles per hour or so on 90 percent nitromethane. We had no idea how much power it would make—if it lived long enough to get a reading—because we had never heard of anyone testing one before."

Norwood and crew rigged up boat headers to the Hemi and piped the exhaust out through the ceiling. Then they hit the starter button. "We were so freaked by this incredible Fueler rattling and knocking you can't usually hear due to the open exhausts on a drag car," says Norwood, "at first we shut it down, but thinking it over, the oil pressure was good, and the engine was winning races, so we decided to go for it." After dealing with a series of minor explosions that blew a header clean off the block in a brilliant flash of light and threatened to launch the blower into orbit, Norwood actuated the throttle manually from another room and brought the Hemi back up to 6,500. Just before punching the nitrous button to inject additional fuel and oxygen, he noted the giant scale on Tugboat Annie's torque meter pushing through 1,600 lb-ft of torque—three times that of a full-race hemi engine on gasoline—and more than 2,000 horsepower!

The nitrous hit with a sound like Frankenstein clearing his throat—followed immediately by an abrupt, dreadful silence. For a second time, men dove for the deck—warily approaching the engine moments later when all seemed clear. What they eventually discovered was every pushrod in the engine folded neatly in half. Black's analysis: Cylinder pressures so extreme the engine could not open its own valves against the force. Undaunted, Norwood and Armstrong immediately installed D&D rods, generated another 300 horsepower with the nitrous, and took it out to the track where the National Hot Rod Association was so impressed by the results they immediately banned nitrous from fuel drag cars.

---

in immense amounts of 115/145 ultra-high-octane enrichment fuel, alcohol-water injection at 50 percent fuel mass, and tons of ignition retard. As you might expect, the scientists used gaseous rather than liquid oxygen. The project was a success in its goal of raising the service ceiling of the engine to altitudes unreachable with air-supercharging alone, but the engine was so severely knock-limited with the oxygen injection active that the engine developed *less* power at lower altitudes than could be achieved if the engine was run on air alone at higher manifold pressure. In the real world, air can be enriched with nitrous to boost engine power, but nitrous must be diluted with air for the engine to perform well and live.

4. Nitrous engines burn a blend of air and nitrous, and the charge gas oxygen content is typically unknown. In fact, when you enrich air with nitrous to boost the power of a variable-speed automotive engine, the oxygen content of the intake charge is a moving target. Although nitrous flow typically remains constant, in theory, at least within stages, mass airflow varies constantly according to engine speed and volumetric efficiency. It's worse than that because, in the real world, most nitrous-injection systems struggle and fail to keep nitrous delivery constant in the face of factors such as temperature-induced changes in nitrous tank pressure, temperature lag, changes in liquid nitrous density that can occur due to nitrous temperature

changes, or foaming during partial phase changes from heat soak or supply line pressure drop (which is why NACA scientists studying nitrous injection in combat aircraft engines during World War II premixed conditioned air and nitrous *vapor* into a precisely formulated "enriched-air" brew of known composition).

True, some sophisticated modern nitrous-injection systems now use pulsewidth-modulation techniques to feather in the nitrous hit "gently" according to a configurable "ramp time" during which nitrous pulses of increasing duration help to prevent smoking the tires or breaking

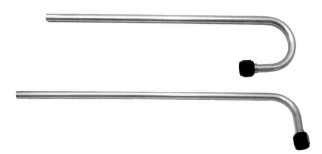

Two vent tubes that attach to the safety blow-out fitting on the bottle control valve of a nitrous tank. You don't want to be breathing nitrous oxide (an inhalation anesthetic!) when you are driving, though opening the windows is usually a fairly good countermeasure if you don't crash due to the lack of visibility in a dense cloud of freezing nitrous vapor. *Nitrous Outlet*

STOICHIOMETRIC FUEL-TO-NITROUS RATIOS FOR VARIOUS COMMON FUELS

Molecules containing carbon and hydrogen combine with oxygen to form carbon dioxide (CO_2) and water (H_2O).

OPTIMUM NITROUS/GASOLINE RATIO

The chemical formula for isooctane (a chemically pure form of gasoline) is C_8H_{18} and the stoichiometric chemical equation for combustion is

Equation 1:

$C_8H_{18} + 25\,N_2O \rightarrow 8\,CO_2 + 9H_2O + 25\,N_2$ (Fuel + nitrous oxide → carbon dioxide + water + nitrogen)

The hydrocarbon fuel (in this case isooctane, a chemically pure gasoline) combines with the oxygen content of nitrous oxide and forms 8 molecules of carbon dioxide and 9 molecules of water plus 25 diatomic molecules (two atoms per molecule) of nitrogen (N_2).

The atomic weights of the above elements are:

Hydrogen	1
Carbon	12
Nitrogen	14
Oxygen	16

Nitrous-to-fuel ratio by weight can be determined by dividing the mass of the oxidizer by the mass of the fuel:

Equation 2:

(nitrogen) (oxygen) (carbon) (hydrogen)
$((25 \times 14 \times 2) + (25 \times 16)) / ((8 \times 12) + (18 \times 1))$

These values are obtained from equation 1; for example, the 25 molecules of nitrogen in the nitrous oxide are multiplied by the atomic weight of nitrogen (14) and that is multiplied by 2, since the diatomic molecules of nitrogen (N_2) contain two atoms. Thus:

$((700 + 400)) / 114 = 1,100/114 = 9.649$

What does this ratio mean? Because the values for the number of molecules were obtained from the stoichiometric chemical equation (meaning that complete combustion will "use up" all of the molecules called for in the equation), the mass figure ratio gives us a relation (by mass; i.e., weight) of how much of fuel must be combined with the oxidizer (nitrous oxide) to obtain complete combustion. Therefore, the above value of 9.649 indicates that 9.649 pounds of nitrous oxide is needed to combust 1 pound of gasoline.

This same relationship can be applied to other fuels, as follows:

OPTIMUM NITROUS/PROPANE RATIO

The chemical formula for propane is C_3H_8 and the stoichiometric equation is

Equation 3:

$C_3H_8 + 10\,N_2O \rightarrow 3CO_2 + 4H_2O + 10N_2$

Therefore
Equation 4:

(nitrogen) (oxygen) (carbon) (hydrogen)
$((10 \times 14 \times 2) + (10 \times 16))/((3 \times 12) + (8 \times 1)) = 440/44 = 10$

This ratio indicates that 10 pounds of N_2O will be required for each pound of propane.

OPTIMUM NITROUS/METHANE RATIO

The chemical formula for methanol is CH_3OH, therefore

Equation 5:

$CH_3OH + 3N_2O \rightarrow CO_2 + 2H_2O + 3\,N_2$

Therefore
Equation 6:

(nitrogen) (oxygen) (carbon) (hydrogen) (oxygen)
$((3 \times 14 \times 2) + (3 \times 16))/((1 \times 12) + (4 \times 1) + (1 \times 16)) = 132/32 = 4.13$

4.13 pounds of N_2O are needed to fully burn 1 pound of methanol.

OPTIMUM NITROUS/ETHANOL RATIO

The chemical formula for ethanol is C_2H_5OH, therefore

Equation 7:

$C_2H_5OH + 6N_2O \rightarrow 2CO_2 + 3H_2O + 6N_2$

Therefore
Equation 8:

(nitrogen) (oxygen) (carbon) (hydrogen) (oxygen)
$((6 \times 14 \times 2) + (6 \times 16))/((2 \times 12) + (6 \times 1) + (1 \times 16)) = 264/46 = 5.74$

5.74 pounds of N_2O are needed to fully burn 1 pound of ethanol.

---

engine parts; but once the nitrous hit has ramped up to full duty cycle, mass flow is usually intended to remain constant (in fact, many solenoids effectively go "static" [i.e., fully on] at duty cycles as low as 60 percent). Assuming a constant nitrous flow, supplemental nitrous enrichment fuel can be calibrated to achieve a target nitrous-fuel ratio, which is a useful concept that simplifies a lot of things. But it's only a concept: Nitrous is blended with supplemental enrichment fuel and a variable quantity of primary charge air and fuel, meaning that the target supplemental fuel-nitrous ratio is part of a much bigger picture that makes the ratio essentially *imaginary*.

REAL-WORLD NITROUS COMBUSTION

Nitrous-boosted combustion in a piston engine occurs as follows:

1. Nitrous oxide blasts into the intake system of a performance engine as a fog of tiny droplets and vapor ("liquid" nitrous may be only 50 percent liquid as it emerges from the injection nozzle) that begins boiling immediately. Injected nitrous is swept up in charge air hurtling toward the intake valves at speeds that can approach 200 feet per second at full throttle and high rpm—creating a race between the time it takes

STOICHIOMETRIC COMBUSTION AND FUEL ENRICHMENT

Regardless of whether an engine is boosted with nitrous injection or other power-adders, in the presence of sufficient air, "gasoline" (which can be a lot of things) and air react chemically in a ratio of 14.65 (usually rounded up to 14.7) moles of air to 1 mole of gasoline during the burn, producing water and carbon dioxide. This chemically perfect air-fuel charge mixture is referred to as *stoichiometric*, and non-gasoline fuels such as methyl alcohol have their own stoichiometric air-fuel ratios that can vary considerably from gasoline. Methanol's is about 6.4:1, and nitromethane's is 1.7:1. Diesel's is roughly 15:1 (but no one ever runs a diesel at stoich mixtures).

The complex numerical variations in stoichiometric ratios of various fuels can be expressed using the lambda system, in which lambda is defined as the ratio of the actual air-fuel mixture to the stoichiometric ratio of the fuel being used, also known as the *equivalence ratio*. Thus, an engine running at an air-fuel ratio of 14.7 air versus gasoline is running at 14.7/14.7 or lambda 1.0. The same engine running at an air-gasoline ratio of 12.5-1 is running at 12.5/14.7 or lambda 0.85. To achieve .85 lambda in a methanol-fueled engine the required air-methanol ratio is $.85 \times 6.4 = 5.44$.

Under ideal conditions with perfectly mixed fuel and oxidizer and no time restrictions, combustion reactants combine at the stoichiometric ratio with nothing left over. But perfect combustion is an ideal rather than a reality, and real-world combustion cannot be perfect and absolute. Stoichiometric combustion in an engine—aye, in a laboratory flask!—always results in some residual exhaust-gas fuel that encountered no oxygen to burn it, some partially burned fuel in the form of carbon monoxide that didn't find enough oxygen, and some residual oxygen that somehow encountered nothing to burn. If there is a surplus of fuel—and therefore insufficient oxygen available to produce complete combustion—combustion results in exhaust with significant levels of unburned waste hydrocarbons and partially combusted carbon monoxide gas, which itself is a significant fuel that burns with a hot blue flame.

Nonetheless, richer than stoichiometric air-fuel mixtures make more power. Why is this?

The reason a spark-ignition engine needs richer mixtures than you'd expect from a mathematical point of view for best torque stems from the persistent air famine in this type of engine and from the fact that real-world internal combustion in a piston engine is messy. Combustion is not some neat thermodynamic or chemical equation; rather it's a swirling, turbulent mixture of high-speed fluids and gases of varying temperature and chemical composition, high-speed flame fronts, sparking electrical energy, and even, on occasion, explosive detonations. Oxygen tends to be scarce in the combustion chambers of a spark-ignition engine at wide-open throttle, particularly if it's a normal-charged engine. In part this is because only about 21 percent of air is the oxygen that's really needed for combustion (the rest being nitrogen gas, which is nearly inert), so you need a lot of air by weight to burn gasoline at stoichiometric air-fuel ratios (14.65 times as much).

Meanwhile, you're always trying to maximize the horsepower available from a given size and weight of the powerplant. It is phenomenally difficult to get a normal-charged engine to charge itself with even the displacement of the engine in cubic feet per minute of air. At higher engine speeds there is very little *time* available to charge the cylinders. The airway into the combustion chambers by necessity consists of twisting, complex, restrictive plumbing, with various obstacles in the way (valves, throttlebodies, and so on) which completely block the airway a high percentage of the time. If you could somehow get more oxygen in the engine, you'd want to inject more fuel to optimize power, and then there'd again be an air shortage. What's more, even if you didn't want more peak horsepower, you'd *need* to inject more fuel to minimize the air surplus at full throttle to keep from

damaging the engine. The air famine in piston engines is the reason for forced-induction and nitrous injection, but even on boosted engines, the goal is still to make maximum use of the available oxygen supply to optimize power.

Which brings us back to the reasons for oxygen-fuel mixtures richer than stoichiometric. Because oxygen is relatively scarce, fuel is easily abundant, and the charge mixture can never be entirely homogenous; the strategy that optimizes power on *any* spark-ignition engine is to make sure that every molecule of oxygen that does make it into the combustion chambers has something to burn. For normal-charged engines running on gasoline fuel, it turns out the way to accomplish this is to enrich the air-fuel mixture from the chemically ideal 14.7:1 to something in the range of 13:1. It's a little like inviting extra girls to a dance to increase the odds every guy can always find a partner. Depending on engine speed, gasoline fuel will produce best torque over a *range* of mixtures, with lean best torque (LBT) as lean as 13.3:1, rich best torque (RBT) as rich as 11.5:1, and mean best torque (MBT) in the 12-12.5:1 area. The range of air-fuel mixtures over which an engine will make maximum torque is referred to as the fuel's *sensitivity*. The sensitivity of gasoline narrows at high engine speeds, when the highest possible flame speed is required in order that combustion can complete in the tiny amount of available time.

In any case, it turns out that the difference between power available at stoichiometric mixtures and richer MBT mixtures is considerable. Many normal-charged street engines with moderate compression ratios work well with a 13.3:1 air-fuel ratio for maximum torque with best fuel economy on street gasoline. Low-pressure turbo engines will safely make more power at 12:5 or richer, because 13.3:1 combustion is hotter, and cooler combustion permits more ignition advance without knock, critical to achieving peak cylinder pressure at the optimal time for delivering maximum torque. (Tuners joke that an engine always makes the best power as you lean it out just before it burns up.)

Alas, high-performance gasoline-fueled engines with power-adders will need even *more* fuel than this. This is a shame because the thermal efficiency resulting from air-fuel ratios richer than 12.5 is increasingly inefficient from the point of view of producing the highest combustion energy per weight of fuel, eventually delivering less torque per weight of *oxygen* as mixtures move richer than RBT.

Unfortunately, even at rich best torque oxygen-fuel mixtures, thermal loading from the enhanced power of boosted combustion quickly becomes a critical problem as manifold pressure increases above a psi or two on engines boosted with turbo-supercharging. This can lead to severe high-power detonation with ordinary gasoline. It's even worse on nitrous engines supercharged with chemical means because of the reduced amount of nitrogen available in the charge to act as a combustion moderator. On such a knock-limited engine, the best strategy for maximizing power turns out to be increasing fuel enrichment to produce a super-rich combustion environment in which excess fuel that cannot be burned due to the oxygen shortage *cools off high-combustion temperatures*. In this odd environment, excess gasoline slows combustion by getting in the way and then absorbs large amounts of heat as drops of fuel vaporize—exactly like water or water-plus-alcohol injection, which was commonly used to fight knock prior to EFI and electronic engine management and has recently made something of a comeback.

The required air-fuel ratio of a turbo engine or a nitrous engine with progressive nitrous injection tends to increase in a relatively linear fashion as the boost effect rises from zero, first to maximize torque and then more steeply as surplus fuel becomes a serious anti-knock and anti-heat countermeasure.

for the charge mass to be trapped in the cylinders by the intake valves and the rate at which liquid nitrous droplets fully vaporize. By the time nitrous oxide has completed its journey from the point of injection to the farthest reaches of the combustion chambers, some or all of the nitrous is gas and charge air has lost heat to the boiling, expanding nitrous ("No one knows how much [is still liquid]," said nitrous maven Butch Schrier). Any combination of operating conditions that succeeds in delivering a substantial "sweet spot" of liquid nitrous to the combustion chambers will reveal itself as a burst of power (assuming there's sufficient fuel). At this point, nitrous oxide molecules are bonded firmly together and incapable of burning anything.

2. Heat soak from internal engine surfaces begins to exert a warming effect on intake air.

3. The cooling effect of boiling gasoline (184 calories per gram) has a counter effect on the heating of pure air.

4. The cooling effect of boiling nitrous (43,002.5 cal per kg at 15 degrees C) continues to exert a tremendous cooling effect on the charge.

5. There is a much smaller but finite cooling effect from continuing expansion of nitrous oxide that vaporized in the nitrous supply system.

6. The continued cooling effect of boiling gasoline has a counter effect on adiabatic heating of the charge as the compression stroke proceeds.

7. A spark (or surface ignition) initiates combustion by raising the local temperature of fuel above the auto-ignition temperature (495–536 degrees F in the case of gasoline), at which point nitrous-enhanced combustion accelerates with unusual speed toward peak cylinder pressure. The enhanced flame speed during nitrous combustion typically demands ignition retard of 1 to 2 degrees F per 50 horsepower gain from nitrous to optimize power and prevent detonation.

8. The combustion heat vaporizes any remaining fractions of gasoline and nitrous liquid, which soaks up additional heat. However, as nitrous molecules cook past 565 degrees F, nitrous is done with cooling and essentially goes over to the other side: Oxygen atoms separate violently from the nitrogen pair, forming nitrogen gas and combustion-ready oxygen in an exothermic reaction that *releases the heat of formation* of nitrous, *accelerating* the temperature rise of combustion and adding to nitrous flame speed by increasing turbulence in the combustion chamber. This reaction occurs as follows:

$$2N_2O \rightarrow 2N_2 + O_2 + \text{18,500 calories of heat per mole } N_2O$$

9. As nitrous oxide breaks apart, unstable free oxygen atoms combine greedily with other nearby oxygen atoms to form molecular diatomic oxygen gas (or in some cases directly attack the chemical bonds of fuel molecules with high energy, initiating combustion). Nitrogen atoms combine to form molecular diatomic nitrogen. Oxygen liberated from dissociating nitrous is greatly diluted by air and recently freed molecular nitrogen, but the net effect is to enrich the overall oxygen content of the charge gases. For example, if nitrous is injected in the quantity of 20 percent air mass (and the mass

Liquid oxygen injection may seem like a good alternative to nitrous oxide for chemical supercharging, but it is not. LOX requires an expensive cryogenic container, which must continuously vent evaporation oxygen, and pure oxygen is very dangerous, due to its ability to make almost anything burn. Nitrous oxide is easily capable of providing all the oxygen enrichment an engine can stand (a few percent) without turning into a blow torch, and a tank of liquid nitrous actually contains more oxygen than a tank of *compressed* (non-liquid) oxygen. MODS 120-190-300 gallon tank weighs 1,800-3,600 pounds when full (not easy to transport!).

Gas

Liquid

Gas

Liquid

Cutaway drawing shows nitrous tanks expelling dense liquid or much-less-dense vapor, depending on whether or not nitrous is pushed out of the gas bubble or "under water." *NOS*

Over the years nitrous oxide has been used in rocketry, in some cases as an oxidizer in liquid-fuel rockets, in other cases as a self-pressurized and catalyzed jet propellant for light satellite navigation. *NASA*

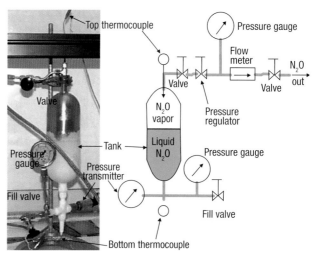

Tsinghua University used this experimental apparatus to investigate the temperature and pressure changes that occurred in a tank as nitrous gas was expelled from the tank over the course of nearly an hour. Note that the stainless steel tank is coated with thick frost: The in-tank cooling effect of boiling nitrous is extremely powerful when gas is expelled from the tank, since all boiling takes place inside the tank. If you ever need to cool a nitrous tank, release some gas (even if you have to invert the tank to accomplish this). *Tsinghua University*

airflow stays constant), then charge gas oxygen increases as follows:

$$(.232\ [O_2\ \text{as \% air}] + (.2\ [\text{nitrous as \% air}] \times .3636$$
$$[O_2\ \text{as \% nitrous}]))/1.2\ [\text{nitrous-air blend as \% air mass}]$$
$$= 25.39\ [\text{\% } O_2\ \text{in combined charge}]$$

10. Flame fronts rip through the combustion chambers, raising cylinder pressure as high at 2,500 psi in the 35-50 degrees of crankshaft rotation between nitrous-on ignition and peak-torque pressure at 15 degrees after top dead center (0.0008 seconds at 7,500 rpm!). With 20 percent nitrous and a 0.75 lambda oxygen-fuel ratio, flame speed is much higher than combustion in plain air. Nitrous combustion produces enhanced cylinder pressure not only by burning more fuel more quickly with more heat, and not only due to the refrigerant effects of nitrous on mass air flow and ignition timing, but due to a more advantageous products-to-reactants combustion ratio (see sidebar "Combustion Products, Reactants, Nitrous Injection, Avogadro's Number and the Ideal Gas Law").

11. Surplus fuel that cannot be burned due to the finite oxygen supply has already had a cooling effect on the charge mixture when vaporizing. During combustion it acts as a moderator on flame speed loading *by getting in the way*, reducing the possibility of spontaneous combustion and detonation. Such "fuel coolant" modestly reduces the peak thermal efficiency of the engine (by lowering combustion heat) but helps protect the engine from overheating damage while simultaneously permitting increased levels of power on knock-limited engines by enabling higher levels of chemical or air supercharging for a given octane fuel.

12. In case of unintended lean oxygen-fuel mixtures, the oxygen surplus ensures that all fuel will burn, leaving none to cool combustion or reduce flame speed. In the harsh combustion environment of a knock-limited nitrous engine that's already on the verge of detonation, the heightened combustion temperature, rapidly increasing pressure, and smaller percentage of combustion-moderating nitrogen in the charge make detonation a certainty. During abnormal nitrous combustion resulting from combustion overheating or overpressure, entire areas of combustion chamber gases spontaneously erupt in flames everywhere at once rather than flame fronts burning smoothly through the charge from the sparkplugs as they should like a fire moving through a field of dry grass. Once detonation begins, it is hard to stop because spark knock magnifies the excessive temperature and pressure problems that led to detonation in the first place, compounding the situation with tremendous spikes of overpressure, out-of-control heat, and parts-busting shock waves. When the charge mixture explodes partway through normal combustion, thermal and mechanical loading increases to critical levels, raising the possibility of preignition at localized hot spots when valves, pistons, and cylinder head surfaces become red-hot and initiate surface combustion before the spark plug fires—radically increasing heat and pressure. In this horrendous, super-heated environment,

COMBUSTION PRODUCTS, REACTANTS, NITROUS INJECTION, AVOGADRO'S NUMBER, AND THE IDEAL GAS LAW

Count Lorenzo Romano Amedeo Carlo Avogadro was an Italian genius who lived from August 9, 1776, to July 9, 1856. Long before it could be proven true in the physical world, Avogadro realized that equal volumes of "ideal" or perfect gases at the same temperature and pressure contain the same number of molecules—and that this concept can be extrapolated into the real world to conclude that the number of molecules in a specific volume of *any gas* is essentially independent of the size or mass of the individual gas molecules when related to an "ideal gas" approximate.

While **Avogadro's Law** is not perfectly true in the real world case, it is statistically very close. To approximate real gas behavior, the trick is to apply an ideal gas or perfect gas definition ("hypothetical gaseous substance consisting of identical point particles of zero size, with no intermolecular forces, but the ability to interchange momentum in elastic collisions with identical gas molecules") to a real gas such as hydrogen or nitrogen. As a tribute to Avogadro, the number of elementary entities (atoms, molecules, ions or other particles) in one mole of a gaseous substance—$6.02214199 \times 10^{23}$—is known as **Avogadro's Number**. A mole is now defined as the amount of a substance containing the same number of elementary units as the number of atoms in 12 grams of carbon-12.

The **ideal gas law** was first stated by Benoît Paul Émile Clapeyron in 1834 as follows:

The state of an amount of gas is determined by its pressure, volume, and temperature according to the equation

PV = nRT

where

P = absolute pressure
V = volume of the vessel
n = amount of substance of gas
R = ideal gas constant, $10.7316 \text{ ft}^3 \cdot \text{psi} \cdot {}^\circ\text{R}^{-1} \cdot \text{lb-mol}^{-1}$ (look it up!)
T = absolute temperature

Thus, equal volumes of, say, lightweight molecular hydrogen, versus nitrogen (with approximately seven times the mass) contain the same number of molecules—as long as they are at the same temperature and pressure and observe ideal or perfect gas behavior.

Since the ideal gas law neglects both molecular size and intermolecular attractions, it is most accurate for mono-atomic gases at high temperatures and low pressures. In the real world case, the law's neglect of molecular size becomes less important for larger volumes, i.e., for lower pressures, and the relative importance of its neglect of intermolecular attractions diminishes with increasing thermal kinetic energy (i.e., increasing temperature).

What this means with respect to boosting engines with nitrous oxide is that a cubic foot of air on its way into an engine has the same number of molecules as a cubic foot of nitrous oxide, or carbon dioxide, or water vapor, or anything else—*as long as they are at the same temperature and pressure.*

The ideal gas law is helpful not only in understanding the implications of replacing air with nitrous in an intake manifold, but in understanding why nitrous combustion tends to generate higher cylinder pressure than combustion with air—*even when the same number of oxygen atoms are involved in either.*

To start with, combustion with nitrous oxide has a different ratio of products to reactants than combustion with air.

Let's say you are going to burn two molecules of gasoline (isooctane) in stoichiometric combustion as follows:

$$2C_8H_{18} + 25O_2 \; [+ \; 47N_2] \rightarrow 16CO_2 + 18H_2O + [47N_2] + \text{heat}$$

Since the nitrogen in air is just along for the ride, the ratio of products (34 total) to reactants (27 total) for combustion with air is 1.259.

Compare this to burning two molecules of gasoline with nitrous oxide as follows:

$$2C_8H_{18} + 50N_2O \; [\rightarrow 2C_8H_{18} + 50N_2 + 25O_2 + \text{heat}] \rightarrow$$
$$16CO_2 + 18H_2O + 50N_2 + \text{heat}$$

The ratio of products (84 total) to reactants (52 total) for combustion with air is 1.615.

Air combustion produces 26 percent more gas particles than were present before combustion, but nitrous combustion produces 61 percent more gas particles than were present before combustion.

Bottom line, nitrous combustion produces 28.27 percent more particles than air combustion. The ideal gas law tells us that more particles at the same temperature will exert more pressure.

But what is the effect of the nitrogen gas in air (which is not involved in combustion)?

Being virtually inert, nitrogen gas in air does not contribute heat to combustion, nor does it multiply in number. When heated, nitrogen increases in pressure, but no more or less so than any gas heated to equal temperature.

But what of this "equal temperature" business? Obviously, the more mass there is in a container of gas, the more heat it takes to raise the temperature of the mass to a fixed point. Comparing stoichiometric combustion of a fixed amount of fuel using pure nitrous oxide versus combustion of the same amount of fuel with ordinary air, the mass involved in stoichiometric combustion of isooctane is

surplus oxygen that has not reacted with fuel attacks overheated metal components like a blowtorch, burning away metal and sending high-velocity molten fragments burning their way through metal like a shaped charge. The engine virtually consumes itself. High-power nitrous detonation or preignition can produce catastrophic engine damage in a matter of two to three seconds. When a nitrous engine is boosting, lean air-fuel-nitrous mixtures must be avoided at all cost.

13. A dangerous shortage of fuel can result from incorrect oversized nitrous injector jetting or undersized wet-nitrous fuel jetting, inadequate fuel pressure, or poorly calibrated engine management electronics.

FUEL CHARACTERISTICS AND NITROUS COMBUSTION

Virtually all spark-ignition engines boosted with nitrous injection or air-supercharging are knock-limited. This

114.23 (atomic weight of fuel) + **1,716.61** (weight 14.7x air) = **1,830.84** (total mass)

Meanwhile, the mass involved in stoichiometric nitrous combustion is

114.23 (atomic weight of fuel) + **1,100.32** (weight 9.6x nitrous) = **1,214.55** (total mass)

There is only 66 percent of the mass to heat during pure nitrous combustion versus combustion with air (and, in pure oxygen combustion, only 28 percent of the mass).

But is the heat from stoichiometric nitrous combustion the same as the heat from air combustion? No. In the first place, we have already discussed the fact that the dissociation of nitrous oxide at 565 degrees F into oxygen and nitrogen contributes the heat of formation of nitrous to the subsequent heat of fuel combustion, so nitrous combustion is already ahead on heat.

But how scarce is heat in a piston engine, whatever the fuel and oxidizer being used? Well, very scarce in the sense that it is heat in combustion gases that does the work of pushing down the pistons, and anything that lowers heat lowers combustion pressure, reduces horsepower, and damages basic thermal efficiency. In another sense, not scarce at all. Only about 25 percent of combustion heat actually can be effectively harnessed to do any useful work, and a lot of heat is going to be wasted. In yet another sense, there's generally *way too much heat* in high-output gasoline-fueled spark-ignition engines boosted with chemical or air supercharging, which are virtually always knock-limited and in constant danger of overheating and burning up internal parts, particularly if the boost lasts more than a few seconds. The whole purpose of fuel enrichment and water injection is to limit combustion overheating by throwing in additional liquid that will not all be burned, which slows down combustion, soaks up some heat when it vaporizes, and then limits maximum combustion temperature by adding to the total mass that must be heated.

Is there a difference in the thermal efficiency of boosting with chemical versus air supercharging? Yes. Nitrous injection produces substantial power gains not just from combusting more fuel but from the improved volumetric efficiency that results from nitrous oxide charge cooling. Unlike air-supercharging, nitrous combustion burns faster and hotter without changing the *compression ratio*—or even the effective compression ratio—of the engine during nitrous boost, as happens during air-supercharging. Nitrous combustion has thermal advantages over air-supercharging, because a higher

percentage of heat energy can be extracted from the expansion phase compared to a similar turbo-supercharged powerplant. In a nitrous engine, increasing the compression ratio not only increases power during combustion due to the increased charge density but simultaneously gains thermal efficiency from the increased expansion ratio. By contrast, turbo-supercharging an engine increases only the *effective* compression ratio, and the *expansion ratio* during the power stroke of a turbo-supercharged powerplant is essentially unchanged from that of an equivalent normal-charged engine. Given the higher fuel burn rate of an engine expending precious energy driving a mechanical blower, a supercharged engine actually tends to be *less* thermally efficient than it was when normal-charged. *Turbo* charged engines are able to reclaim some of the waste heat energy in the exhaust, and are thus able to approach the thermal efficiency of a normal-charged engine. Turbo engines gain efficiency almost exclusively from their increased dynamic range, which permits smaller engines with fewer cylinder and reduced internal friction to deliver very high specific power, *but only when it's required for hard acceleration, towing, or maximum performance hill climbing.* The rest of the time a turbocharger is freewheeling, and the engine functions as a small, low-output normal-charged powerplant. When not boosting, nitrous engines lose their superpowers and revert back to normal-charged efficiency.

Other differences? Again, there is a different ratio of products to reactants in nitrous combustion versus combustion with air, with the advantage going to nitrous injection. There is a difference in energy wasted turning a mechanical supercharger to pack the cylinders with oxygen air versus effortlessly receiving the oxygen for free from a nitrous tank. Obviously, for a *given required amount of charge-gas oxygen*, there is more total charge mass from the added nitrogen dilution of air induction versus the lower nitrogen content of nitrous oxide (which is the whole point of nitrous!), meaning that the effective compression ratio of air-supercharging is higher, compression heating is higher, and there is an advantage to heat spent raising the temperature of charge-gas-nitrogen because it contributes to cylinder pressure in a way that heat lost into the cooling jacket does not. The additional nitrogen mass and higher effective compression ratio reduce thermal leakage due to differences in the ratio of combustion chamber gas mass versus surface area when an air-supercharger has packed the combustion chambers with a large amount of inert nitrogen that is not involved in producing heat, but retains heat and contributes to cylinder pressure once it *is* heated. Obviously, if the cooling system has to be run cooler in the case of nitrous to stop detonation or cylinder head overheating, this reduces the thermal efficiency of the engine.

means that maximum power is not limited by the engine's ability to ingest more oxygen and fuel to make more torque (i.e., volumetric efficiency), but by the need to prevent engine damage from detonation. Detonation occurs when oxygen-fuel mixtures explode violently in the cylinders rather than burning normally. Nitrous injection is about increasing cylinder pressure to make power—and anything that increases cylinder pressure and heat (they go together) increases the risk of detonation.

If an engine is experiencing detonation, the choice is switching to a fuel with a higher octane rating (i.e., higher auto-ignition temperature), limiting boost, or retarding ignition timing to limit peak combustion pressure (which kills torque). Longer term anti-detonation countermeasures involve reducing the compression ratio or taking other steps to reduce the octane number requirement of the engine (see the sidebar "The Octane Number Requirement [ONR] of Performance Engines" on page 50).

Fuel	Oxidant	Temperature (C)	Flame Speed (meters/sec)
Acetylene	Air	2,400	1.60 - 2.70
"	Nitrous Oxide	2,800	2.60
"	Oxygen	3,140	8.00 - 24.80
Hydrogen	Air	2,050	3.24 - 4.40
"	Nitrous Oxide	2,690	3.90
"	Oxygen	2,660	9.00 - 36.80
Propane	Air	1,925	0.45
Natural Gas	Air	1,950	0.39
Gasoline	Air	?	10.0 – 25.0
Gasoline	Nitrous Oxide	?	?
Gasoline	Oxygen	?	?

Combustion characteristics of various fuels and oxidizers

In general, combustion with nitrous oxide tends to magnify any problematic characteristics of a motor fuel.

GASOLINE

Gasoline, a natural stew of hydrocarbons in the 6- to 12-carbon range, has specific heat in the neighborhood of 125,000 British thermal units (Btu) per U.S. gallon—which exceeds that of all other common motor fuels with the exception of diesel. The downside is that many gasoline-sized hydrocarbons have a fairly low auto-ignition temperature (500 to 600 degrees F), and thus a nasty tendency to explode.

Alas, it is difficult (and therefore expensive!) to manufacture gasoline with high octane. Street premium gasolines range from 91 to 94 octane ((R+M)/2), but 91-octane fuel is somewhat problematic for boosted engines. Toluene, an aromatic hydrocarbon and carcinogen with octane of 114 ((R+M)/2) and auto-ignition temperature of 849 degrees F, is about as good as it gets as an octane booster short of deadly tetra-ethyl lead or blending in a lot of oxygenated fuels like alcohol or ether that are not legal in some classes of racing. Commercial unleaded racing fuels tend to max out at either 100 (not oxygenated) or 107 octane (somewhat oxygenated). Leaded racing fuels (which are illegal for street use and will damage catalytic converters and wideband O_2 sensors) are available with octane ratings in the 110 to 120 range. Racing fuels typically cost several times as much per gallon as street premium, and are usually available only in 55-gallon drums.

Adding nitrous to any engine always increases the risk of detonation. Apart from using higher-octane racing gasoline, the best anti-detonation countermeasure is to lower combustion temperatures, and the easiest and most straightforward way to do that is with fuel enrichment. Aggressively retarding ignition timing will defeat knock at the cost of lowering peak combustion pressure, but will not help with surface ignition (pre-ignition).

In an effort to control nitrous tank temperature and pressure, climate-control systems have been developed by nitrous kit suppliers like Nitrous Express. This "Fire and Ice" solid-state electronic heat pump system uses Peltier Junction technology to cool or heat the nitrous tank as conditions require. These systems are virtually never powerful enough to overcome the tremendous vaporization heat sucked from the tank as nitrous boils during boost to maintain vapor pressure. *Nitrous Express*

Nitrous oxide requires robust plumbing to contain the high vapor pressure. Plumbing has traditionally used aircraft-quality Teflon-core braided-stainless steel hose as shown here, but some nitrous suppliers are now providing high-pressure reinforced-rubber "race hose," with its improved insulation capabilities, or high-pressure nylon hose, which can be cut and plumbed without specialized, expensive equipment. *Nitrous Express*

Air Density

°F	°C	lb/ft³	kg/m³
14	−10	0.0837783	1.342
23	−5	0.0822176	1.317
32	0	0.0806569	1.292
41	+5	0.0792211	1.269
50	+10	0.0778477	1.247
59	+15	0.0764743	1.225
68	+20	0.0751633	1.204
77	+25	0.0739147	1.184
86	+30	0.0727286	1.165

As this chart of air density versus temperature shows, one important benefit of injecting liquid nitrous oxide is that the cooling effect of nitrous boiling in the airstream of an engine induction system can actually make additional power beyond the oxygen-enrichment combustion effects by increasing the density of charge air, in some cases resulting in engine volumetric efficiency gains of 10 percent *even after the net effect of some intake air volume being displaced by the injected nitrous.*

Boiling nitrous has such a powerful cooling effect that nitrous oxide is sometimes used to improve horsepower by increasing the effectiveness of a turbo intercooler heat exchanger with liquid nitrous sprayed against the *exterior* of the intercooler. This Nitrous Express "N-tercooler" kit delivers liquid nitrous from a huge spraybar that mounts directly on the intercooler. *Nitrous Express*

A fairly common boosting strategy for modern gasoline-fueled engines with EFI and nitrous injection is to run a dual-fuel-injection architecture in which a small auxiliary tank of supplemental racing gasoline or alcohol provides ultra-high-octane nitrous enrichment fuel—thereby saving the expense of constantly burning ultra-expensive race fuel. An even more effective anti-detonation strategy is to install a complete secondary set of port fuel injectors pressurized from an independent fuel rail and tank, with electronic controls seamlessly switching entirely from the primary street-premium fuel supply to 100 percent race gas when the nitrous-injection system is active.

GASEOUS FUELS

Propane and natural gas have inferior heating value per gallon compared to gasoline (about 65 percent) but are typically less expensive per gallon and per calorie of heat delivered, resulting in a cost structure that makes them attractive to fleet operators capable of setting up their own fuel distribution infrastructure. Propane and natural gas are exceptionally clean-burning, and thus benefit from lenient state and federal requirements for add-on emissions control devices. Some

Physical Properties of Fuels, Water, Nitrous Oxide

	Fuel Type	Specific Gravity	Boiling Point	Vapor Press. 68F	Thermal Decomp.	Oxygen Content	Dielectric Constant	Freeze Point	Latent Heat	Energy
H_2O	Water	1.000	212F	17.54	3,500F	88.89%	80.10	32F	2,256 kJ/kg	
C_8H_{18}	Gasoline (Isooctane)	0.690-0.780	100-400F (244F)	10.44		00.00	1 .0-2.0	-10 to -80F (-224F)	350 kJ/kg	18,400 Btu/lb
CH_3OH	Methanol	0.796	148F	97.48	867F	50.00%	32.6	-137F	1,109 kJ/kg	9,500 Btu/lb
C_2H_5OH	Ethanol	0.794	172F	43.89	685F	35.00%	24.3	-104F	904 kJ/kg	11,500 Btu/lb
CH_3NO_2	Nitromethane	1.140	214F	27.80	890F	52.50%	39.4	-83F	560 kJ/kg	5,000 Btu/lb
$C_2H_5NO_2$	Nitroethane	1.045	255F	15.60	690F	42.70%	19.7	-131F		
N_2O	Nitrous Oxide	0.629	-128F	750.00	565F	36.36%		-132F		

Since they all require heat to boil, liquid fuels, water, and nitrous oxide can all have an important cooling effect on engine combustion. Water, of course, does not contribute energy to combustion, but nitrous oxide actually does contribute a modest effect, since the heat required to form nitrous oxide is released when the molecules break apart.

Air, Fuel, and Nitrous Chemistry (www.o2-technology.com)

Fuel		Gasoline C_8H_{18}		Ethanol/E85 C_2H_5OH		Methanol CH_3OH	
Atomic Weight	Carbon	12 × 8 = 96		12 × 2 = 24		12 × 1=12	
	Hydrogen	1 × 18 = 18		1 × 6 = 6		1 × 4 = 4	
	Oxygen	0 = 0		16 × 1 = 16		16 × 1 = 16	
	Total Weight:	114		46		32	
Air/Fuel Ratio		12.8		7.7 (E85)		5.7	
Components	Oxygen	2.69		1.62		1.20	
	Nitrogen	10.11		6.08		4.50	
	Oxygen	2.69	19.49%	1.92	22.07%	1.70	25.37%
Percentage	Nitrogen	10.11	73.30%	6.08	69.89%	4.50	67.16%
	Fuel	1.00	7.21%	0.70	8.04%	0.50	7.46%
Total Parts		13.8		8.7		6.7	
Oxygen/Fuel		2.69/1		2.74/1		3.40/1	
Nitrous/Fuel Ratio		5.50		3.75 (E85)		2.50	
Components	Oxygen	1.98		1.35		0.90	
	Nitrogen	3.52		2.40		1.60	
Percentage	Oxygen	1.98	30.46%	1.65	34.74%	1.40	40.00%
	Nitrogen	3.52	54.15%	2.40	50.53%	1.60	45.71%
	Fuel	1.00	15.38%	0.70	14.73%	0.50	14.28%
Total		6.50		4.75		3.50	
Oxygen/Fuel Ratio		1.98/1		2.36/1		2.80/1	
Volume/Sec/HP		115cc/10sec/100hp		155cc/10sec/100hp		229cc/10sec/100hp	

*Gasoline assumed to be 6 lb/gal; air assumed to be 21 percent oxygen

Air, fuel and nitrous oxide combustion chemistry with gasoline (isooctane), ethanol, E85 (85 percent ethanol, 15 percent gasoline), and methanol. Alcohol fuels contain less energy per gallon than gasoline, but they run much cooler, have very high knock resistance, and require much less air or nitrous to burn, meaning the power available for a given mass of oxidizer is much higher.

performance enthusiasts and racers have decided the low cost, high octane, and emissions flexibility make it worthwhile dealing with the availability and storage disadvantages of gaseous fuels.

Propane (C_3H_8) and natural gas—a natural blend of methane (CH_4) and ethane(C_2H_6)—are too small and lightweight to remain liquid at ambient temperatures, but the compact molecular structure provides excellent resistance to detonation due to auto-ignition temperatures as high as 1,170 degrees F—which makes propane injection feasible for boosting the power of *diesel* engines that are out of diesel injection capacity! Depending on the specifications,

natural gas may have an octane rating as high as 120, and propane's octane rating of 110 puts it above almost all unleaded gasolines.

The downside of methane/ethane or propane/butane as motor fuels for engines boosted with nitrous injection or turbo-supercharging is that there is no heat of vaporization available for combustion cooling since both fuels are a gas at working temperatures. Without supplemental combustion cooling, the magnitude of power boost available from nitrous injection without risking component failures is much less than what's available from a comparable mixture of nitrous and liquid fuel.

The solution is injecting water or water-alcohol fluid during nitrous or turbo boost, which creates the best of all worlds: economical fuel cost, very high octane, clean emissions, emission legality, comparatively low combustion temperatures, and excellent power boost.

ALCOHOL

Alcohol fuels such as methanol (CH_3OH), ethanol (C_2H_5OH), and propanol (C_3H_7OH) are essentially partially combusted (oxidized) hydrocarbons. In fact, methanol was originally discovered as a byproduct of heating wood underground to make charcoal.

Methanol doesn't have much energy (it is effectively already partially burned!), so you need to burn a lot to make much power, but it is an excellent racing fuel because it provides high specific energy (heating per weight of inducted air), relatively high octane (100) and wonderful combustion cooling properties when used at rich oxygen-fuel ratios—making methanol the fuel of choice for race engines that need to make tons of specific power. All light alcohols have high heat of vaporization (which is why rubbing alcohol feels cold on the skin). Methanol, the lightest alcohol with the most exaggerated characteristics, provides approximately four times the combustion cooling of gasoline—making methanol the perfect fuel for cooling nitrous combustion.

As you'd expect with any fuel, injecting nitrous into an engine burning methyl or ethyl alcohol lowers the detonation limits of the engine, but methanol can be run at very rich oxygen-fuel ratios to fight knock. That said, methanol is actually more prone to pre-ignition than gasoline—meaning that if a methanol-fueled engine was on the verge of pre-ignition from combustion chamber hot spots, injecting nitrous will immediately instigate surface ignition and detonation.

NITROMETHANE AND NITROPROPANE

Nitromethane (CH_3NO_2) and nitropropane ($C_2H_3NO_2$) are nasty fuels with a high potential for destruction. These are essentially light gaseous hydrocarbons with one of the hydrogen atoms replaced by a relatively heavy nitro group (NO_2)—thereby increasing density into the liquid range and providing two oxygen atoms that can potentially be freed from the nitro group and used to combust carbon or hydrogen. Nitropropane, which has more hydrocarbon characteristics than nitromethane, is rarely used because it makes far less specific power than nitromethane. Nitropropane's main virtue is that it will mix with gasoline (nitromethane will not) to generate modest amounts of "liquid horsepower." Nitromethane is the more extreme version of the breed. It is prone to detonation but has a much higher proportion of oxygen (and thus poor heating value), allowing it make a lot of power in a piston engine because the fuel can burn without very much oxygen—or even none at all!

Both nitro fuels are already partially oxygenated, or, you could say, already partially burned. Nitromethane can dissociate in a fairly strong exothermic reaction as a monopropellant without any oxygen at all, releasing water, carbon dioxide, carbon monoxide, hydrogen, nitrogen, and heat as follows:

$$CH_3NO_2 \rightarrow 0.25CO_2 + <F>0.75CO + 0.75H_2O + 0.75H_2 + 0.5N_2 + \text{heat}$$

More efficient stoichiometric combustion of nitromethane in air produces water, CO_2, diatomic nitrogen, and a lot more heat as follows:

$$CH_3NO_2 + 1.5\,O_2 + 2.82\,N_2 \rightarrow CO_2 + 1.5H_2O + 2.82N_2 + \text{heat}$$

Air-Fuel Ratio And Energy Density of the Stoichiometric Air-Fuel Mixture ($\lambda = 1$)

Fuel	Air-Fuel Ratio	Mixture Density	Energy Density	Rel. Energy Density
	(-)	(kg/m³)	(MJ/m³)	(-)
Hydrogen	34.00	0.94	3.21	0.84
Methane	17.20	1.24	3.40	0.89
Propane	15.60	1.32	3.68	0.96
Methanol	6.40	1.49	3.98	1.04
Ethanol	9.00	1.44	3.85	1.01
Gasoline	14.70	1.38	3.83	1.00
Diesel	14.50	1.38	3.79	0.99
Diesel ($\lambda = 1.3$)	18.90	1.36	2.92	0.76

(λ = actual air-fuel ratio/theoretical air-fuel ratio)

Although nitromethane contains only a quarter of the heating value of gasoline (again, it's already partially burned), due to the high oxygen content, a mass of air will burn *eight times* more nitromethane than gasoline, giving the fuel much higher specific energy per air mass than gasoline.

Nitromethane is usually cut with methanol to (1) counteract a vicious tendency to detonate and (2) improve combustion properties—one being nitro's tendency to operate at such rich mixtures that Top Fuel drag engines are constantly at risk of inhaling so much noncompressible fuel that the liquid fuel can overfill and hydro-lock the combustion chamber, with the hydralocked piston blowing the head off the engine on the compression stroke. The properties of nitromethane are highly dependent on the precise alcohol-nitro blend.

Since the main advantage—some would say the *only* advantage!—of nitromethane is that it doesn't need much air to burn (nitromethane is already almost 70 percent oxygen!), and since virtually all nitro engines are also supercharged or turbocharged, the enhanced oxygen content of nitrous oxide would appear to be more or less wasted on nitromethane, with the downside that nitrous is certain to make nitromethane even more prone to detonation.

However, it is possible to imagine some circumstances where a particular blend of air, nitromethane, methanol, reduced supercharger boost, and injected nitrous

THE WANDERING OXYGEN RATIO OF NITROUS INJECTION

In many cases there is no practical alternative to constant nitrous injection for variable-speed engines.

It is possible in theory to feed an engine a blend of charge air enriched on the fly with nitrous to a heightened, fixed, known percentage of oxygen mass—kind of a "super air" that facilitates the kind of precision full-authority fuel management that is now routine on many modern factory performance engines. In fact, scientists actually did deliver homogeneous oxygen-enriched air with fixed oxygen content for wartime testing of chemical supercharging by feeding pure oxidizer (oxygen or nitrous) and air into giant surge tanks at a precise mass flow rate, with the test engines breathing enriched intake charge from the surge tank.

Alternately, it is theoretically possible to achieve the opposite: precisely *varying* charge oxygen content on the fly under computer control using precision variable nitrous or oxygen injection to produce a "designer" torque curve—say, using a speed-density table of target "charge-gas oxygen" (CGO) ratios as the basis of an engine-management strategy designed to optimize fuel, spark, and *oxygen* for perfect performance, traction, and emissions.

In either case, you'd be abandoning constant-flow nitrous delivery in favor of a nitrous architecture that dynamically pulses one or more nitrous solenoid valves with variable frequency to vary duty cycle and, thus, nitrous flow rate in order to inject liquid nitrous oxide as a known ratio of mass airflow the same way that electronic fuel injectors vary pulsewidth in accordance with mass airflow to deliver extremely accurate air-fuel ratios. Alternately, we might imagine a continuous-flow variable nitrous injection system based on variable-orifice or metering architecture, similar to the old Bosch K-Jetronic (CIS) fuel injection that mechanically varied fuel delivery with airflow by moving the plunger in a barrel valve.

In practice, there are tremendous problems even attempting such a strategy:

- An engine injects fuel in a ratio of 7 or 8 percent mass airflow, but a nitrous hit can easily be 20 or 30 percent of airflow, and this is typically delivered though a single solenoid valve rather than one injector per cylinder.
- Nitrous pressure is at least ten times higher than port-EFI fuel pressure.
- Therefore, nitrous solenoids are huge (and slow!) compared to electronic fuel injectors, and thus limited in their ability to achieve

precise flow control across a wide dynamic range. Many nitrous solenoids are really only able to accurately vary the duty cycle in the middle 30-60 percent of the range.
- Even modest pressure bottlenecks in nitrous plumbing can become expansion valves that cause a pressure drop that allows liquid nitrous to fizz with vapor, making it impossible to accurately meter liquid flow that is partially foam.
- Any such vaporization will cause chilling, which can change both liquid and gas density.
- The relatively high boiling point (100 degrees F to 400 degrees F) and low vapor pressure of gasoline components makes it easy for fuel delivery systems to deliver fuel at a reliable 30- to 60-psi pressure in a hot engine compartment with zero fuel boiling problems (what used to called *vapor lock* on old carbureted engines that ran very low pressure fuel supply systems). On the other hand, the temperature gain or loss between, say, 70 and 97.7 degrees F changes nitrous vapor pressure over 300 psi (but nitrous liquid density as well, from 783 to 450 kg/m^3, a negative change of .4528).
- Nitrous components on or near the engine can easily heat-soak to above nitrous' critical temperature of 97.7 degrees, turning liquid nitrous into a gas-like supercritical fluid, with potentially large density changes—which is why it is common to see nitrous racers purging gas (or gas bubbles!) from the nitrous lines in a cloud of freezing mist just before a drag launch.

Even using sophisticated modern electronic controllers and ruggedized nitrous solenoids, it has so far not been practical to vary nitrous delivery in precision concert with changes in engine airflow in order to maintain a consistently heightened but static percentage of oxygen in the charge during nitrous injection.

Which is why no one even tries (except NACA scientists in wartime research, and they did it with nitrous oxide vapor using a huge apparatus); it's a horrendously difficult task simply maintaining a consistent, unvarying constant mass flow of injected nitrous. But assuming nitrous mass flow *can* be held constant, it is still the case that basic non-nitrous mass airflow varies greatly with changes in engine speed, temperature, turbo boost, and other factors (not to mention throttle position—though on most nitrous systems wide-open throttle (WOT) is a critical required state and trigger for nitrous delivery).

oxide, would produce superior power to, say, increased supercharger boost and zero nitrous, or, say, fuel economy improved enough to eliminate a pit stop—or some other esoteric, subtle, advantage available in some particular brand of racing under some particular circumstances. In most cases this blend would probably involve a limited amount of nitro, a lot of methanol, and nitrous replacing or enhancing a certain proportion of turbo-supercharging a certain amount of the time. Only a few pro supertuners and racers have the expertise and financial resources to play this game with enough finesse to derive a worthwhile benefit.

Fuel + oxidizer + AMG Mercedes = Tire smoke

Thus, no matter what you do, the oxygen content of the nitrous-air charge blend is all over the place as an engine accelerates. Consequently, the basic strategy of modern air-fuel engine management—measuring mass airflow (which, more to the point, tells you mass oxygen flow!) and other engine parameters in real time and using this data to derive the precise injection pulsewidth and spark advance required in the next cylinder's power stroke to achieve a target oxygen-fuel combustion ratio for the current engine conditions—is essentially impossible when nitrous is involved.

Engine management for many nitrous-boosted powerplants is a schizophrenic strategy designed to treat nitrous combustion and air combustion as if they were logically independent. Common practice is to determine fueling requirements for injected nitrous as though supplemental fuel could be calibrated to deliver a particular nitrous-fuel ratio without regard for the oxygen and fuel arriving independently in the cylinders through normal means, then depending on the stock engine management algorithms and calibration tables to fuel the basic engine airflow during nitrous boost in the same manner as it does when nitrous injection is disabled. Historically, the most common case is that all nitrous delivery systems are controlled independently of the main engine management systems, as well as some or all fuel delivery components. Some or all electrical or electronic control systems for fuel and nitrous may be completely isolated from air-fuel engine management systems.

Targeting completely independent oxidizer-fuel ratios for basic air-fuel engine operation versus nitrous boost has the virtue of being logically simple, and relatively straightforward to implement. However, this strategy relies on an oversimplified model of the complex interactions that occur in a powerplant—especially in light of the fact that nitrous injection introduces dynamic changes to (1) overall charge oxygen content, (2) combustion fire chemistry, (3) engine octane number requirement (ONR), (4) engine performance, and (5) thermal and mechanical stresses on the engine.

As an example, depending on how and when nitrous is injected into an engine, there may or may not be an opportunity cost to the engine's basic volumetric efficiency when charge air is displaced by nitrous oxide (and, in some cases, supplemental nitrous fuel), which could disrupt certain kinds of stock electronic engine management under some circumstances. As another example, dual-fuel considerations can and will have an effect on combined octane. The reduced percentage of moderating nitrogen gas and higher percentage

of oxygen in the charge can be a greater constraint on safe nitrous combustion in the *lower* part of the powerband during a nitrous pull when constant-delivery nitrous is a bigger percentage of the charge blend than it would be at higher rpm. Ideally, this deserves a more sophisticated engine management response than simply throwing in more fuel or water injection throughout the entire pull or simply prohibiting nitrous injection below 3,000 rpm.

In the end, air-fuel and nitrous-fuel delivery may or may not be physically distinct (and the engine management strategies to deal with each logically independent), but actual combustion is something else entirely—a hybrid of both. This is why it is ideally appropriate and functional for the main EMS to not only provide basic, integrated open-loop fuel and timing during nitrous boost, but also to detect and respond to nitrous-induced changes in engine status quickly enough to provide precision modern full-authority closed-loop engine management in real time rather than requiring that a piggyback nitrous management system have the sophistication to deliver plausible nitrous and supplemental enrichment fuel delivery and the ability to conceal all nitrous activity from the main EMS to the extent required to prevent dysfunctional EMS countermeasures. At the very least, a piggyback controller should have the ability to detect and defeat EMS countermeasures if they arise during nitrous boost.

Many sophisticated standalone aftermarket and racing engine-management systems actually can integrate nitrous control with basic engine management, but because the oxygen content of the combined nitrous-air mix is unavoidably dynamic and the "massmatics" of nitrous delivery and combustion are complex, it is problematic for such systems to directly measure and respond optimally, and in time, to variations in charge-gas oxygen, combustion temperature, and charge-gas nitrogen.

What is ultimately important is the *overall* composition, weight, and temperature of the oxygen-nitrogen-fuel charge arriving in the combustion chambers during nitrous or non-nitrous combustion, but achieving near-perfect consistency working with liquid fuel, gaseous air, and a gas-liquid oxidizer that is also a refrigerant is exceedingly complex and difficult, which is why real-world nitrous-air-fuel ratios ideally must be dialed in on a dyno or track by trial and error and tend to be *uniquely imprecise by modern standards for street-legal engines*. Since this is out of the question for many hot rodders, street nitrous systems are almost universally designed to deliver a safely rich oxygen-fuel ratio targeted at worst-case combustion conditions when charge oxygen content is highest but suboptimal elsewhere.

Chapter 3
Nitrous Performance Potential

You name the vehicle, someone has given it super powers with nitrous injection: cars, pickups, boats, water-craft, bikes, go-carts, sleds, aircraft, dragsters, speed-record vehicles, road-racers, pulling tractors, monster trucks, Wankel engines, even lawnmowers. Powerplants as small as a 90cc scooter engine and as large as a 55-liter radial air-race powerplant have been granted super powers with nitrous injection in amounts ranging from as little as 5 horsepower on up to thousands. Feeding an engine nitrous is like feeding spinach to Popeye or switching on a jet fighter's afterburner. And if an engine already has heroic power as a deep-breathing high-rpm superfreak or an air-supercharged boost addict, nitrous can turn it into a god. Almost any engine can be nitrous injected.

But should it?

Everyone in the world who's been within spitting distance of a "spray" hot rod or who's read Chapter 1 of this book knows that nitrous injection is about cheap power—and lots of it. But what are the ultimate limits and constraints on nitrous injection, and how does it stack up next to alternate methods of adding power with turbos, blowers, deep-breathing all-motor tricks, or big displacement? Is nitrous compatible

Nitrous as a Power-Adder

Advantages	Disadvantages
Cheap to buy	Runs out in two minutes
Cheap to install	Refills cost money
Stealth fairly easy	Hot combustion pro-knock
Installs easily	Heat hard on engine components
Works on complex late-model engines	Hard hit shocks components
Fast flame speed good for high rpm	"On-off switch" smokes tires
Good thermal efficiency from higher heat	Wet systems can cause distribution problems in EFI engines
Doesn't rob power from crankshaft or VE from exhaust	
Intercooling effect increases air VE	
Dual-fuel conceptually easy	
Adds horsepower across the powerband	
Peak torque occurs at low-to-medium engine rpm	

Nitrous versus Air-Supercharging

Nitrous	Turbocharging
Relatively cheap purchase and installation price	Maximum boost easily adjusted, on the fly
Easier to install	May require internal engine changes for enough boost to justify expense
Great low-end torque above threshold rpm (peak torque in low-to-mid rpm range)	Spooling to make boost introduces "lag" time
Cheap enough that very low boost is cost-effective, with no internal engine mods required	Low exhaust energy at low rpm means a threshold below which there is no boost (though this can be calibrated with A/R size and VATN design)
Must be refilled regularly if used much, which adds considerably to the cost (but don't have to use!)	Tradeoff between good low-end torque (small turbine nozzle) and high-end power (large nozzle or A/R)
Threshold low-end boost limited by knock	Stresses oil with higher thermal loading
Adding horsepower with jet changes is trivial	Adiabatic heating of charge requires intercooling
System could potentially be moved to another vehicle	0-60 a challenge due to lag and boost threshold
Implicit charge intercooling from heat of vaporization cools the intake charge during boost	Requires special first gear for max acceleration
Quickest 0-60 times	Nitrous oxide requires special safety precautions
Boost can be electronically controlled using pulsewidth-modulations	Boost can be electronically controlled using PWM
No parasitic drag on engine from nozzle or pulley	Heats the intake charge during boost
Internal engine modifications not required with progressive nitrous to 100-horsepower boost	

T&T Racing's Celica dragger burning out at Redline Drag Strip in Texas. The mild-mannered four-banger was capable of more than 1,200 horsepower on methanol. Tuner Bob Norwood has often used nitrous oxide injection to provide accelerated turbocharger spooling off the line.

with other power-adding gadgetry? If so, are they additive—or something else? How do we compare the horsepower? And what do we really mean when we talk about the "power" in "power-adder"? In fact, what is horsepower, anyway, and how is it different from torque? Is nitrous horsepower the same as turbocharged horsepower, or "all-motor" horsepower? Does a 100-horse nitrous kit always add 100 horsepower? When and where? At the crankshaft? At the wheels? Inquiring minds want to know.

Hot rodders and racers talk a lot about horsepower, but horsepower begins with torque. Torque is the instantaneous measure of an engine's ability to exert twisting force against the crankshaft at whatever speed, and this is precisely the same type of twisting force that you exert when you employ a torque wrench as a lever to tighten, say, the crank pulley bolt. Torque is a measure of the pounds of pressure exerted to twist the crankshaft, multiplied by the leverage in feet from the centerline of the crank, which is why engineers talk about pound-feet of torque, or sometimes foot-pounds (they're the same). Nothing need be moving to produce torque; a mechanic or an electric motor can sustain torque against the crank even when nothing is moving. An internal combustion piston engine, however, must normally be turning to deliver torque, and it must definitely be moving to make horsepower, which is a measure of work done per time.

Depending on engine speed, a certain amount of torque delivered over time can move a certain amount of weight a certain distance, which defines the engine's horsepower output, with one horsepower being the ability to lift 550 pounds one foot in one second. The faster the engine is turning, the more horsepower it will make for a given amount of torque input. At a constant engine speed, it makes

zero difference which engine and power-adder tricks are at play to deliver the torque and horsepower (a horsepower is a horsepower is a horsepower). But the dynamic range of modern engines is very large, and the ability for land vehicles to accelerate quickly at almost any engine speed is critical to market acceptance. It is the instantaneous twisting force of torque that delivers impressive acceleration, which is why it is important that automotive engines deliver excellent torque not just at one sweet spot but across a wide range of engine speeds.

POWER AND POWER-ADDING

Like all power-adders, nitrous injection is not just about adding power to an engine, but about adding serious power. Nitrous is about adding enough power at full howl to give an engine a new soul—but doing it at a bargain price that can be 10 percent or less than the cost of a turbo or supercharger conversion kit.

In theory, the performance character of a typical nitrous powerplant is pretty simple. It's an on-off horsepower switch that's usable at full throttle anywhere between about 2,500 rpm and redline. Nitrous engine performance is a simple function of the engine's basic full-throttle power capabilities overlaid with the nitrous-injection strategy, limited by the fuel octane and the blow-up limits of the engine. In the simplest theoretical case of a constant-flow nitrous system providing a relatively modest power boost on a healthy engine that is not detonation-limited, the nitrous system hits hard and fast to inject a continuous, fixed amount of nitrous oxidizer and fuel per time—which adds a fixed, predictable quantity of horsepower to the stock power curve across the board. In theory, you can accurately model a plausible nitrous horsepower curve with a hand calculator simply by adding a fixed amount of incremental horsepower to the engine's stock power curve across the nitrous operating range. The nitrous contribution to torque, however, actually declines as a function of increases in engine rpm due to reduced time per power stroke for continuous nitrous injection, causing the fixed flow rate of nitrous and supplemental fuel to be distributed over an increasing number of power strokes. Conversely, at slower engine speeds, the horsepower boost must be generated with fewer and fewer power strokes and a heavier and heavier nitrous load, until combustion and mechanical loading become damaging (which is why most nitrous venders recommend never triggering constant nitrous injection below about 2,500-3,000 rpm). Modeling engine torque during nitrous boost is more complicated than a simple addition, but torque can be computed starting with the calculated nitrous-augmented stock horsepower curve for a representative set of points according to the formula **Torque = Horsepower × 5,250/rpm**.

That is how typical nitrous injection works in theory, and because the street nitrous marketplace is highly price-sensitive, this type of simple, inexpensive single-stage on-off nitrous kit is the typical case: For an X-horse nitrous kit, boosted power @ any rpm = Stock horsepower + X. On the dyno, unfortunately, the results are seldom that simple, as we shall see. Nitrous kits that are designed and installed with a threshold minimal competency will indisputably make significant power, but it is unfortunately not uncommon for nitrous conversion kits to fail to achieve their advertised power increase under some or all conditions.

THE RAW MATERIAL

These days, the raw material for a nitrous engine is often a late-model street or modified-street automotive powerplant with port or direct-injection electronic fuel injection. The design goals of a modern street engine include great drivability, low exhaust emissions, and excellent fuel economy—plus power adequate to the application (which can be *a lot*, in the case of a street engine like Chevy's 625-horse supercharged Corvette ZR1!). Although the design considerations of factory automotive engineers are not necessarily the same as those of hot rodders and racers, it is worth considering the reasons why factory-stock street engines are designed the way they are, especially since aftermarket tuners looking to increase

---

GET A HORSE: HORSES, LOCOMOTIVES, AND "5250": TORQUE VERSUS HORSEPOWER

Everyone knows that the power-torque conversion formula is

HP = (Torque × rpm) / 5,250

The purpose of the formula is to derive **horsepower** from **torque** at a specific engine speed. Conversely, torque can be derived from horsepower and engine speed as follows:

Torque = (HP × 5,250) / rpm)

But what is the "5250" in these formulae?

The oft-repeated, seldom explained 5,250 number lumps together several different conversion factors and is based on something called *radians* per second.

Let's start at the beginning. One horsepower is defined as the ability to lift 550 pounds 1 foot in one second or 33,000 pounds 1 foot in one minute.

Torque is normally a measurement of instantaneous force and leverage—usually twisting power, represented as force in pounds available to rotate an object—multiplied by the leverage in feet from the center point of the object against which the force is being applied (say against a lever, a torque wrench, or perhaps a crankshaft). This is why torque is represented as *pound-feet*.

James Watt's original experiments compared his new steam engine to the output of a workhorse pulling in a circle against a 12-foot lever attached to a central capstan (used, for example, to pump water from mines in eighteenth-century England). Watt calculated that a typical horse could pull with about 180 pounds of force at just over 3 feet per second. At the center of the 12-foot lever, the horse's force would be multiplied to roughly *2,187 lb-ft of torque*, and the shaft was thus capable of lifting 550 pounds 1 foot in one second. The horse's forward rate added up to 2.4 revolutions around the circle per minute. By contrast, when pulling directly against, say, a plow, with *no leverage*, the force the horse exerts is just that, with no multiplication factor. Using Watt's baseline number, the horse would only have 180 lb-ft of torque (though still 1.0 horsepower).

Horsepower is defined in feet per second. Piston-engine speed is normally represented in revolutions per minute. Getting from one to the other is not perfectly straightforward.

First we will need to convert from minutes to seconds, but that is a trivial division by 60.

Beyond that, since engine speed is measured in *revolutions*—rather than *distance*!—per time, and the definition of a horsepower is represented in *distance* rather than *revolutions*, we're going to need a "dimensionless" conversion factor that doesn't involve "feet." We'll need to convert horsepower away from feet per second to something per second that is not a distance. That something is called a *radian*.

If you take the radius of a circle (distance from the center to the outside) and superimpose this length around the arc of the circumference of the circle, it turns out there are 2-pi (pi is 3.14159) radians per circle, such that a radian is about 57.3 degrees. To convert a revolution per minute to radians per second, we divide 1 revolution by 2 × 3.14159 and divide that by 60 seconds. One revolution per minute is thus 0.10472 radians per second, *no dimension involved*. Dividing 550 lb-ft by 0.10472 radians per second yields the conversion factor 5,250.

Therefore, applying the conversion formula, in the case of the horse

Horsepower = (Torque × rpm) / 5,250

Since torque is defined as pounds of force against a lever of X feet,

Horsepower = 180 [pounds of force] **× 12** [feet leverage]
× 2.43 rpm) **/ 5,250**

horsepower with nitrous or other power-adding tricks are—like it or not—up against many of the same considerations, constraints, and tradeoffs.

These days, factory street engines are built to maximize cylinder filling (volumetric efficiency) across the rpm range using a variety of tricks that were formerly considered too exotic and expensive to be deployed in mass-production cars and trucks, including:

- Individual-cylinder fuel injection
- Sophisticated electronic engine management
- Variable cam timing and lift under computer control
- Variable-volume intake systems
- Transmissions with continuously variable ratios or lots of torque-multiplying gears that keep the engine running as close as possible to the sweet spot

The result is that at full throttle most modern street engines ingest about the same amount of air per intake stroke across the rpm range such that the force or torque exerted against the crankshaft at any particular instant—a function of the mean effective cylinder pressure, bore, stroke, and

rod length—is quite stable across the usable powerband. The result is a nearly flat, gently convex torque curve, which delivers high average power, also known as the "area under the curve."

Unlike continuous-flame jet engines, most internal combustion engines deliver torque to the crankshaft in pulses dispersed throughout the combustion cycle of one or two turns of the crankshaft. The inertia of the engine's flywheel is quite effective at smoothing and redistributing torque, but input to the crank nonetheless varies as the crankshaft turns and various cylinders enter the combustion and expansion cycles and generate intermittent positive cylinder pressure. This produces cyclical variations in engine torque and micro-changes in crank acceleration and deceleration through the combustion cycle. At full throttle, each combustion event occurs in approximately the same discrete slice of real time required for flames to consume the entire air-fuel mass in a cylinder, and this does not vary significantly with changes in rpm (though flame speed does vary according to changes in the air-fuel ratio and charge density at part-throttle or as positive boost pressure rises and falls on some engines with forced induction). Bottom line, each full-throttle combustion

This is approximately 1.0 horsepower, *exactly* what you'd expect (given that this is a tautology, Watt's definition of 1 horsepower).

A horse plowing a field with a force of 180 pounds—straight ahead, no revolutions or leverage involved—and able to move 3.05 feet in one second, still moves a total of 550 lb-ft per second, achieving 1 horsepower (it's still one horse). If the horse could move farther in the same time, plodding a circle to pump water, say *4* feet, it would achieve

$$rpm = (feet / minute) / circumference \ of \ circle \ [radius \ circle \times 2\pi]$$
$$= (4 \times 60) / (12 \times 2\pi)$$
$$= 240/75.4$$
$$= 3.18$$

$$Horsepower = 180 \ [pounds \ of \ force] \times 12 \ [feet \ leverage]$$
$$\times 3.18 \ rpm) / 5{,}250$$
$$= 1.64 \ horsepower$$

On the other hand, if the horse could pull with 200 pounds of force and still move 3.05 feet in a second, it would be capable of

$$Horsepower = 200 \ [pounds \ of \ force] \times 12 \ [feet \ leverage]$$
$$\times 2.43 \ rpm) / 5{,}250$$
$$= 1.11 \ horsepower$$

However, it is easy to see that increased speed or distance with a fixed amount of torque vastly multiplies the work done per time, meaning it greatly increases horsepower, which is why an automotive engine with "only" 500 lb-ft torque at 5,000 or 6,000 rpm (a lot of radians or many, many feet per second) can do so much more work than a horse on a 12-foot capstan that's producing **2,187 lb-ft torque at 2.43 rpms.**

A 5,000 horsepower railway locomotive will lift 2.75 million pounds 1 foot in one second. If it did this at 5,250 rpm, torque would also be 5,000 lb-ft. If it was rated 5,000 horsepower at, say, *1,000* rpms—like a typical turbo-diesel locomotive engine—required torque is 26,250 lb-ft as follows:

$$Torque = (HP \times 5{,}250) / rpm)$$
$$= (5{,}000 \times 5{,}250) / 1{,}000$$
$$= 26{,}250 \ lb\text{-}ft$$

On the other hand, if you have just 1 pound of torque, the rpm required to make 1 horsepower and move 550 feet is roughly 525 revolutions per second, or 31,514 rpm. This type of torque multiplication is how turbocharger turbines—which typically need to deliver dozens or even hundreds of horsepower to drive the compressor wheel to boost an automotive engine—can get away with such thin, lightweight shafts. The turbine shaft of a turbocharger boosting an engine by 500 horsepower, for example, must supply (and withstand!) at least 150 horsepower to the compressor. Fortunately, because the turbine shaft speed is so high, the torque loading on the shaft required to deliver the power is quite low: 150 horsepower delivered through a turbine shaft at, say, 90,000 rpm requires less than 9 lb-ft of torque!

On the other hand, a gas turbine designed to supply 5,000 shaft horsepower at 45,000 rpm needs vastly less torque than the locomotive engine:

$$Torque = (HP \times 5{,}250) / rpm)$$
$$= (5000 \times 5{,}250) / 45{,}000$$
$$= 583 \ lb\text{-}ft$$

Max Mad Racing's awesome nitrous sled prepares to leave the line. At the time of this writing, some wheel-equipped snowmobiles drag racing on hard pavement have used over 400 horsepower of nitrous or turbo power to run the quarter mile in the 8-second range at over 160 mph.

event of a modern spark-ignition street engine without power-adders is approximately equal in duration and force, varying only in the number of degrees of crank rotation consumed as rpm changes.

A spark-ignition piston engine's intermittent delivery of full-throttle power pulses contrasts radically to the situation of a jet engine—in which combustion is continuous and there is typically a huge air surplus, making the total amount of fuel that can be burned relatively insensitive to changes in engine speed and limited mainly by thermal loading considerations—or even a compression-ignition engine—which can often be calibrated to increase power by burning more of the typical diesel's large air surplus. With a normal-charged spark-ignition factory automotive engine, the only way to get more full-throttle horsepower is to run the engine faster, producing more combustion events per time and more power until the negative effect of declining volumetric efficiency and torque at high rpm overwhelms the positive contribution of additional combustion events.

When this peak horsepower is not enough, it's back to the factory drawing board: Increase displacement by adding more cylinders. Or add a positive-displacement supercharger. Or install one or more turbochargers with a wastegate to clamp peak torque at the maximum safe boost limit. You'll note that I do not mention increasing engine size with large increases in bore and stroke. True, car factories will sometimes modestly increase bore and stroke on modern street engines. GM's 2.0-liter Ecotec, for example, is also available in 1.8- and 2.2-liter displacements, a 10 percent variation. However, factory displacement changes are generally kept within fairly narrow limits due to physical constraints and because there is a "natural" bore size range that works well for street engines in balancing detonation resistance, torque, friction, noise-vibration-harshness (NVH), thermal efficiency, expense, and engine length:

Typical Nitrous Plumbing Diagrams For EFI Applications

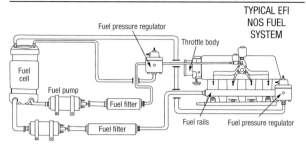

Typical EFI direct-port nitrous system injects fuel and nitrous directly into the individual intake runners where excellent distribution is virtually guaranteed. High-output direct-port nitrous systems often have entirely independent fuel systems, in some cases even fueled from an auxiliary high-octane fuel tank located in front of the engine where acceleration G's assist in fuel delivery.

Lance Wester's "Bonds" spray-Z06 'Vette purges the nitrous system in preparation for activating a combined three-stage nitrous shot totalling 350 horsepower on the streets of Dallas, Texas. The car has easily exceeded 200 mph using roughly 915 crankshaft horsepower (863 at the wheels on a Dynojet chassis dynamometer).

- A smaller bore is an excellent anti-detonation countermeasure because the shorter flame travel of a smaller piston increases the likelihood combustion will complete before detonation can occur.
- A larger bore size increases torque.
- Fewer cylinders reduces overall internal friction, even if displacement remains the same.
- Fewer cylinders reduces engine cost by decreasing the number of parts.
- Fewer cylinders of larger bore have a larger volume-to-surface ratio for increased thermal efficiency.
- Smaller bore and stoke produces less NVH, while larger displacements may require balance shafts on some inline-4s and V-6s for acceptable vibration characteristics.
- A design with fewer cylinders permits reduced engine length, allowing the powerplant to fit more easily in smaller vehicles with smaller engine compartments.
- Piston stroke is limited on the large end by piston speed at higher rpm or block deck size constraints, and by torque considerations on the small end.

Such tradeoffs are the reason why most modern factory four-cylinder engines are sized between 1,500 and 2,400 cc, most six-cylinder engines between 2,400 and 3,600 cc, and most V-8s between 3,600 and 4,800 cc or larger. Very small V-8s and V-6s are relatively expensive compared to sixes and fours of similar displacement (though Ferrari marketed 2.0-liter flat-crank V-8s circa 1980 in the 208, and Porsche produced 2.0-liter flat-six powerplants for the 914-6, both of which had very high performance for their time).

Engines with a large number of cylinders (V-10s and V-12s) are more expensive, have more internal friction, and tend to be more difficult to shoehorn into compact engine compartments. Forced induction is relatively expensive, but valuable when a factory vehicle needs more power and engines with more cylinders will not fit the engine compartment or transmission configuration, or when the sex appeal of turbos and blowers provides a compelling justification when marketing to performance enthusiasts.

This is the raw material and context for modern hot rodding, in which everything on a factory engine is the way it is for a good reason. The days when car factories left power on the table with needlessly inefficient intake or exhaust systems and dysfunctional emissions controls are *long* gone. Of course, there are still ways to add power. . . .

Such serious "full-monty" hot-rodding tricks include:

1. Large increases in displacement from difficult custom engine swaps or massive bore-and-stroke engine rework projects that replace an engine's entire reciprocating assembly,
2. Optimizing engine breathing apparatus for extreme high-speed operation at the cost of large sacrifices to low-end torque, the need for exotic, super-duty components, and loss of street legality, or
3. Extreme levels of manifold pressure from air-supercharging that require high-octane gasolines or even conversions to high-power, high-octane oxygenated fuels—and are illegal for street use without an exemption order.

Every one of these adds power as some function of engine speed, because the same mechanism that makes the power

---

BOOST ME

To understand the consequences and implications of a nitrous conversion, let's compare the advantages and disadvantages of normal-charged versus boosted powerplants.

Things nitrous engines do better than normal-charged powerplants:

1. Nitrous injection enables engines with fewer cylinders and smaller displacement to make as much peak torque and power as bigger displacement engines with more cylinders, but provides improved mechanical efficiency and fuel economy due to less internal friction. Nitrous engines are more efficient than air-supercharging because other than modestly increased electrical requirements to open nitrous and fuel solenoids, they do not rob engine power to drive the power-adder system.
2. A nitrous engine represents a smaller package for a given power output, providing improved handling, better gas mileage, or better acceleration.
3. If nitrous engines have PWM "progressive" nitrous controls, these can provide dynamic adjustment of maximum power, enabling the engine to safely "overboost" for brief periods of super-high-output performance while avoiding internal damage from excessive thermal or mechanical loading. Maximum boost and torque can be dynamically limited under computer control according to gear, engine temperature, air temperature, or other factors in order to protect transmissions from damage, provide traction control, or achieve other performance goals.
4. Compared to high-output all-motor engines with traditional hot cams and a lumpy idle, a well-designed nitrous engine of similar or greater maximum power output can be smooth and tractable, with good city drivability and far better acceleration at low- to mid-range rpm due to greatly improved average power.
5. Nitrous engines tend to "lug" well, because torque normally *climbs* as engine speed drops to maintain the steady horsepower boost (don't

try this at home; nitrous engines that are loaded too hard to freely accelerate require *very* robust architectures).
6. Compared to normal-charged diesel engines, turbo-diesel powerplants have more air-surplus than is needed to achieve maximum power levels without black smoke emissions or excessive combustion temperatures. Nitrous injection will add power and reduce exhaust emissions on any diesel engine that is smoking, but will have no effect on turbodiesel engines unless overfueling has depleted the air surplus.

Problematic aspects of nitrous engines

1. Extracting more power from a given displacement engine increases the thermal and mechanical loading on virtually all engine systems, from cooling and lubrication to pistons, rods, crankshaft, rod and main bearings, exhaust valves, and so on. Even when using expensive super-duty parts, nitrous engines tend to take more abuse, and in the best case nitrous conversions in particular tend to have at least a slightly shorter engine life than an unboosted normal-charged engine. World War II aircraft with nitrous injection had a much shorter time between overhauls (TBO).
2. Nitrous engines with moderate boost require modestly more maintenance than similar normal-charged engines.
3. Nitrous boost will definitely increase the octane number requirement (ONR) of a powerplant, due to the increased thermal loading, higher flame speed, and higher combustion pressures. Preventing engine damage from spark knock thus requires higher octane fuel or specific countermeasures to lower engine ONR, such as reduced static compression ratio, boost-based ignition retard and aggressive fuel-enrichment to cool combustion during boost. Any nitrous engine with a lot of power boost will require special tuning to prevent detonation, which can add expense and hurt drivability, power, and fuel economy, and mandate compromises to the tuning of carbureted engines during all-motor operation.

(a reciprocating piston) is critically involved to at least some extent in the process of charging itself with air for the next power pulse. The cost of this type of increased performance is cash, reliability, longevity, or another aspect of performance that's significantly reduced, which is why the faint-of-heart, faint-of-wallet, congenitally lazy, or get-rich-quick types install custom wheels, big chrome mufflers, or fancy car stereos and make do with the power they've got.

And it's why people with a light wallet and a heavy foot bolt on a nitrous tank.

NITROUS DELIVERY CHARACTERISTICS

Nitrous injection is unique as an automotive power adder because it is not limited by normal engine volumetric efficiency (VE) constraints due to the concentrated power of the freezing nitrous oxidizer and because nitrous injection is self-powered and thus has no parasitic effect on engine power. Nitrous injection is the one and only power-adder that is intrinsically time-oriented rather than at least partially rpm and load based like all-motor or air-supercharged engines. As such, nitrous adds a predictable (and usually constant) augmentation to horsepower rather than torque.

Although "progressive" nitrous systems that modulate nitrous flow rate and pressure by electronically controlling the frequency and duration of intermittent nitrous pulses are becoming more common, for reasons discussed in detail elsewhere in this book progressive nitrous is still mainly used to feather in the initial nitrous hit rather than to precisely regulate nitrous flow at full power for long periods of time. At this time of writing, most nitrous systems were constant-flow, constant-rate injection systems, even if nitrous arrived in

Wester's spray-Z06, complete with an auxiliary fuel tank located inside the engine compartment to provide supplemental race gasoline during nitrous boost.

several stages of increasing constant-flow kick-ass on some drag-race and high-power street nitrous system.

A constant rate of nitrous injection has huge implications for the performance character of an engine with nitrous super powers. The fallout of constant-rate injection is that nitrous injection has a disproportionately large performance impact at lower engine speeds: The slower the engine turns, the more supplemental horsepower nitrous injection delivers (and must deliver) per power stroke—in other words, an increase in torque at lower engine speeds is achieved through higher and higher relative concentrations of nitrous and supplemental fuel in the charge mixture. The ironic result is that even though the greatest relative power increase of nitrous boost is at lower engine speeds, nitrous cannot be deployed to lug the engine at *too* low an rpm without risking engine damage due to overpressurizing, overheating, and detonating the combustion chambers, or overloading the pistons, connecting rods, or other mechanical components until something dies and goes to hell.

Lower-rpm performance aside, nitrous injection is highly efficient at adding peak horsepower at higher rpm because no engine power is wasted turning a supercharger and no engine exhaust-side VE is lost pushing pressurized exhaust gases through the turbine nozzle of a turbocharger. At modest to moderate levels of nitrous power boost, internal engine modifications such as compression ratio reductions are not required, allowing nitrous engines to remain optimized for high efficiency during nonsupercharged conditions so that nitrous injection has no adverse effect whatsoever on fuel efficiency and engine VE during non-boosted operations.

NITROUS POWER-MAKING CAPABILITIES

Nitrous oxide is a powerful oxidizer that enriches the oxygen content of charge gases, allowing more fuel to be combusted per power stroke than would be possible with air alone, thus

The NOS Pro-shot multi-stage direct-port nitrous system can be used for racer cars or evil street predators like Lance Wester's spray-Z06. With the right controls, a "two-stage" nitrous system can actually provide three stages of nitrous boost: a small initial stage of power from one set of solenoids, a larger stage of power from a second set of solenoids with larger nitrous and fuel jetting, and then both stages together, providing additive horsepower. *NOS*

substantially increasing cylinder pressure and horsepower. Nitrous oxide is 50 percent more dense than air at equal temperatures, and nitrous consists of 36 percent oxygen versus the 23 percent oxygen mass in air. The bottom line for nitrous oxygen enrichment is that nitrous oxide has 2.3 times more oxygen than air, giving nitrous a theoretical power capacity that's 230 percent that of an equal volume of air based solely on oxygen content. The effect of nitrous charge-gas oxygen enrichment, induction air volume displaced by nitrous, and the refrigerant effect of boiling nitrous on charge air density (see section on "Nitrous as a VE-improver," page 61) may or may not provide a net reduction or increase in the volumetric efficiency of *air induction* during nitrous boost, but since nitrous is a much more powerful oxidizer than air, the net effect of nitrous injection is a highly effective power boost, whether or not it's done with maximum efficiency. A modest amount of nitrous can go a long way as a power-adder.

But it isn't even necessary that nitrous injection be efficient to compete effectively with other methods of adding power. Given the relatively compact volume of concentrated liquid nitrous oxide and supplemental liquid fuel compared to the breathing capability of an engine in cfm, it is rather easy to build nitrous system plumbing that will add as much power as you have the guts to add by dumping into the intake system whatever quantity of "liquid horsepower" is necessary even if air VE is degraded. There are Pro Comp drag racers dumping 1,500 horsepower worth of juice in a stroker big-block. For all practical purposes, the physical delivery of nitrous and supplemental fuel is not a constraint on power because nitrous injection is capable of making more power than almost any engine or chassis can tolerate.

Dyno testing reveals that nitrous injection can actually make even more power than you'd expect based purely on the theoretical advantages of oxygen enrichment. In fact, when injecting nitrous oxide at a ratio of 10 percent the mass flow of air induction, a nitrous system (done right) is capable of making 20 percent more power. Why? Several factors combine to increase power beyond what's available from oxygen enrichment: Refrigerant effects on the volumetric efficiency of air induction (producing an air-supercharging effect), energy liberated by the exothermic breakdown of nitrous into oxygen and nitrogen at 565 degrees, and improved engine thermal efficiency from the higher flame speed and combustion temperatures of the more radical fire chemistry of enhanced-oxygen fuel combustion.

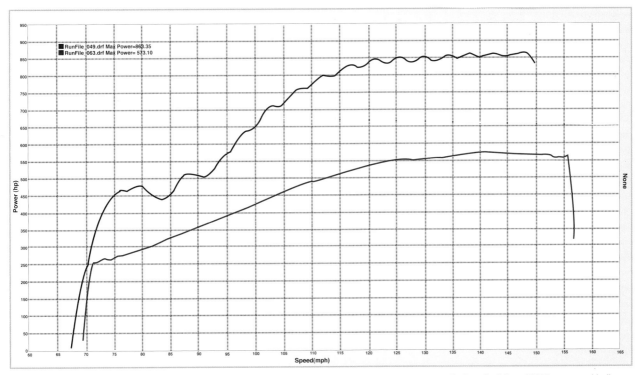

Lance Wester's hot rod Z06 proved capable of 573 horses at the wheels on the motor only. Following nitrous system purge, the Corvette delivered 863 horsepower. Ideally, nitrous injection's horsepower graph would exactly parallel the all-motor power line at a higher level. But it can be very difficult to prevent some surging due to refrigeration effects, foaming and nitrous density changes, and changes in the air-fuel ratio during boost as boiling liquid nitrous in the tank lowers temperature and pressure and sometimes cannot keep up with the mass rate of nitrous expulsion from the tank. A very large tank, partially full, provides the least pressure drop. Even better is multiple tanks, as was the case with this Corvette.

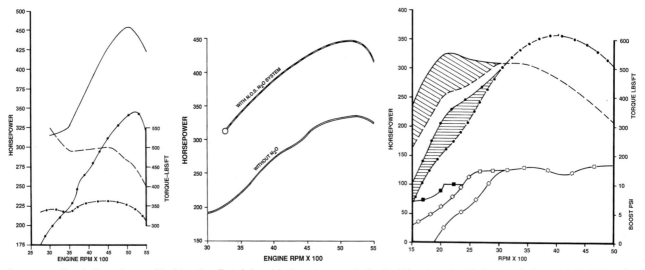

Horsepower, with and without nitrous, and the interesting effect of nitrous injection on torque production (the highest torque is at the lowest activation rpm). In the third graph, nitrous injection is used temporarily to wallop-up engine torque on a turbo engine below the boost threshold. The lower lines in the third graph show boost pressure, with and without nitrous injection, with the highest line revealing the *effective* boost pressure produced with nitrous injection (the boost that would be required to deliver the higher torque line without nitrous injection).

KNOCK LIMITS

Detonation is typically the first unintended constraint on nitrous horsepower boost to become operative in almost any engine, especially when the fuel is pump gasoline. Horsepower increase is a result of higher cylinder pressure, temperature, or both, producing higher torque, but temperature and pressure increase as combustion heats fuel closer and closer to the auto-ignition temperature (495 to 525 is typical for gasoline), meaning as combustion proceeds there is an increasing likelihood for remaining unburned charge to explode all at once before normal combustion is complete—also known as detonation or spark knock. Oxygen enrichment from nitrous oxide will increase the flame speed of high-compression racing engines that were already operating near the knock threshold, producing added thermal loading in the combustion chamber that will result in severe detonation in the absence of countermeasures such as higher octane fuel, ignition timing retard, extra fuel enrichment, water injection, or engine design changes to lower the octane number requirement (ONR). The same is true when injecting nitrous into air-supercharged engines with high *effective* compression ratios that are already on the verge of knock. As you'd expect, detonation is much less of a problem with nitrous-injection on early emissions-era (1973 to 1984) vintage engines with particularly low specific power and low compression ratios that are nowhere near being knock-limited at peak power, and were capable of performing well in stock form with regular-octane gasoline.

In addition to the inherent pro-knock aspects of nitrous injection resulting simply from combustion heat and pressure, some nitrous-injection systems are prone to detonation from nitrous or supplemental fuel *distribution problems*. The nitrous systems that are least expensive to purchase and install normally use single- or central-point injection for the nitrous oxide and single- or central-point injection for the supplemental fuel. Any gaseous or liquid substance with markedly higher specific gravity than air injected into an engine intake will have a tendency to be centrifuged outward when navigating turns in the intake system, with heavier liquids "understeering" and following a different route from lighter gases when there are alternate pathways available on the way to the various cylinders—with a high probability that there will be distribution problems. Keep in mind that when most engines used single-point carburetion to mix fuel with air, intake manifolds were carefully designed with special geometry, add-on ribs, and air dams that helped to prevent fuel puddling in the intake and to achieve acceptable distribution of "wet" air-fuel mixtures to the various cylinders (and, even so, fuel distribution was often not equal). Modern port- and direct-injection intake manifolds are designed within the context of freedom to improve engine volumetric efficiency by optimizing air-only intake manifolds for excellent *air distribution* and higher airflow than was formerly achievable within the requirement to manage the flow and distribution of *wet* mixtures.

Nitrous kits with single- or central-point supplemental fuel introduction are still relatively common, but even when Dry nitrous systems deliver supplemental enrichment fuel through factory multi-point fuel-injection systems, it is common to inject the nitrous oxide at a single point. Single-point nitrous *gas* injection should not be significantly better or worse than air distribution (after all, the gaseous components of air do not have equal specific gravity, but manage to stay mixed). However, many nitrous systems strive mightily to keep at least some nitrous oxide in *liquid* droplet form all the way into the combustion chambers, meaning that single-point nitrous distribution could be a problem. (You can find out by measuring exhaust gas temperature with individual exhaust-port EGT sensors).

Particularly when fuel droplets are relatively large, nitrous-system supplemental fuel distribution to individual cylinders is extremely important in preventing detonation in cylinders with lean oxygen-fuel mixtures from too much nitrous or too little fuel. Single-point fuel enrichment can be acceptable on relatively low-power nitrous-injection systems where kit designers have carefully tested and specified precise injector location, but unless racing class rules prohibit it, any high-power nitrous system adding much more than 25 to 30 percent power should provide fuel distribution to individual ports via (1) the stock pulsed electronic fuel injectors, (2) special under-injector ("NOSzle"-type) bosses with built-in fuel introduction plumbing and nozzles, or (3) individual-port auxiliary nitrous/fuel nozzles. Some injection systems have attempted to improve supplemental fuel atomization by aiming the 900-psi nitrous injection nozzles directly at the fuel delivery nozzles. This tends to shear the fuel into really tiny droplets but can also result in chilled fuel droplets that are slower to vaporize, with the potential to exacerbate any intake system distribution problems.

The first indication of an oversupply of liquid horsepower is usually severe detonation, but there is very little latitude for detonation on nitrous engines without nearly immediate internal engine damage to exhaust valves, ring lands, or pistons. How much is "too much" nitrous? This depends on the engine design (for example, engines with 4-valve pentroof combustion chambers have improved knock resistance due to the reduced flame travel from spark plugs to the farthest "end gases"), head gasket design, the strength of the pistons, and even the rods and crank.

MECHANICAL LIMITS

Given that nitrous oxide and supplemental fuel delivery systems are not an important constraint to delivering *insane* levels of power-boost, if you can avoid detonation, the physical strength of various internal engine components will eventually become a constraint on power, in many cases before exhaust system and ignition constraints come into play to stop further horsepower increases. In recent years, excellent Failure Mode and Effects Analysis and other modeling/simulation software have allowed automotive engineers to reduce the cost of modern engines by eliminating unneeded excess mechanical strength with high reliability, reducing the mechanical headroom for significant power-adder hot-rodding tricks like nitrous injection. In one drag-race R&D engine build-up project, a stock GM-Racing inline-4 2.0-liter inline-4 Ecotec failed catastrophically at 200 percent stock power (100 percent power boost). With stronger pistons and rods, the engine ran up against exhaust-side breathing constraints that effectively halted additional power increases at 250 percent stock power. The Ecotec was a strong modern engine with a design that had been "protected" for future turbocharging, which subsequently arrived in 2006. But older "overbuilt" pushrod engines with relatively low specific factory power also have mechanical limits that govern maximum safe nitrous boost.

Many engineers postulate that the theoretical maximum average cylinder pressure (a.k.a. brake mean effective pressure,

Norwood Racing twin-turbo 325-inch nitro/methanol-fueled four-cylinder drag engine takes time to spool, but nitrous injection wakes up the turbochargers plenty quickly, at which point nitrous injection progressively fades to zero.

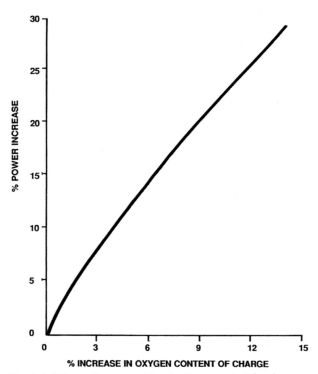

The effect of nitrous oxide oxygen enrichment on the power output of an air-supercharged powerplant. *NACA*

THE OCTANE NUMBER REQUIREMENT (ONR) OF PERFORMANCE ENGINES

Avoiding detonation is *critical* on nitrous engines because detonation will damage a boosting nitrous engine faster than you can believe. At a minimum, high-octane street gasoline is mandatory, but super-high-output nitrous engines will probably require racing gasoline or air-race fuel.

What is octane, and what are the factors that determine how much octane an engine needs to avoid detonation?

A fuel's octane rating is a measure of its ability to resist abnormal combustion (detonation, preignition, post-ignition, or dieseling). When an engine detonates, combustion typically begins normally with flame fronts burning smoothly away from the spark and moving progressively through the air-fuel mixture until all has been consumed. But as combustion proceeds and pressure and temperatures rise, there is an increasing tendency for unburned "end gases" to suddenly and violently explode all at once rather than combustion completing normally. This produces high-pressure shock waves in the combustion chamber that can accelerate engine wear or even cause immediate catastrophic failure. Mild knock is seldom disastrous, but knock can lead to preignition, a deadly related form of abnormal combustion in which the air-fuel mixture is ignited by something other than the spark plug. Knock increases thermal loading, which can lead to glowing combustion chamber deposits, red-hot sharp edges or burrs on the head or block, or overheated spark plug electrodes—any of which can act like a glow-plug to produce surface ignition. Early surface ignition that occurs prior to the plug firing is called preignition, while late surface ignition that occurs after normal combustion has started is called post-ignition. Preignition is deadly because it causes ignition timing to be early and out of control. The upward movement of the piston on compression stroke is opposed by too-early high-combustion pressures, resulting in power loss, engine roughness, and severe heating of the piston crown. Preignition can result from knock, or trigger knock. Dieseling (also known as run-on), is usually caused by compression ignition of the air-fuel mixture due to unusually hot temperatures in the combustion chambers of a spark-ignition engine, but it can also be caused by surface ignition.

The octane number requirement (ONR) for a particular engine is established in a test lab by making a series of wide-open-throttle dyno pull with design spark timing using a precise blend of two primary reference fuels with successively lower octane ratings until a mixture is found that produces trace knock as measured by vibration sensors in the block or cylinder heads. The percentage of isoctane in the mixture is the octane number requirement of the engine. The quality control of factory-built engines is now superb, but aftermarket-assembled powerplants and older apparently identical vehicles from the same assembly line can have octane requirements that vary by as much at 10 octane numbers.

The factors influencing an engine's octane requirements are effective compression ratio, atmospheric pressure, absolute humidity, air temperature, fuel characteristics, air-fuel ratio, variations in mixture distribution among an engine's cylinders, oil characteristics, spark timing, spark timing advance curve, variations in optimal timing between individual cylinders, intake manifold temperature, head and cylinder coolant temperature, condition of coolant and additives, type of transmission, and combustion chamber hot spots.

Compression Ratio

The single most important internal engine characteristic demanding specific fuel characteristics is compression ratio. Each ratio increase in the 8.0 to 11.0:1 range increases the ONR 3 to 5 points, meaning that 11.0:1 engines typically require octane that is 9 to 15 points higher than those with 8.0:1. Higher compression ratios squash the inlet air/fuel mixture into a more compact, dense mass, resulting in a faster burn rate, more heating and less heat loss into the combustion chamber surfaces, and higher consequent cylinder pressure. Turbochargers and superchargers can produce *effective* compression ratios far above the ordinary static compression ratio by forcing much greater quantities of charge into the cylinders, which multiply boost pressure to much higher levels during compression. Either way, high compression results in an increased density of oxygen and fuel in the charge gases, which burns faster and produces more pressure against the pistons but has increased tendency to explode as the heat and pressure rise in the unburned portion of the charge. Nitrous injection also increases charge oxygen density by chemical means.

Until 1970, high-performance cars often had compression ratios of up to 11 or 12 to 1, easily handled with vintage high-octane leaded gasolines readily available with 98 to 99 octane ratings ((R + M)/2)). By 1972 engines were running compression ratios between 8 and 8.5-1, which produce less peak torque and thermal efficiency but tend to emit less NOx pollution. Other side-effects of low compression include burning more fuel at idle because there is more clearance volume in the combustion chamber to dilute the intake charge with exhaust. What's more, because fuel is still burning longer in the expansion cycle as the piston descends, lower compression raises exhaust temperature, which increases stress on the cooling system. In the 1980s, compression ratios in computer-controlled fuel-injected factory vehicles again began showing up with compression ratios between 9.0 and 11.5-1, based on port electronic fuel injection's ability to provide the precise distribution and air-fuel control on catalyst-equipped vehicles required to keep emissions low and tolerate higher compression ratios without detonation. Maximum compression ratios in exotic high-speed competition engines burning ultra-high-octane gasoline fuels are even higher, with compression in the 14.0-1 to 17.0-1 range. Effective compression above 14.0-1 demands not only extremely high-octane fuel (which might or might not be gasoline), but low coolant temperature, uniform coolant temperature around all cylinders, and *reverse flow cooling*. Extremely high compression ratios also require excellent fuel distribution to all cylinders, retarded timing under maximum power, very rich mixtures, and probably individual cylinder optimization of spark timing, air-fuel ratio, and volumetric efficiency.

Air-Fuel Ratio

Air-fuel ratio has a major impact on engine ONR, increasing octane requirements by 2 points per one increase in ratio (say from 13:1, to 14:1). Optimal air-fuel ratio varies according to the amount of air in a particular cylinder at a particular time, i.e., volumetric efficiency. Richer air-fuel ratios combat knock by the combustion-cooling effect of the heat of vaporization of liquid fuels and a set of related factors. The volatility of fuels affects not only octane number requirement but drivability in general.

The chemically ideal air-fuel mixture (by weight), at which all air and gasoline are consumed in combustion, occurs with 14.7 parts air and 1 part fuel. This ratio is referred to as stoichiometric. Stoichiometric mixtures vary according to fuel, from a low of nitromethane at, say, 1.7:1, to methanol's 6.45:1, ethanol's 9:1, up to gasoline at 14.6:1, and beyond to natural gas and propane, which are in the range of 15.5 to 16.5:1. Mixtures with a greater percentage of air than stoichiometric are called lean mixtures and occur as higher numbers. Richer mixtures, in which there is an excess of fuel, are represented by smaller numbers. At high loading and wide open throttle, richer mixtures give better power by making sure that all air molecules in the combustion chamber have fuel to burn. At wide-open throttle, where the objective is maximum power, all four-cycle gasoline engines require mixtures that fall somewhere between lean and rich best torque in the 11.5 to 13.3 air-gasoline range. Since the best-torque mixture spread narrows at higher speeds due to the increased importance of flame speed, a good goal for naturally aspirated engines is 12 to 12.5, or richer if fuel is being used for combustion cooling in a boosted engine. Typical air-fuel ratios providing best street drivability, fuel economy, and emissions characteristics range between 13.0 and 14.5 for gasoline engines, depending on speed and loading.

The ideal air-fuel ratio to fight knock and optimize power tends to vary slightly from cylinder to cylinder. Engine management with individual-cylinder-adjustable electronic port fuel injection really shines on extremely high output engines with high effective compression ratios. For peak power, any engine must be treated as a gang of single-cylinder engines, each of which should be optimized for peak power, and individual-cylinder air-fuel calibration is typically good for as much as 50 horsepower on some super-high-output small-block V-8. Not only does individual-cylinder calibration improve power, but it saves engines from knock damage while allowing a higher state of tune. Common practice for ordinary performance tuning and nitrous jetting is to tune for the leanest cylinder (i.e., the best flowing). Testing some years ago by Smokey Yunick for *Circle Track Magazine* showed that a carbureted small-block V-8 test engine was prone to detonation on three of the eight cylinders—assumed to be due to unequal fuel distribution or coolant circulation that caused those cylinders to run hotter. "We could have cut these three cylinders to 14:1 [compression]," wrote Yunick, "and maybe run the other five cylinders at 15:1 and gained some power. Don't know, but I do know this, you are going to get a safer, more powerful engine if you adjust the compression, timing, and distribution to each cylinder." These days it's done with electronic engine management changes to the timing and injection pulsewidth of individual cylinders.

Jacket Coolant Temperature
Increases in coolant temperature raise octane requirements by roughly 1 octane number per 10 degree increase from 160 to 180 degrees F.

Absolute Humidity
Humidity, which increases the amount of water vapor in the combustion chamber, decreases octane requirement by 1/3 octane number per 10 grains (1/7,000th of a pound) increase per pound of air.

Altitude, Air Density, Fueling, and Forced-induction
Air density varies with temperature, altitude, and weather conditions. Higher altitude reduces octane number requirements by about 1.5 octane numbers per 1,000 feet above sea level. Forced induction, which provides a denser breathing atmosphere, has the opposite effect. The higher ONR of engines operating with higher manifold pressure is often intensified in forced-induction powerplants by the adiabatic heat of pressurizing charge air and the higher effective compression ratio. For any given indicated manifold pressure, hotter air (with greater molecular activity) is less dense. Air is less dense in warm weather, and air that is heated for any reason on the way into the engine becomes less dense and will impact the weight of fuel required to achieve a correct air-fuel ratio. Intake system layout can have a great effect on the volumetric efficiency of the engine by affecting the density of the air the engine is breathing. Air cleaners that suck in hot engine compartment air will reduce the engine's output and should be modified to breathe fresh cold air from outside for maximum performance. Intake manifolds that overheat the air will produce less dense air, although a properly designed intake manifold that is heat-soaked at lower engine speeds will very quickly be cooled by intake air at high speed. Heat tends to improve wet-mixture distribution at part throttle and idle. Air is less dense at high altitude, as is air with a higher relative humidity. Turbo-superchargers, which deliver heated, turbulent air, are known to enhance air-fuel mixing and fuel atomization.

Combustion Chamber Deposits
Depending on engine design, fuel, lubricant, and operating conditions, combustion chamber deposits can increase ONR by 1 to 13 numbers.

Ambient Temperature
Inlet air temperature increases octane requirements by .5 octane number per 10 degree increase. Temperature affects fuel performance in several ways. Colder air is more dense than hotter air, affecting cylinder pressure. Colder air inhibits fuel vaporization. But hotter air directly raises combustion temperatures, which increases the possibility of knock.

EFI systems normally have sensors to read the temperature of inlet air and adjust the injection pulse width and spark timing to compensate for density changes and fuel volatility limitations. Engines will make noticeably more power on a cold day because the cold dense air increases engine volumetric efficiency, filling the cylinders with more molecules of air. This is bad news for a carb, which has no way of compensating (other than manual jet changes—one size per 40 degrees temperature change). Airplane pilots must always know the ambient air temperature in order to estimate take-off distance (much shorter on colder days). Aircraft carbs allow dynamic manual adjustments of air-fuel mixture. As you'd expect, racing automotive engine designs always endeavor to keep inlet air as cold as possible, and even stock street cars often make use of cold air inlets, since each 11 degrees F increase reduces air density 1 percent.

Cold engines require enrichment to counteract the fact that only the lightest fractions of liquid fuel may vaporize at colder temperatures, while the rest exists as globules or drops of fuel that are not mixed well with air. (The actual vaporization/distillation curve of various gasolines and fuels differs, depending on the purpose for which the fuel is designed. Gaseous fuels like propane and methane do not require cold running enrichment and have no intercooling effect once in gaseous form.) But in a cold engine, most of a fuel like gasoline—in liquid form— will be wasted. At temperatures below zero, optimal air-gasoline mixture may be as low as 3 or 4 to 1 for best drivability and during cranking as rich as 1.5 to 1!

Liquid fuels do not vaporize well in cold air (although the oil companies change their gasoline formulation to increase the vapor pressure in cold weather, which formerly could lead to a rash of vapor lock in sudden warm spells in winter). Choking systems in carbureted vehicles and cold-start fuel enrichment systems on EFI vehicles are designed to produce a rich enough mixture to run the vehicle even when much of the fuel exists not as burnable vapor, mixed with air, but as drops of non-burnable liquid fuel suspended in the air or on the manifold walls. Most air pollution is produced by cold vehicles burning super mixtures. EFI systems sense coolant temperature in order to provide cold start enrichments (cold prime, cranking, after start, and warm-up). Electronic port injection systems usually spray fuel straight at the intake valve into the swirling turbulent high velocity air that exists there—which greatly improves atomization and vaporization. In general, the higher the injection pressure, the better. Experiments have shown pressure as high as 300 psi produces excellent shear of fuel droplets for the best quality atomization. EFI does not normally need the exhaust-gas intake heating that street carbs require to provide acceptable warm-up operations. EFI manifolds may use coolant heating of the manifold to increase vaporization at idle in very cold weather.

Unlike carburetors, which are susceptible to fuel starvation if ice forms in the carburetor as vaporizing fuel removes heat from the air and metal parts in cold weather, EFI systems will deliver fuel even if ice forms in the throttle body. In any case, EFI is not as susceptible to icing since fuel vaporizes (stealing heat) at the hot intake valve, not at the throttle body. EFI systems don't require a choke stove to heat inlet air for cold start driving like carbureted vehicles.

Spark Advance, Flame Speed, Volumetric Efficiency, and Air-Fuel-Nitrous Ratio

There is a complicated interrelation between timing, flame speed, volumetric efficiency (VE) and oxygen-fuel ratio, all of which have an effect on whether a performance engine will experience detonation. Spark advance, which is optimized to achieve best torque by producing peak cylinder pressure at about 15 degrees ATDC, increases octane requirements by 1/2 to 3/4 of an octane number per degree of advance. Spark advance increases peak cylinder pressure and allows more time for detonation to occur. Dynamically retarding spark timing to fight knock by lowering peak combustion temperature and pressure is *the* main operational anti-knock countermeasure on premium-fuel factory vehicles. Boosting turbo-supercharged engines and nitrous engines on the bottle almost always require boost-retard timing strategies to prevent detonation. Unfortunately, understanding and optimizing ignition timing sufficient to maximize power—or even tune without engine damage—can be quite complicated.

Engine speed range and fuel burn characteristics have a dominant effect on ignition timing requirements, but other factors are also critical. As an engine turns faster, the spark plug must fire sooner in order to allow time for a given air-fuel mixture to ignite and achieve a high burn rate and maximum cylinder pressure by the time the piston is positioned to produce best torque. Optimal timing for best torque is

dependent not only on engine speed but on flame speed, which, in turn, is dependent not only on the type of fuel, but on operating conditions such as the air-fuel ratio (which changes dynamically) and the ratio of oxygen to nitrogen in the charge (which changes abruptly when nitrous boost kicks in). An independent variable affecting the need for spark advance as rpm increases is the need to modify ignition timing corresponding to engine loading and consequent volumetric efficiency variations that demand dynamically variable mixtures. Throttle position, for example, impacts cylinder filling, resulting in corresponding variations in optimal air-fuel mixture requirements and ignition timing. Activating nitrous boost immediately and dramatically increases flame speed.

Valve timing and lift have a large effect on volumetric efficiency, flame speed, air-fuel ratios, and detonation, though variable cams have eliminated lift- and timing-based rpm and power tradeoffs on some modern engines. Valve timing has a large influence on the rpm at which an engine develops its best power and torque, though intake and exhaust geometry are also critically important. Adding more cam lift and overlap allows an engine to breathe more efficiently at high speeds, but a traditional big-cam engine may start hard, idle badly, bog on off-idle acceleration, and produce bad low-speed torque. The increased valve overlap that improves high-rpm VE allows exhaust gases in the clearance volume of the combustion chamber at higher than atmospheric pressure to rush into the intake manifold (exactly like EGR), diluting the inlet charge. This continues to occur until rpm increases to the point where the overlap interval is so short that reverse pulsing is insignificant. Short cam engines typically run stoichiometric mixtures at idle for cleanest exhaust emissions, but big cams result in gross exhaust gas dilution of the air-fuel mixture at idle, which consequently burns slowly and requires a lot of spark advance and a mixture as rich as .78 lambda (11.5-1 on gasoline) to counteract the lumpy uneven idle resulting from partial burning and misfires on some cycles. Valve overlap also hurts idle and low speed performance by lowering manifold vacuum, since the lower atmospheric pressure of high vacuum tends to keep fuel vaporized better. High output engines with carburetion or

a.k.a. BMEP) practical for *sustained operations* in conventional gasoline-fueled piston engines without engine failure is 460 to 500 psi, and up to 700 psi with methanol fuel, but that detonation limits become operative as a constraint before mechanical factors. GM Racing switched to methanol fuel when promoting the then-new 2.0-liter inline-4 Ecotec in drag racing when the target was 800 horsepower at 8,500-plus rpm and torque approaching 475 lb-ft, which would require BMEP approaching 590 psi.

My own mild-cammed hot rod 2.1-liter '91 Toyota MR2 Turbo magazine project car proved itself capable of 439.9 lb-ft torque at roughly 6,000 rpm and 31 psi boost on a Dynojet chassis dynamometer, which calculates out to almost 553 psi BMEP. Where do these BMEP numbers come from? BMEP is a function of torque and engine displacement per the following formula:

BMEP = torque × 150.8/displacement (CID)
= 470 × 150.8/128.15
= 553.07

. . . in which BMEP is a simple multiple of torque per cubic inch of displacement, and 150.8 represents 1.0 lb-ft per cubic inch of displacement in a 4-stroke engine. The turbo MR2 result was a figure achievable on a dyno on 118-octane leaded racing gasoline with highly effective total-loss intercooling—but certainly could not have been considered "sustainable." Obviously, quick dyno pulls and drag racing would not be considered sustained operations.

Reworking the formula allows torque to be computed from a known BMEP and engine displacement as follows:

Torque = displacement (CID) **× BMEP/150.8**

Assuming a maximum BMEP of 500 psi for the same 2.1-liter turbo engine and the optimistic maximum BMEP of 500, the maximum "sustainable" torque for this powerplant is:

Torque = 128.15 × 500/150.8
= 424.90 lb-ft

throttlebody injection that have low manifold vacuum can thus have distribution problems and a wandering air-fuel mixture at idle, which may require an overall richer mixture in order to keep the motor from stalling. Carbureted vehicles with hot cams may not have enough signal available to pull sufficient fuel through the idle system, which will lean out the mixture, requiring a tuner to increase the idle throttle setting. This may put the off-idle slot/port in the wrong position, causing an off-idle bog. Obviously, this is not a problem with port fuel injection unless standoff is extreme enough to permit fuel to migrate between velocity stacks in an intake plenum.

A big-cam engine may require off-idle mixtures nearly as rich as idle to eliminate surging, beginning at .85 to .88 lambda (12.5-13.0 on gasoline) and leaning out with speed or loading. Mild cams will permit lambda .95 to 1.2 (between 14 and 15:1 air-gasoline ratio) mixtures off-idle and at slow cruise. As engine speed continues to increase, flame speed starts to become important. Denser and richer mixtures (to a point) burn more quickly, but poor VE at low- and mid-range rpm results in slow combustion and exhaust dilution, lowering combustion temperatures and reducing the tendency to knock. Hot cams can produce problems where air-fuel mixture is inconsistent or poorly atomized, causing flammability to suffer and affecting many other variables; the bad effects of big cams diminish at medium rpm, resulting in less charge dilution, allowing the engine to happily burn mixtures at or close to stoichiometric, with additional spark advance required with leaner mixtures to counteract the slower flame speed. The onset of nitrous boosting in this speed range (many systems permit nitrous boost to begin at or below 3,000 rpm), of course, changes everything.

Turbulence and swirl are extremely important factors affecting both flame speed and detonation. Within limits, turbulence and swirl are more important than mixture strength or exact fuel composition. Automotive engineers have long made use of induction systems and combustion chamber geometry to induce swirl or turbulence to enhance flame speed and, consequently, the anti-knock characteristics of an engine. Wedge head engines, with their typical large quench area, have long been known to generate turbulence and swirl as intake gases are aggressively squeezed out of the quench area as the piston approaches top dead center.

In the 1970s, automotive engineers began to de-tune engines to meet emissions standards that were increasingly tough. They began to retard the ignition timing at idle, for example, sometimes locking out vacuum advance in lower gears or during normal operating temperature but permitting more advance if the engine was cold for drivability reasons. Since oxides of nitrogen are formed when free nitrogen combines with oxygen at high temperature and pressure, modestly retarded spark reduces NOx emissions by lowering peak combustion temperature and pressure, and can also reduce hydrocarbon emissions. However, retarded-spark combustion is less efficient, resulting in poor fuel economy and increased heating of the engine block as thermal energy escapes through the cylinder walls into the cooling jacket. Torque is down due to lost heat, and fuel economy is damaged because some of the fuel is still burning as it blows out the exhaust valve, necessitating richer idle and main jetting to get decent off-idle performance and prevent leaner, hotter combustion temperatures from defeating the purpose of ignition retard by producing more NOx! Combustion inefficiency under such conditions requires more throttle or throttle bypass to achieve adequate idle speed. By removing pollutants from exhaust gas, three-way catalysts tend to allow more ignition advance at idle and part throttle. Undesirable products of combustion include formaldehyde, NOx, CO_2, and fragments of hydrocarbons.

High-performance and racing gasolines can vary significantly in chemical composition in ways that go far beyond differences in nominal octane ratings. Some may contain fairly large amounts of oxygenated components such as ether or alcohol that affect mixture requirements and burn characteristics, particularly with respect to flammability, flame speed, and emissions—all of which affect spark timing requirements. These parameters are powerfully affected by nitrous injection, dual-fuel systems, and conversions to propane, natural gas, or alcohol fuels, all of which have important differences in combustion flame speed and mixture requirements.

If this engine were run on methanol fuel instead of racing gasoline, then it could be boosted with air-supercharging or nitrous oxide to BMEP of 700, then

Torque = 128.15 × 700/150.8
= 594.86 lb-ft

Assuming that 90 percent of peak torque can be sustained to 6,250 rpm, maximum sustainable gasoline-fuel horsepower at peak BMEP can be calculated using the formula

HP = torque × rpm/5,250
= 382.41 × 6,250/5,250
= 455.25

With methanol,

HP = torque × rpm/5,250
= 535.37 × 6,250/5,250
= 637.35

If you re-cammed the engine to maintain 90 percent of this torque to 7,000 rpm (within the stock MR2 redline of 7,250 rpm)—382.41 lb-ft, then absolute peak "sustainable" power with turbocharging *or nitrous* can be calculated with gasoline using the formula

HP = torque × rpm/5,250
= 382.41 × 7,000/5,250
= 509.88

With methanol fuel,

HP = torque × rpm/5,250
= 535.37 × 7,000/5,250
= 713.83

Unquestionably, conventional gasoline engines can survive delivering 2.0 to 2.5 lb-ft torque (average MEP) per cubic inch from nitrous boost (305 lb-ft on a 2.0-liter engine), or 3.5 to 4.0 lb-ft with alcohol-gasoline fuel blends, and thoroughbred racing engines have definitively survived delivering 4.0 horsepower per cubic inch (about 244 horsepower per liter). For perspective, consider that a de-boosted version of GM Racing's turbocharged 2.0-liter Ecotec drag powerplant set several land speed records at Bonneville running at approximately 750 horsepower (6.15 horsepower per cubic inch), down from the 1,200 to 1,400 horsepower available at higher boost in short-duration drag racing (11.5 horsepower per cube!). On street engines where it is unacceptable for nitrous injection to compromise powerplant reliability, significantly given the relatively rare occurrence of nitrous boost, 30 to 50 percent power increases are easily feasible with decent reliability, though this is more than the power-adding capability of many factory or aftermarket air-supercharged versions of engines with strengthened internal engine components. A turbocharged long-block is great raw material for a nitrous motor.

Factory automotive engines and, even more so, aviation engines are *always* ruggedized for high-output applications and air-supercharging boost applications with super-duty parts— forged pistons and rods, steel cranks, billet, piston-cooling oil-squirters, and so on. But the fact is, *any* engine can be boosted *some* without significantly compromising reliability, and the fact that nitrous kits are as cheap or cheaper than a set of custom wheels makes a small power-boost of 10, 20, maybe 30 horsepower (and *much* more favorable torque characteristics for street acceleration!) justifiable in a way that it would not be with a multi-thousand-dollar air-supercharging conversion kit. That said, if you are like most people, you will almost definitely *not* remain satisfied with a small power boost. When the initial (safe) power boost has lost its thrill, the availability of more horsepower from a nitrous system with a five-minute jet swap is more than most grown men can resist. There are plenty of engines that have been incrementally overboosted to levels beyond (or *far* beyond) what's optimal for the design—because there is always hot rodder gravity pulling in the direction of pumping up the juice a little more, and then a little more, and then a little *more*, and so on.

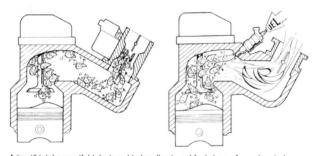

A "wet" intake manifold designed to handle air and fuel charge for carbureted or throttle body-injection engines must be equipped with features that take into account the disparate fluid flow characteristics of gasoline and air. A "dry" intake manifold with optimized air-only gas flow may be unable to provide good mixture distribution if gasoline and nitrous are sprayed into the manifold at a central point near the throttle.

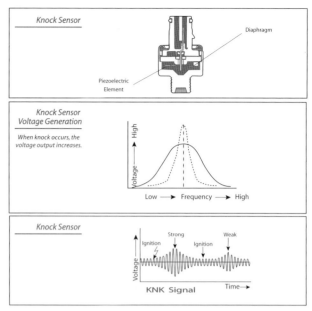

Retarding timing is extremely effective at killing knock, because full combustion pressure is delayed until the piston is already moving away from top dead center. All modern street premium-fuel engines are equipped with knock-sensor systems to retard ignition timing in case the knock sensor detects vibration frequencies characteristic of knock. Add-on knock sensor systems are great insurance for preventing engine damage on nitrous installations.

Stock cast pistons are not viable for the BMEP that results from more than a 110- to 125-horsepower boost. A 125-horse nitrous boost, for example, increases 6.0-liter LS2 Corvette specs from 400 horsepower at 6,000 and 400 lb-ft at 4,400, to 525 horsepower at 6,000 and 550 lb-ft at 4,400. Assuming peak torque stayed at the same rpm (don't count on it), BMEP at 4,400 would increase from approximately 165 psi to 225 psi. If these exact same numbers could be achieved with a larger 7.5-liter Chevy big-block (454 CID), then BMEP at 4,400 would be down to about 183 psi. A 454 crate motor is more likely to deliver 400 horsepower at something like 4,900 and 470 lb-ft at 3,200 (at which point it's making 286 horsepower with 164.8 psi BMEP). Adding a 125-horse nitrous kit that's fully kicking ass by 3,200 rpm on the big block would increase power at 3,200 to 411 horsepower, which equates to 674 lb-ft torque, and BMEP of—surprise!—225 psi.

If an engine was designed to maximize normal-charged volumetric efficiency, peak power with nitrous boost will be limited by detonation or mechanical failure. A conventional competition engine can typically absorb a nitrous power boost of at least 0.5 to 0.75 horsepower per cubic inch, which works out to, say, 150 to 275 horsepower for a small-block V-8, and 200-340 for a large, raised-block V-8. Nitrous venders commonly market streetable turnkey nitrous kits with up to 300 to 400 horsepower boost (the largest of which would probably utilize two or three stages). Many tuners consider 300 to be the maximum sustainable power boost for a normal-charged V-8 unless the engine is expressly

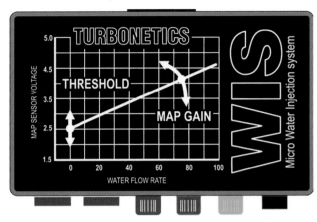

The fire chemistry of oxygen-enriched nitrous combustion is hotter and faster than ordinary combustion, but water or alcohol injection can fight knock by cooling combustion by forcing the fire to boil water into steam. NACA testing during World War II found that a mixture of water and alcohol was as effective in fighting knock in large nitrous-injected engines equipped with air-supercharging as forcing the engine to boil large amounts of supplemental fuel that could not burn due to the lack of oxygen. This Turbonetics controller enables a tuner to provide a threshold and gain for water injection to prevent knock and increase nitrous horsepower without sub-optimal ignition retard. *Turbonetics*

purpose-built to survive a very high nitrous boost with lowered static compression ratio (in some cases reduced from 12 to 14:1 or more to as little as 8 to 9:1), low-silicon forged pistons, and thicker ring lands located extra-far from the piston crown. A 300 to 400 horsepower nitrous boost is more practical for a big-block V-8 engine, though 300 horsepower of boost has been successfully implemented on some race-type normal-charged small-block V-8s that must achieve very high performance during non-boosted conditions. However, it may not be practical to achieve a net power gain that adds up to the all-motor power plus 100 percent of the theoretical nitrous boost unless engine management is fully adaptable to both normal and nitrous-boost conditions. In one interesting example, a carbureted big-block racing engine achieved roughly 650 all-motor horsepower when tuned for maximum non-boosted performance, but only about 550 in non-boosted operation when the tuning was reworked to be compatible with nitrous operations. When boosted, the engine delivered 872 horsepower, a 320-horse jump but a net gain of only 220 over the fully optimized all-motor tuning. Some computer-controlled engines, of course, are able to optimize

The ideal antidetonation countermeasure is to burn very high octane fuel, which is very resistant to auto-ignition from high heat and pressure. Auxiliary fuel tanks like this filled with super-high-octane leaded race gas or aviation fuel are very effective in optimizing the power of nitrous boost without detonation getting in the way, while permitting the engine to burn ordinary (relatively inexpensive) pump gasoline during normal all-motor operations.

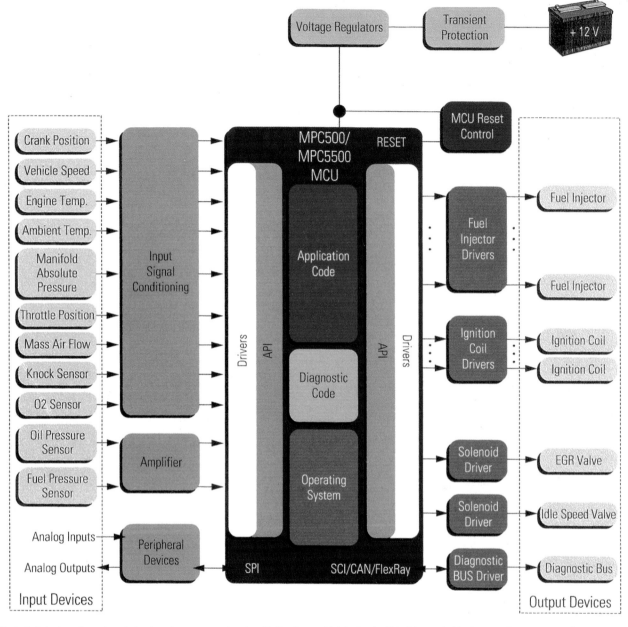

The logical structure of a modern electronic engine management system. Ideally, nitrous oxide injection should be integrated with primary engine management for optimal power, efficiency, and safety. Modern aftermarket engine management systems are now usually capable of managing progressive nitrous delivery and coordinating this with supplemental fuel delivery through the primary electronic injectors.

tuning for both all-motor and nitrous operations, including altered valve timing and lift, (and some experimental engines can even change the compression ratio dynamically under computer control!).

In the real world, a good rule of thumb is that a nitrous system delivering 1 pound of nitrous into the engine every 10 seconds provides sufficient oxygen for a 100-horsepower boost. Thus, 1.25 pounds every 10 seconds provides a 125-horse boost. Assuming the nitrous flow could be maintained in the face of the refrigerant effect of boiling nitrous on nitrous tank temperature and pressure, a 20-pound nitrous tank would provide a 125-horse boost for a total of $(20/1.25) \times 10$ seconds = 160 seconds—i.e., 2 minutes and 40 seconds of boost. Fuel flow required to make horsepower is similar to the full-throttle fuel consumption of turbocharged engines with the same horsepower (assume 0.4 to 0.5 brake specific fuel consumption [fuel mass per hour divided by horsepower] for naturally aspirated engines,

0.5 to 0.6 for nitrous and turbocharged engines, 0.6 to 0.7 for supercharged and rotary engines). Meanwhile, at this level of boost, fuel consumption remains unaffected on a V-8 engine when nitrous boost is inactive because knock can be controlled without lowering the compression ratio.

NITROUS INJECTION PERFORMANCE

On a normal-charged powerplant, the same mechanism that produces the power must charge itself with air and fuel using the weight of the earth's atmosphere, resulting in a nearly insurmountable air famine in the neighborhood of 100 percent VE that can only be partially ameliorated using very high engine speeds with resonation-effects intake and exhaust tuning—a strategy that requires exotic (expensive!) engine components designed to cope with tremendous reciprocating forces. Even so, an all-motor engine with the same peak horsepower as a nitrous-injected powerplant delivers *much less* performance due to the fact that a nitrous horsepower-boost improves power by the amount of the shot *across the powerband* from threshold boost on up. The *average*

horsepower of a nitrous-boosted powerplant (sometimes referred to at *the area under the curve*) is far greater.

That said, why is it sometimes difficult or impossible for a nitrous kit to deliver the advertised or expected performance you'd expect based on the jet size of the nitrous-injection nozzles?

1. In the first place, nitrous tank pressure will vary according to temperature and the ability of nitrous to boil fast enough during boost to maintain pressure (boiling, of course, has its own chilling effect on tank pressure).

2. Beyond this, since rated nitrous system performance is almost always dependent on achieving *liquid* nitrous injection into the intake, nitrous system heat soak and tank pressure fall-off can result in nitrous boiling in cavities in the system plumbing, resulting in unintended multiple bi-directional nitrous phase changes between liquid and gas as cavities boil and gasify, temporarily producing dysfunctionally rich mixtures and a power

Three relatively small Garret turbochargers provide good low-end turbo boost, but a small shot of low-end progressive nitrous provides a quick blast of heat to wake up the turbos in record time, at which point nitrous injection stops and the turbos take over. At this rate, a 15-pound tank of nitrous provides many hundreds of acceleration assists.

A very large shot of direct-port nitrous injection can destroy traction, so the cute trick is to bring in nitrous in three stages. This SX2 system from Nitrous Express provides all stages of injection through single fogger-type injectors in each intake port. *Nitrous Express*

bog. Such nitrous gas or foam pockets are subsequently flushed into the engine as boost continues and replaced with liquid, resulting in a burst of power—possibly followed by another power bog, and so on (which can easily result in surges of up to 50 horsepower in a second or two on street nitrous systems, a process known as thermo-hydraulic resonance).

3. Assuming liquid nitrous is injected at the proper mass flow rate, depending on the type of nitrous-injection system, it can be difficult to achieve precision mixing of nitrous oxide and supplemental fuel.

4. And even when there is a good fuel-oxidizer mix, it can be difficult on some intake systems to achieve equal nitrous/fuel distribution to the various cylinders.

5. Beyond that, nitrous- and fuel-injection nozzles that are located too far from each other (particularly on single- or dual-point nitrous systems) can cause mixture distribution problems or fluctuating oxygen-fuel ratios that make some or all cylinders run lean.

6. And finally, nitrous systems with distribution problems that cause individual-cylinder lean conditions may force tuners to increase the global fuel enrichment of *all cylinders*, reducing power in some cylinders that run grossly rich.

Unfortunately, it can be very difficult to troubleshoot fuel distribution problems during nitrous boost. A wideband O_2 sensor with datalogging can be helpful, though one wideband sensor will not distinguish between cylinders. Multiple wideband sensors or individual-port EGT probes with datalogging are standard procedure on modern nitrous-injected draggers equipped with electronic engine management, but for tuners with thinner wallets, the old-school method of chopping power at various stages of boost and reading the plugs is mandatory (see Chapter 6).

About the smallest nitrous boost that's usually practical per injection nozzle is about 5 horsepower, meaning an

All direct-port nitrous systems need a distribution manifold to split the stream of nitrous (and fuel, when required) into multiple tubes feeding the individual-cylinder nozzles. You cannot, however, assume that the distribution manifold provides perfect distribution, particularly in the case of traditional "distribution blocks." For this reason, some tunersnow prefer "showerhead" or radial distribution manifolds, but is it still hard to beat the appearance and geometry of a rectangular manifold? *Nitrous Outlet*

engine with a single point nitrous-injection system could be boosted as little as 5 horsepower, while a 4-cylinder engine with port nitrous injection could be boosted as little as 20 horsepower. Nitrous has reportedly been used to boost engines as small as 90 to 100 cc (which is smaller than a 3.5-cid Briggs and Stratton lawnmower engine!). As discussed elsewhere in this book, engines with very small cylinder bores are more resistant to detonation than larger engines due to the shorter combustion flame travel and subsequent increased likelihood that normal combustion will burn up all the oxygen-fuel mixture before any significant portions reach auto-ignition temperature and cause trouble by exploding (detonation can damage engine parts and does not produce optimal power).

Nitrous can certainly be deployed to add power on air-cooled powerplants found in older Volkswagen and Porsche automobiles or many current motorcycles and other small ATVs, snowmobiles, watercraft, etc. But *conservatively*: Air-cooled engines have much less thermal momentum in the form of a large liquid coolant reservoir that can absorb large amounts of heat with little temperature rise, so the temperature of air-cooled powerplants can rise *very quickly* in the face of lean-mixture problems. Air-cooled 2-stroke

NOS's "VTEC Cheater" nitrous kit is a little unusual in that it can be considered a plate system with fuel and nitrous injected from orifices in an intake manifold spacer-plate, a direct-port injection system that introduces fuel and nitrous into individual intake runners, and a wet-EFI system all in one. NOS makes a similar system for the 5.0 Ford V-8 that installs between the upper and lower intake manifold pieces. *NOS*

engines have the same problem, but it is exacerbated by the fact that 2-stroke engines will seize more easily than 4-stroke powerplants.

FUEL SUPPLY AND IGNITION CONSTRAINTS

Horsepower results from burning fuel. You cannot make power without fuel, but additional fuel enrichment is also required on engines boosted with air-supercharging or nitrous injection to prevent detonation and engine damage by keeping combustion at safe temperatures. A powerful spark is required for efficient combustion during boosted operations.

There are a variety of potentially problematic issues related to fuel-supply hardware which, without modifications, could be fatal to a nitrous-injection project. As well, ignition can eventually become a constraint on a boosted engine. The details of nitrous engine management are described in detail elsewhere in this book, but there are several problematic issues related to fuel supply.

Dry-manifold nitrous systems deliver supplemental fuel through stock or upgraded primary electronic fuel injectors, but stock injectors have a finite maximum sustainable flow at rated fuel pressure, and the realistic maximum flow is less because injectors can overheat when held open continuously. A good rule of thumb is that each electronic injector can deliver a maximum of 1 horsepower per pound of injector flow capacity, meaning eight 25-pound/hour injectors can deliver about 200 horsepower worth of fuel. Maximum horsepower, of course, includes basic power delivery plus

4 Cycles of Operation

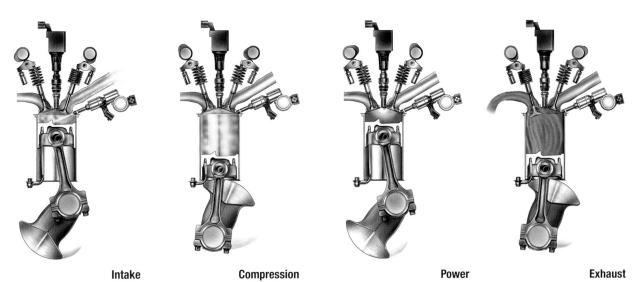

| Intake | Compression | Power | Exhaust |

Ecotec 2.0L Turbo (LNF) Highlighting Direct Injection and Piston Oil Spray Cooling

GM's 1.8-2.4L I4 Ecotec was designed to be strong so it could be used in factory turbo applications, making it a good candidate for nitrous injection as well. In turbo versions the pistons are cooled with oil-squirter jets, and the crank and block structure are very robust. When GM Racing decided to build up the engine for super-high-output drag racing, they searched for the limits of the engine with ever-increasing amounts of nitrous injection. *GM* nitrous boost. When supplemental fuel is not delivered through the stock fuel injectors, or if the primary injectors cannot provide 100 percent of fuel delivery during nitrous boost, additional injection capacity is required. A lot of "wet" nitrous systems have been sold with a single supplemental fuel nozzle, but it is not the best idea to inject supplemental nitrous fuel from a single nozzle at the throttle body or manifold plenum of an engine with multipoint electronic injection due to the fact that multipoint EFI manifolds are *not* designed to handle "wet" air-fuel mixture, and a single-point supplemental nozzle injecting fuel into a dry manifold may not distribute liquid fuel correctly to all of the various cylinders—though it can often be made to work acceptably well with sufficient research and development if the boost is not too radical. Injecting supplemental fuel using the stock electronic injectors is a great way to achieve excellent fuel distribution, but unfortunately there is not normally a lot of excess injector capacity between maximum stock injector duty cyle and the point at which the electronic injectors are effectively wide open (static) and it is *not trivial* to upgrade injector size while maintaining functional correct air-fuel ratios at all combinations of engine speed and loading in both boosted and non-boosted operations.

To *increase fuel delivery*, **electronic injectors** may be run at higher-than-rated pressure to supply supplemental fuel during nitrous boost by various means (usually with an add-on variable-rate-of-gain fuel pressure regulator). Many experts suggest running a maximum of 80- or 90-psi fuel rail pressure, but actual maximum operable fuel-injector pressure will vary depending on injector design, the electrical characteristics of the driver circuitry, and the manifold

GM's basic 140-plus-horsepower 2.0L Ecotec I4 easily handled nitrous boost in the 50 to 80 percent power increase without trouble, but all four rods failed at once at 200 percent of stock power. Then, by upgrading the rods, pistons, and rings, GM Racing had an engine mechanical configuration that was a zero constraint on maximum nitrous horsepower. At this point the engine's exhaust became the operative constraint on the nitrous power boost, and the Ecotec absolutely would not make more than 370 horsepower with the stock exhaust valves, headers, and cam, no matter how much nitrous and fuel GM packed into the engine. With upgrade intake and exhaust systems installed, however, power increased and the basic semi-floating structure of the cylinder block eventually became a constraint on head-sealing and ring performance. *GM*

pressure into which the injectors are squirting. And, of course, the latest electronic injectors for Gasoline Direction Injection powerplants inject fuel directly into the cylinders at over 100 atmospheres (roughly 3,000 psi).

The maximum horsepower that a given injector can make on an engine at design fuel pressure can be computed using the formula

Horsepower = flow rate (lb-hr) × number injectors × maximum injector duty cycle (%)/brake specific fuel consumption

Changes in fuel pressure impact fuel delivery according to the following:

New flow rate (lb-hr) = square root [new pressure/old pressure] × old flow rate

Regardless of whether fuel is delivered through a carburetor, electronic injectors, direct-injection injectors, or one or more supplemental nitrous fuel nozzles, the **electric fuel pump** itself on a vehicle has a rated maximum fuel flow volume. The fuel pump capacity varies inversely with pressure, such that the higher the head of pressure the pump is pushing against, the *less* fuel mass or volume it can deliver. If the total combined fuel flow for normal and

Technicians at Rousch Performance near Detroit working to build a high-output Ecotec for use in Sport Compact drag racing and Land Speed Record trials. The build-up is a great example of what modifications it takes to boost engine power by nearly a factor of ten.

nitrous-boost horsepower is higher than what the fuel pump can supply at a given pressure, fuel pressure at the injector rail will drop until flow reaches an equilibrium volume the pump *can* deliver at reduced pressure, which could result in engine-damaging lean mixtures, since pressure-based fuel delivery devices will deliver less fuel than they should. Besides pressure and volume, another variable affecting fuel pump performance is the electrical voltage supplied to the pump. As voltage increases, the pump will run faster with greater power, and can thus pump more fuel at higher pressure. Add-on power-supply devices are available that kick in to overdrive a fuel pump (stock or aftermarket) with super-normal voltage when fuel demand is high to maintain or increase the fuel delivery during nitrous boost. It is also common to increase the fuel delivery capacity of an in-tank pump by adding a second-stage inline fuel pump in series to boost pressure, or the vehicle fuel supply can be doubled using two fuel pumps installed in parallel. Obviously, the diameter of fuel supply and return plumbing itself can become a restriction to fuel delivery.

The fuel pressure on port-EFI systems is normally determined by a *fuel pressure regulator*. The regulator's job is to ensure fuel delivery at a conditioned pressure to the injectors by pinching off return fuel flow exiting the fuel rail into the fuel tank return line to the degree required to maintain a target pressure upstream of the regulator in the fuel rail. Some fuel pressure regulators are adjustable to a limited degree by turning a bolt that alters preload against the internal diaphragm spring, which will then hold the regulator

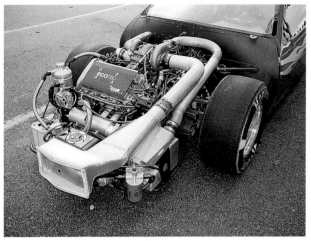

Boosted with a Garret turbocharger, GM Racing's Ecotec dragger quickly proved capable of 7.853 seconds in the quarter at 188.33 mph. There is no reason why similar performance couldn't be achieved with nitrous injection.

closed to a higher pressure. Such a pressure regulator is also typically—but not always—referenced to manifold pressure in order to supplement the power of the regulator spring as manifold pressure increases toward atmospheric so that fuel pressure at the injector inlets stays a fixed amount above manifold pressure, continuing to rise linearly with manifold pressure if a turbo or blower starts making boost. Some modern engine management systems now have an embedded ability to manage fuel pump speed or regulation in order to maintain required injection pressure via voltage changes that are calculated based on internal demand tables and feedback from a fuel rail pressure sensor.

A special aftermarket variable-rate-of-gain fuel pressure regulator (sometimes called a "Fuel Management Unit" or FMU) can be deployed downstream of the standard fuel pressure regulator in the fuel tank return line with the goal of providing supplemental fuel during power boost by increasing fuel pressure as a *multiple* of manifold pressure increases as a turbo kicks in and manifold pressure becomes positive, or when nitrous boost kicks in. During normal-charged operation when the VRG regulator is inoperative, the standard regulator manages fuel pressure as always.

Gasoline direct injection (GDI) engines, which inject fuel straight into the cylinders rather than the intake runners, run radical, quasi-diesel injection pressures, typically in the 1,500-3,000 psi range (these days diesel injection can be as high as 24,000 psi!). GDI Piezo hydraulic injectors open and close using an electrical current that slightly changes the *volume* of a substrate surrounding a microscopic fuel channel such that it functions as a valve. This tiny valve is much too small and weak by itself to supply the fuel for a full-blown injector squirt, so fuel pressure from the Piezo orifice is used to hydraulically actuate a larger servo valve in the injector that opens and closes to spray fuel into the engine at extreme pressure. Some

Ecotec drag-race block with thick, pressed-in custom cast-iron cylinder sleeves and O-ring grooves machined into the block deck. With a pool of epoxy poured around the bases of the super-duty cylinder sleeves, the block proved capable of 1,200-plus-horsepower for short-duration drag racing, and 750 horsepower for Land Speed Record Trials at Bonneville. GM Racing tried filling the block completely with epoxy in a quest for 1,400 reliable drag-race horsepower, as seen in this photo, but this was not considered a successful experiment, and was not continued in competition.

Ecotec-powered LSR vehicles at the Bonneville Salt Flats. GM Racing's effort are a textbook example of what it takes to achieve one of the most radical power increases imaginable, and are highly applicable to understanding how and when parts break, and what it takes for radical nitrous powerplants to live when the power is multiplied.

Bob Norwood has to be one of the few people on earth who proved long ago that nitrous oxide can be combined successfully with nitromethane in Hemi-powered Funny Cars, and the concept was recently reprised in this solid-block twin-turbo nitrous-nitro-methanol dragster with electronic and constant fuel injection.

GDI systems work under a constant high pressure, while other "demand control" GDI systems dynamically manage fuel pressure to the injectors under computer control based on feedback from a fuel pressure sensor.

Mass airflow sensor (MAF) units on modern EFI engines can be critical to achieving good engine management (though some of the most modern EFI engines have redundancy in the form of *both* MAF and manifold absolute pressure (MAP) sensors. Nitrous oxide should never be injected upstream of an MAF sensor, since the added (nitrous) mass as detected by the sensor will confuse the EMS as to how much *air* is being inducted into the powerplant. The increased mass would tend to result in unneeded fuel enrichment, but it could also trigger a trouble code and limp-home mode if the combined nitrous and air mass is greater than the EMS will tolerate.

(Some nitrous vendors are now supplying special MAF units with integral nitrous/fuel nozzles on the downstream side; MAF airflow data may alternatively be tweaked to result in the main fuel system automatically delivering supplemental fuel during nitrous boost.)

Assuming ignition timing has been properly retarded during nitrous boost to reflect the faster flame speed and the need to delay ignition to lower cylinder pressures on knock-limited engines, the high-voltage spark delivery system downstream of the coil-driver must be powerful enough to fire through the combination of normal charge gases and the additional mass of nitrous and supplemental fuel. Keep in mind that with the increased noise level and power during nitrous boost, it can be very difficult to detect misfires, particularly on V-8, V-10, or V-12 engines. Stock ignition

Nitrous system builders have been ingenious in ways of introducing nitrous oxide into an engine. This NX kit injects nitrous oxide and fuel from orifices integral to a special replacement mass air flow (MAF) sensor in such a way that the MAF unit continues to provide accurate information to the engine management system regarding mass air flow into the engine during both all-motor and nitrous-boosted operations. *Nitrous Express*

systems vary in power, but can become a power constraint even at surprisingly low nitrous boost on some engines. When installing a nitrous-injection system, you will almost definitely want to upgrade to a more powerful ignition and/ or decrease the plug gap.

NITROUS AS A VE-IMPROVER

When evaluating the *effectiveness* of a competition nitrous powerplant, the bottom line is total horsepower, which depends ultimately on achieving target maximum charge gas *oxygen* from a particular blend of air and nitrous within the constraints of knock-limited horsepower and the physical ability of the powerplant internals to survive the onslaught of power.

When evaluating the *efficiency* of a nitrous powerplant, the criteria is ultimately the gain in horsepower per *weight of injected nitrous* (fuel efficiency is a separate issue). Once again, this is heavily dependent on the sum total of nitrous-induced changes in engine VE. Obviously, all port- or manifold-injected *nitrous* makes it into the cylinders, but depending on whether the dominant effect of nitrous injection is charge air cooling or air intake displacement, there might be an overall loss or a gain in volumetric efficiency.

NITROUS PATENTS

Air amplifier for nitrous oxide injection application - Patent 6240911
Automated electrical switching system - Patent 4869132
Computer controlled flow of nitrous oxide injected into an internal combustion engine - Patent 5287281
Computer controlled flow of nitrous oxide injected into an internal combustion engine - Patent 5444628
Control system for an engine supercharging system - Patent 6378506
Control valve for nitrous oxide injection system - Patent 20060157108
Control valve for nitrous oxide injection system - Patent 7150443
Direct nitrous injection system operable from zero to 100 percent throttle control - Patent 6260546
Electronic pre-combustion treatment device - Patent 20080006249
Engine control system using an air and fuel control strategy based on torque demand - Patent 6298824
Fuel charging system for high performance vehicles - Patent 4494488
Fuel injector nozzle adapter - Patent 6997401
Fuel pump system with precision variable restrictor - Patent 20060231075
Fuel pump system with precision variable restrictor - Patent 7278413
Fuel-nitrous oxide injection plate - Patent 6955163
Intake manifold plate adapter - Patent 20070017492
Internal combustion engine with barometric pressure related start of air compensation for a fuel injector - Patent 5848582
Laminar flow nozzle - Patent 6116225
Liquid injection system for internal combustion engine - Patent 5499603
Method and apparatus to provide oxygen enriched air to the intake manifold of an internal combustion engine - Patent 7128064
Method for controlling an internal combustion engine with nitrous oxide injection - Patent 6758198
Method for controlling an internal combustion engine with nitrous oxide injection - Patent 6758198
Method of controlling an engine with a pseudo throttle position sensor value - Patent 6250292
Nitrous oxide and fuel control valve for nitrous oxide injection system - Patent 20060157106
Nitrous oxide and fuel control valve for nitrous oxide injection system - Patent 7228872
Nitrous oxide fuel injection safety system - Patent 4683843
Nitrous oxide injection system - Patent 20040250804
Nitrous oxide injection system - Patent 20070261685
Nitrous oxide injection system - Patent 7171958
Nitrous oxide plate system - Patent 5743241
Nitrous oxide precooler - Patent 4572140
Nitrous oxide vapor delivery system for engine power enhancement - Patent 7210472
Nitrous oxide-fuel injector for air intake to internal combustion engine - Patent 20050081827
Nitrous oxide-fuel injector for air intake to internal combustion engine - Patent 6935322
Nitrous-oxide system - Patent 20060225671
Nozzle for emitting nitrous oxide for fuel to engines - Patent 6520165
Nozzle for mixing oxidizer with fuel - Patent 5699776
Pressure compensating orifice for control of nitrous oxide delivery - Patent 6938841
Pulse width modulated controller for nitrous oxide and fuel delivery - Patent 5269275
Spray bar pair assembly - Patent 6279557
System, method, and device for nitrous oxide injection - Patent 5967099
System, method, and device for nitrous oxide injection - Patent 6105563
Temperature control system for nitrous oxide pressurized bottle - Patent 6889513
Valve apparatus and method for injecting nitrous oxide into a combustion engine - Patent 20020029769
Valve apparatus and method for injecting nitrous oxide into a combustion engine - Patent 6349709

In the case of the 5.0L V-8, Ford made it easy for hot rodders to install direct-port nitrous by conveniently splitting the intake manifold into two parts, between which hot rodders can install an annular-orifice spacer plate with integral nitrous and fuel injection nozzles, one per intake port. *Nitrous Express*

- Intake manifold surface temperature
- Engine rpm
- Intake air speed
- Intake tract length from the point of nitrous injection
- Intake runner length
- Engine coolant temperature
- Nitrous plumbing thermal leakage
- Nitrous-air mass ratio
- Air-fuel ratio
- Engine mass airflow
- Intake manifold pulse-resonation effects and turbulence
- Manifold pressure
- Intake-runner pressure
- Cylinder pressure
- and more . . .

How do we evaluate nitrous efficiency? One way is to compare dyno numbers with and without nitrous boost, and carefully monitor nitrous mass flow during boost. Another way is simply to compare data-logged mass airflow stats with and without nitrous boost. Unfortunately, dyno results from state-of-the-art maximum-effort competition nitrous motors reveal that such engines have very poor efficiency of power per injected nitrous mass. High-end Pro Comp nitrous drag racers targeting a larger horsepower increase from nitrous than the basic unboosted output of the engine report that adding, say, a 1,400-horse (7-stage!) nitrous "shot" to a dual-quad-carbureted 750 cubic-inch 1,250-horse powerplant might yield 2,250 rather than the 2,650 horses you might expect—obviously due to supplemental fuel and nitrous displacing intake air in spite of temperature-based gains in air density from nitrous refrigeration.

What factors determine whether there is a net supercharging effect on engine volumetric efficiency from nitrous phase change refrigeration? This is ultimately contingent on such factors as the nitrous mass-air mass ratio and how fast injected nitrous vaporizes. Depending on intake geometry, charge temperature, and distance to the combustion chambers, shrinking droplets of liquid nitrous streaking toward the intake valves at up to 200 feet per second may or may not make it all the way into the cylinders before they evaporate completely—which can have a large effect on VE. It is fabulously difficult to predict what percentage of nitrous oxide will remain liquid when the intake valves slam shut to trap liquid nitrous droplets (or very dense cold nitrous gas) and charge air in the cylinders before the nitrous liquid can fully expand, dependent as this is on a set of dynamically changing factors that include:

- Nitrous tank temperature and pressure
- Intake air temperature upstream of nitrous injection
- The cooling effect from vaporizing liquid nitrous
- Liquid-nitrous distribution inequalities to various cylinders

The best-case nitrous VE improvement occurs with low nitrous-to-air-mass ratios, and about the best you can expect is a 10 percent mass airflow gain with a 10 to 20 percent nitrous-air mass ratio. If you dump a tremendous amount of nitrous and supplemental fuel into a motor, there are diminishing returns. And not just from charge volume lost to nitrous: The more you enrich the oxygen content of the charge mixture, the more *supplemental fuel* mass you have to dump in to realize additional power and keep the engine from burning its insides out from all that oxygen—and fuel takes up space and displaces charge air too.

Of course, the simplest way to know precisely how much nitrous liquid is getting into an engine is to make sure *none gets in* by injecting nitrous *gas* at a controlled temperature (see Chapter 8 regarding the controlled conditions of NACA's World War II experiments with *nitrous oxide supercharging of an aircraft engine cylinder*), or to make sure that *100 percent liquid nitrous gets in* by injecting nitrous liquid straight into the cylinders with nitrous direct injection (see sidebar "Nitrous Patents" on page 62). Unfortunately, neither strategy will do anything to increase the net volumetric efficiency of air induction (though, of course, liquid nitrous direct injection will still help lower combustion temperatures via nitrous boiling in the combustion chambers).

System control panels like this unit for Chevrolet Camaros with nitrous injection make it easy to arm the nitrous system, turn a bottle heater on or off, open or close a remote bottle opener, and purge the nitrous line. Rock 'n' Roll!

THE EXTREME EVOLUTION
OF GM'S BOOSTED 2.0-LITER ECOTEC

What does it take to convert a mild-mannered stock four-cylinder engine into an extreme-boost terror?

Using gasoline and then methanol, GM engineers and racers incrementally hot-rodded the 2.0-liter Ecotec four-cylinder through every possible stage of horsepower and torque from stock to the far outer reaches of hot-rodding hell. This effort employed the experts' best tricks to make an engine live and scream.

The Ecotec arrived brand-new in Y2K in some Saturn models as a 140-horsepower normally aspirated powerplant. Within a few years, GM offered the 1.8-2.0-2.2-liter engine in car and SUV brands around the world from Pontiac to Saab, ranging from the basic 140-horse versions to higher-output, bigger displacement engines with 15 to 25 percent more power, to a 205-horse supercharged Chevy Cobalt, a 260-horse turbocharged version of the Pontiac Solstice, and more. Eventually GM began marketing Stage 1 and Stage 2 upgrade kits for supercharged engines that boosted power to 235 horsepower and 205 lb-ft, or to 241 horsepower and 218 lb-ft.

Meanwhile, starting in 2001, GM Racing developed the Ecotec for an all-out crash drag-racing program. That group tweaked and tuned and ramped and boosted until output reached nearly 1,400 horsepower!

As raw material, the Ecotec was reasonably impressive. Although the original aluminum-block design was not turbocharged, it was "protected" for future turbocharging (as well as direct-injection gasoline and variable cam phasing), meaning it was built to be strong, with features like six-fastener main caps (four studs plus cross-bolting) integrated into a die-cast girdle structure and buttressed by a structural aluminum oil pan. The semi-floating block deck was designed with pressed-in cast-iron cylinder sleeves. All Ecotec blocks and heads were originally manufactured with lost-foam casting and included oil gallery passages machine-able for piston-cooling oil jets ("oil squirters"), and the engine was factory-readied to receive an oil cooler. GM's design employed extra-thick main bearings to resist the differential expansion of the nodular iron aerodynamic crankshaft and aluminum block. Eventually, based on lessons learned from the racing effort, GM would enlarge the block bulkheads that act as attachment points for the main bearing caps, as well as the bore walls in the "Gen II" version of the Ecotec used in the Pontiac Solstice GXP 2.4-liter 260-horsepower factory turbo package. Some of the higher-output cylinder heads would be die cast.

Seeking a 10,000-rpm powerplant that could survive at least 20 to 40 drag runs making 800 horsepower, a GM Racing team working in an advanced southern California skunkworks set about to find the limits of the brand-new Ecotec the old-fashioned way: By progressively blowing more and more nitrous through the powerplant on a dyno until something broke, repairing the engine with stronger parts (and sending the damaged pieces to a lab for forensic analysis), and pushing on until the next weakest link died and went to hell. When the engine's intake and exhaust systems inevitably became too constipated to make more power, the team would abandon nitrous and switch exclusively to turbocharging as the power-adder. That was the plan, and engineers began making bets about what was going to break first as the GM Racing team geared up to begin destroying engines.

GM's team set up a stock Ecotec on a Hienen-Freud water-brake engine dyno and wired the powerplant for engine management using a DFI/Accel programmable system that controlled fuel, spark, and a cold spray of nitrous and enrichment fuel entering the induction

system from a single point near the throttlebody supplied by a three-stage nitrous delivery system. With a fire crew standing by, GM Racing began a rigorous series of tests. The Ecotec would receive a passing grade for a given level of power only if it survived a set of 8 to 10 full-power dyno "sprints" from peak torque to maximum power in rapid 50-rpm steps, each test concluding with at least six seconds at full power—for a total of at least 20 seconds of engine-raping flog per dyno run.

The stock-block Ecotec—running premium gasoline, a custom free-flow exhaust, and no accessories but the alternator—immediately ripped off a 168-horsepower baseline run without nitrous (up from the stock advertised 140 horsepower). Boosted with nitrous, the engine survived happily at 200, 225, and 250 horsepower, at which point the Ecotec was making 80 percent more power than stock! The bet at GM Racing was still that the first thing to fail would be the head gasket.

Not so. As the Ecotec pushed through 283 horsepower at 4,400 rpm (twice stock power as installed in early USA-spec cars), all four rods failed simultaneously and smashed through the side of the block. Lab analysis subsequently revealed a mid-beam compression fracture of *all four* powder-metal connecting rods. This was *not* a high-rpm stretch failure, *not* a fastener failure, *not* a lubrication failure. And all rod bearings, wrist pins, and ring packs checked out fine.

The obvious conclusion is that with proper engine management, premium fuel, and good engine cooling, you can figure conservatively on boosting a healthy Ecotec at least 50 percent above stock power without killing anything right away. The Ecotec's stock components tolerated a 110-horsepower nitrous boost from the stock 140 output to 250 horsepower—an 80 percent increase—without incident. The rods failed when GM pushed output to 200 percent of stock. Of course, without upgraded components, any increase in maximum power may shorten the life of a stock engine.

Starting over again with a brand-new engine, GM Racing installed a package of parts typical of what any serious performance enthusiast or racer would want if you were taking the trouble to open the engine to upgrade the connecting rods: Super-duty X-beam Crower rods, 10:1 JE forged pistons with thicker (4.5 millimeters versus 3.0 millimeters) top ring lands, and moly ring packs.

The 10-1 pistons are about as high a compression ratio as you're likely to see on a gasoline-fueled turbo engine and much higher than ever found on older street turbo engines from the 1970s and 1980s (the 1976 930 Porsche Turbo ran less than 6.5:1!), but modern four-valve pentroof engines running street premium fuel with a *lot* of fuel cooling are knock-resistant enough to run a 10- to 15-psi boost with 93 octane premium fuel and excellent engine management. GM, of course, was now running super-high-octane racing fuel. The GM Team also installed larger fuel injectors and then continued to lean on the engine.

With the new parts installed, and before anything else could break, the nitrous engine ran out of breathing room on the exhaust side at 350 horsepower. In terms of engine gas flow, nitrous produces an extremely high ratio of products to reactants, constipating the exhaust long before the intake. The stock exhaust manifold became so restrictive at about 350 horsepower that if you weren't careful, more nitrous would actually make less power. "We actually made 370 to 375 horsepower on nitrous," said team leader Stephen Bothwell, "but the engine was really pissed off." So far, the head gasket had not failed.

Chapter 4
Nitrous System Architecture

Having covered the theory and basics of how nitrous oxide injection works, we can now examine real-world nitrous system architecture in more detail. All nitrous systems are equipped with a subsystem that provides nitrous and a subsystem that delivers supplemental enrichment fuel. All have systems that control when nitrous boost will be active and most have systems that modify engine management during nitrous boost. The nitrous delivery circuit for modern automotive applications universally consists of:

1. A high-pressure nitrous tank with manual or electric bottle control valve
2. A flexible, robust, high-pressure line that routes nitrous from the bottle valve to the engine
3. A normally closed solenoid valve at the end of the line activated by an electrical switching mechanism to start and stop nitrous flow
4. A restrictor jet or orifice that precisely meters the flow of nitrous oxide into the engine when the solenoid valve is open
5. One or more orifices designed to inject pressured nitrous oxide into the engine intake system in a precise geometric fog of homogenous atomized droplets

All nitrous systems have this much in common, but, depending on the application, there are a variety of architectures and options that complete the system.

"Megabuck" was a 1972 Pantera with the mid-engine Ford 351C V-8 replaced by a big-block SOHC Ford 427 "Cammer" V-8 with twin turbochargers. The engine was fueled by a variable-venturi Predator carburetor and was equipped with individual-port direct nitrous injection.

Tuners, hot rodders, racers, and nitrous venders commonly describe nitrous systems with names such as **single-point**, **throttle-injection**, **dry**, **EFI**, **constant**, **standalone**, **direct-port**, **plate**, **wet**, **progressive**, **proportional**, **multi-stage**, **carbureted**, **spray bar**, **nozzle**, **tightly integrated**, **computer-controlled**, **electrically controlled**, and **stealth** or **hidden**. Unfortunately, some of these descriptors are mutually exclusive, some overlap, and some—such as single-point and throttle-injection—refer to essentially the same thing. Classifying nitrous systems can get confusing because a nitrous system cannot, for example, be both **wet** and **dry**, but it can definitely be both **dry** and **progressive**.

The basic distinctions of nitrous system architecture relate to (1) where and how the nitrous circuit injects the nitrous oxidizer, (2) where and how the system delivers enrichment fuel, (3) what mechanism and strategy is used to determine when and for how long nitrous and supplemental fuel are turned on to provide a horsepower boost, and (4) any additional tricks used to modify engine management during nitrous boost to prevent engine or drivetrain damage and achieve optimal boosted performance. The most important factor in nitrous system effectiveness and reliability is, without a doubt, the functioning and calibration of the supplemental fuel system, which is why computer-controlled nitrous injection has so much potential.

Most articles and books about nitrous oxide injection kick off their survey of nitrous architectures with a discussion of traditional wet spraybar constant nitrous, an architecture that has been installed on many thousands of carbureted and EFI performance engines for 50 years. From a hardware point of view, however, the simplest and most elegant type of nitrous system is definitely not the original "wet" nitrous system that made its way into drag racing and history back in the 1960s with its brutal ability to dump a huge self-contained jolt of "liquid horsepower" into large carbureted V-8s with 4-barrel carburetors when the driver squeezed a shifter-mounted push-button. Old-school **spray bar** nitrous systems designed to snap your neck back by injecting a constant-rate burst of nitrous and supplemental enrichment fuel from a spacer **plate** under the carburetor can be pretty rudimentary, but even the most basic spraybar systems require not only a nitrous supply subsystem to deliver and spray the liquid nitrous oxide, but a *complete auxiliary fuel subsystem* to inject

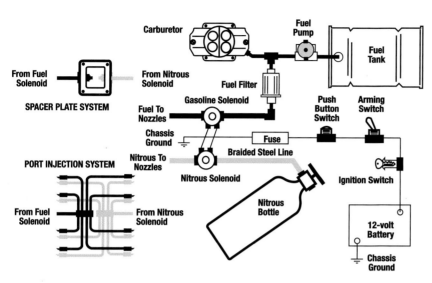

SPACER PLATE SYSTEM
From Fuel Solenoid
From Nitrous Solenoid

PORT INJECTION SYSTEM
From Fuel Solenoid
From Nitrous Solenoid

Carburetor
Fuel Pump
Fuel Tank
Fuel Filter
Gasoline Solenoid
Fuel To Nozzles
Chassis Ground
Fuse
Braided Steel Line
Nitrous To Nozzles
Nitrous Solenoid
Nitrous Bottle
Push Button Switch
Arming Switch
Ignition Switch
12-volt Battery
Chassis Ground

As this system diagram indicates, it is usually a simple matter to convert carbureted engines from wet plate nitrous systems to direct-port injection, since both systems are identical as far as the solenoid valves. In fact, many late-model EFI engines can similarly be converted from a single plate or fogger-type nitrous system to direct-port nitrous injection. The same goes for single-point dry EFI nitrous systems, which are generally convertible from one central-point nitrous nozzle to individual-port nitrous injectors.

the supplemental enrichment fuel that makes the power on any nitrous boosting system.

But why not boost an EFI powerplant by programming the engine management computer to activate and trigger nitrous oxide spray at full throttle while adding supplemental enrichment fuel through the *primary electronic port fuel injectors* by increasing the duration of the basic injection pulse? Why not fully integrate nitrous injection and supplemental enrichment fueling with the primary computer-controlled engine management?

Why not, indeed? At its simplest, computer-controlled dry nitrous requires only basic nitrous hardware, no auxiliary fuel hardware whatsoever, and no add-on control hardware other than an arming switch: Simple, elegant, logical, powerful. Computer-controlled dry nitrous is the logical starting point for a detailed survey and analysis of real-world twenty-first-century nitrous system architectures. By comparison, everything else can be seen as a compromise, a departure from the ideal.

COMPUTER-CONTROLLED DRY NITROUS

All nitrous-injection systems that deliver supplemental enrichment fuel through the primary electronic fuel injectors of a multi-port EFI powerplant are classified as **dry** nitrous systems because the intake manifold plenum is not required to distribute liquid fuel. Technically, of course, the only truly "dry" intake manifolds are the ones found on powerplants with direct-injection, where 3,000-psi piezoelectric or mechanical fuel injectors bypass the intake manifold completely by firing directly into the combustion chambers to deliver outstanding atomization and more efficient combustion. Port-EFI intake manifolds are not *literally* dry, in that these systems *do* inject liquid fuel into the intake manifold, albeit very far downstream in the runners near the intake valve where airstream has already been split and distributed equally to the various cylinders. Assuming port injectors are in good condition with properly matching flow rates, unless there

is *tremendous* reversion and standoff in the intake plenum, correct fuel distribution is inevitable. With dry nitrous injection, this remains true during nitrous boost because the primary electronic injectors continue to provide 100 percent of engine fuel requirements.

Some nitrous vendors use the designation "dry nitrous" to refer exclusively to a particular type of common nitrous-injection architecture that this book calls pressure-regulated dry nitrous, in which the nitrous system delivers supplemental enrichment fuel through the primary electronic injectors by transiently increasing fuel-injector-rail pressure during boost. This book uses the term "dry" to refer to *any* nitrous-injection architecture that introduces supplemental enrichment fuel exclusively through the primary port-EFI electronic injectors rather than using add-on continuous injection equipment in the ports or at a central point farther upstream. By this definition, dry enrichment architectures include what I call pressure-regulated dry nitrous, piggyback-controlled dry nitrous, and computer-controlled dry nitrous. You'll notice this list does not include direct-port nitrous, which is unique in that it keeps the intake plenum every bit as dry during nitrous boost as garden-variety port-EFI (and may achieve equally good fuel distribution), but delivers supplemental enrichment fuel with individual-cylinder add-on continuous injection rather than by manipulating the output of the primary electronic injectors. We have not yet discussed where the *nitrous* is injected, because this is not a factor in the "dryness" of nitrous architecture.

The most rudimentary computer-controlled dry nitrous systems are constant-injection systems that deliver a fixed mass of nitrous per time. The hardware consists of little more than a nitrous tank, high-pressure hose, solenoid valve with relay, fixed-size metering jet, and nitrous-injection nozzle. There is no *add-on* nitrous fuel enrichment system whatsoever. In the simplest case, there are no hardware modifications to the stock EFI fuel system. When the bottle control valve is open, a

MAJOR NITROUS SYSTEM COMPONENTS

Nitrous Supply Subsystem
- High-pressure *nitrous oxide tank with bottle control valve and mounting system* (on-board storage of chemical horsepower)
- High-pressure *nitrous line* (transports liquid nitrous from the tank to a control solenoid in the engine compartment: nylon hose, Teflon braided-steel hose, or metal pipe)
- *Electrically controlled solenoid valve* (closed by default) (start and stop flow out of the nitrous line, with wiring kit and relay)
- *In-line nitrous restrictor jets* (meter the rate of nitrous flow; global or one per cylinder)

Throttle-Injection Nitrous
- *Central-point supplemental nitrous injection device* (spacer-plate spray bar, diffuser, or injection nozzle) (deliver, atomize, and mix nitrous oxide with charge air, or air and fuel, in the engine intake system)

Direct-port Nitrous
- *Individual-cylinder nitrous injectors* (nitrous-only or nitrous-fuel fogger nozzles) to deliver, atomize, and mix nitrous oxide with air (or air and fuel) in the engine intake runners
- *Nitrous oxide distribution manifold* with individual-cylinder metal hard lines or nylon pipes

Options
Tank
- *Tank pressure gauge, tank temperature gauge*
- *Remote-controlled electrical bottle valve*
- *Nitrous debris filter*
- *Multi-stage nitrous delivery* (phase in nitrous hit more gradually to improve traction and protect powertrain parts)
- *High-flow bottle control valve* (for super-high boost applications without pressure drop)
- *Electrical tank heater* (maintain nitrous pressure and density)
- *Insulating tank cover (bottle blanket)* (keep heat in or out of the liquid nitrous oxide mass)
- *Additional nitrous tanks* (increase system time-to-empty and increase thermal momentum of liquid nitrous)
- *Carbon-fiber nitrous tanks* (reduce weight)
- *Quick-disconnect tank connectors* (quick installation of full nitrous tank)
- *External pressurization system* (eliminate large pressure drops on self-pressurized nitrous systems)
- *Purge-based nitrous line (and tank) cooling sleeve* (refrigerate away heat-soak in nitrous tank and supply line)
- *Incremental tank overpressure pressure-relief safety valve and tank-cooling system* (prevent overpressure tank explosions without venting the entire tank, while producing large temperature drop)
- *Nitrous refill kit with large donor-cylinder*
- *Manual inline nitrous auxiliary shutoff valve* (fail-safe nitrous shut down and quick turn-on without trip to trunk)

Solenoids
- *Fail-safe anti-leak backup solenoids* (eliminate leakage or stuck-open nitrous)
- *Axial-flow solenoids* (more direct nitrous pathway)
- *Anti-lag nitrous gas purge system* (eliminate nitrous vapor from initial hit)
- *CO_2 faux-purge system* (cool-looking blast of mist without wasting nitrous oxide)

Injectors
- *"Crossfire" nitrous/fuel nozzles* (improve nitrous-fuel mixing by blasting nitrous spray across fuel spray from both directions)
- *Straight-through jetspray-type nozzles* (good for straight shot into floor V-8 intake runner on hidden nitrous system)
- *Ninety-degree fan spray-type nitrous nozzles* (side blast of nitrous into airway)
- *Multi-orifice nitrous injectors* (improve nitrous atomization and mixing with multiple annular orifices)
- *Stealth nitrous injectors and components*

Controls
- *Nitrous triggering with fail-safe fuel pressure detection* (disarms nitrous injection if subnormal fuel pressure)
- *Dynamic nitrous-fuel metering via PWM solenoid controller* (variable nitrous metering with pulsewidth modulation of nitrous solenoid)
- *Turbo-boost nitrous oxide cutout system* (stops nitrous boost as turbocharger boost rises enough to provide required torque)
- *Multi-stage activation circuitry* (triggers multiple stages of increasing nitrous boost according to time, rpm, load, linear, and so on)
- *Secure (key-operated) arming switch* (slow down the valet)
- Indicator lights for solenoid-on and system-armed (lets you and emergency responders know if the nitrous system is armed or active)
- *Ignition delay start-up system* (sucks leaked nitrous from intake system by extended cranking before start)
- *Oil pressure-based nitrous disarming system* (prevents the nitrous system from flowing nitrous if the engine has stalled)

Miscellaneous
- *Waterproof nitrous system components* (keeps the nitrous circuitry running in harsh marine environments)
- *Total-loss external intercooler refrigeration spray* (chill turbocharging intercooler before or during turbo boost)

Supplemental Fuel Delivery and Engine Management Subsystems
- *Vehicle fuel pumping system* (deliver sufficient fuel mass at working pressure for 100 percent of ordinary all-motor requirements plus nitrous boost)
- *System arming switch* (disable nitrous boost when you don't plan to go mental)
- *Nitrous activation switch* (triggers nitrous boost if system is armed using full-throttle micro-switch, manual pushbutton, MAP pressure switch, or TPS-triggered throttle switch)

nitrous storage tank delivers nitrous oxide at full tank pressure into a supply line routed to a normally closed solenoid valve near the engine that opens under computer control to boost the engine by delivering a precisely metered constant blast of ultra-high-pressure nitrous oxidizer through a single orifice in a nozzle fixture aimed into the intake air stream.

Controlling a basic dry nitrous system without adding supplemental hardware or electronics requires an engine management system (EMS) equipped with the internal logic necessary to calculate and integrate nitrous enrichment fuel and ignition requirements as modifications or offsets to basic or air-supercharged engine management.

Computer-Controlled Dry-EFI Nitrous
- *Nitrous-capable standalone aftermarket EMS* (activates and triggers nitrous injection plus EFI-based enrichment fuel, optimizes engine management for nitrous boost)
- *Primary fuel injectors with surplus duty-cycle* (supply normal *plus* boost fuel requirements through primary electronic injectors)
- *Nitrous-enabled EMS configuration* (nitrous-capable aftermarket EMS must be configured properly to control nitrous injection)

Standalone Dry-EFI Nitrous
- *Auxiliary pressure-sensitive nonlinear fuel pressure regulator* (significantly increases stock fuel rail pressure during nitrous boost—and, thus, fuel mass delivered per injector squirt—to satisfy 100 percent of all-motor and supplemental nitrous fuel or requirements through the primary EFI fuel injectors) . . . or
- *Additional-injector-controller with add-on individual-port electronic fuel injectors* (provides boost enrichment fuel by pulsing auxiliary electronic injectors installed in each intake port)

Interceptor-controlled dry nitrous
- *Nitrous-capable auxiliary electronic interceptor* (installs between stock EMS and main wiring loom; activates nitrous flow and provides special nitrous-boost engine management by extending stock EMS fuel-injection pulsewidth, delaying ignition signal, or other means)

Auxiliary Continuous-Injection Enrichment Fuel Delivery
- *Fuel-metering jets* (restrictor-orifice provides precise volumetric flow)
- *Electrically controlled solenoid valve with wiring* (start/stop the fuel flow)
- *Supplemental fuel plumbing with micro-filter and pressure conditioning* (transports sufficient fuel at precise pressure to provide correct boost enrichment)

Direct-port nitrous (wet or dry intake manifold)
- *Supplemental fuel nozzles* (fogger-type nozzles install directly into individual intake manifold runners to provide constant fuel injection and nitrous during boost)
- *Fuel distribution manifold* (distributes fuel to direct-port constant injection nozzles through nylon hoses or steel "hard lines") . . . or
- *Under-EFI individual-injector nitrous/fuel fogging nozzles* (NOSzle-type fixtures install into the manifold beneath individual electronic injectors to deliver supplemental nitrous and fuel with connections for nitrous and fuel supply) . . . or
- *Intake manifold spacer plate* with individual-runner nitrous/fuel spray

Throttle-injection wet nitrous (preferably carbureted or throttlebody-injection intake manifold)
- *Central-point supplemental fuel-injection device* (nozzle, spacer plate spray bar, or spacer plate diffuser-plate) to deliver, atomize, and mix nitrous oxide with charge air (or air and fuel) in the engine intake system

Nitrous Controller-controlled Nitrous
- *Standalone auxiliary electronic nitrous controller* with primitive user interface manages direct-port or throttle-injection nitrous and supplemental fuel delivery, ignition delay, and any other nitrous system requirements on a variety of EFI, carbureted, direct injection–gasoline, or even diesel powerplants

Options
- *Additional or upgrade fuel pumps*
- *Fuel pump voltage-overdriving power supply* (increase existing pump flow rate)
- *PWM fuel pump controller* (manage fuel-pump flow rate by effectively reducing pump duty cycle)
- *Rpm window switch* (disarm nitrous system below safe minimum and maximum safe rpm)
- *Ignition timing interceptor* (retard timing during the faster flame speed of nitrous combustion)
- *Knock detection and control system* (retard ignition timing to kill detonation if knock sensor detects dangerous-frequency vibrations)
- *Auxiliary supplemental fuel tank* (supply special race gasoline or alcohol only during nitrous boost to kill knock and make power)
- *Bypass-fuel pressure regulator* conversion kit (provides modern high-pressure fuel loop for accurate, repeatable fuel delivery, and long pump life)
- *High-flow electronic fuel injectors* (increase the fueling capacity of the stock electronic injection system with upgrade injectors)
- *Boost additional-injector controller* (provide enrichment fuel during nitrous boost by pulsing additional electronic injectors)
- *PWM solenoid controller* (provides dynamic fuel or nitrous metering and fade-in by pulsing nitrous/fuel solenoids)
- *High-power ignition system* (deliver spark without misfire through dense air-fuel-nitrous charge mixtures)
- *High-amp upgrade alternator*
- *Fuel pressure sensor*
- *Gauges* (dash view of boost fuel pressure, auxiliary fuel tank level)
- *Rich-lean pinch valve* (manual valve pinches off EFI fuel loop to provide higher fuel pressure and additional fuel enrichment)
- *Nitrous-injection duration timer/nitrous-level computer* (counts elapsed boost time since last tank refill/reset and estimates time-until-empty using calculations and sophisticated nitrous-usage table)
- *Gasoline direct-injection fuel pressure control* (200-bar direct-injection EMS manages fuel rail pressure according to rail pressure sensor)
- *Engine-driven fuel pump* (mechanically driven fuel pump automatically increases capacity at higher engine speeds and can supply extremely high volume of fuel for engines running oxygenated fuels)
- *Methanol/ethanol-compatible nitrous system components* (resist corrosion from oxygenated fuels)
- *Nitrous-blast booster-venturi fuel enrichment* (stealth nitrous system produces fuel enrichment for modest but critical power boost by blasting nitrous spray through the booster venturis of a four-barrel carburetor)
- *Cockpit-adjustable manual ignition retard system* (allows driver to manually dial back ignition timing in case of audible knock during boost)

Translation: You need a nitrous-capable aftermarket engine management system.

The EMS must be capable of detecting when a nitrous arming switch is turned on and then triggering the nitrous supply system under configurable circumstances (full throttle, rpm within range, and so on). When nitrous is flowing, the engine management system must simultaneously deliver supplemental enrichment fuel through the primary fuel injectors by incrementing injector open time as an offset to the base EFI injection pulsewidth calculation. Nitrous engine management thus requires logic capable of predicting how much nitrous oxide the nitrous supply circuit will deliver in

Dry nitrous injection—in which the intake manifold does not handle liquid fuel—was invented after automakers began phasing out single-carb induction systems on performance engines in the late 1970s and early 1980s in favor of computer-controlled multi-port electronic fuel-injection systems that injected fuel far downstream within the individual intake runners.

With the advent of port EFI, nitrous venders had both a problem and an opportunity.

The *problem*—only it certainly didn't show up as a problem for most drivers—was that although port-EFI induction systems are more effective at getting air into an engine, they are not designed to handle fuel. With no need to manage liquid fuel in the intake manifold, port-EFI allowed factory automotive engineers the freedom to improve engine volumetric efficiency with a variety of tricks.

In pursuit of colder, denser intake charge, EFI engine designers not only eliminated intake-manifold heating previously required to prevent fuel condensation in the intake systems of carbureted engines but eventually switched to modern *plastic* intake manifolds that are less susceptible to ordinary heat-soak from the long block and engine compartments. The most important VE-improving impact of EFI was that by eliminating the need for "wet" intake manifolds purpose-built to manage the asymmetrical flow characteristics of both liquid fuel and dry air, port-EFI gave engineers the freedom to design better-breathing air-only intake manifolds that required none of the airflow compromises previously required to distribute fuel effectively and keep it suspended in the air without puddling. Dry EFI manifolds did not have to flow charge downhill to the engine. They could be equipped with large plenums and very long, equal-length, equal-geometry tuned runners that improved volumetric efficiency across a broad rpm range and thus significantly improved average torque compared to what was possible with wet carburetion or wet throttlebody fuel injection. Eventually, high-performance EFI intake manifolds could be equipped with EMS-controlled variable-length runners, variable-size plenums, and variable-diameter dual-ported runners.

Improved VE was not the only advantage of port EFI, which further improved power on otherwise identical engines by delivering more precise fuel delivery and intrinsically superior fuel distribution than single-point carburetion. A second-order effect of more precise fuel delivery and more sophisticated timing controls (or even sensor-based anti-knock subsystems) was that EFI engines could run higher, more efficient compression ratios without knock.

For most people, EFI was purely a blessing. For nitrous vendors, injecting both nitrous and supplemental fuel with old-style methods at a central location near the throttle into an unheated air-only EFI intake manifold that had none of the tricks previously used to successfully (more or less) manage wet charge mixtures was unlikely to provide equal distribution of heavy liquid fuel to the various cylinders. The result of injecting supplemental fuel into an EFI manifold was all too often a terrible combination of overly rich cylinders and dangerously lean cylinders—particularly when a nitrous system was designed, adapted, installed, tested, or debugged by non-scientists.

The *opportunity* of EFI for nitrous vendors and others in the performance-racing industry was that computer-controlled EFI provided much better and more straightforward fuel management than carburetion. Improved fueling precision and distribution under computer control meant that not only did EFI engines run cleaner and more efficiently (the existential reason for EFI), but that super-high-output hot-rod and race EFI powerplants with extreme power-adder systems could ultimately run much closer to the ragged edge of melt-down with high reliability and good drivability, and thus deliver much higher levels of usable power. What's more, with the arrival of the first digital engine controllers in the early 1980s, tuning EFI was conceptually far more straightforward, flexible, and powerful than carburetion, mechanical fuel injection, or analog electronic fuel injection because EFI used the onboard microcomputer—*not* some fabulously complex interaction of aerodynamic and hydraulic forces in the guts of a mechanical carburetor!—to determine what the air-fuel ratio should be for a particular combustion event based on up-to-the-millisecond engine status sensors and internal tables of calibration and configuration data. In fact, EFI engine fuel and spark tuning could be changed radically just by changing some *numbers* in a computer-resident data table or warping the shape of a graphical representation of the table using the arrow keys or mouse on a laptop PC.

Table-driven engine management is marvelously simple and straightforward compared to mechanical engine management devices like the carburetor. In response to a certain **event** (a certain amount of time passes and the onboard computer system's clock interrupts the CPU, or perhaps the crankshaft arrives at a certain position and a sensor generates an interrupt, and so on), the engine management computer executes logic designed to evaluate the current **state** of the engine by reading sensors that report engine status: rpm, throttle position, engine position, coolant temperature, air temperature, airflow, and so forth. Based on the current engine **state** and the nature of the **event** that generated the interrupt, an internal **state transition table** tells the computer the next **action** that should take place, and the computer makes it happen. Rinse and repeat ad infinitum.

If the required action is **inject fuel** (or, say, **inject fuel from injector #5**), the computer calculates how long and when the appropriate electronic fuel injectors must be held open to deliver the correct air-fuel ratio in the upcoming combustion cycle for the cylinder (or *all cylinders* in the case of batch fuel injection). The basic fuel-injection calculation uses engine sensor data as an index into a multi-dimensional **calibration table** of rpm versus load data stored in non-volatile memory. The array of entries in the fuel and timing tables consists of discrete fuel-injection pulsewidth and ignition timing data points representative of the entire operating range of a particular engine or class of engine. Factory engine management systems are designed to discourage casual tampering with the calibration tables, but once you know how to hack your way in (or have laptop software that knows how!), it is trivial to hit a few keystrokes on a PC connected to the engine-management system to overwrite or modify injection pulsewidth or timing at any designated breakpoint of engine speed and loading.

the upcoming combustion cycle at the current engine speed. Based on an estimate of the nitrous mass present in the current gulp of inducted charge gas (computed as a function of the jet size, time available for constant injection, and possibly changes in nitrous mass flow or tank pressure or temperature as the tank empties), the EMS not only calculates an appropriate increase in basic all-motor fuel-injection pulsewidth to supply the required enrichment fuel for nitrous combustion, but also determines how much the spark timing should be retarded as an offset to the basic timing calculation in order to match the higher flame speed of oxygen-rich nitrous combustion and prevent detonation.

Assuming you're starting with an existing aftermarket EMS with an excellent all-motor or air-supercharged calibration, you'll

The EFI injection event actually begins when the computer commands driver circuitry through the appropriate fuel injector(s) to be grounded, causing an electromagnet in the injector(s) to pull open a tiny spring-loaded valve, which allows pressurized fuel in a supply manifold or fuel *rail* regulated to a precise increment above manifold pressure to rush through the injector valve and spray out the nozzle in a cone of fuel droplets that blast against the hot intake valve, thus delivering vaporized fuel for combustion in the next intake stroke in the required proportion to charge-gas oxygen. When the computed injection pulsewidth time is up, the EMS computer switches off the injector circuit. With no electromagnetic force holding the injector open, spring pressure snaps the valve closed and the fuel-injection event is over.

The new digital EFI engines of the early 1980s performed more efficiently than carbureted powerplants in virtually every respect, but for hot rodders and performance tuners the icing on the cake of digital fuel injection was that injection pulsewidth could be *any length of time the computer wanted it to be* up to 100 percent of the time available in one engine combustion cycle of two revolutions at the given engine speed. What's more, EFI systems were completely scalable, in the sense that the electronic injectors provided fuel in variable-sized slices across the operating range from idle to redline at all levels of engine loading. This was not like carburetors, which needed idle jets, idle passages, main jets, main and secondary venturi barrels, booster venturis, power valves, secondary air barrels, emulsion tubes, needle jets, jet needles, and various other complex mechanical systems to calibrate air and fuel delivery across various subsets of the engine airflow range, any of which could become an irreconcilable bottleneck in the face of radical-enough engine modifications. No need to tune EFI by iteratively ripping apart carburetors to swap parts, and even then not necessarily getting it really right without junking the entire carburetor for something more appropriate to the application—and starting the tuning process from scratch. By contrast, anyone able to hack into the EMS fuel and ignition tables could effortlessly recalibrate fuel delivery or ignition timing to be compatible with hot-rodding modifications and power-adders—in some cases *while the engine was running*. The internal data structures of the PROM chip that held the data tables that calibrated early performance factory engine management systems were rather quickly reverse-engineered by engineers in the performance aftermarket, at which point EFI could be intelligently modified for performance modifications that resulted in radically different volumetric efficiency curves or to accommodate larger fuel injectors and power-adder conversions. Performance and custom PROMs were the order of the day.

But it got even better. If you only needed 20 or 30 percent more fuel for a power-adder application—say, a blower kit—you didn't even need to hack the internal EFI fuel and timing calibration tables. With port EFI, it was possible to provide enrichment fuel for moderate power increases simply by increasing fuel pressure to the injectors during boost. It wasn't long before inventers developed pressure-sensitive auxiliary fuel pressure regulators with a multiplicative rate of gain designed to be installed in the return segment of the main EFI fuel loop downstream

of the primary regulator. A variable-rate-of-gain regulator could be referenced to manifold pressure and adjusted so it came into play only during turbo boost to jack up fuel rail pressure as a configurable *multiple* of positive manifold pressure. The VRG regulator could be adjusted so that each 1-psi increase in turbo boost pressure jacked up fuel pressure by, say, 5 psi, a 5:1 ratio. Eventually, some regulators were even developed with electronic controls that could dynamically manage fuel rail pressure using very sophisticated firmware logic.

It wasn't long before someone figured out that an auxiliary regulator could be referenced to *nitrous pressure* and configured so that when the nitrous valve opened up, regulated nitrous pressure was delivered to the VRG regulator, would automatically amp up fuel rail pressure to match the nitrous shot with supplemental enrichment fuel delivered through the stock fuel injectors from, say, a 40-psi rail pressure *gain*.

Necessity is the mother of invention, and it turned out there were additional cute tricks available to modify the fuel delivery of electronic fuel injection. If the EFI engine control logic wasn't too clever (in the early days EFI logic was universally very dumb!), you could often trick the computer into commanding longer injection pulsewidth or retarded ignition timing during power-adder boost simply by *lying* to it about engine sensor status (and this even worked with the pre-digital analog EFI systems built between 1967 and 1982). On the occasions when a power-adder required enrichment fuel, you could, for example, substitute alternate electrical voltages in place of true mass airflow, manifold pressure, or engine temperature data on a transient basis using a variable resister circuit or voltage clamp (. . . the computer notices the temperature is suddenly minus-30 degrees F and lengthens injection pulse to provide "warm-up enrichment").

Tuners also began jacking with *outbound* computer commands to the fuel injectors, and it wasn't too long before entrepreneurs were selling tiny adjustable microcomputers that piggybacked onto EFI output circuitry to dial-in extended injection pulsewidth under configurable circumstances by keeping the injector grounded for an adjustable incremental time period.

Eventually, aftermarket inventors developed extremely sophisticated and flexible standalone electronic engine management systems to facilitate user-friendly configuration and calibration by laptop computer, providing tuners the option to junk the factory computer entirely and manage hot rodded engines almost any way they wanted. Some aftermarket engine management systems were soon equipped with logic that could provide sophisticated nitrous oxide injection control and boost-on engine management.

In the end, some of the most highly evolved aftermarket engine management devices would turn out to be sophisticated piggyback computers more powerful than the primary EMS (increasingly a *vehicle* management system) to the extent that they could run circles around sophisticated factory engine management strategies, creating a virtual-reality bubble that kept the factory computers fully happy and functional in the face of extensive piggyback-instigated manipulations, modifications, and extensions to primary engine management.

have to reconfigure the EMS to enable nitrous functionality and specify the nitrous flow rate or jet size. Assuming the total fuel requirements are within the scope of the existing EFI fuel supply system and injector flow capacity, you'll need to test the calibration during nitrous boost (if not, you'll need to upgrade the appropriate fuel supply components first). From this point on, any time that engine status meets the preconfigured trigger

conditions—for example, nitrous arming switch "On," throttle position above 95 percent, engine rpm above 2,500, engine rpm below 7,000, manifold pressure *below* 5-psi turbo boost (or whatever other combination of constraints is appropriate to the engine application)—the EMS will switch on an electrical circuit that opens the nitrous solenoid to begin injection while simultaneously delivering supplemental enrichment fuel through the primary electronic fuel injectors in a calculation that synchronizes *time-based nitrous delivery with rpm/cycle-based fuel delivery* as an offset to the basic fuel-injection pulsewidth calculation. Programmable logic allows more complex tricks to improve nitrous performance and safety (i.e., a flow table of corrections for changes in nitrous mass flow as the tank empties and cools), but the basic logic is not tremendously complex. Unfortunately, nitrous functionality does not exist as such on factory engine management systems, meaning true computer-controlled dry nitrous mandates a nitrous-capable standalone aftermarket engine management system (some turbocharged factory engine management systems might potentially be reworked to treat constant nitrous boost like an increase in turbo boost).

Unless you're a glamour-class racer or richer than most, you're probably not very interested in spending the bucks for an aftermarket EMS just to have a really elegant nitrous system—particularly since there are less expensive ways of implementing dry nitrous injection if you aren't already running a programmable aftermarket EMS. But let's say you are running a turbo conversion that's controlled by an aftermarket programmable EMS: Adding basic computer-controlled dry-nitrous hardware that will eliminate turbo lag and lower the boost threshold (or even bump up peak power if you run out of turbo compressor airflow), is simple, cheap, accurate, and effective. Anyone who has or can justify adding aftermarket EMS can very easily use it to implement nitrous injection.

As we shall see, computer-controlled dry nitrous architecture can be upgraded with additional features to improve performance and render the system more reliable, fail-safe, and convenient, or if you want a full-bore radical

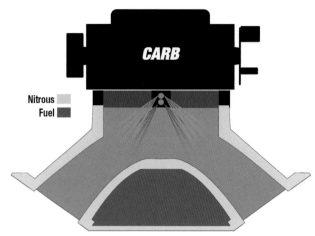

Typical carbureted V-8 engine with a plate spraybar wet nitrous system. Nitrous and fuel spray from a perforated pipe located in the dead air between the barrels of the carburetor, where the pipes will not significantly degrade air flow into the engine. Ideally, spray bars should have a tear-drop profile, but this is less important in a quad-throttle 4-barrel carb or throttlebody. *Edelbrock*

nitrous vehicle that retains the reliability and performance advantages of precision electronic engine and nitrous management. It is worth noting that the elegance of computer-controlled dry nitrous can also be *stripped-down or transmogrified* to lower the price or deliver nitrous functionality from factory EFI, carbureted engines, direct injection gasoline, or even propane-injection diesel powerplants by transferring nitrous engine management functionality out of the main EMS computer to purpose-built auxiliary subsystems—in which case the nitrous system is no longer integrated into a centralized engine management strategy and cannot be considered fully "computer-controlled." Examples of this include:

- One or more electronic interceptors activates nitrous system, and tampers with factory-stock EMS fuel delivery, mass air flow data, timing, or fuel pressure to provide correct engine management during nitrous boost. This book considers this type of system to be interceptor-controlled dry nitrous.
- A special nonlinear auxiliary fuel pressure regulator provides supplemental boost fuel delivery mechanically via fuel rail pressure changes. This book considers this extremely common architecture to be pressure-regulated dry nitrous.
- Arrays of micro-switches and on-off electrical circuits provide or augment nitrous safeguards or control algorithms (i.e., the oil-pressure disarming switch prevents nitrous injection if the engine has stalled but the ignition remains on, etc).
- Standalone constant fuel injection with electro-mechanical controls or an additional injector controller supplies supplemental enrichment fuel for nitrous boost (this

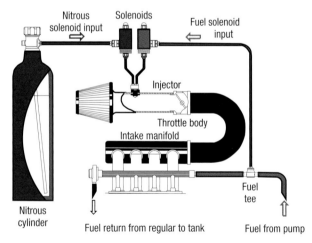

Wizards of NOS (WON), located in the United Kingdom, softens the hit on its street nitrous systems by locating the nitrous and fuel jets at the solenoid discharges rather than at the entrance to the injection nozzle(s). It was common at one time to tune the hardness of the nitrous hit by lengthening the solenoid-to-nozzle hose, which tends to provide the initial nitrous shot as less-dense vapor rather than liquid, and may also cause the engine to bog slightly in a momentary rich condition as the enrichment fuel arrives in the engine before the full force of the nitrous hit. *WON*

is no longer "dry" nitrous, and may or may not be computer-controlled). This book considers these systems to be direct-port nitrous or central-point wet nitrous, and both are workable with either EFI or carbureted engines, which need not have electronic engine management.

- Standalone electronic nitrous controller with configuration user interface manages all nitrous functionality (direct-port or throttle-injection nitrous plus supplemental wet or direct-port fuel delivery, ignition delay, and any other nitrous-system requirements) on EFI, carbureted, direct injection-gasoline, or even diesel powerplants. Electronic nitrous controllers typically provide sophisticated controls and safeguards not found in a simple electro-mechanical nitrous system, providing traction control and reduced powertrain shock with progressive or multi-stage nitrous injection.

Let's examine the subsystems and permutations of computer-controlled dry nitrous in more detail.

Injecting Nitrous. The simplest dry nitrous systems use a **central-point architecture** that injects liquid nitrous through one nozzle fixture installed in the air intake, typically 4 to 12 inches *upstream* of a single throttle body feeding air to all cylinders. Vee engines like the V-10 Dodge Viper that have independent throttle and intake for each cylinder bank would still be considered throttle nitrous systems even though such engines obviously require dual independent throttle nitrous injection for each bank. In other cases, nitrous systems have been designed to inject nitrous farther upstream at the intake of a turbocharger compressor (which, spinning at 50,000 to 250,000 rpm, makes an excellent mixing device).

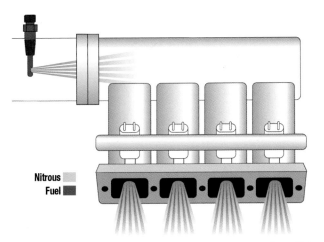

Dry nitrous systems are conceptually very simple, because fuel enrichment is provided through the stock fuel injectors. In practice, most dry nitrous kits require pressure regulators, additional solenoids, and pressure switches to provide nitrous fuel-enrichment by transiently increasing fuel pressure to the stock fuel injectors during nitrous boost. Some dry nitrous systems are now equipped with special MAF units that over-report mass air flow during nitrous boost to provide fuel enrichment. *Edelbrock*

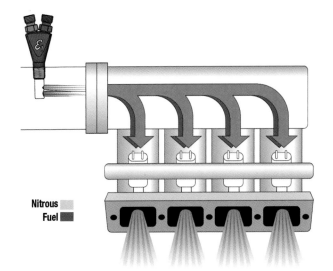

Wet-EFI nitrous systems typically inject nitrous oxide and supplemental fuel through a fogger-type nozzle at least 4-6 inches upstream of the throttlebody. When the nitrous and enrichment fuel are well mixed, the system functions safely, even if the nitrous-fuel mixture is not evenly distributed among the cylinders. The problem is that port-EFI manifolds are not designed to manage wet mixtures of air and fuel, so there is a potential for lean and rich cylinders if the nitrous and fuel do not go to the same places. Nitrous system designers do not recommend wet EFI systems on certain engines known to have fuel distribution problems in dry intake manifolds. *Edelbrock*

Throttle-injection nitrous nozzles in particular have the critically important task of shearing high-pressure liquid nitrous into a symmetrical cone of micro-droplets that mix well with air in the plenum of a dry intake manifold so that the nitrous oxide distributes evenly amongst the various cylinders as it exits the plenum chamber and separates into the various intake runners. Nozzle installation geometry can be extremely important to achieving good nitrous distribution with some intake systems, so it is wise to go with a layout that has already been tested and proven in the application and/or verify nitrous distribution with individual-cylinder EGT probes and spark-plug reading. Like all nitrous architectures, this type of nitrous supply system should deliver nitrous oxide to the injection nozzle without excessive heat soak at or very near full tank pressure (760 psi at 70 degrees F in self-pressurized tanks).

Single-point throttle-injection nitrous nozzles typically have male National Pipe Tapered (NPT) threads machined into the discharge end for easy installation into an appropriately sized bung hole drilled and tapped directly into a thick cast-metal air intake or a thick boss welded to a thinner sheet-metal air intake. Alternately, the nitrous nozzle can be installed in a plastic or sheet-metal intake using a jam-nut "sandwich" or high-temp epoxy or other super-strong glue that's compatible with the particular breed of plastic. The supply end of a throttle-injection nitrous nozzle may be machined to accept a high-pressure nitrous supply hose from the solenoid valve equipped with flare connection. Alternately, the nozzle supply

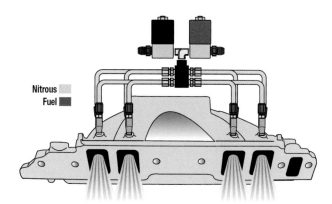

NITROUS SYSTEM ARCHITECTURE

Direct-port nitrous systems usually deliver nitrous and fuel to the individual ports of an engine via integrated "fogger" nozzles that use 950-psi nitrous pressure to atomize fuel into tiny droplets and mix it well with the fog of nitrous droplets. *Edelbrock*

Nitrous ☐
Fuel ■

end may be machined to accept a male NPT adaptor that would, in turn, attach to the flare connector on a braided-steel hose or the compression fitting on a nylon hose.

Throttle-injection nitrous nozzles are available in a number of configurations.

Some nozzles spray nitrous directly out of a single orifice. An example of this is the NOS "jet spray" nozzle, a highly compact fixture available in straight, 90-degree, or blank (drill your own) spray configurations with integral or external metering. NOS has provided nitrous metering orifices as small as .008 inch, good for flowing enough nitrous to oxidize roughly 2.9 horsepower worth of fuel.

Annular-orifice nozzles are designed to improve atomization in some applications by injecting nitrous through a tight ring of six or more smaller orifices (often in close proximity to one or more fuel jets, if it's a wet nitrous system) in order to improve nitrous-fuel mixing.

Yet another type of nozzle intrudes part way into an intake airway perpendicular to airflow, delivering a 90-degree sideways fan spray pattern by blasting nitrous spray against an integral deflector that forces the nitrous to bounce sideways and fan out into a homogenous cone of tiny droplets.

There is a short conceptual distance from a fan injector nozzle protruding partway into an airway to a spray bar injection pipe that completely transects the airway and sprays nitrous oxide not from a single orifice but from multiple tiny openings arranged along the bar to improve distribution by spreading nitrous injection across a larger area. Nitrous spraybars are most often integrated into a spacer plate in close proximity to a fuel spray bar, with both spray bars tucked in the dead air underneath the space between the multiple throttle bores of a 4-barrel carb or TBI throttle body, perpendicular to the throttle shaft where the pipes will do the least damage to volumetric efficiency: An unshielded spray bar naked in the airstream is *terrible aerodynamically* (which is precisely why slide throttles can significantly improve airflow at peak power on radical high-rpm engines compared

to shaft throttles). The severe aerodynamic problems of cylindrical objects perpendicular to high-speed air flow are why aeronautical engineers envelop the spindly wheel struts of fixed-landing-gear aircraft inside much larger teardrop shrouding: Shrouded gear struts have a larger cross-section but far less drag. The lesson is clear: Any spray bar naked in the airstream should really have a teardrop cross-section. Alternatively, you see improved aerodynamics in some "spraybar-less" plate systems where the plate and injection fixes are part of a single casting.

Yet another single-point nitrous injector design is the diffuser-plate system, typically used in super-high-output throttle-injection wet nitrous systems on large carbureted racing V-8s. High-pressure nitrous (and fuel, usually) emanates in a 360-degree pattern between a pair of conical diffuser plates centered between the four throttle bores in a spacer plate below the carb or throttle body.

Some engine applications do not work very well with single-point nitrous injection. Single-point nitrous distribution eccentricities in a dry manifold can vary greatly depending on intake manifold geometry, nitrous tank temperature, air temperature, engine temperature, engine speed, the quality and design of the nitrous injector, throttle position, the length of the intake tract from the point of injection, how long nitrous droplets stay liquid on the trip to various cylinders, and other factors. Correcting single-point nitrous distribution problems requires iterative development and testing of injection nozzle location, aim, and spray pattern under controlled conditions, manifold changes, or a change to individual-cylinder nitrous injection. You hope extensive iterative testing has been done in the R&D process

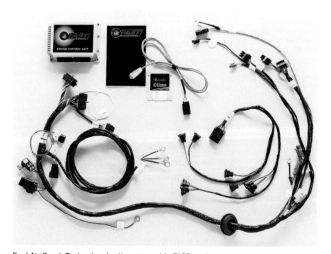

Fuel Air Spark Technology's nitrous-capable FAST engine management system provides total control over all engine functions, including nitrous injection, if installed. Nitrous boost fuel requirements can be a part of the basic fuel calculation that determines how long the primary fuel injectors should be pulsed open to deliver fuel on a power stroke-by-stroke basis. FAST and most other modern nitrous-capable engine management systems can also control multiple stages of direct-port or plate nitrous delivery.

Gen VII Accel EMS installed in GM Racing's Cobalt LSR racer. If the main consideration is using the best technology, all nitrous systems should be computer-controlled and integrated with primary EFI engine management.

when you buy a turnkey throttle-injection dry nitrous kit. It is possible to engineer central-point nitrous-injection systems that add huge amounts of power, as evidenced by the results when some drag-race sanctioning bodies thought they would even the playing field by banning super-high-output direct-port nitrous systems, which had the unintended consequence of spawning a new generation of wildly powerful throttle-injection wet nitrous systems good for as much as 400 to 750 horsepower!

Keep in mind that these systems are designed to run on a wet manifold purpose-built to handle air-fuel mixtures of asynchronous mass. Single-point throttle-injection nitrous distribution can be problematic enough in amateur dry nitrous installations that nitrous vendors do not usually recommend a nitrous shot much greater than about 35 percent of unboosted horsepower in stock engines due to the potential for unstable nitrous distribution and the consequential need for excessive, cylinder-washing global fuel enrichment to make certain that the cylinders with the most nitrous get sufficient fuel during boost (to prevent detonation and catastrophic overheating under worst conditions). Occasionally you'll see a Stage 2 dry kit that is sanctioned for jetting to 50 percent above stock power and run on premium gasoline or unleaded race gas.

In the case of computer-controlled dry nitrous, nitrous-fuel ratio problems in certain cylinders that are predictable and repeatable can be eliminated using individual-cylinder fuel pulsewidth corrections available on most really sophisticated aftermarket engine management systems. But this is academic outside of situations where racing class rules require single-point nitrous injection: No one is going to implement Band-Aid correction strategies on radical dry EFI nitrous engines that exceed the recommended single-point nitrous boost constraints because it is much easier, better, and ultimately cheaper to replace single-point

nitrous injection with individual-cylinder **direct-port nitrous**. In fact, apart from turbocharged applications where low-output computer-controlled nitrous is being used exclusively to accelerate turbine spool-up, particularly in the case of large, complex V- or flat-cylinder-configuration turbo powerplants with a lot of cylinders where individual-cylinder nitrous injection plumbing is complex with no significant upside, most people with expensive EMS-controlled nitrous are going to run nitrous lines direct to each intake port. Turbochargers, by the way, are great as a kind of *100,000 rpm Waring Blender* for massively whipping charge mixtures into a homogeneous blend.

Up to a point, direct-port nitrous is identical to throttle-injection nitrous. But instead of nitrous oxide flowing out of the solenoid discharge plumbing and directly into the intake charge gases near the throttle body through a single metering jet and central-point nitrous injection fixture, individual-cylinder liquid nitrous exits the solenoid plumbing into a miniature distribution manifold designed to split the flow into multiple streams which then travel via individual pipes or hoses to the various intake runners where the nitrous passes through cylinder-size metering jets to spray into the air stream through individual injection nozzles. Almost any throttle-injection nitrous system can be upgraded to individual-cylinder nitrous without too much difficulty, though the cost of precision-machined direct-port components is typically not trivial.

Individual-cylinder nitrous injection can be implemented in various ways. Direct-port nitrous systems have traditionally

There are many great reasons to retain the factory EMS on street cars, not the least of which are drivability and emissions legality during unboosted operations. Nitrous-capable piggyback computers work with the factory EMS, turn on the added functions like nitrous injection, and typically intercept several signals to and from the factory EMS, which can often be modified or disregarded in order to cause the factory EMS to work well with power-adders like nitrous injection or turbochargers. Note the boost ignition retard module that can retard timing during nitrous or turbo-boosted operations. *ProECM*

used cubical "distribution blocks" to distribute nitrous oxide into a maze of **steel "hard pipes"** similar to brake lines that connect to injection nozzles identical to single-point dry nozzles but installed directly in the individual intake runners. Hard-pipe distribution systems are what you see on show vehicles, and when the pipes are carefully bent and routed by someone with an artistic sense of style, the geometrical grid of pipes can really add exotic visual appeal to an engine compartment. However, doing hard pipes right requires experience or a great deal of patience because even subtle geometric flaws can detract tremendously from the appearance, which is why some people prefer to farm out hard-pipe-fabrication to a specialist. In recent times, nitrous vendors have developed improved radial and "shower-head" distribution manifolds intended to deliver very even flow and pressure to the various nitrous injectors using equal-length internal passages while eliminating or minimizing asymmetrical distribution-block expansion cavities that could produce adverse, unequal gasification and refrigerant effects. Anyone building a radical, state-of-the-art nitrous powerplant should try hard to eliminate tiny expansion chambers in the design of direct-port nitrous plumbing.

Rather than flaunting a gorgeous hard-line setup, someone may want to *conceal* the fact that an engine is

This Nitrous Express system is typical of the extremely simple systems required for computer-controlled dry nitrous or diesel nitrous injection. One tank, one solenoid, one nozzle with nitrous jet, a couple hoses, and arming switch. That's as simple as it gets, and simpler, even, than old-style carbureted plate nitrous systems, which must provide both fuel and nitrous. *Nitrous Express*

In some cases, piggyback interceptors like this Unichip system from Dastek of Australia simply plug inline between the factory onboard computer and the main wiring harness, permitting a highly sophisticated interceptor to be tightly coordinated into primary engine management. In this case, the Unichip provides the following piggyback features: ignition timing, fuel quality, boost control, rpm and turbo boost limits, dual maps, water injection control, nitrous oxide control, additional injectors, idle speed stabilization, variable valve timing control, variable induction control, launch control, full throttle gear changes, road speed de-limiting, speedo conversion, electronic speed calibration, shift light activation, and 476 map breakpoints of speed-loading engine control. *UNA*

equipped with individual-cylinder nitrous injection. At one time it was fairly common for street-racing hustlers with hot rodded muscle cars to improve the odds of a financially advantageous stoplight-drag upset by running a **stealth** or **hidden nitrous system**. Obviously, a computer-controlled dry nitrous fuel system is easy to conceal, because there are no hardware changes to the stock fuel system (other than upgrade components, where required, such as larger high-flow electronic injectors and fuel pump). But many vee engines have enough space between the underside of the intake manifold and the top of the short block to install the nitrous nozzles, hard lines, distribution block, and nitrous supply plumbing required for a computer-controlled dry nitrous system with direct-port nitrous injection. Obviously, severe heat soak can have adverse consequences on the performance of this type of stealth setup by gasifying the initial nitrous hit in such a way as to produce bog and surge problems, which is why concealment is the only justification for installing nitrous components in such a hot location.

Nitrous lines must be able to handle working pressures of at least 1,000 to 1,100 psi and overload pressures approaching 2,000 psi, but it is not necessary to use steel hard lines to supply direct-port nitrous nozzles. In fact, you can substitute thin, **flexible nylon hose**, which has the distinct advantage that it is much easier to install than steel pipe and has much better insulating qualities. That said, nylon is also more vulnerable to mechanical or heat damage than steel, and it looks about as good (or bad!) as brightly colored 1/4-inch insulated wiring snaking around the engine compartment (4.0- to 5.0-mm outside diameter, 2.0- to 2.5-mm inside diameter). Sectioning nylon hose for port-nitrous use requires a razor blade or scalpel rather than the pipe cutter and flare tool needed to build steel hard lines.

In some cases, individual-cylinder nitrous injection can be implemented by installing special direct-port adaptor nozzles beneath the primary electronic port fuel injectors. These adaptor nozzles can be as expensive as the electronic injectors themselves but save the trouble and expense of removing all or part of the intake manifold, machining threaded bosses in the runners, and installing direct-port nitrous nozzles (which they don't give away for free either). A good example is Holley's NOSzle, a one-per-cylinder three-piece billet aluminum injection nozzle precision-machined to channel nitrous spray (and, usually, supplemental enrichment fuel) into the individual intake runner while housing the existing port fuel injector. Adaptor nozzles of this type eliminate the distribution danger of single-point "fogger" nitrous/fuel nozzle systems and the hassle of installing direct-port injection nozzles. Each NOSzle fits between the port fuel injector and its injector boss in such a way that the electronic injector is relocated a short distance outward from the original position in the injector boss but remains aimed in exactly the same direction (which might or might not require modifications to relocate the stock injector fuel rail). NOSzles use an annular-orifice spray pattern for delivering supplemental nitrous (and, usually, fuel) in a ring around the stock injector pintle, with high-pressure nitrous blast intersecting the spray of both supplemental enrichment fuel and the stock electronic injector during boost. NOSzles have connections for both fuel and nitrous hoses, but in the case of a computer-controlled *dry* nitrous application the NOSzle fuel supply input would not be required and could be capped off. Admittedly, this would be an easy but expensive solution.

An alternative to direct-port nozzles on some engines is an individual-cylinder **spacer plate** system. The vast majority of plate nitrous systems are designed to provide central-point spraybar nitrous injection between the intake manifold inlet and the throttle body or carburetor, but in some cases it is possible to install an individual-runner spacer **plate** between the upper and lower halves of a two-piece EFI intake manifold on some V-8s or between the intake manifold and cylinder head on certain inline engines. One advantage of pro-built individual-runner plate systems is that

There are now *large* electronic injectors like this side-solenoid unit that is capable of delivering as much as 350 pounds per hour of gasoline or methanol per cylinder!

the design is virtually certain to reflect extensive scientific testing in an R&D environment, which is often not the case with do-it-yourself direct-port nozzle installations. Individual-cylinder plate systems eliminate the expense of removing and precision-machining the manifold for nozzle locations with perfect, equal geometry that has the least negative impact on engine volumetric efficiency.

At the time of this writing, nitrous vendors were selling prefabricated individual-runner plate systems with integral nitrous-fuel spray bars or annular orifice nitrous-fuel injectors for a number of engines, including Ford's 5.0-liter EFI V-8 and Honda's 16-valve 1.8-liter VTEC I-4. Individual-runner plate systems are usually bundled into complete kits designed to provide both nitrous and fuel, but most nitrous venders will sell the individual components, potentially allowing a computer-controlled dry system to be scratch-built around the plate fixture, or a single-point nitrous system to be upgraded to individual-cylinder nitrous. In this situation, the constant-injection *fuel* spray bar would obviously not be utilized, and might even be removed. Again, convenient, but you pay for it.

Metering Nitrous. All nitrous delivery systems—computer-controlled dry nitrous included—are calibrated for volumetric nitrous oxide flow rate by the area of the most restrictive bottlenecks in the supply plumbing that delivers nitrous flow. This is normally either the actual nitrous injection orifice, restrictor-jetting in the injector feed plumbing, or, in the case of progressive systems, the average area of the solenoid valve at a specified pulsewidth-modulated duty cycle. Poorly engineered or over-jetted systems could have an unintended

Electronic port fuel injectors embody tiny pulse width–modulated electrical solenoid valves, which typically are capable of opening and closing hundreds of times per second. Fuel delivery is determined not by fuel pressure but by varying the length of the opening event. Dry nitrous systems increase injection pulse width during nitrous injection to provide supplemental fuel, or manipulate fuel rail pressure so the injectors deliver more fuel per injection pulse.

This BEGi variable-rate-of-gain fuel pressure regulator is capable of radically increasing fuel pressure as a 5-7 psi multiple of turbo boost manifold pressure, or in a single leap if regulated nitrous pressure is fed to the reference line when nitrous kicks in. There is a severe limit to that amount of fuel that can be delivered using this method, since most electronic fuel injectors cannot function reliably much above 70-90 psi fuel pressure.

and whenever nitrous oxide expands in the supply circuit a certain proportion of it will vaporize, producing tiny bubbles (foaming) and refrigeration of the nitrous and downstream plumbing components between the restriction and the injector nozzle. The heat-soak versus refrigeration effects on nitrous phase downstream of a restrictor jet (or any nitrous supply bottleneck!) in a hot engine compartment add an element of uncertainty to how fast and hard the nitrous hits—unpredictability magnified by the transient nature of nitrous boost. When boost stops, nitrous oxide in the delivery system downstream of the solenoid loses pressure, boils and dissipates, initially chilling components, after which the resulting void immediately begins heat-soaking back up toward engine temperature. In general, a relatively low-temperature nitrous supply tank combined with a sharp temperature increase in the final nitrous plumbing and injection fixture will adversely impact engine torque because the abrupt nitrous temperature increase reduces nitrous density but is too localized to have a significant effect on global system pressure. The result is reduced nitrous mass flow and maximum power—at least temporarily. Unless the goal is to intentionally cushion the initial nitrous hit mass by starting injection with foaming nitrous, restrictor jets of any type should be located as close as possible to the point of injection.

Despite the mass-flow advantages of metering nitrous through the actual injection orifices, calibrating a nitrous system in the course of a horsepower R&D project can be *a lot* more convenient if you don't have to R&R the entire nitrous injection device every time you want to adjust nitrous flow. It is much easier and cheaper to stock a set of replaceable restrictor-jet inserts encompassing the entire plausible range of nitrous jetting for an engine application than it is to order a

critical bottleneck in the bottle valve, supply plumbing, or any solenoid that effectively governs nitrous flow and thus prevents the intended metering device from having any effect. The total nitrous metering area at the critical bottleneck determines the maximum theoretical horsepower boost of a nitrous system and is an independent variable capable of modifying the final oxygen-fuel ratio during boost if supplemental fuel delivery is held steady and nitrous metering adjusted.

Another independent variable affecting nitrous mass flow is pressure in the nitrous supply line and tank, which you might expect would force a greater volume of nitrous liquid per time through a given-size metering orifice when pressure is higher. Fortunately for the existence of affordable nitrous systems, except in the case of nitrous oxide tanks that are externally pressurized above self-generated vapor pressure with regulated high-pressure nitrogen or compressed air, equilibrium vapor pressure in a self-pressurized nitrous tank is entirely a function of temperature, and the same temperature increase that raises vapor pressure in the tank also causes *thermal expansion* of the liquid nitrous mass exactly like mercury or alcohol in a thermometer. When the volume of a given mass of nitrous oxide *increases*, the density per cubic centimeter *decreases*. As long as liquid remains in the tank and the nitrous supply remains below the critical temperature but not too far below normal cockpit temperature, temperature-induced pressure and density changes to the nitrous oxide to a great extent cancel each other out. The result is that the flow through the nitrous delivery system can be relatively independent of tank pressure. It's the metering area that counts.

The ideal location to meter nitrous flow is at the actual point of injection. The reason for this is that *any* bottleneck further upstream in the nitrous supply system will cause nitrous oxide liquid to expand rapidly as it travels past the restriction,

This microswitch has been positioned to switch on nitrous flow when throttle position is at or near wide open throttle (WOT). This type of switch cannot handle large electrical current, meaning the switch must activate heavy-current nitrous solenoids by triggering a 30-amp relay. *Edelbrock*

Typical EFI return-type fuel pressure regulator with manifold pressure reference port and adjustment bolt. This type of regulator pinches off fuel return flow back to the fuel tank until rail pressure overcomes the force of the regulator spring. Manifold pressure or vacuum applied to the reference port may increase or decrease the force of the regulator spring, keeping rail pressure a fixed increment above manifold pressure, so the amount of fuel injected is not directly affected by the manifold pressure. Some dry nitrous systems jack up fuel pressure during nitrous boost by applying (regulated!) pressure from the nitrous tank to the reference port of this type of regulator. *MSD*

replacement injection fixture with a different integral metering orifices when you are working to precisely calibrate power, traction, and nitrous-fuel ratio (and drilling an orifice larger, obviously, is a one-way calibration tactic). Modern nitrous injectors of almost all types are equipped with a replaceable brass metering jet located in the inlet, which allows a tuner to recalibrate nitrous delivery simply by detaching the supply hose and swapping jets. Most nitrous jets slide into place in the nitrous-feed connection of a nozzle, spraybar, diffuser, or other injection fixture; attaching and tightening the nitrous supply hose also clamps the jet in place and forms a robust seal against the tapered surface exactly like a flare fitting. At least one vendor offers nitrous systems that incorporate a threaded jet similar to a carb main jet that screws into place further upstream than usual in a special discharge fitting on the downstream side of the solenoid valve; this approach increases distance, thus softening nitrous onset with an initial hit of less dense nitrous gas or foam.

Single-point nitrous jets must be sized to supply the correct amount of oxidizer for the entire engine, whereas individual-runner jets are sized to provide nitrous for only one cylinder—in either case down to a minimum orifice size representing about 3 to 5 horsepower per cylinder (or engine). In a few cases, sophisticated race tuners have calibrated direct-port nitrous jet orifices on an individual-cylinder basis (synchronized, obviously, with the supplemental fuel metering for the individual cylinders) to compensate for powerplant design flaws such as uneven block cooling or unusual variations in volumetric efficiency.

Some nitrous nozzles designed to fit in very cramped space are their own metering jet. In some cases, there simply isn't room for a replaceable jet and surrounding plumbing, so the nozzle itself must be swapped out to recalibrate nitrous flow. A good example of a size-constrained circumstance is the situation on some compact V-8 engines where there are stealth Direct-port nozzles spraying directly at the intake valves from threaded ports machined into the *floor* of the intake runners from underneath the manifold. To change nitrous jetting in some cases, you need to remove the intake manifold, distribution block, all hard lines, and then swap out eight injection nozzles.

It is critical that any nitrous jet be sized to have a lower flow rate than the actual injection orifice, or the jet will not be the critical bottleneck and cannot actually meter nitrous—one more reason to avoid trouble by acquiring officially sanctioned jets from a nitrous system vendor rather than drilling out jets in the expectation that doing so will flow more nitrous. (Unless you are a competent machinist, do not try to drill out injection nozzles. Machining marks or a wobbly or worn drill could fatally damage the spray pattern or metering rate.) It is critical in the process of changing or upgrading any and all nitrous supply circuit components to make certain that nitrous flow remains entirely a function of the area of the *metering orifice*. With one exception (progressive PWM solenoid pulsing designed to implement variable-calibration dynamic nitrous metering), this means that components upstream of the jet (solenoid, delivery line and plumbing, and bottle valve) must never be permitted to become a bottleneck.

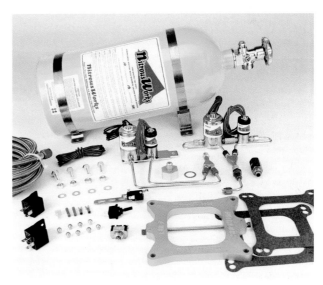

A modification to the traditional wet plate nitrous system for carbureted or four-barrel-type throttle body V-8 engines is this dual-stage system from Nitrous Works, which ramps up the nitrous and fuel flow in separate stages through spray bars in a single spacer plate. In the simplest control system, the first stage is activated by a full-throttle switch, and the second stage activated manually by a push-button switch on the shift lever. *Nitrous Works*

The PWM exception is an interesting one. Although the purpose of computer-controlled dry nitrous on turbocharged engines is usually to improve low-end torque by lowering the boost threshold and decreasing spooling time with a sudden jolt of nitrous boost, in addition to commencing nitrous boost at unusually low rpm, it may be desirable under some circumstances to maintain traction off the line or reduce stress on mechanical parts by throttling back on the restrictor-jet's *initial* delivery rate of nitrous oxide to limit low-end torque and prevent detonation. Pulsewidth-modulation (PWM) techniques can turn most electrical nitrous solenoid valves into a metering device by buzzing the solenoid open and closed rapidly at a frequency that might be as high as 50 times per second. PWM techniques effectively vary the solenoid's flow area by lowering the percentage of time the pathway through the valve is available to flow nitrous—i.e., the *average* flow area. Variable-calibration metering is the one situation in which something other than the jet is legitimately restricting nitrous flow, and this is usually of brief duration during a modulated ("progressive") ramp-up to full boost. PWM solenoid metering, like any restriction in the nitrous line, will tend to refrigerate downstream components, introducing secondary thermal effects that can temporarily destabilize nitrous mass flow.

Nitrous solenoids: starting, stopping, (or metering!) nitrous boost. In the early days of the first primordial automotive nitrous systems, boost was sometimes triggered using a cable that opened spring-loaded manual nitrous and enrichment fuel valves exactly the way the accelerator pedal manually opens the throttle on engines not equipped with drive-by-wire electronic throttles. Not any more. These days, computer-controlled dry nitrous-injection kicks in when an

Multi-stage nitrous systems with as many as six or seven stages can gobble battery or alternator power by the end of a drag run, causing some nitrous mavens to switch to gas-actuated nitrous and fuel solenoids powered by the CO_2 system of a drag car or a high-pressure air tank. A small low-draw electrical pilot solenoid allows CO_2 pressure to bang open the main solenoids. This dual-carb '68 Camaro big-block uses Combo-flo Airnoids, seen here between the second and third intake runners. *Combo-Flo*

aftermarket EMS decides it should and triggers a robust 12-volt automotive relay to energize a normally closed inline electrical solenoid valve located in the engine compartment at the end of the nitrous supply line. Nitrous solenoids (along with fuel solenoids on wet or direct-port systems) are normally situated as close as possible to the actual injection device in a relatively cool place where they will heat-soak as little as possible.

Solenoids are analogous to giant electronic port fuel injectors, with a spring-loaded plunger normally held closed against a seat by a combination of spring and fluid pressure. Solenoid valves open only "momentarily"—for as long as a 12-volt electrical current from the battery energizes a coil in the solenoid to create and maintain an electromagnetic field powerful enough to overcome spring and fluid pressure in order to yank the plunger off its seat and allow fluid to shoot through the valve. The instant the circuit through the coil goes dead, the solenoid snaps closed in a tiny fraction of a second and the fluid delivery stops. On engines lacking a nitrous-capable aftermarket EMS, nitrous-capable piggyback, or a standalone nitrous controller, the solenoid relay can be triggered with a momentary full throttle micro-switch or simply a manual pushbutton on the shifter.

A nitrous solenoid's electromagnet must be very strong in order to pull the valve open quickly against the force of the return spring and pressure from the nitrous tank. Solenoids are designed to harness nitrous tank pressure to assist in keeping the valve closed using the same principle that allows increasing water pressure at the bottom of a filling bathtub to keep a rubber ball or stopper pressed into the drain.

Nitrous solenoids can be used as both an on-off switch and a mechanism to meter nitrous flow. Depending on the design, nitrous solenoids are capable of rapidly pulsing open

When some race cars began making too much power with direct-port nitrous injection, some race sanctioning bodies thought they could dial back speeds and produce more competition by banning direct-port nitrous. They were wrong. The move spawned a new generation of radical plate nitrous systems like this quad-spraybar system from Edelbrock. Some plate systems are now capable of delivering as much as a 750-horsepower nitrous shot from the plate! *Edelbrock*

and closed to achieve a particular average duty cycle and flow rate, with the maximum frequency typically somewhere between 8 and 50hertz (cycles per second). A nitrous solenoid is, thus, vastly slower than an electronic fuel injector, which can have a frequency as high as 250 hertz (though a nitrous solenoid is regulating a system with roughly 25 times the pressure of typical port EFI). Nitrous solenoids are available in a number of sizes, depending on the required flow rate. As you might expect, bigger ones react more slowly due to the increased inertia of the larger, heavier plunger and thus have a slower maximum frequency when pulsed progressively.

In order to overcome spring and nitrous pressure very quickly and maximize opening performance, nitrous solenoids require a robust power supply. Rated solenoid performance typically requires 5 to 30 amps of current delivered at or near the high end of the voltage rating of the solenoid—which is why nitrous solenoids are usually switched by heavy-duty relays with thick-gauge wiring. Some electronic power supplies are capable of improving solenoid or injector performance by delivering a higher initial *peak* current that opens the device very fast, after which the current is allowed to fall back to a lesser specification that can *hold* the device open with less thermal loading on the coil and controller circuitry. This circuit is called a **peak and hold** driver.

A nitrous solenoid's two electrical leads connect directly to ground and to a high-current automotive relay wired to a robust (+12- to +14-volt) electrical source. The relay triggers nitrous injection at the solenoid when an arming switch and some type of switch or control circuit complete a +12-volt circuit through the coil of the relay trigger. The arming switch of a computer-controlled dry nitrous system would typically be connected to switched +12-volt battery power, such that, when in the "on" position, the arming switch delivers power to the relay coil and to an auxiliary input pin on the EMS that tells the computer that the nitrous system is armed. Most modern aftermarket EMS computers typically have multiple

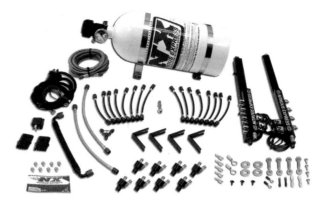

For people who cannot or will not drill their intake manifold for direct-port fogger nozzles, Nitrous Express offers the LS1NXL system, in which special O-ringed injection nozzle-adaptors (foreground) fit underneath the stock electronic injectors to fog nitrous and fuel into the intake runners. Individual hoses transport fuel and nitrous from special rails to the injection nozzles. NOS provides a similar capability in its NOSzle systems. *Nitrous Express*

auxiliary output circuits that can be configured to provide a variety of functionality, ranging from controlling additional fuel injectors, to activating electric fuel pumps, to managing PWM turbo boost controllers, to providing On-Off or PWM nitrous solenoid control plus appropriate supplemental fuel. When the EMS has determined all systems are "Go" for nitrous boost, an EMS circuit grounds the relay trigger circuit causing the relay to close, activating the nitrous solenoid.

Any time a nitrous solenoid is in the process of opening or closing—or in the case that it is an unintended bottleneck when fully open—the solenoid becomes a restriction and begins to function like an A/C expansion valve, producing a pressure drop that refrigerates the solenoid discharge and downstream plumbing. In the freezing cold produced by nitrous expansion, a solenoid not specifically designed for controlling nitrous oxide flow could seize and stick open. Because the consequences of unintended nitrous release into an engine (running or not) can be disastrous, nitrous solenoids must be very robust, and they must have the ability to function properly across a wide temperature range from below zero to hot engine compartment temperatures.

The length and volume of the plumbing between a solenoid valve and a nitrous-injection device can have a significant effect on how hard and fast the nitrous boost hits as well as on the the stability of the torque and power boost throughout the course of a hard nitrous pull. Longer plumbing will tend to soften the nitrous hit by vaporizing more of the initial liquid nitrous shot into foam for a longer time. A softer hit will help to prevent powertrain component failures and can actually *improve* traction/hook-up compared to a wild, lightning-fast tire-smoking hit. The biggest problem with softening the nitrous hit by increasing the volume of the void between a solenoid and an injection orifice is that when liquid nitrous blasts into a longer line between the solenoid and injection fixture and boils into a foam or

This SpeedTech nitrous system combines a two-stage wet plate system using a central diffuser-plate injector with a third stage of direct-port nitrous injection. *SpeedTech*

Edelbrock's 5.0 plate system provides direct-port nitrous and fuel with 16 individual-runner spraybars. All-motor torque and power will be affected by the spraybar impact on intake gas flow. *Edelbrock*

vapor in the heat-soaked supply line—ramping up nitrous mass flow more gradually—the unintended consequence is usually "nitrous lag," i.e., a rich power bog caused by a combination of an immediate full-force *fuel* hit combined with substandard, low-mass *nitrous* delivery, followed by a surge of power as nitrous liquid fills the void and the nitrous mass flow ramps up. This is followed, in some cases, by pulsating thermo-hydraulic resonance with additional cycles of power bogging and surging.

That is, unless the nitrous and fuel do not *trigger* at exactly the same time or ramp up at the same rate. Some nitrous controllers are able to delay or feather-in the fuel hit to better synchronize its arrival with supplemental nitrous delivery, and the length of nitrous and fuel supply lines can be tuned asynchronously. Unfortunately, when nitrous mass flow is significantly impacted by *unpredictable* variable heat and cold soak in the line downstream of the solenoid, it is essentially impossible to calibrate the supplemental fuel *lead-time* and *ramp-up* profile in such a way as to negate the lean-mixture danger of nitrous hitting first without creating a high risk of rich bog some of the time. The whole thing can be particularly serendipitous with a dry nitrous system if the nitrous supply line volume is large and the solenoid and restrictor jet are significantly farther from the intake valve than the fuel injectors.

Rigorous installation of heat shields around hot engine components, good insulation around nitrous plumbing, or even engine compartment exhaust fans will help to improve the repeatability of nitrous-hit performance by controlling and stabilizing heat soak. Some drag racers have gone to great lengths to exert control over nitrous supply heat-soak with tricks such as self-cooling post-solenoid nitrous plumbing by constructing an expansion chamber sleeve around the line with

an expansion valve that is fed by a controlled rate of nitrous leak-down prior to nitrous system activation. For calibration and debugging purposes, virtually all modern aftermarket engine management systems that are sophisticated enough to manage computer-controlled dry nitrous would have the ability to datalog information from high-speed auxiliary temperature and pressure sensors located on the nitrous supply line downstream of the solenoid.

If nitrous supply line heat-soak can be controlled with insulation or design factors to produce repeatable nitrous ramp-up, and particularly if it is possible to synchronize the phase-in of supplemental fuel with sluggish nitrous onset (this could be a configurable parameter on nitrous-capable aftermarket EMS), the length and inside diameter of the nitrous line between the jet and orifice can potentially be *tuned* to impact the aggressiveness of the nitrous hit—a simpler solution than variable-calibration progressive solenoid pulsing that saves wear on the solenoid.

As always, good R&D practice is to start with the nitrous solenoid very close to the injection device with the nitrous jet immediately upstream of the injection nozzle, design the plumbing to rigorously control heat soak, and begin the tuning process with a modest-horse shot nitrous jet and aggressive fuel enrichment so the oxygen-fuel ratio starts on the rich side. A nitrous hit that's reliably too hard can be softened up by incrementally increasing the length of the supply hose(s) or with progressive nitrous solenoid pulsing or multi-stage nitrous. On the other hand, an unintended chronically mushy hit that cannot be controlled with insulation or by

Progressive controllers limit nitrous or fuel flow by pulsing solenoids like big electronic fuel injectors to modify the effective output of the solenoid. Obviously, this type of system can only decrease flow relative to the maximum flow of the system metering jets, but this is extremely effective at improving traction at activation on big-hit nitrous vehicles by fading in full nitrous boost, and is very effective at permitting nitrous flow to begin at a much lower engine rpm without the risk of detonation when tremendous wallops of nitrous oxide are delivered to the cylinders at every power stroke by a constant-flow nitrous system. *Edelbrock*

NOS's Launcher progressive controller system can be configured to control up to four stages of nitrous using a laptop or the dedicated 3.5-inch color LCD with touch screen, stylus, and mini SD card to log data and make changes right up to race time. User-friendly graphical interface software is designed to make Launcher easy to program, and you can download free software updates from the Internet. The system is designed to store data files for optimized operation at different race tracks. The NOSbus 2-wire network interface allows seamless integration with other Holley/NOS products. *NOS*

reducing the supply line void might have to be eliminated on the fly prior to boost using a nitrous line vapor *purging system* to bleed the line empty of all nitrous gas and foam.

All nitrous supply systems should have an inline nitrous **debris filter** to prevent any particulate matter from damaging sealing surfaces or plugging tiny orifices in the solenoid, jet, and injection components. How does debris get into a nitrous system? It accumulates over time from (1) metal filings on the fitting that connects your tank to the donor cylinder at the speed shop when you refill it, (2) your own filthy connections when you R&R the tank for refill, (3) junk in the hoses when you assembled the system the first time, and (4) metal shavings created the times you were in a hurry reconnecting the tank. You want a filter, but they are not all created equal. Some will only trap large particles, while others are effective at trapping the tiniest bits of debris. A fine filter is better, but the filter must always be capable of flowing more nitrous than the metering orifice—*even when partially blocked with debris*—or the size of the nitrous shot will be regulated by the filter rather than the metering jet! The downside of a debris filter is that the volume must be high enough to support a large filtering area, meaning the debris filter could become a refrigeration expansion chamber if there is any pressure drop through the filter. A large filter that is not a bottleneck inevitably contains a pool of nitrous in the filter that could heat-soak and vaporize, and might have to be wasted into a nitrous purge system.

Over the last 40 years, nitrous solenoids have evolved from generic, low-speed industrial valves with Teflon seals to high-tech units purpose-built with special neoprene seals to survive the high-pressure and refrigeration effects intrinsic to the life of a nitrous oxide solenoid. Nitrous solenoids definitely live a *hard* life, particularly in the case that they're being *pulsed* to provide variable-calibration nitrous metering. Seals eventually start to leak under 900-psi pressure from thermal and mechanical shock. Moving metal parts begin to wear out. The consequences of a leaking or stuck solenoid

can be catastrophic, which is why some racers treat solenoids the way the FAA treats certain essential moving parts on helicopters—that is, as limited-life components that must be replaced at certain intervals even if they appear to be perfectly healthy. A solenoid with a slow leak can waste a tank of expensive nitrous oxide, but there are worse fates than losing $50 worth of nitrous: If you are too lazy (or forget) to close the bottle control valve when the engine is shut down, the intake manifold and any cylinders stopped with the intake valve open could slowly fill up with nitrous oxide, which could be dangerous the next time you crank the engine and it sucks in a huge gulp of pure nitrous (which won't burn, but is a lot better than air at making *other things* burn, with fierce fire chemistry). If a solenoid sticks open when the engine *is* running, the powerplant will continues to receive oxygen from the nitrous bottle even when the throttle is closed. A stuck solenoid could zing the engine if you disengage the clutch quickly, and it could cause an accident if you don't.

If you're into nitrous for the long haul, and you like being safe or can't risk the consequences of a solenoid failure, you may want to install a Hobbs meter capable of counting seconds, minutes, or hours of time during which the solenoid is open and making nitrous boost. Alternatively, digital timers are available from various nitrous system vendors, some with sophisticated mass-flow correction tables built in. If the digital timer has a "Life Timer" feature, you could potentially use this as an indication of when it's time to rebuild a nitrous solenoid. Even better, buy a meter at Fry's or Radio Shack

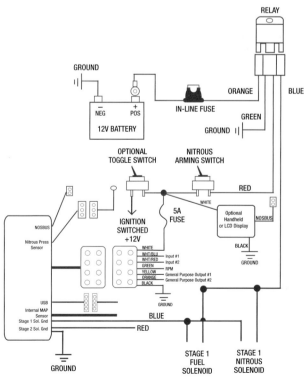

NOS Launcher progressive controller installation schematic. *NOS*

that keeps track of how many times a solenoid has *opened* (including metering pulses, if progressive) by incrementing the count each time the solenoid circuitry comes alive—and then rebuild the solenoid when the open-event count reaches some fraction of the solenoid manufacturer's specified Mean Time Between Failures (MTBF), which will reduce the possibility of failure to a statistically insignificant level.

Redundancy is a great way to create a fail-safe system when the consequences of failure are unacceptable. Think of skydivers and reserve parachutes, or piston-engine aircraft with twin spark plugs on every cylinder fired by separate isolated ignition systems. Installing an anti-leak *backup* solenoid that works in concert with the primary solenoid to positively halt all nitrous flow if the primary solenoid valve should leak or stick is a powerful safety measure, especially if you are incessantly forcing the primary solenoid to pulse rapidly open and closed to deliver progressive boost on start up. If the chance of one device failing in a certain length of time is 1 in 10,000, the chance of *two* failing at once is multiplicative, i.e., 1 in 100,000,000.

Multiple solenoids are useful not only to provide fail-safe redundancy when installed in series, but to manage multi-stage nitrous systems when installed in parallel in a system that is essentially two or more complete nitrous kits with coordinated control systems that bring on the power boost more gradually than is possible in a single stage. Sophisticated aftermarket EMS computers usually have the capability to customize auxiliary control tables that determine

This NX spacer plate delivers nitrous and fuel to the overhead-cam 4.6 Ford V-8 through 16 orifices in the divider. Tests have shown that multiple orifices typically improve distribution in a plate nitrous system. *Nitrous Express*

when to activate a three-stage nitrous system (which is really two nitrous systems of asynchronous shot size controlled by two separate solenoids, which allow a tuner to increase power sequentially by activating the small-shot nitrous circuit alone in stage 1, the large-shot nitrous circuit alone in stage 2, and both circuits together in stage 3).

You may decide you want solenoids purpose-built for PWM nitrous metering. Some solenoids are better able to tolerate extensive pulsing than others, and solenoids can vary greatly in their ability to pulse with a high frequency against very high pressure. Many nitrous solenoids cannot effectively achieve the very lowest or highest duty cycles in the theoretical range as fluid flow approaches fully closed or fully open. Solenoids effectively go "static" when there is too little time to open or close at the intended duty cycle at a frequency quick enough to avoid uneven nitrous throughput, pressure, and harsh pulsing. The speed of nitrous solenoid opening and closing events determines the lowest and highest nitrous flow the solenoid can achieve within the available period. The pressure of the fluid being controlled by a solenoid has a powerful effect on opening and closing performance, as does the design of the solenoid coil and the voltage and current energizing the coil. Identical solenoids metering nitrous versus fuel (in a wet or direct-port nitrous system) have different ranges due to the pressure differential of the substances being metered (40 psi fuel versus, say, 900 psi nitrous). A solenoid that could achieve a duty-cycle ranging from 10 percent up to 95 percent when metering fuel might actually have an effective range as poor as 30 to 60 percent when metering nitrous oxide—meaning the nitrous solenoid effectively stays wide open at 61 percent while the fuel solenoid continues restricting fuel flow all the way to 95 percent duty cycle. If you install or convert to progressive nitrous control, make

The NOS Mini 2-Stage Progressive Nitrous controller activates dual stages of nitrous depending on throttle position and user-definable progressive ramps. The Mini 2-Stage effectively acts as an rpm window switch by prohibiting nitrous triggering at user-definable high and low rpm thresholds, and two programmable output signals allow the unit to control timing retard units or other auxiliary control devices. A hand-held programmer interface makes configuring the device quick and simple and allows you to mount the main box remotely. *NOS*

sure the solenoids can handle the job. English nitrous maven Trevor Langfield dubbed his latest Wizards of NOS (WON) solenoid design the "Pulsoid" to emphasize that it is targeted at progressive applications. WON claims the solenoid can achieve nitrous flow metering from 5 to a 95 percent duty cycle without overheating or rapid failure.

All nitrous solenoids force fluid to change direction as it moves through the solenoid valve, but nitrous vendors like WON have touted **axial-flow solenoids** that are supposed to produce less fluid turbulence in the solenoid body. Reduced fluid turbulence could help to reduce kinetic vaporization when the solenoid opens and "superheated" nitrous (held in liquid phase to artificially high temperatures with extreme pressure) blasts through the valve into a heat-soaked solenoid body. It is not clear if anyone has conclusively *proven* the efficacy of axial or non-standard solenoid designs in reducing vaporization and foaming, but anything that reduces turbulence in a nitrous supply line certainly couldn't hurt.

The electrical consumption of a complex multi-stage nitrous system can be substantial: A radical 3,000-horsepower drag-race nitrous system might have as many as eight solenoids, each having electrical current requirements as high as 30 amps—totaling as much as 240 amps without counting nitrous controller, fuel pump, or other engine management power requirements. In an effort to get electrical requirements under control, some drag racers have deployed CO_2-actuated solenoids built by companies like Combo-Flo that greatly amplify the power of a small, low-power electric *pilot solenoid* by using it to switch gas pressure from the onboard CO_2 drag-race shifting system to open the solenoid valve(s) with great authority.

Nitrous Plumbing. Nitrous oxide typically flows to the engine compartment and solenoid through a flexible high-pressure nitrous supply line with inverted-flare connectors that attaches to adapter fittings on the nitrous bottle valve and solenoid (or debris filter). The supply line must be flexible so it can be routed around or through the various structures between the nitrous tank and engine, and must be robust enough to resist external mechanical damage and handle freezing and hot temperatures and over-pressure as high as 2,000 psi—which is why nitrous supply lines are usually built from aircraft-quality **Teflon-core braided-stainless hoses** with power-crimped connectors purpose-built for nitrous-injection systems. Teflon is great for nitrous applications due to its outstanding performance at extreme temperatures. Teflon's chemical properties remain stable at temperatures ranging from -400F to 500 degrees F. Above 500 degrees F, Teflon begins to degrade but the initial melting point is nearly 650 degrees F (which is, however, well below exhaust-gas temperature, which can easily reach 1,500 degrees F or higher on gasoline). *Never, ever* substitute standard neoprene-rubber braided-steel hoses (the ones that hot rodders commonly duct-tape and cut to length with a hacksaw and then assemble with screw-together compression connectors) for purpose-built power-crimped braided-steel Teflon-core nitrous hoses. This type of hose cannot handle the high working pressure of nitrous systems, and ordinary neoprene hose can become brittle if refrigerated by nitrous even though special neoprene is used in street nitrous solenoids.

A nitrous supply hose and its connectors should have the same inside diameter in order to prevent cavities or choke-points in the plumbing from inducing phase changes that refrigerate the line and alter the nitrous mass-flow rate. Ideally, hose and connector flow area should exactly match the flow area of the solenoid, bottle valve, and all additional plumbing beside the metering jet and injection orifice. In the real world, there are sometimes cavities in the nitrous supply plumbing where the flow path widens and then narrows (such as a debris filter, or at the exit of the bottle control valve itself where the discharge bore widens as nitrous passes through an adapter fitting and into the hose). Downstream flow-area *reductions* as nitrous moves farther through the system will not refrigerate the line, though reductions obviously increase

Twin Nitrous Works fogger-type nozzles are imbedded in a throttle spacer plate in this two-stage wet nitrous kit with rpm window switch. *Nitrous Works*

NX delivers nitrous and fuel with injectors and solenoids integral to a special Z06 Corvette MAF unit. *Nitrous Express*

Speedtech's spacer-plate nitrous systems deliver fuel and nitrous spray to the intake manifold in a 360-degree pattern from a central diffuser plate located below the carb. *SpeedTech*

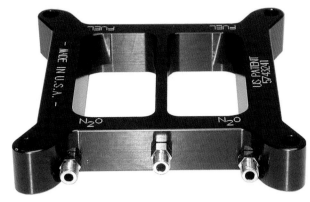

This dual-stage nitrous plate injects fuel and nitrous from both a central bar and from annular orifices around the periphery of the outer plate. *Nitrous Express*

friction and pressure-drop, which can become significant on nitrous circuits delivering a very large horsepower shot. Ideally, *everything* should match. The nitrous supply line should be as short as possible to minimize heat-soak as nitrous moves through the line but since the nitrous tank may be in the trunk at the opposite end of a vehicle from the engine, prefabricated 14-foot nitrous supply lines are common in nitrous kits because they are long enough for almost any automotive application.

The high density and high pressure of nitrous oxide liquid allows relatively small hoses and lines to move a lot of nitrous mass, but the supply line must be large enough to flow enough nitrous oxide and avoid friction sufficient to cause significant pressure drop, which can easily be 25 psi per 4-foot section of line. Typical prefabricated nitrous lines are standard AN 3, 4, 5, and 6 sizes, with inside diameter (I.D.) 3.5 to 6.5 millimeters. Even if the area of the hose is greater than the combined area of all nitrous-injection orifices, there will still be friction as liquid flows through the hose, but the ratio of hose inside area to circumference increases with larger hose sizes. Bigger is better when it comes to reducing or eliminating pressure drop, and only pressure gauges or fast sensors upstream and downstream of the supply hose will reveal the true scope of pressure drop. Depending on the architecture, higher volume hoses can soften the hit and add to a nitrous system's sluggishness. Multi-stage nitrous systems typically use a separate tank with independent supply hose for each stage.

Some nitrous vendors are now aggressively marketing **nylon nitrous supply lines** for applications of less than 150-horsepower boost. Nitrous lines must be able to handle working pressures of at least 1,000-1,100 psi and overload pressure of 2,000 psi, but it is not necessary to use 5,000-psi braided steel hoses. In fact, you can now substitute thin, flexible *nylon* hose (nylon hose, in some cases, can support up to 5,000 psi!) that functions almost identically to braided steel other than using compression rather than inverted flare fittings.

The downside of nylon is that it is far more vulnerable to mechanical and heat damage, which is why modern aircraft use Teflon tubing sheathed in braided stainless steel. When it can kill you if a hose fails, they don't mess around. On the other hand, nylon hose has the distinct advantage that it is *much* easier to install in a neat package of perfect length because sectioning nylon hose requires nothing more than a razor blade or scalpel. In most cases, the only practical way to change the length of a one-piece power-crimped braided-steel hose is to replace it with a new one of the correct length, which can be fairly expensive. When you consider that factory fuel lines (which are considerably more dangerous than nitrous hoses, should they rupture and spray fuel all over the place) have often included segments made out of relatively vulnerable fabric-reinforced synthetic rubber, it is clearly possible to build safe nitrous supply systems from nylon if you make sure that nylon hoses running underneath a vehicle are never routed where they could be subject to damage from heat, high-centering, or flying debris (plastic PVC or steel pipe makes excellent conduit as a countermeasure against debris damage). Obviously, nylon hose should never be routed near anything really hot like exhaust components . . . but then you don't want braided stainless hose anywhere near extreme heat either because (1) the Teflon core can be damaged by hot exhaust components, and (2) anything that heat-soaks the line will heat the nitrous flowing through it, which is bad from all points of view. Braided steel, by the way, can be extremely dangerous if the steel covering comes in contact with any +12-volt battery source: Braided-steel metal connectors are typically *very* well grounded, and it is *very easy* for electric arcing to burn through the steel sheathing and damage the Teflon core. A 4.0-mm hose with a 2.0-mm inside diameter or a 5.0-mm hose with 2.5-mm I.D. will typically do the job for a nitrous kit making less than a 150-horse boost.

Stainless steel pipe is routinely used to build the distribution hard pipes for direct-port nitrous injection, but it can also be used to transport nitrous from the tank to the solenoid and beyond. Unlike nylon or even braided-steel hose, steel pipe has the advantage that high pressure will not produce waves of expansion, contraction, or even resonation back and forth as the system gains and loses pressure in the course of an episode of nitrous boost. Stainless steel pipe is normally more robust and damage-resistant than any type of flexible hose, but it heat-soaks more easily and should ideally be insulated. Like braided-stainless hose, steel pipe conducts electricity and must never come in contact with live positive voltage to prevent failure from severe electric arcing.

Nitrous tank. Given the relatively large size of automotive nitrous tanks big enough to provide even two minutes of boost for a 100-horse shot powerplant, nitrous kit installers working with street vehicles typically have limited options when it comes to locating the tank. Most applications require installing the nitrous tank in the luggage compartment. The tank typically mounts in one or two purpose-built automotive nitrous brackets that bolt or screw to the body of the vehicle and must be strong enough to support the tank at both ends securely enough that the tank cannot break loose and become a deadly, forward-moving high-speed projectile in a high-G crash. Automotive tank brackets—whether they are basic dip-painted mild steel brackets or expensive, gorgeous, single-piece billet aluminum—are almost always designed to keep the tank oriented at a high enough angle above horizontal that a pickup tube running from the bottle control valve to the deepest part of the bottom of the tank can extract nearly every drop of liquid nitrous oxide and will not be easily uncovered during severe acceleration. In most cases, nitrous tanks are clamped in place by pinch-bolts or quick-disconnect fasteners.

All U.S.-market nitrous tanks are D.O.T.-certified to the rated working pressure. Nitrous tanks require periodic inspection and then pressure-testing at the conclusion of the certification period before they can be legally refilled. No one wants to haul around extra dead weight in a high-performance vehicle, so nitrous oxide tanks are generally made of light-weight aluminum. An **aluminum tank** capable

of being filled with 10 pounds of liquid nitrous (a bit over 1.5 gallons at room temperature) has an empty weight of about 15 pounds. Unlike the situation of scuba tanks (in which stronger steel cylinders can pack the same mass of compressed air as larger aluminum tanks into a smaller space at a higher pressure), **steel nitrous tanks** must be just as large as aluminum tanks because both are carrying noncompressible liquid nitrous. Steel tanks, however, are stronger and work fine if you don't mind the weight. Aluminum and steel differ somewhat in their ability to sink and transfer heat, which can be important if you are planning to use a bottle heater. For the "cool" factor—or where every pound is critical—lightweight aluminum-core carbon-wrapped tanks are available with an empty weight that's only about 50 percent that of an 100-percent-aluminum tank of similar capacity. **Carbon fiber tanks** are round on the bottom to improved structural integrity and maximize capacity for a given weight.

Metal automotive nitrous cylinders usually have a flat bottom to maximize the capacity for a given length of cylinder and because a flat bottom allows the tank to stand up on its own. Composite carbon tanks can be expected to have a slower rate of thermal transfer compared to painted metal tanks, reducing the effectiveness of tank heaters or environmental heat-soak in fighting liquid-nitrous heat-loss during boost. All nitrous tanks taper to a narrow neck, which is machined with internal female threads. Unless ambient temperature is below -128 degrees (ha!), nitrous tanks need a valve to keep the liquid from boiling furiously and evaporating while the tank is being reconnected to the nitrous system after refill, not to mention protecting the hands of the installer from frostbite.

A male-threaded **bottle control valve** screws into the neck of the tank through a Teflon washer that compresses to provide a perfect seal. Bottle control valves are extremely reliable. Many automotive nitrous bottle valves dump 90 degrees sideways through a large male-threaded discharge,

WON's "Black Widow" Spider Plate competition plate system spews nitrous and fuel into a V8 engine from a 16-tube fixture located below a four-barrel spacer plate. As always, the goal is lots of nitrous-fuel mixture and excellent distribution and mixing. *Wizards of NOS*

though there are straight-through valves that discharge nitrous longitudinally and do not require nitrous to change direction as it flows through the valve. Obviously, the main consideration for most applications is which type of valve allows the most convenient, sanitary external plumbing, given limited options for tank orientation. In automotive applications, the bottle valve almost always connects internally to a pickup tube running to one side of the bottom of the tank. The pickup is normally clocked so that it sits at the lowest point of the tank when the valve discharge is pointing down.

The pickup (sometimes called a siphon tube, though the term is not technically accurate for a nitrous pickup) must remain immersed in nitrous liquid at all times to prevent the tank from dispensing low-density nitrous vapor rather than high-density nitrous liquid. Tank orientation is thus critical to good boosted performance, particularly since violent acceleration will slosh the liquid nitrous rearward and uncover the pickup if the tank is mal-oriented. With a pickup tube installed, the tank obviously cannot be mounted upside-down. Ideally, the tank should be oriented at an angle with the bottle valve facing forward in order that acceleration pushes nitrous *toward* the pickup and sideways G-forces during turns will not have an important effect. Bottle control valves sans pickup tube are available for the situation in which a nitrous installer wants to orient the tank upside-down, which can be particularly useful for small vehicle applications like motorcycles and snowmobiles where the horsepower shot is relatively small and there is only room for a very small nitrous tank.

Most nitrous bottle valves open manually by rotating a wheel that first lifts the precisely contoured tip of a threaded shaft off its seat and then progressively uncovers more and more of the valve discharge bore to increase flow. In most cases, several full turns counter-clockwise moves the valve from fully closed to fully open. The bottle control valve must be open for nitrous to flow, but it should always be closed when the engine is stopped to prevent a worn solenoid control valve downstream from potentially leaking nitrous through the injection system and into the intake manifold; on some types of nitrous systems nitrous oxide buildup in the manifold could result in an explosion in case the engine backfires on

There are a plethora of nozzle designs that "fog" together high-pressure nitrous and 5-50 psi fuel in a single unit designed to vastly atomize fuel and nitrous oxide droplets into a homogenous mixture. This is an Edelbrock titanium wet nozzle. *Edelbrock*

restart. Not all bottle valves have equal flow rates, so you need one large enough that it can never become the critical bottleneck to nitrous flow in relation to all other components in the nitrous circuit. Nitrous vendors commonly offer two choices: standard and high-flow bottle valves.

A nitrous tank must never be mounted in a hot engine compartment, in direct sunlight in the vehicle interior without insulation, or anywhere else where its temperature could rise above 120 degrees F. Overheating a nitrous tank increases both vapor pressure and thermal expansion. Vapor pressure in a seriously overheated tank could eventually threaten the structural integrity of the tank, but *overfilling* a completely sealed tank is even more dangerous because it leaves insufficient room for thermal expansion, which can easily burst a strong aluminum or steel tank. In the absence of countermeasures, overheating a nitrous tank could result in a catastrophic tank explosion at temperatures as low as 130 degrees F.

A tank explosion, by the way, is capable of causing unbelievable damage, totaling a vehicle as surely as if it had been hit by a Panzerfaust. Nitrous tanks sold in the United States are required to have a safety valve that screws into a port in the bottle control valve assembly upstream of the main valve in order to release overpressure in an emergency. The safety valve is usually an all-or-nothing device in which a blow-out disk lets go when tank pressure reaches approximately 1,200 psi so as to vent the entire contents of the tank. You occasionally hear a rumor of some moron removing or tampering with the safety valve in the hope that overpressure will get more nitrous in the engine (it will not, however, because the *only* way a self-pressurized nitrous tank increases in pressure is from a temperature rise, but any temperature rise above 97.7 degrees F will exceed the critical temperature of nitrous oxide and result in the tank discharging 100 percent gas rather than liquid, with a great loss in refrigeration effect).

NOS Dry Fanspray nitrous nozzle sprays NO_2 sideways into the inlet airstream, at a central point or into the individual runners. This nozzle is for systems that deliver fuel enrichment through the EFI electronic injectors. *NOS*

Blow-out disks work very well, which is why there have apparently only been two automotive nitrous tank explosions in history. If the blow-out disk does do its thing, however, keep in mind that nitrous oxide ("laughing gas") is not just liquid horsepower but also an inhalation anesthetic that can cause uncontrollable giggling or even unconsciousness—which will probably not help your driving skills. High-enough concentrations of nitrous oxide with insufficient oxygen can kill you (if you didn't already die in the crash). But you won't actually be laughing, because automotive nitrous in the United States is manufactured by Airgas and branded as Nytrous+, which is nitrous oxide denatured to prevent substance abuse with 100 ppm of oxides of sulfur, a disgusting-smelling irritant.

There are a large number of **tank options** that can help improve nitrous system performance, and enhance safety and reliability. Tanks come in a variety of sizes. The most commonly used tanks hold 10, 15, or 20 pounds of nitrous oxide when full; empty aluminum tanks in these sizes weigh roughly 15, 24, and 27 pounds, their "tare weight." Larger tanks, 40 or 50 inches long, hold up to 50 pounds of nitrous. For motorcycles or other small vehicles where space is at a premium, smaller tanks are available that hold 5, 2, or less than 1 pound of nitrous, with empty weights in the range of 8, 4, and 2 pounds. Some multi-stage nitrous systems use more than one tank.

Removing or swapping your tank will be much quicker and easier if you fit **quick-disconnect fixtures**. With quick-removal connectors and tank brackets, a nitrous tank can be out and a new one installed in seconds.

Many adaptor fittings are available to attach the bottle control valve to a variety of pipes and hoses. The adaptor is typically a large female NPT fitting that threads onto the bottle valve discharge, with the other end equipped with a flare or inverted-flare connection for Army-Navy (AN) size 3 to 8 braided-steel hoses or a compression fitting for 4.0 or 5.0 millimeter nylon hose. Some adapters are equipped with an NPT-threaded plug that can be removed to install a **pressure gauge** or **electronic pressure sensor**. Keep in mind that below the critical temperature of 97.7 degrees F, tank pressure is

Close-up of NXL wet injection nozzle. This expensive little jewel fits into an electronic injector boss and relocates the injector outward a short distance. Fuel and nitrous hoses attach to the dual fittings, with nitrous and fuel spraying into individual intake runners around the periphery of the electronic injectors. *Nitrous Express*

exclusively a function of temperature as long as any nitrous liquid remains in the tank after boiling has generated equilibrium vapor pressure. Indicated gauge pressure under static conditions is a function of the temperature, and indicated gauge temperature conversely translates predictably to pressure.

That said, conditions are *not* static during boost, and the *location* of a temperature gauge can be important. The metal mass of the tank itself is a significant heat-sink with a temperature that may not correspond to nitrous temperature under some conditions. What's more, temperature will not be uniform throughout the mass of nitrous liquid and gas contained in the tank during boost when in-tank boiling is causing the nitrous to refrigerate itself and the tank from the inside, or when a nitrous bottle heater may be doing its best to cook the tank from the outside. A typical nitrous pressure gauge reads from 0 to 1,500 psig. Maximum tank temperature could range from -128 degrees F to 150 degrees F. The advantage of a high-speed tank pressure or temperature *sensor* is that a nitrous-capable aftermarket EMS can usually datalog the sensor data stream along with other engine status data during the course of nitrous boost for tuning or coordination purposes. Even more critical, a computer-controlled nitrous system can usually be configured to prevent engine damage by aborting nitrous boost if tank temperature or pressure goes out of a tuner-defined acceptable range.

If you need an on-board **nitrous contents indicator**, there are electronic controllers with sophisticated bottle flow algorithms designed to predict how many seconds of boost are available based on configuration data specifying the nitrous system's metering jet size and bottle capacity. The contents indicator must be reset each time the tank has been refilled, from which point it will display an estimate of the remaining contents (in seconds until empty) on the display screen. To be accurate, a contents indicator requires logic that understands that displaying the time left before the tank is empty is not a linear function of time, but can vary according to a complex set of interrelated factors. The contents indicator logic is

Cutaway of NX Piranha injection nozzle with nitrous and fuel connectors and metering jets. *Nitrous Express*

NX's Direct-port Piranha LS1 intake manifold attaches direct-port fogger-type injection nozzles to combination fuel and nitrous rails with high-pressure braided-stainless hose. *Nitrous Express*

typically based on a sophisticated mass-flow correction table that may take into account factors such as total elapsed time (since bottle refill), elapsed time since last boost event, elapsed time of the current boost event, past depletion history, current environmental factors, average solenoid duty cycle, etc.

Pressure and temperature control. The higher pressure in a warmer nitrous tank pushes a greater volume of liquid nitrous through a metering jet, but each cubic millimeter of liquid contains correspondingly fewer molecules of nitrous oxide as temperature increases. The equilibrium **mass flow** rate of nitrous remains approximately the same (within a few percent) at ambient operating temperatures.

Given the critical importance of achieving precise oxygen-fuel ratios during nitrous boost, an increasing number of modern racers and hot rodders have decided it is desirable to control the pressure and temperature of the nitrous tank. Why not *make sure* nitrous delivery pressure into the nitrous supply line stays constant by installing, say, a pressure regulator in the supply line upstream of the nitrous solenoid? Why not *make sure* that bottle pressure stays constant by thermostatically regulating the temperature of the nitrous bottle with a bottle heater kit—or even manage the activity of the bottle heater based directly on a nitrous tank pressure sensor? In fact, why not normalize nitrous tank pressure under all circumstances using regulated external pressurization? There are real-world products designed to do each of the above, some of which function more effectively than others. It is *critical* to analyze the utility of each of these control tactics in the intended application.

The real benefit of a **nitrous tank pressure regulator**, says one commercial vendor's website, is that it eliminates the typical horsepower loss that occurs when bottle pressure begins to drop after 3 to 5 seconds of spraying. The regulator can be adjusted to deliver pressure ranging from 500 to 1,100 psi

according to the pre-load of an adjustment screw against an internal diaphragm. Obviously, a regulator can never deliver more pressure than what's available from the tank, so if the tank gets too cold or the rate of boiling can't keep up with self-pressurization requirements during really heavy nitrous delivery, a pressure regulator cannot maintain pressure. The operational theory behind a regulator is to lower regulated pressure far enough below pre-boost equilibrium tank pressure that tank-pressure drop during nitrous injection will never reduce tank pressure below the regulated pressure, which therefore stays fully under control. Like any bottleneck in the nitrous supply line that induces a pressure drop, a pressure regulator becomes a de-facto expansion valve that causes some of the nitrous liquid to boil and foam as it leaves the regulator.

In this situation there are a number of possible effects, the consequence of which is to change liquid nitrous mass flow: (1) the regulator lowers supply line pressure, which reduces the volume of nitrous liquid pushed through a metering jet; (2) the pressure drop refrigerates supply components and liquid nitrous downstream, which tends to increase the density of the nitrous liquid; (3) expansion dilutes the liquid with vapor bubbles, and this foaming action makes it impossible for a jet to accurately meter liquid volume let alone mass. What is the net effect on a given day in a given application? Who can say? To minimize adverse effects, a nitrous pressure regulator should not be installed at the bottle control valve but as far downstream as possible in close proximity to the nitrous solenoid valve where refrigeration and vaporization effects will have less impact. As always, if there is an unexpected *increase* in mass flow and you do not compensate by increasing supplemental fuel delivery, the result could be dangerously lean combustion.

Variable-orifice nitrous nozzles are designed to choke down the flow of nitrous oxide in the face of higher pressure,

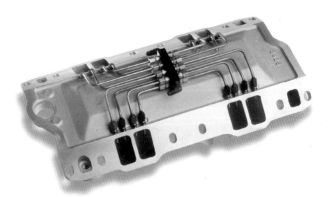

This hidden nitrous architecture fits on the underside of a traditional V-8 intake manifold and provides direct-port nitrous and fuel injection through individual (non-fogging) jet spray nozzles drilled into the floor of the intake runners. The fuel and nitrous nozzles should be directed slightly toward each other for best mixing. The hit from this type of system tends to be lazy due to the high potential for heat-soak, but it can defeat the stealth purpose of this type of system if there is a visible nitrous purge. Some people have concealed this by purging into the hot exhaust system. *NOS*

This NX "Incognito" hidden nitrous system delivers no fuel enrichment and often depends on extremely rich all-motor fuel tuning to deliver a small power boost. The tank is small and easy to hide. With auxiliary fuel enrichment delivered by an EFI system misled by a trick coolant temperature sensor that reports very low temperature during nitrous boost, or a rigged carb power-valve, the system can deliver up to a 50 horsepower boost. *Nitrous Express*

or increase the volumetric flow when pressure drops off. A patent has been issued for an adjustable variable-orifice nozzle that modifies nitrous flow inversely to pressure at the point of injection in such a way that the refrigeration effects and gasification are not a factor.

Another pressure-control option is a **bottle heating kit**. These kits are onboard systems that typically envelop the center section of the tank in what is essentially a small electric blanket—optionally augmented by an **insulation jacket** (a.k.a., "bottle blanket") to improve the efficiency of an electric bottle-heater by slowing heat loss into the environment and prevent *overheating* in the sun. Some heating systems house the entire tank in a climate-controlled, insulated box. Nitrous systems with electric heaters should be well-insulated in cool weather to keep the heat in the nitrous tank and out of the vehicle, and nitrous systems without heaters should be insulated during warm or hot weather to prevent overheating from direct sunlight or to keep heat out of the tank if it is being kept below the critical temperature by self-refrigeration tricks. There is no point whatsoever in insulating a nonheated nitrous tank as long as the environment is even slightly warmer than the temperature of the liquid nitrous in the tank, as this will prevent the tank from heat-soaking from the environment to help counteract internal cooling once boost starts and nitrous begins boiling in the tank to maintain vapor pressure.

As of this writing, most onboard bottle heaters were rated in the 240- to 400-watt range and typically consumed at least 20 amps of power when heating at full strength (which is two to three times the current drain of two headlights and will run

down a battery fairly quickly if the engine is not running). It can take quite a while to heat a nitrous tank enough to raise the pressure significantly, even when the tank is not dispensing nitrous and therefore self-cooling. One real-world testing regime found that a 400-watt bottle heater required 18 to 20 minutes to increase the pressure of a full 15-pound nitrous tank from 700 to 900 psi by heating the tank from 64 degrees F to 88 degrees F. Unfortunately, no practical onboard bottle heater can heat a tank of nitrous fast enough to keep up with the powerful refrigeration effect of boiling nitrous when a self-pressurized system is making boost.

The best bottle heaters are the ones equipped with automatic controls that regulate heating on the basis of a temperature or pressure sensor, because a manually controlled heater can cause serious trouble if you leave it running too long (the *worst* type of bottle heater is the open flame of a torch, which can damage the integrity of the tank, but that doesn't stop people from doing it when the weather is cold and they want to win races). In one incident a manual electric heater on a stopped vehicle with the engine shut down had a gasoline generator running to keep the battery charged. The bottle heater cooked the nitrous until the safety disk blew out, at which point nitrous was sucked into the *generator*, which went nuts and destroyed itself.

Pressure-normalized heaters have the advantage that they stay on continuously until pressure reaches the target psi, and thus heat at the fastest possible rate, but this type of system will cook the tank to blow-out if accidentally left running with the bottle control valve closed because the pressure sensor will not see any pressure no matter how hot the tank gets—a good reason to design-in an over-temperature override switch or a timed switch of the type found on many commercial battery chargers.

Temperature-normalized heaters are somewhat slower than pressure-based automatic heaters due to the on-off nature of thermostatically controlled systems heating objects that have massive thermal momentum. A heating element cannot warm a tankful of nitrous everywhere at once, and thermal transfer from the heating element to the (somewhat)

The NOS "Top Shot" hidden nitrous system fits inside the air cleaner of a four-barrel carb or throttle body, directing nitrous and enrichment fuel into the engine through the carb venturis or individual throttles. *NOS*

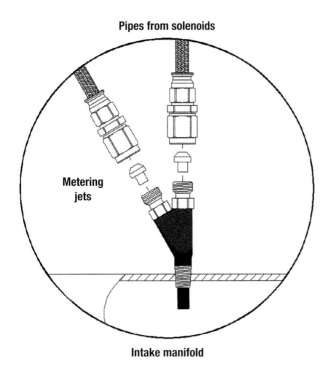

Pipes from solenoids

Metering jets

Intake manifold

Wet fogger-type injection nozzles illustrates how the metering jets slide into the connectors and form a flare-type seal with the braided-steel supply hoses.

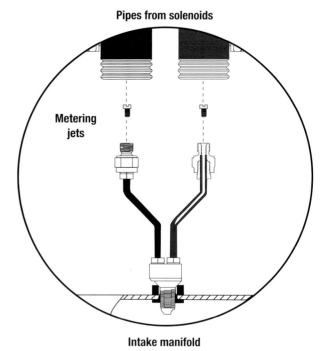

Pipes from solenoids

Metering jets

Intake manifold

WON's street nitrous system locates the metering jets at the outlets of the fuel and nitrous solenoids. *Wizards of NOS*

remotely located thermostat (temperature sensor) is not instantaneous. To keep from constantly hunting on and off for the right temperature, thermostat control systems must overshoot the target sensor temperature by a certain margin, then shut down the heating element and wait until enough heat migrates away from the temperature sensor for it to cool to a margin below the target temperature, at which point the system activates the heating element again, and so on, until the tank reaches target temperature.

Keep in mind that bottle-heating systems virtually always do what their name implies: they heat the nitrous *tank*, not the nitrous oxide itself, and temperature control systems sense the temperature of the outside *metal surface* rather than the nitrous liquid inside it. Not only will a metal tank heat unevenly as thermal energy migrates away from the heating element to the temperature sensor and farthest reaches of the tank, but heat must soak through to the inside surface of the tank and from there throughout the liquid and gaseous contents. Nitrous oxide has significantly slower thermal transfer properties than water (though the specific heat required to raise the temperature is less), causing nitrous to act as a big, sluggish heat sink for a heated metal tank. One testing regime found that although one pressure-controlled tank heating system reached 1,000 psi after 15 minutes of heating, liquid near the bottom of the tank was 13 degrees F cooler than liquid near the surface. Even with the nitrous system dormant, pressure dropped in fairly short order once the heating system shut down as heat spread more evenly throughout the liquid, causing vapor pressure in

the tank to fall. Some tests found that it typically required two full hours of heating for a blanket-style heater to achieve even heating throughout a nitrous tank and its contents. On the other hand, once a tank is warm, there is a fair amount of thermal momentum: A tank heated to 100 degrees F held its temperature for nearly an hour in 63-degree air when not making boost.

Unfortunately, neither a 240- nor 400-watt bottle heater is close to being powerful enough to keep up with the massive heat required to boil nitrous oxide from a liquid into a gas. For example, a 100-horse nitrous kit that requires injecting 0.1 pounds per second of nitrous oxide into the engine requires that 0.02569 lb/sec of nitrous liquid boil to keep the tank at full pressure. Boiling 0.02569 lb/sec of nitrous liquid, in turn, requires approximately 1,875 watts/sec of energy. This energy is normally donated by the mass of nitrous liquid that is not boiling and the aluminum tank, which are ultimately heated by the environment around the tank, including a heater if present. The heat required to maintain self-pressurization in a 15-pound mass of nitrous in a tank spewing liquid at 0.1 lb/sec is initially about 0.75 degrees F per second temperature drop (though in the real world heat would also be available from the aluminum tank). Unfortunately, as boost continues the temperature drop per second must accelerate because (1) the mass of liquid nitrous is continuously depleted, (2) the heat for vaporization must come from less and less nitrous liquid, and (3) the nitrous liquid cools and the heat required to vaporize it increases. Ignoring heat available from and through the metal tank, in this example nitrous would self-cool at a rate exceeding 45 degrees per minute!

The bottom line is that nitrous bottle heaters in the 240- to 400-watt range are not effective in stabilizing the temperature and pressure of a nitrous tank during boost. Even if there was theoretically enough power available on board to maintain temperature against the powerful cooling effect of boiling nitrous, it would nonetheless be difficult or impossible to maintain uniform in-tank temperature and pressure with an external-surface electric blanket when we notice that steam boilers, air-water intercoolers, and other devices with major heat transfer requirements need a massive, intricate heat exchanging interface replete with multiple tubes, finned "turbulators," and fluid agitators or pumps to jack up thermal transfer efficiency to an effective level.

The latest trick in nitrous tank temperature control is using **Peltier Junction** electronic heat-pump technology to target an ideal nitrous tank temperature and pressure—whether this involves adding or *subtracting* thermal energy from the nitrous tank. How Peltier technology works is that junctions of certain dissimilar metals are arranged in large arrays to create a thermo-electric heat pump. Electrical current flowing through the grid of junctions sends heat in one direction and coldness in another, depending on the polarity of the circuit, allowing heat and coldness to be collected on a continuing basis and put to use as required. A fluid (air, water, and so on) pumped through the Peltier array can be cooled or heated as required to normalize the temperature of a nitrous tank or bottle housing. One commercially available Peltier-technology nitrous temperature control system consists of an insulated, climate-controlled "environmental chamber" designed to house a single nitrous tank and preheat or precool it as required before racing to achieve a designated temperature. NX's "Fire and Ice" unit straps onto the outside of the tank, something like a bottle heater. Unfortunately, like ordinary electric bottle-heating kits, onboard Peltier temperature-maintenance kits are not powerful enough to maintain nitrous liquid temperature during nitrous boost when nitrous is actually boiling in the tank.

Nitrous external pressurization. If a tank of nitrous oxide is kept below the critical temperature of 97.7 degrees F and externally pressurized with compressed nitrogen or air above the vapor pressure of nitrous at the ambient temperature, 100 percent of the nitrous oxide in the tank will be liquid. Precision external pressurization guarantees that the mass flow rate of liquid nitrous delivery is a function purely of the density of the liquid nitrous (a function of temperature, assuming there is no nitrogen or air foam in the nitrous liquid) and the average area of the nitrous metering orifice. Maintaining a constant nitrous tank pressure is straightforward using an external source of ultra-high-pressure air or nitrogen from an auxiliary tank conditioned by an adjustable gas pressure regulator. Assuming the nitrous supply plumbing is large enough to eliminate pressure drop and insulated against heat soak so that the liquid nitrous remains at a constant temperature, as long as there's any liquid nitrous remaining in the tank, a constant nitrous mass flow is guaranteed.

Constant-temperature nitrous, of course, is a *big* assumption, given things like . . . well, weather and engine heat soak. The consequences of temperature variation are significant. Liquid nitrous oxide is non-compressible, but it shrinks significantly at lower temperatures and expands significantly

Nitrous bottle and accessories kit includes a vapor-pressure gauge to provide information about the volumetric flow currently available from self-pressurization, vent tube to route over-pressure nitrous gas outside the vehicle passenger compartment, and a low-pressure sensor to disarm the nitrous system if system pressure drops below a minimum. *Nitrous Works*

Nitrous tank bottle control valve with pickup tube. The tube is normally clocked opposite the bottle label so the tank can always be oriented with the pickup tube at the lowest point. If the tank will be mounted inverted, the pickup tube must be removed or deleted from the system when ordering the tank or kit. *Nitrous Works* at higher temperatures, exactly like the liquid mercury or alcohol in a thermometer. The result is substantial change in density. The density of self-pressurized superheated liquid nitrous is roughly 450 kg per cubic meter at 97.7 degrees, but as temperature drops density increases in a parabolic fashion to more than 1,200 kg/m3 at -130 degrees F. This means that liquid nitrous oxide 6.0 inches deep in a tall iced tea glass at 97.7 degrees F (and 72.5 atmospheres of pressure) shrinks to just 2.25 inches of depth at -130 degrees F. If the temperature of nitrous liquid changes, a metering jet will continue to deliver the identical *volume* of nitrous oxide into an engine, but the volume will contain a different *mass* of nitrous. (The thermal expansion properties of nitrous oxide make it critical to never overfill a nitrous tank: If you pump the tank *full* of liquid at, say, 68 degrees F, and it warms to 97.6 degrees, thermal expansion reduces the density of the nitrous from 783 to 450 kg/m3, a whopping 75 percent change. If the tank was full at 68 degrees F, thermal expansion will unquestionably try to explode the tank, blowing out the safety disk!)

If a nitrous tank is externally pressurized, and the supply line to the engine is designed so it is insulated from heat soak and contains no significant bottlenecks, nitrous oxide will arrive at the metering jet as an ambient-temperature liquid (at least after any initial vapor is driven out of the line). However, keep in mind that at any temperature above -128 degrees F, pressurized nitrous oxide liquid in a storage tank exists in a *superheated* state, meaning that the temperature of the liquid is far above its boiling point at atmospheric pressure. Room-temperature

The Billet 6160T-6 "Lightning 45" bottle valve is designed to exceed the flow capacity of ordinary bottle control valves with reduced turbulence, and eliminates the need for adaptor fittings common on some nitrous systems. *Nitrous Express*

liquid nitrous in a tank may appear superficially stable, but the molecules are dying to boil furiously at the first possible opportunity. When nitrous liquid sprays out of an injection nozzle into an engine intake at 850 psia, the droplets are suddenly in a low-pressure environment vastly above the boiling point of nitrous at room temperature. Injecting nitrous in an engine is like misting water against a red-hot frying pan: Nitrous droplets immediately begin to sizzle, boil, and expand, stealing heat energy from anything in the vicinity to fuel the phase change into vapor, exactly the way a water spray will cool off a hot frying pan as it vaporizes into steam.

Externally pressurized nitrous systems are equipped with a small auxiliary cylinder containing extremely high pressure (4,500 psi is typical for a carbon-wrapped tank, 3,000 psi for an aluminum tank) nitrogen gas or air of sufficient mass to pressurize the main nitrous oxide tank to the regulated working pressure (925-1,050 psia, in the case of NANO's system). The auxiliary tank bottle valve connects via a short high-pressure braided-steel hose to an adjustable variable-rate-of-gain pressure regulator referenced to nitrous tank pressure, which connects through a one-way valve to a secondary port on a special nitrous bottle control valve. The one-way valve allows the external pressurization system to be detached from the nitrous tank without venting nitrous oxide. The nitrous tank need not be totally empty before refilling with nitrous oxide. The refill procedure (assuming a standard nitrous valve with extended liquid nitrous pickup tube) is to disconnect the partially empty nitrous tank, invert it, and then crack open the nitrous valve to bleed off the lighter external pressurization gas until visible nitrous vapor is expelled from the tank, at which point the bottle valve can be closed with the tank purged of contaminants and ready for refill.

Bottle remote arming valve and hardware allows the driver to enable nitrous flow from the tank without having to manually open the bottle control valve so that the nitrous can flow if the nitrous electrical system is armed and the nitrous solenoid triggered. *Edelbrock*

The proper functioning of any external pressurization system is critically dependent on the quality and design of the pressure regulator that manages external pressure delivery as well as the one-way check valve that together deliver external pressurization. Many pressure regulators cannot maintain static "resting" pressure once gas begins flowing, so pressurization typically drops about 10 percent before stabilizing under dynamic conditions. During heavy nitrous outflow, reference pressure from the nitrous tank may be employed by a nonlinear-rate-of-gain regulator to improve the ability of the external pressure system to deliver a steady liquid nitrous mass flow. There is evidence in some cases that excessive external pressurization during dynamic conditions can produce foaming in the nitrous tank, possibly due to changes in the surface tension of the nitrous liquid—which, obviously, would reduce nitrous mass flow in unpredictable ways, which could adversely impact the oxygen-fuel combustion ratio. NANO, for example, limits the maximum pressure of their system to 1,040 psi, which is actually almost 30 psi under the maximum nitrous vapor pressure as temperature approaches the critical point. In general, external pressurization systems undoubtedly add mechanical complexity, and some people have claimed that racers using "push" pressurization systems on nitrous-injected powerplants have experienced a higher-than-expected number of catastrophic engine failures. Some race sanctioning bodies have responded by outlawing external pressurization systems. NANO makes the distinction that their system is an energy conservation measure rather than a "push" system.

Adjustable nitrous pressure regulator. The theory is that by normalizing nitrous tank delivery pressure to a lower initial value, nitrous pressure can be maintained throughout the boost event. Potential problems with this strategy are liquid nitrous density reductions resulting from vaporization and foaming that may result from the pressure drop through the regulator. On the other hand, nitrous mass flow tends to be impacted in the opposite direction due to liquid nitrous density increases resulting from thermal contraction that is a result of the temperature drop produced by liquid nitrous boiling in the tank *or the supply line* during boost to maintain vapor pressure. This may not be eliminated by regulating nitrous pressure. *ZEX*

Some nitrous vendors market a **remote-control bottle valve** actuated by an electric motor controlled by a two-position cockpit switch. This valve can even be set up to open and close the bottle automatically: Starting the engine, oil pressure going positive, or manually arming the nitrous switch could automatically trigger a relay to activate the electric bottle valve opener. The absence of any of these essential prerequisites to nitrous flow would automatically close the valve as a safety measure.

An alternate to the remote-control electrical bottle valve is to route the nitrous supply line near the driver's seat on the way to the engine and install an **auxiliary in-line manual shut-off valve**. This enables the main bottle control valve to be left on constantly except when you R&R the tank for refill.

Bottle control valves can become a bottleneck if nitrous mass flow gets high enough. Most nitrous vendors now offer off-the-shelf .325-inch **high-flow bottle valves** designed to provide nitrous mass flow sufficient for 500 horsepower without significant pressure drop—beyond which most people would, in any case, be using multi-stage systems. Whatever the flow rate, bottle control valves are available with 90-degree or straight-out discharge, and the valve can be installed with or without an extended pickup or "siphon" tube depending on whether the tank will be installed with the valve up or down.

Some nitrous vendors are now offering the option to replace an all-or-nothing overpressure safety blow-out disk with a **pressure relief valve** of the type traditionally used to vent air or steam pressure. Nitrous systems from WON employ a spring-loaded valve that can be forced open by overpressure *on a temporary basis* to vent just enough nitrous oxide from the tank to avoid exceeding the tank's pressure limit. The relief valve stays open only until pressure is back down to a safe level, at which point a spring forces the valve closed to save the remaining nitrous oxide. As is the case

EFI-pressure fuel pressure gauge provides an immediate indication if fuel loop pressure drops below normal or if total fuel usage exceeds the capacity of the fuel pump(s). To be useful, a fuel pressure gauge must be installed where you can see it—meaning in the cockpit. Electrical gauges make this easier and safer than having to route plastic hoses all the way from the fuel rail to the dashboard. *Edelbrock*

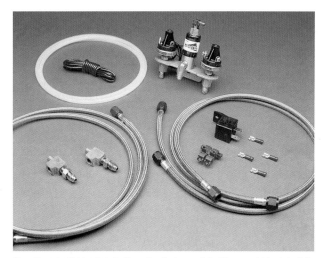

Given the potential for disaster if an oil or fuel pump fails, it is a great idea to install fail-safe protection. This NW nitrous safety kit includes two pressure-activated inline switches that disable the nitrous system if fuel or oil pressure fall below preset conditions—which will also prevent the nitrous system from continuing to flow nitrous into the engine if the engine stalls. For example, if you stall the engine burning a burnout and then press the gas to the floor while cranking, it could cause a nitrous explosion on restart from accumulated nitrous oxide in the intake or cylinders. *Nitrous Works*

with an ordinary blow-off valve, the pressure relief valve on a tank in the passenger compartment should be equipped with what is sometimes called a "Safety Blow-Down Kit." This component routes any vented nitrous outside the passenger compartment so occupants do not breathe it.

Additional auxiliary nitrous tanks. These can be plumbed together in parallel into the primary nitrous stage through a common nitrous solenoid or isolated in separate stages. A larger mass of nitrous delivered in a single stage increases the time until a tank runs empty, helps to reduce tank pressure drop at onset of boost (heavily dependent on the volume of the in-tank nitrous vapor bubble [ullage]); the more volume, the less immediate pressure drop), and provides a larger mass of liquid to donate heat for vaporization in the tank to maintain pressure.

Computer-controlled dry nitrous systems with sufficient fuel capacity may activate successive nitrous stages while simultaneously increasing fuel delivery through the primary injectors or supplemental direct-port constant-injection. **Multiple nitrous stages** normally consist of independent self-contained nitrous supply systems (each with its own tank, bottle control valve, supply hose, solenoid, metering jets, and nitrous-injection fixtures) that share a coordinated control system. Where the maximum nitrous delivery requirement is within the capacity of a singe tank and nitrous supply circuit, it usually makes more sense to vary nitrous delivery with progressive PWM nitrous solenoid control (to reduce driveline shock or improve traction) than to deploy all the additional hardware and complexity of a multi-stage system.

In order to maximize the repeatability, accuracy, and explosiveness of a hard nitrous hit, it has become quite common to install a nitrous supply line vapor-purging system. A **nitrous purge system** consists of an auxiliary nitrous solenoid that T's into the main nitrous supply line as close as possible to the nitrous-injection nozzle, a restrictor orifice, and discharge plumbing that routes the purge blast away from the vehicle (usually sideways from the wheel wells, or over the car from the wiper area like an out-of-control windshield washer jet). Squeezing a spring-loaded momentary switch energizes the auxiliary purge solenoid and holds it open as long as the switch is depressed to clear heat-soaked nitrous vapor and foam from the supply line so it ends up filled with pure liquid nitrous. Purging vapor improves the density of the initial nitrous hit and eliminates the rich bog that can occur if the full-force initial fuel hit is accompanied by a weak nitrous hit contaminated by low-density gas bubbles (or even completely gasified). Purge systems produce an impressive blast of visible vapor with a "psy-ops" benefit—competitors who witness it will realize that the car has a serious nitrous system and that its owner has no problem wasting a little extra nitrous to clean their clock.

If it turns out that you are frequently bleeding nitrous to cool the tank, it could make sense to build or obtain a nitrous bottle control valve with a secondary port that bleeds nitrous vapor, which is *far* more economical in the amount of nitrous wasted to achieve a given level of cooling (because all boiling takes place inside the tank). A nitrous purge system that vents nitrous vapor and foam into an expansion-chamber sleeve surrounding the supply line can be used to reduce heat-soak by chilling the supply plumbing.

If you use a lot of nitrous oxide or might want to sell it, you may decide to acquire a **nitrous tank refilling kit**. You can rent a nitrous donor cylinder and acquire industrial- or food-grade nitrous oxide from nitrous kit builders or direct from commercial chemical companies like Airgas, Inc. Medical-grade nitrous oxide, which has very high standards for purity, is more difficult and expensive to buy, has no advantages when it comes to boosting an engine.

As is the case with an onboard nitrous bottle, it is critical that a nitrous donor cylinder dispense liquid nitrous oxide.

Inline nitrous debris filters remove extraneous particles before they can reach the tiny metering jets used to boost individual cylinders of a direct-port nitrous system. *Nitrous Works*

WON Radial distribution manifold, designed to provide improved distribution to the individual-cylinder supply lines of a direct-port nitrous system. It is not automatic that a distribution manifold—particularly the rectangular "distribution blocks"—will distribute nitrous liquid evenly to all cylinders. *Wizards of NOS*

Thus, donor tanks are commonly inverted in a special stand with the bottle valve and plumbing at the bottom, though a donor cylinder with a "siphon" tube will also work—it is obviously critical to know which you have. Inverted donor nitrous cylinders without a siphon tube are somewhat more efficient at delivering the maximum refill mass with minimal waste.

A refill is easier if you have a pump to transfer nitrous from the donor cylinder, but a nitrous tank can be refilled without a pump, which is the most common method for do-it-yourselfers. The refill plumbing attaches to both the donor and recipient tanks and incorporates an inline shut-off valve. After weighing the recipient tank and carefully purging air from all hoses by cracking the donor nitrous control valve while the connectors are only loosely tightened (wear gloves to prevent frostbite from the-128 degrees nitrous), open all valves, and pressure and gravity will force liquid nitrous out of the donor tank into the lower-pressure recipient tank until pressure is equal in both tanks or until you stop the flow with the shut-off valve. Remember, you're aiming for the maximum allowable weight, not a full tank—too much nitrous liquid will expand in warm weather and blow out the safety disk! If it is difficult or impossible to achieve the gross fill weight by the time pressure equalizes, cooling the recipient bottle by inverting it and bleeding off some gas or cooling the bottle for a while in a freezer will help, as will warming the donor cylinder (as long as it stays below the critical temperature).

Nitrous Oxide Systems, among others, sells a pneumatic nitrous pump powered by 50- to 125-psi automotive shop air pressure that forces gulps of liquid nitrous from the donor tank into the recipient nitrous bottle until the recipient bottle is at gross weight.

Injecting supplemental fuel. Total nitrous boost is limited by the necessity to avoid detonation and damage to the mechanical structure of the engine. But a computer-controlled dry nitrous system uniquely integrates supplemental nitrous enrichment fueling with the primary fuel supply system. This means the fuel pump, electronic injectors, fuel supply plumbing, and fuel pressure regulator require especially large dynamic delivery range and are themselves independent constraints on the ability of a nitrous engine to make power. Port-EFI fuel systems pump gasoline from the fuel tank at 30 to 80 psi through a loop into the engine compartment, after which surplus fuel returns back to the tank by way of a pressure regulator that pinches off return flow to the extent required to maintain target pressure upstream in the loop. Electronic port fuel injectors—attached to a "rail" section of the fuel loop near the intake ports using O-ring or hose-barb technology—are more or less a miniature version of a nitrous solenoid, with electromagnetic force employed to overcome spring pressure and pull open the valve for a precise slice of time to permit fuel to spray through into the intake port. Electronic injector flow is a function of fuel loop pressure, injector open time, and the total area of the injector metering orifice.

Most modern vehicles with electronic fuel injection are equipped with in-tank rotary electric fuel pumps capable of supplying roughly 130 to 150 percent of the maximum stock fuel requirements at 40-55 psig. The volumetric pumping efficiency of an EFI fuel pump is inversely proportional to the pressure it must deliver, meaning that the pump delivers its highest volume of fuel at zero pressure, with the gallons-per-hour delivery rate declining as pressure increases. If an existing in-tank fuel pump will not provide sufficient fuel for required horsepower plus cylinder cooling and anti-detonation needs, the easiest solution is often to install downstream auxiliary in-line fuel pump in series with the stock pump. With this setup, the stock pump supplies maximum fuel against what is essentially a zero head of pressure, while the auxiliary performance fuel pump boosts pressure to the fuel loop.

"Lightning" 90-degree fuel and nitrous solenoids from NX. Nitrous solenoids eventually wear out, but many are now designed to "fail safe," whereby flow stops if the seals begin leaking. Some experts recommend installing backup solenoids to positively stop nitrous flow if the primary solenoid valve fails, particularly if it is being pulsed to achieve progressive nitrous control. *Nitrous Express*

If lengthening injection pulse or increasing fuel pressure is not sufficient to provide enough supplemental fuel for the required nitrous horsepower boost, the primary electronic **injectors can be upgraded** to a larger size. Electronic injectors have been available for many years with mass flow ranging from about 15 to 152 pounds per hour at 43.5 psig or higher, but the latest side-armature designs provide flow rates of more than *300 lb/hr*! The impedance (resistance) of an upgrade injector must be within the range of the electronic controller's driver circuitry to avoid damaging the controller. In some cases it may be desirable or necessary to install **multiple *staged* electronic injectors per cylinder** to achieve the dynamic range needed to provide the maximum fuel flow while retaining the ability to inject a small enough amount of fuel within the minimum repeatable injector open time to idle well.

Yet another option to increase supplemental enrichment fuel is for a computer-controlled nitrous system to activate individual-cylinder continuous-injection fuel nozzles instead of—or in addition to—extending the primary fuel-injection pulsewidth during nitrous boost. In this case, pressurized fuel enters a manifold that distributes it into individual-cylinder hard lines or nylon hoses that are identical to what's used for distributing direct-port nitrous; from there the fuel passes into constant-injection delivery nozzles, which are often integral with high-pressure nitrous-injection nozzles that "fog" together liquid nitrous and fuel into a homogeneous mist. As is the case with continuous individual-cylinder nitrous, the fuel circuit must be equipped with one or more jets to meter the fuel, and fuel delivery must ultimately be synchronized with nitrous injection to produce safe, viable oxygen-fuel ratios.

Nitrous system controls. All nitrous systems must limit when nitrous boost may deploy and provide special engine

Nitrous purge kits "tee" an auxiliary nitrous solenoid off the main nitrous supply line upstream of the primary nitrous solenoid. A push button opens the solenoid to purge nitrous vapor from heat-soaked nitrous supply lines so that cool, dense nitrous liquid produces a harder "hit" when nitrous boost begins. *Edelbrock*

management when it does (which usually includes ignition retard, and virtually always includes fuel enrichment). Modern nitrous systems can be classified as **progressive**, **constant**, **multi-stage**, **standalone**, **tightly integrated**, **computer-controlled**, or **electrically controlled**, according to the methods used to manage when and for how long nitrous and enrichment fuel are allowed to flow into the engine. Computer-controlled dry nitrous systems in particular have the ability to deploy not only special timing and fuel delivery software algorithms during boost (including variable (progressive) nitrous and fuel delivery), but special hardware that provides additional robust protection against engine damage.

Sophisticated aftermarket engine management systems can monitor a fuel rail pressure sensor and immediately discontinue nitrous boost if fuel pressure drops below a target pressure. Alternately, the EMS can command a special variable power supply (Boost-a-Pump) to increase battery voltage to the fuel pump prior to nitrous boost or if fuel pressure has started to drop (fuel pump performance is directly related to battery voltage and current).

Many nitrous-capable engine management systems can monitor a knock sensor (essentially a crystal microphone sensitive to a particular frequency and intensity of vibration that correlates to the shock waves from spark knock on a particular type of engine) and protect the engine with immediate aggressive ignition retard or cessation of nitrous boost.

A sophisticated aftermarket EMS can synchronize nitrous boost with electronic turbocharger controls, for example, deploying nitrous injection (progressively, if necessary) to provide very rapid turbocharger spool-up, then phasing out nitrous injection as turbo boost ramps up. In the simplest case, nitrous boost activates at the threshold rpm and

Pressure-actuated solenoid from Combo-Flo. Instead of using a powerful electromagnet to hold open the solenoid against spring and nitrous pressure, a small electrical valve supplies gas pressure to open the main solenoid, thereby drastically reducing the electrical current draw on multi-stage nitrous systems that may have as many as 8 to 10 solenoids. *Combo-Flo*

throttle position and terminates at a configurable maximum manifold boost pressure. This is usually effective in providing greatly enhanced low-end torque and a smooth transition to high levels of air-supercharged boost, but progressive nitrous controls will phase in or remove nitrous boost more gradually using PWM progressive nitrous/fuel pulsing.

If an electronic engine management system is not fully nitrous-capable or if the nitrous system is not fully computer-controlled, it may be necessary or wise to supplement or implement control logic with external sensors or switches. For example, an adjustable boost pressure sensor that opens an electrical switch at, say, 3 to 5 psig intake manifold pressure can be used instead of or in addition to EMS manifold pressure logic to terminate nitrous boost. An oil-pressure switch (which is open below, say, 5 to 10 psi) could be wired in series with the nitrous arming switch to make sure nitrous injection is disabled if the engine stalls or is damaged in a crash. The logic would be opposite of the above boost switch, with power *disabled* through the gate if pressure drops below the threshold.

Anyone who is concerned about adverse consequences of nitrous leaking past the solenoid may want to install an ignition delay circuit, which prevents the engine from starting before it has sucked the intake manifold gases through the engine and sent them out the exhaust and has the additional benefit of creating plenty of positive oil pressure before the engine starts. The right way to do this is to install a timed counting switch that cuts off +12-volt battery power to the fuel injectors for a configurable amount of time so cylinder walls are not washed with gasoline while the engine cranks. The logic is: If [Time is Less Than X], then [Turn Off Coil Power], else [Leave Coil Power On].

The nitrous arming switch itself is a critical nitrous system control—usually a two-position toggle switch that provides critical permission when "on" to an electronic nitrous controller to enable nitrous injection (assuming the other prerequisites have been fulfilled) and locks out the nitrous solenoid relay circuit on all types of nitrous systems when disarmed. Some arming switches have a flip-up safety cover that prevents the switch from being turned on accidentally

This external pressurization system from NANO (nitrogen-assisted nitrous oxide) uses a small steel cylinder of 4,500-psi nitrogen or air regulated down to the 950-1100 psi range to normalize nitrous oxide tank pressure. The vast advantage of this system is that there can never be a pressure drop in the nitrous tank, nor is there any refrigeration effect from nitrous liquid boiling in the tank to maintain vapor pressure. An external pressurization system that is also climate controlled is currently the only method of ensuring a consistent mass outflow of liquid nitrous for eliminating horsepower drop in the course of a nitrous boost event. The downside is added cost. *NANO*

and automatically forces the switch into the off position when the cover is flipped shut. Some arming switches are toggled by a key switch, thereby providing a "valet" mode by which the system can be disarmed and the key removed to lock out the nitrous system.

Most nitrous systems are equipped with an **indicator light** that's on when the system is armed (some arming switches automatically illuminate the switch itself when on). Some systems are also equipped with a second light of a different color, wired in parallel with the nitrous solenoid, that glows when the nitrous solenoid is actually open and delivering boost. Many progressive nitrous controllers have a **sophisticated display** that provides a readout of the current duty cycle of the nitrous solenoid and estimated Time-Until-Empty for the nitrous tank and system. Many nitrous-capable engine management systems can control a check-engine-type indicator light or a small dash-mounted user interface with configurable data display. Virtually all nitrous-capable aftermarket engine management systems provide a very powerful user interface through a laptop computer that enables a tuner to change the behavior of the EMS in real time via tuning or configuration changes, to view engine and system sensor status, and to access other powerful functionality.

An alternative to nitrous-capable aftermarket engine management, particularly for carbureted drag cars, is the competition **nitrous controller**. This is a multiple-output combination ignition interceptor/retarder and sophisticated multi-stage (typically four to seven) controller of nitrous injection, enrichment fuel, and lean-out solenoids that provides nitrous and ignition delivery according to a configurable combination of rpm, speed, load, 1/1000th seconds timer, shift status, and so on. Nitrous controller architecture may be based on microprocessor technology or

Most nitrous bottle heaters are essentially small, thermostatically-controlled 240-400 watt electric blankets that wrap around the bottle and keep the contents warmed to 75-85 degrees during cold weather. Twelve-volt bottle heaters are generally not powerful enough to warm a cold bottle very quickly, and none are powerful enough to maintain temperature during significant nitrous boosting when the bottle is self-refrigerating. *NOS*

an electrical switching arrangement similar to the type of controls found on pre-electronic washing machines. Some nitrous controllers provide not only multi-stage coordinated switching of multiple outputs, but progressive solenoid pulsing with or without multi-stage nitrous and fuel triggering. The nitrous controller is a standalone black box that must be wired to the nitrous actuators (solenoids, additional injectors, ignition delay, and so on) and a set of dedicated engine and driver information sensors (throttle position, arming status, gear, line-lock solenoid position, clutch position, vehicle speed sensor, and so on and so on). Street nitrous controllers provide a subset of this functionality for modern street EFI engines using microprocessor technology.

OTHER DRY NITROUS ARCHITECTURES

When it comes to achieving very high streetable performance with excellent drivability and reliability, computer-controlled dry nitrous controlled by a nitrous-capable aftermarket EFI provides the ultimate in flexibility and power. But the drivability of factory EFI is generally unbeatable, and most people can't justify the expense, hassle, and legal issues of converting to nitrous-capable aftermarket EFI on a street vehicle. Fortunately, there are other dry nitrous options.

Piggyback-controlled dry nitrous. These days, there are some tremendously clever piggyback microcomputers designed to front-end the most sophisticated port-EFI and direct injection-gasoline factory engine management systems in order to extend the capabilities of the EMS so it can perform well with a power-adder conversion or significantly enhanced factory boost. The most advanced piggybacks install between the main EMS onboard computer multi-pin connector and the main wiring loom connector in order to

intercept and manipulate sensor and actuator signals in such a way as to create a bubble of false virtual reality (VR) around the stock EMS when turbocharger conversions or nitrous oxide injection power-adders are making boost. This keeps the EMS from freaking at unusual, out-of-range, or inconsistent engine sensor values related to manifold pressure, exhaust-gas oxygen, rate-of-speed increases, or other factors. Within the right VR bubble, the piggyback will not only keep the EMS working normally and thus prevent it from actively interfering with add-on nitrous boost and supplemental fuel activities managed exclusively by the piggyback, but can often trick the EMS into providing spark retard appropriate to nitrous boost and some or all of the required enrichment fuel.

In some cases, a piggyback is equipped with large, expensive connectors required to plug seamlessly into the main EMS multi-pin connector and wiring harness; in other cases the piggyback simply taps or splices into a subset of wires in the harness in one or two places, some of which typically must be cut so the piggyback has the possibility to completely block some signals and fabricate substitute data. During non-boosted conditions, a piggyback typically allows engine management to proceed as stock by passing through all signals to and from the EMS.

A nitrous-capable piggyback must monitor a variety of EMS input and output signals, and block, intercept, modify, or replace these as needed during boost to retard timing, inhibit full-authority closed-loop EMS, increase injection pulsewidth, and prevent check-engine codes and limp-mode EMS countermeasures. The piggyback must have supplemental circuitry to control add-on nitrous hardware (arming switch, nitrous solenoid, and so on) exactly like a nitrous-capable standalone aftermarket EMS. The most sophisticated modern piggybacks are capable of substituting

UPS AND DOWNS OF COMPUTER-CONTROLLED DRY NITROUS

Advantages
- No supplemental fuel hardware required (lowers cost, reduces complexity of installation)
- With tested and matched primary electronic injectors, eliminates fuel drop-out and puddling at high boost to deliver excellent fuel distribution
- Compatible with direct-port nitrous injection for excellent nitrous distribution
- Sophisticated programmable fuel enrichment strategies are integral to nitrous-capable EMS software, but user interface is relatively simple and straightforward.
- Sophisticated fail-safe controls easily implemented on basic system
- Many have built-in progressive nitrous capabilities.

Disadvantages
- A factory-stock EFI calibration is as good as it gets in most cases, and legal.
- Calibrating aftermarket EFI to factory standards is not trivial.
- Port fuel injectors may not have equal flow rates without testing, cleaning, and matching.
- Single-point nitrous injection may produce nitrous distribution problems and combined with perfect fuel distribution could produce dangerously lean mixtures in some cylinders.
- Primary EFI fuel supply system (injectors, pump, and so on) will require component upgrades for high nitrous power boost.
- Injector and fuel pressure upgrades may require primary fuel calibration changes.
- Aftermarket EMS is usually illegal for street use in the United States and might have difficulty passing emissions testing.

NITROUS SYSTEM ARCHITECTURE

This "pressure on demand" control system is designed to regulate a nitrous bottle heater based not on temperature but on nitrous bottle pressure. In equilibrium conditions, tank temperature and pressure are perfectly coordinated, but tank heaters cannot warm the entire tank or contents at once. Thermostatic controls thus have the problem that the heating is slowed as the system turns on and off and the temperature sensor is heated and cooled, while localized heating spreads throughout the tank. Pressure-based systems have the potential problem that the system will stay on until the tank heats to overpressure and the blow-out disk blows and vents the tank if you forget to open the bottle valve so the pressure sensor has access to tank temperature. *NOS*

plausible but false data to the EMS regarding crank position, wideband exhaust gas oxygen content (reliable indicator of air/fuel ratio), and more.

Sophisticated piggybacks are typically capable of retarding ignition timing during nitrous boost by delaying the coil-driver signal from the EMS or by introducing a delay in crank position sensor data. Assuming there is sufficient surplus fuel injector duty-cycle, piggybacks easily extend fuel injection pulsewidth (by keeping port injectors grounded after the EMS has released ground) to provide supplemental nitrous enrichment fuel. In the case of modern direct-injection gasoline engines (where fuel pressure and injection pulsewidth are under EMS control), piggybacks typically report falsely low fuel pressure from the rail fuel pressure sensor, causing the EMS to unknowingly drive up rail pressure to super-normal levels, thereby delivering supplemental nitrous enrichment fuel.

Obviously, piggyback-controlled dry nitrous systems encounter the same rpm-based limits to the time available for a longer fuel injection pulsewidth encountered by standalone computer-controlled dry nitrous systems, which is the ultimate constraint on the maximum horsepower (boost-derived or not) that the fuel system can deliver without upgrade EFI components. Fortunately, modern engine management systems commonly generate fuel-injection pulsewidth based on parameterized injector flow rate data loaded into working storage at startup from flash memory, allowing the flow rate to potentially be reconfigured with a few keystrokes on a user-interface laptop computer so the

EMS correctly fuels the engine during non-boosted operation with upgrade high-flow fuel injectors—a situation which then provides a nitrous-capable piggyback with more headroom to deliver larger amounts of supplemental enrichment fuel for power-adders like nitrous injection. Alternately, some piggybacks can intercept and shorten the injection pulse (ground) signal to correct basic fueling for upgrade injectors.

Like computer-controlled dry EFI, a nitrous-capable piggyback monitors the on/off position of a nitrous arming switch, and activates nitrous solenoid circuitry at a configurable minimum rpm and throttle position, exactly like a computer-controlled dry nitrous system. Like the nitrous-capable standalone EMS, a piggyback-controlled nitrous system may be designed to "listen" for threshold fuel pressure before triggering (or continuing!) nitrous injection— or a fuel pressure switch can be wired in series to defeat the arming circuit if fuel pressure drops below the threshold.

In general, piggyback EMS computers typically allow a tuner to specify global calibration changes to EMS injection pulsewidth and ignition timing as percentage offsets to the stock EMS calibration, with the piggyback deciding which lies to the main EMS and what outbound data tweaks are required to implement global changes. Piggyback-controlled dry nitrous is not particularly esoteric, given that engine management for street nitrous boost is very much an offset to ordinary engine management. You tell the piggyback what the nitrous shot is, and the piggyback monitors engine status, dynamically calculates the nitrous content of the charge, and from that, the required fuel and timing offsets to primary engine management. In general, the piggyback user interface also allows a tuner to tweak the base nitrous fuel and timing calculations globally or at specific combinations of rpm and engine airflow if that's what it takes to accommodate engine volumetric efficiency (VE) increases or decreases as a result of the opportunity cost or gain from the intercooling effect of boiling nitrous introduced into the induction system. Piggyback-controlled dry nitrous provides the ability to set boundary conditions for nitrous delivery, including low and high rpm thresholds.

As is the case with high-end nitrous-capable aftermarket engine management systems, the most sophisticated piggyback-controlled dry nitrous systems provide the ability to pulse a nitrous solenoid to provide progressive nitrous boost (simultaneously tweaking supplemental fuel delivery to match the duty cycle of pulsed nitrous injection).

Modern direct-injection (DI) gasoline systems now use ultra-high pressure **piezoelectric** electronic injectors that are conceptually similar to port injectors except that DI injectors spray a timed fuel pulse directly into the cylinders at hundreds of atmospheres absolute pressure instead of into the intake ports at 3 to 7 atmospheres absolute pressure.

Some piggyback systems are capable of pulsing **additional electronic fuel injectors** to deliver supplemental fuel enrichment during boost conditions.

As is the case with nitrous-capable aftermarket engine management systems, nitrous-capable piggybacks are able to trigger constant-flow direct-port fogger fuel- and nitrous-injection solenoids to deliver additional large nitrous boost that is independent of the maximum fuel delivery capacity of the primary electronic injectors. In most cases the direct-port system would be implemented as a second nitrous stage. A single fuel pump could provide the fuel supply to both the normal EFI fuel-injection loop and the supplemental continuous nitrous fuel enrichment system. The direct-port supplemental nitrous enrichment fuel circuit would normally have its own deadhead fuel pressure regulator located at the entrance to a direct-port fuel cul-de-sac hung off the main fuel loop. The direct-port regulator would be adjusted to drop fuel pressure below the lowest possible fuel pressure of the EFI loop in order to maintain constant fuel pressure to the direct-port nitrous system as the loop regulator varies primary fuel pressure to keep it at a fixed increment above manifold pressure.

Pressure-regulated dry nitrous. To keep the cost down, the most common dry nitrous systems are designed with controls that require neither an aftermarket EMS or a sophisticated piggyback. For a nitrous power boost that's 25 to 35 percent of the all-motor horsepower and not usually much more than 75 horsepower, standalone dry nitrous kits function more or less independently of the stock EFI engine management system.

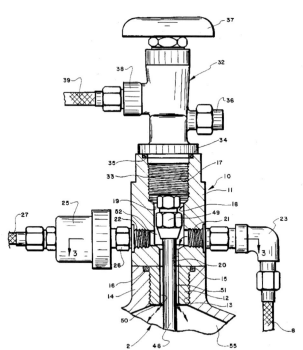

This drawing was featured in the 1985 Wheatley patent (US4494488) for the original externally-pressurized nitrous design. Instead of an ordinary bottle valve containing the main valve and blow-off disk, the system has additional ports that allow pressurized nitrogen to enter the nitrous tank. This type of system is normally equipped with a check valve that allows the nitrous tank to be removed for refill without venting nitrous through the pressurization port.

In the simplest pressure-regulated dry nitrous systems, the nitrous supply circuit hardware consists of a solenoid-controlled constant-flow setup that is a superset of the basic computer-controlled dry nitrous architecture. In this case, however, the nitrous solenoid is controlled not by a nitrous-capable aftermarket EMS but by an interesting standalone electro-mechanical circuit that triggers nitrous delivery and fuel enrichment using four switches and a small secondary nitrous solenoid. The system begins the boost sequence when an add-on micro-switch (or a programmable switch triggered by data from the throttle position sensor) completes a circuit indicating the engine is at or near full throttle.

Some pressure-regulated dry nitrous systems deliver **supplemental enrichment fuel** using what amounts to an electro-pneumatic auxiliary fuel pressure regulator located downstream of the primary EFI fuel pressure regulator in the main fuel loop. Either regulator is capable of throttling the return flow of fuel to the fuel tank to increase pressure delivered by the electric fuel pump. Under non-boosted conditions, the secondary fuel pressure regulator is inactive, passing through all return fuel flow, but during nitrous boost it comes into play to increase fuel pressure to super-normal levels, at which point the primary regulator is not the critical bottleneck and thus has no effect on fuel pressure. In other cases, the stock fuel regulator increases fuel delivery when conditioned nitrous pressure is fed to the reference port. Rather than being referenced to manifold pressure like the primary regulator, during boost the secondary regulator diaphragm is temporarily referenced to *nitrous* pressure by way of a small dedicated electrical solenoid valve hung off the nitrous supply line upstream of the main nitrous supply solenoid. When this control solenoid opens, it delivers nitrous tank pressure through an auxiliary nitrous pressure regulator against the stock fuel pressure regulator diaphragm, at which point the regulator begins to increase fuel rail pressure. The moment the EFI fuel rail pressure begins to rise, the electronic injectors begin to deliver additional fuel per injector squirt. When fuel pressure rises to a threshold level, a pressure switch activates the secondary nitrous solenoid and boost begins. The moment the driver releases the throttle, the throttle switch opens, the control solenoid closes, the secondary fuel pressure regulator stops throttling the fuel return rate, and fuel pressure control returns to the primary EFI fuel pressure regulator.

Like any port-EFI system, this type of fuel enrichment provides excellent, precise fuel *distribution* under all conditions through the primary electronic port injectors. Unfortunately, the system has some intrinsic flaws. It provides relatively crude supplemental enrichment fueling *that is constant only in the most approximate sense*: Supplemental nitrous enrichment fuel ends up as a function not only of rail pressure but of stock fuel injection pulsewidth, which varies according to the full-throttle volumetric efficiency curve of the stock, non-boosted engine. This will probably not translate perfectly to a rate of nitrous injection that is constant under all conditions—meaning the nitrous-fuel ratio will usually not remain constant as the engine accelerates. Meanwhile, the relatively low pressure ceiling on electronic injector operability (usually not much more than 70 to 90 psig max) means that pressure-based fuel enrichment offers only a modest amount of headroom to deliver supplemental power boost using fuel delivered through the stock electronic injectors. For example, raising fuel pressure from 40 to 75 psi through an injector that was originally capable of 50 lb/min occurs as follows:

New flow = square root of (new pressure/old pressure) × old flow

$$= \text{SQR } (75/40) \times 50 \text{ lb/min}$$
$$= 68.47 \text{ lb/min}$$

The new flow rate, 68.47, is roughly 137 percent of the original 50 lb/min rate. Some of the fuel will probably be needed for combustion chamber cooling to fight detonation, but you could certainly figure that this method of providing supplemental fuel would, in this case, support at least 25 to 30 percent more horsepower.

Another way to look at the power potential of a pressure-regulated dry nitrous system begins with the observation that constant nitrous boost will be a percentage of the maximum horsepower capacity of the stock fuel-injection system. Consider that a 40 horsepower boost on a 200-horse engine represents 20 percent additional horsepower, meaning that fuel flow through the injectors must increase by at least 20 percent during nitrous operations. Again, it's actually more, due to the need for fuel combustion cooling on a nitrous powerplant, but let's keep it simple for now. If the engine makes 200 stock horsepower, the stock fuel pressure is 39 psi, and nitrous boost is 40 horsepower, then the new fuel pressure required through the stock injectors to fuel the boost will be:

New pressure (psi) = old pressure × (old power + power boost)/old power)²

$$= 39 \times ((200 + 40)/200)^2$$
$$= 56.16 \text{ psi}$$

By raising fuel pressure from 39 to a little more than 56 psi, the injectors will squirt out enough additional fuel for a 40-horse nitrous power boost. Now, let's assume you need at least 10 percent additional supplemental fuel for combustion cooling, increasing the effective fuel enrichment requirement from 40 horsepower worth of fuel to, say, 45 horsepower worth:

New pressure (psi) = (old pressure × (old power + power boost)/old power)²)

$$= (39 \times ((200 + 45)/200)^2)$$
$$= 58.52 \text{ psi}$$

Inline Walbro centrifugal port-EFI-pressure fuel pump from MSD. Approximate fuel pump flow is 43 gph (282 lb/hr) gasoline (specific gravity 0.788) at 40 psi and 12 volts/5.4 amps. The pump has a 3/8-inch hose nipple inlet, and a 5/16-in. hose nipple outlet. The package includes two cushioned mounting clamps and 4 mounting bolts. This type of add-on pump is commonly found boosting the capacity of intank pumps to provide enough fuel for significant power-adder installations. Two pumps in series are much more capable than one, allowing the intank pump to pump provide maximum flow against zero head of pressure, and the MSD Walbro pump to boost the pressure. *MSD*

In this case, a 20 percent power boost requires about 59 psi fuel pressure to meet boost fuel requirements.

Most dry nitrous kits arrive with a factory-calibrated VRG regulator and nitrous jetting designed to achieve *very* conservative oxygen-fuel ratios, which is why the Sport-Compact hot rod that screams massively by you on the freeway is probably blowing massive black smoke out the exhaust: The nitrous system is configured to run *very rich*.

Meanwhile, pressure-regulated dry nitrous systems need nitrous. And the way nitrous triggers is also interesting. As always, in order to activate nitrous boost, the nitrous bottle valve must be open and the nitrous arming switch set to "On." Arming the nitrous system sends +12-volt current to a full-throttle switch which is open at lower throttle settings. At or near full throttle, the switch closes. But a TPS-actuated trigger switch or simple full-throttle micro-switch cannot handle the 5 to 30 amps of current typically required to energize one or more high-pressure nitrous solenoids, so the full-throttle switch instead completes a low-current circuit that energizes a high-current relay. The relay, in turn, energizes an *auxiliary nitrous control solenoid* that delivers nitrous pressure through a mini nitrous regulator as to the diaphragm of the secondary (VRG) fuel pressure regulator as discussed above. Fuel pressure ramps up very quickly, which immediately begins to enrich the air-fuel mixture by increasing the amount of fuel that is injected into a cylinder for a given length injection pulse. When fuel pressure achieves a threshold pressure (50 psig is common), a pressure switch in the fuel rail closes, energizing a second relay that opens the main nitrous solenoid, allowing nitrous oxide to rush into the engine. Nitrous oxide and supplemental fuel arrive in the cylinders and the horsepower boost begins. The engine has Super Powers.

Most pressure-regulated dry nitrous kits are low-boost systems designed to work on vehicles where engine

MSD Digital SCI Plus ignition delivers high output capacitive discharge (CD) sparks for more complete fuel mixture combustion, especially at high rpm. It features a retard stage to handle nitrous to ensure you don't get detonation from increased cylinder pressure, and a rev limiter that assists with firm launches. The 15 MHz micro-controller is the fastest of all digital ignitions, and provides a smooth rev limit and precision timing. Rotary dials make adjusting the launch limit and retard amount simple and easy. The SCI Plus is designed to install easily on most 4, 6, or 8-cylinder engines with a distributor. *MSD*

management systems use closed loop feedback fuel control strategies only at idle or light cruise (an increasing number of late-model factory engine management computers are equipped with full-authority control strategies designed to trim air-fuel ratios all the way to full-throttle—*not* a good thing if nitrous is installed). The most basic nitrous systems are designed for installation on early EFI powerplants where static ignition timing can be manually recalibrated by re-clocking the distributor in order to eliminate detonation during nitrous boost. Mildly retarded static ignition timing is effective as a full-throttle anti-detonation countermeasure on mildly boosted nitrous engines during boost, although retarded timing will reduce engine efficiency and power during non-boosted conditions.

A better option is to install (in series with the main arming switch) a simple programmable **boost-retard interceptor**, some of which are also equipped with an **rpm window switch** that disarms nitrous boost if engine speed is too high or too low for safe nitrous operation. The typical boost-retard system is packaged in a small standalone metal or plastic box and equipped with several electrical connections for power, ground, ignition signal in, ignition signal out, and, optionally, arm-in and arm-out. One type of boost-retard circuit requires cutting the EMS coil-driver wire and connecting both ends to the boost retard box in order that the coil-driver signal can be intercepted and retransmitted after a delay calculated according to a speed-density timing offset curve defined by three or more swappable variable resisters or a user-defined digital data table stored in non-volitile memory.

Another type of boost retard box does its work by introducing a delay in the crankshaft position signal (which, therefore, delays spark timing as well as the timing of variable cam and sequential fuel-injection subsystems, which may or may not matter during nitrous boost). An rpm window switch—whether or not bundled into a boost retard system—monitors the frequency of the coil-driver or crank position signal to determine engine rpm, flip-flopping a secondary nitrous arming switch according to the values in two user-selectable resisters that install like bus fuses to define the upper and lower rpm limits of permissible boost. The input and output RPM window connections are then wired in series with the main nitrous arming switch.

Standalone pressure-regulated dry nitrous is, obviously, not applicable to carbureted engines, which require a direct-port or wet nitrous system.

WET NITROUS SYSTEMS

If an intake manifold is specifically designed to handle the disparate fluid dynamics of a "wet" charge mixture consisting of both fuel and air (as it must be on a powerplant equipped with a single carburetor or throttle body injection), injecting nitrous oxide at a central location near the throttle inherently permits injecting liquid enrichment fuel at the same place, allowing the architecture to be described as a "wet" nitrous system. Wet nitrous architectures can often be made to work acceptably well on some engines with dry, multi-port EFI manifolds if the horsepower boost is not too large.

Wet nitrous systems add a standalone fuel-delivery-and-injection system to the simplicity of the nitrous-only auxiliary delivery hardware found on a computer-controlled dry nitrous system. Unlike a computer-controlled boosting system, where all nitrous subsystems are under the control of an aftermarket engine management system, wet nitrous systems require auxiliary add-on switching/control systems to trigger both nitrous and supplemental fuel injection. The triggering circuit straightforwardly opens two solenoid valves. One solenoid releases nitrous into the engine through an injection device at a central point near the throttle plate. The other delivers supplemental fuel straight from the main fuel supply system to a continuous-injection device in the immediate vicinity of nitrous injection. Precisely modulated fuel pressure is critical to the proper functioning of a continuous-flow fuel injector on a wet nitrous system, since many wet systems run only a few pounds of fuel pressure, and pressure is one of the two important variables that determine how much fuel is injected per time (the area of the metering orifice is the other; temperature-based *fuel* density changes are less important and generally not practical to control).

There are a number of ways of supplying pressure-conditioned fuel to a wet nitrous system. The simplest is to tap into the primary fuel circuit upstream of the carburetor and its deadhead regulator (if so equipped) or, on a fuel injected engine with return fuel loop, upstream of the EFI pressure regulator. Under all circumstances the nitrous fuel subsystem should have its own independent fuel pressure regulator.

If it's an EFI engine with a fuel loop, a pinch-type pressure regulator, and a fuel-tank return line, you'll need to run either a completely independent fuel supply system (pump, regulator, and plumbing) or fuel tapped from the main EFI fuel loop that's conditioned through an auxiliary "deadhead" inline fuel pressure regulator on the way to the constant injection nitrous fuel subsystem. The purpose of the additional regulator is to eliminate intentional pressure variations introduced by the EFI regulator to maintain rail pressure a fixed amount above intake manifold pressure, though 900 psi nitrous injection pressure is minimally impacted by manifold pressure. Most multi-port EFI systems run 30- to 50-psi fuel pressure, while most throttle body injection systems run about 15 psi.

Carbureted engines often run very low fuel pressure in the 3- to 15-psi range. They are not typically equipped with a EFI-type fuel loop, but there are some good reasons to consider *installing* a fuel loop that returns unused fuel to the tank, high pressure (30 to 100 psi) electric fuel pump and a pinch-type regulator. With a loop fuel system installed, you can then feed the carb by regulating down pressure with a secondary deadhead regulator tapped into the fuel loop (the regulator need not be referenced to manifold pressure in this application as it would be on a port-EFI engine). High-pressure fuel systems have the advantage that any unintended variations in fuel pressure represent a much smaller percentage of 40 psi than 4 psi. Fuel loops with pinch regulators are also much easier on centrifugal fuel pumps than deadhead systems with regulators, which may need to choke off the fuel supply totally at times to limit pressure. An alternative is to retain the stock carbureted fuel supply, and fabricate a totally independent fuel supply system for the nitrous boosting system.

Wet nitrous systems inject enrichment fuel through a nozzle, spraybar, or plate fixture near the throttle body, with one or more jets of high-pressure nitrous aimed directly at the fuel enrichment spray to enhance mixing and atomization. As is the case with dry nitrous injection, central-point of nitrous oxide injection is theoretically compatible with injecting the supplemental enrichment fuel farther downstream in the individual intake runners, but no one's going to do this because the availability of integrated nitrous-fuel fogger nozzles means that the machine work required to install direct-port constant fuel injection automatically allows for the possibility of direct port *nitrous* injection.

Ironically, if you can overcome wet-system fuel distribution problems, some experts have claimed that the increased distance from the point of injection to the cylinders on single-point nitrous architectures tends to *improve* air-fuel-nitrous charge *mixing,* resulting in more homogeneous combustion mixtures within a particular cylinder, and thus superior *power*. Other credible experts report that careful testing demonstrates that if the oxygen-fuel masses arrive at individual cylinders in the correct ratio, improved mixing makes no practical real-world difference.

Some central-point nitrous systems inject nitrous and fuel (or just nitrous) from a single **nozzle** drilled into the intake tract just *upstream* of the throttle body or carburetor, or even *inside* the air cleaner, a morphology that makes it fairly easy to hide the nitrous system. It is also fairly common to introduce nitrous and fuel—or, again, just nitrous—using a constant injection system built into a **spacer-plate** that bolts between the intake manifold and the carb or throttle body.

Plate systems need not be central-point. Nitrous systems for multi-port EFI engines sometimes inject nitrous and fuel from a spacer plate that bolts *between the upper and lower intake manifold sections* on engines with two-piece intake manifolds (Ford's 5.0-liter pushrod V-8, for example), resulting in an individual-port nitrous plate system with guaranteed excellent distribution. On in-line engines, a plate can sometimes be installed between the intake manifold and cylinder head if heat soak can be controlled. It's not normally feasible to install spacer plates between the intake manifold and cylinder heads on a V engine because anything thicker than a head gasket alters the geometry of the head-manifold interface in such a way that the manifold no longer fits the block. Obviously, there *must* be an injection orifice for each intake runner in this type of plate system.

Traditional central-point **spray bar** throttle-injection—a subcategory of plate nitrous system that was ubiquitous on performance 4-barrel carbureted V-8 engines of the past—is still commonly available for specific carbureted or throttle body-injected V-8s and V-6s, or in "universal" guise drilled

MSD Ignition Retard Module Selector allows you to select from 12 retard amounts by turning a dial, and the purpose is to modify spark timing during nitrous or turbo boost for optimal power or to eliminate detonation. The selector plugs into the retard module receptacle of any MSD Timing Control. *MSD*

to fit several common 4-barrel carburetors. Spray bar systems deliver nitrous boost using an under-carb spacer plate transected by tandem over-under perforated metal tubes centered in the dead air between the primary throttles of the carb in such a way that the negative aerodynamic effect on engine volumetric efficiency is minimal or nil. Each of the spray bars (there's at least one for nitrous, one for fuel, sometimes more) is drilled with multiple tiny orifices in proven locations to meter and aim fluid into the high-speed airflow roaring past the throttles in such a way as to mix the nitrous and supplemental fuel and and achieve acceptably equal nitrous and fuel distribution among the various cylinders (which can be a cute trick to get right).

In most cases, spray bar systems are designed with swappable restrictor orifices (jets) at the entrance to the nitrous and fuel spray bars that can be changed to allow some adjustment in the level of horsepower boost or air-fuel ratio. As the name implies, restrictor jets can really only de-rate or *subtract* horsepower from the basic, unrestricted flow capacity of the spray bar, and this can only be done to a certain extent (75-, 100-, and 125-horse jets are common options on mild street spray bar systems) without inducing a large pressure drop upstream of the actual injector orifices that causes nitrous oxide to boil excessively with possible bogging, surging, and reduced performance.

The nitrous spray bar should *always* be positioned slightly upstream of the fuel spray bar to make sure that nitrous oxide will never arrive at any cylinder ahead of enrichment fuel and damage pistons or valves with lean, overheated combustion. In fact, it is mandatory on *every* type of nitrous architecture that enrichment fuel must *never* be introduced upstream of nitrous injection unless the onset of nitrous and enrichment fuel injection can be precisely synchronized using a time-delay for nitrous start up. Accepted nitrous spray bar doctrine is that performance is improved by aiming ultra-high-pressure nitrous spray directly at the fuel spray orifices so that high-velocity 900-psi nitrous blasts apart fuel droplets to enhance atomization and promote improved nitrous-fuel mixing.

Ideally, nitrous and fuel spray bar design should be optimized not just for a specific engine architecture, but for the specific intake manifold installed on a particular individual engine. You do this by testing and calibrating the boosted powerplant on an engine dynamometer equipped with individual-cylinder exhaust gas temperature (EGT) probes that permit accurate calibration of spray bar orifice geometry and size to optimize nitrous and fuel balance and equalize distribution at the individual-cylinder level. More than a few generic ("universal") spray bar systems have been sold and successfully adapted to a variety of engines, but it is likely that many powerplants with do-it-yourself (DIY) or universal nitrous spray bar systems are making suboptimal power because they are operating with an unholy combination of rich cylinders, where excessive fuel is washing cylinder walls and accelerating wear, and leaner cylinders that are running significantly hotter.

Unless you know what you are doing and have extended access to a dyno and individual-cylinder test equipment, the rich-lean situation is a great argument for buying a kit from a vendor who has thoroughly optimized it for your engine and then following nitrous-vendor recommendations *exactly* with respect to permissible induction modifications. If the individual-cylinder air-fuel ratio is questionable on a particular engine, it is critical to prevent detonation and overheating by making sure the overall *global nitrous flow* through the nitrous spray bar is carefully matched to *global enrichment fuel flow* through the fuel spray bar to the extent that the leanest cylinder runs adequately rich—typically a function of total orifice area in the spray bars as well as swappable upstream metering jets on many systems. As you'd expect, commercial street spray bar nitrous kits out of the box run on the rich side, but jets are easy to change. It is surprising how many people fail to respect the importance of fuel cooling until they torch a few exhaust valves or even melt a piston or two.

Where peak power and reliability are critical, really high-performance competition nitrous engines have traditionally run port nitrous systems. The best of these have nitrous and enrichment fuel *calibrated at the individual-cylinder level* to optimize torque at each of the 4-, 6-, 8-, or more "single-cylinder engines." Eventually, racers with direct-port nitrous systems began running so hard in competition that some race sanctioning bodies decided to outlaw port systems in a vain effort to restore class equilibrium by slowing down

NOS Digi-Set Time Delay Relay Switch allows you to activate a second or third stage of nitrous (or other electronic device) as a function of time. Delay is easily set from 1/10th of a second to almost two minutes, in 0.1 second increments, by setting the small dip switches on the timer. Available with DIP switch settings. *NOS* the fastest spray-cars. Not gonna happen: nitrous vendors simply developed and marketed a new generation of central-point **plate** designs that upped the ante for wet nitrous from classic spray bar designs that generally maxed out in the 100- to 250-horse range to new designs capable of delivering more than 600 horsepower that ran every bit as well as direct-port systems of similar power. Nitrous system designers accomplished this by improving distribution, injection quality, and engine volumetric efficiency with tricks like (1) fogging nitrous oxide and fuel into an intake manifold plenum using **annular-discharge** orifices drilled around the entire perimeter of an open-chamber plate, (2) conical **diffuser-plate** injector units centered in the downstream side of a 4-bore spacer plate matching the venturi bores of a 4-barrel carburetor, (3) **crisscrossed or outboard dual spray bars** with as many as 88 orifices, (4) a combination of the above, or (5) other innovative arrangements. Even where direct-port systems are legal, some high-end Pro-Mod drag racers have moved to diffuser-plate arrangements as the primary stage of multi-stage mega nitrous systems on super-high-output draggers.

Nozzle systems. Wet nitrous systems on some 4- and 6-cylinder powerplants very often inject fuel and nitrous from a single fogger nozzle installed upstream of the throttle body. There are several classes of nozzle design, but it is fair to say that compared to the complex multi-orifice wet plate systems found on super-high-output competition engines with highly developed wet intake manifolds, single-nozzle systems that blast nitrous and fuel into the airstream from one fogger-type nozzle are more suited to providing mild nitrous boost.

INDIVIDUAL-PORT NITROUS SYSTEMS

Any decision to inject nitrous into the individual intake runners usually *mandates* that supplemental fuel must *also* be injected in the individual runners *downstream* of the nitrous-injection point, to prevent any possibility of nitrous arriving in cylinders too soon and transiently producing dangerous lean combustion. Single-point nitrous injection can be successfully combined with port-injected enrichment fuel as it is on many inexpensive dry nitrous systems that introduce supplemental fuel through the primary electronic injectors, but the reverse would be very problematic, with no technical advantages compared to the alternatives.

Most **direct-port nitrous systems** now deliver supplemental fuel through integrated constant-flow nitrous and fuel delivery nozzles installed in the individual runners near the intake valve that blast a concentrated "fog" of liquid horsepower into the air stream. Fuel and nitrous flow through separate distribution networks of individual hard pipes or nylon hoses that transport the fluids to individual ports where nitrous and fuel finally come together immediately at the point of injection. Constant-flow direct-port nitrous

RPM-Activated Switches can perform a variety of different functions, from turning on a bulb or solenoid to activating an ignition timing control at a desired rpm. Rpm-activated switches normally have two activation wires, one of which can ground a circuit, the other that can open a circuit. Simply plug in an rpm module and wire the switch to the circuit you want to activate. MSD's 8956 RPM Window Activation Switch has two rpm adjustments. The first activates a circuit, while the other deactivates the same circuit, by supplying, then removing ground to a circuit. This is a great feature to activate nitrous above a threshold detonation rpm and then deactivate nitrous before the engine hits the rev-limiter under nitrous boost, which can be disastrous. *MSD*

systems are essentially identical to wet nitrous systems with the exception of the more complex individual-cylinder distribution plumbing downstream of the solenoids.

It is not unheard of for individual-cylinder enrichment fuel to be injected with **pulsed direct-port injection** via add-on auxiliary electronic fuel injectors managed by a programmable additional-injector controller or a standalone nitrous controller. Like dry nitrous systems, all direct-port nitrous systems keep liquid fuel out of the common-plenum section of the intake manifold. The advantage of pulsed fuel delivery from EFI injectors is that it potentially allows sophisticated supplemental fuel delivery to be trimmed very accurately across the rpm range of the engine to provide additional fuel-cooling in problem areas.

HIDDEN NITROUS SYSTEMS

There are two major categories of hidden nitrous systems. The first is a stealth system used in street situations, where the required power advantage to kick ass and take names might be in the range of 75 to 100 horsepower. As is the case when the nitrous system is not hidden, this type of power boost requires a fairly large nitrous storage bottle, with a large solenoid, and a substantial nitrous supply line. Such a system is difficult to hide completely, and would never pass muster in a sanctioned racing environment. That said, there's no such thing as a teardown tech inspection in a street-race environment, so a stealth system that is not absolutely hidden but simply not obvious may do the job. The other type of hidden nitrous system is used in serious competition on a race track where 15, 20, or 30 horsepower can make all the difference in close competition to win a race or deliver an unusually fast qualifying lap. This type of miniature nitrous system is much easier to conceal, although designing a system that will not be found in a teardown is, obviously, extremely difficult.

As discussed previously, direct-port nitrous nozzles and plumbing can often be hidden underneath the intake manifold of a V-8 engine between the manifold and block, with fuel and nitrous injected through the floor of individual intake runners. Such a system is not detectable without a teardown, but, of course, it will be found immediately if there is a teardown. NOS sells a nitrous system that is hidden within the air cleaner of a carbureted V-8. Either still leaves the question of how to hide the other components of the system, the tank in particular. Without getting further into specifically *why* you might want to conceal the existence of a nitrous system (to cheat in some type of competition or money racing, of course), the following are some tactics that have been used in the past to make it difficult or impossible to determine whether a vehicle is boosted with nitrous. Keep in mind that hiding the hardware will not conceal the sudden surge of power from a nitrous-boosted powerplant, nor will it conceal the second or two of black exhaust smoke that usually results when a heat-soaked nitrous system is not purged before boosting (though people have designed purge systems that emit no tell-tale plume of freezing nitrous vapor).

- Install direct-port nitrous nozzles, distribution plumbing, or even solenoids underneath the intake manifold of a V-8.
- "Fire extinguisher" is a nitrous bottle.
- Nitrous tank hidden in the spare tire
- Nitrous tank hidden inside the fuel tank
- Nitrous tank hidden inside a pneumatic air tank
- Nitrous tank hidden in the dry sump oil tank
- Nitrous bottle hidden in a gym bag or backpack
- Nitrous tank hidden in a hollow battery, with supply line through a battery "cable"
- Nitrous purge plumbed into the exhaust system
- Nitrous purge injected into the intake manifold (during idle or deceleration)
- Nitrous hidden in the center console or inside dash behind false floor or bulkhead
- Roll cage tubing conceals a liquid nitrous reservoir.
- Nitrous tank with quick-connectors concealed in the driver's pants.
- Tiny nitrous bottle hidden beneath a false bulkhead in the trunk or other location in the unibody, in a fender well,

underneath the driveshaft hump, underneath a seat or behind rear seat, etc.
- Nitrous container and solenoid concealed in a false wall in a hood scoop in a composite hood, with the wiring circuit for the nitrous running through two Dzus fasteners (nitrous blast enters the carb mouth but also produces mild pressurization of the float chamber and, therefore, fuel enrichment)
- Nitrous supply line runs inside a fuel line.
- Nitrous supply line is hidden inside a coolant hose to the intake manifold.
- Nitrous enters a modified carburetor through a previously unused float chamber fuel inlet to be dumped into the airstream below the throttles, with nitrous pressure providing enrichment fuel by pushing open an auxiliary power valve.
- Nitrous plumbed through the bellhousing and through the bulkhead at the rear of the block
- Nitrous components other than the tank are obvious; driver shows unattached nitrous "hose connections" and empty nitrous tank bracket, claims vehicle set up for nitrous but currently de-installed; there is a hidden tank.
- Nitrous nozzle in the front bumper points toward the air cleaner inlet for very small nitrous boost
- Nitrous enters engine through a false EGR valve.
- Nitrous is armed using the still-functioning rear-window defroster switch.

The Magnum X dual-stage nitrous system was originally designed to provide the highest horsepower capability of any spray plate system. A unique two-stage cross bar design incorporated in a 1-inch plate provides ultra-high volumes with improved fuel distribution from discharge clusters positioned for delivery to all corners of the plenum. An adjustable fuel supply and heavy duty engine components are necessary with this type of radical plate system. Power levels are adjustable in pairs from 150/300, 150/375, 200/400, 200/475, 250/500 to 300/550, with the second number referring to the total horsepower when both stages are engaged. *Nitrous Works*

Chapter 5
Installing Nitrous Oxide Injection

When implementing a massive nitrous power boost, it is important to start with the right engine platform because you are eating into the existing margin of safety, and, in the long run, almost certainly reducing the life of the engine. No vehicle manufacturer builds a factory nitrous engine (there have been warranted new vehicles with nitrous provided by tuners like Saleen), but many engine manufacturers have developed *turbocharged* and normal-charged versions of the same basic engine. It can be highly enlightening to peek under the skirts and see the hidden differences, because whatever thermal

and mechanical margin of error exists in the normal-charged version of the engine *cannot* be maintained in the turbo version without upgrading parts directly impacted by the increased mechanical and thermal loading. What's more, when it's a turbo engine there's always the possibility of *overboost* intentionally or unintentionally increasing power due to something as innocuous as a failed or disconnected vacuum hose. Factory engineers always design turbo engines to survive not only the intended maximum boost, but a certain amount of overboost, so *they always engineer factory turbo engines with super-duty parts not*

THE DOS AND DON'TS OF NITROUS OXIDE FROM NOS

Do . . .
- Make sure your fuel delivery system is adequate for the nitrous jetting you have chosen. Inadequate fuel pressure or flow will result in engine damage.
- Use 14-gauge (minimum) wire when installing electrical system components.
- Use high-quality connections at all electrical joints.
- Use Teflon-based paste on all NPT fittings.
- Make sure your engine and related components are in good working condition.
- Remove the engine coil wire or otherwise disable the ignition, open the throttle, and crank the engine 10 to 15 seconds before starting if nitrous is accidentally injected into the engine when it is not running. Failure to do so can result in an explosive engine failure.
- Make sure the nitrous system only triggers at wide-open throttle and at engine speeds above 2,500 to 3,000 rpm.
- Install a proper engine-to-chassis ground. Failure to do so may result in an explosive failure of the main nitrous supply line.
- Use a high-quality, high-octane gasoline unless special fuel system components are installed to handle alcohol fuels.

Don't . . .
- Engage your nitrous system with the engine off. Severe engine damage can occur.
- Overtighten AN-type fittings.
- Use Teflon tape on any pipe threads. Pieces of Teflon tape can break loose and become lodged in nitrous or fuel solenoids, solenoid filters, or jets. Debris lodged in a nitrous or fuel solenoid can cause catastrophic engine failure.
- Use sealant of any kind on AN-type fittings.
- Allow nitrous pressure to exceed 1,100 psi. Excessive pressure can cause swelling or in extreme cases failure of the nitrous solenoid plunger (solenoid plungers are designed so that pressure-induced

failures will prevent the valve from operating, but no leakage should occur with this type of failure).
- Inhale nitrous oxide. Death due to suffocation can occur.
- Allow nitrous oxide to come in contact with skin. Severe frostbite can occur.
- Use octane boosters that contain methanol. Fuel solenoid failure may occur, producing severe engine damage.

Beware . . .
- Do not attempt to start the engine if nitrous has been injected while the engine was not running. Disconnect the coil wire and turn the engine over with the throttle wide open for several revolutions before attempting to start. Failure to do so can result in extreme engine damage.
- Never permit oil, grease, or any other readily combustible substances to come in contact with cylinders, valves, solenoids, hoses, and fittings. Oil and certain gases (such as oxygen and nitrous oxide) may combine to produce a flammable condition.
- Never interchange nitrous and fuel solenoids. Failure to follow these simple instructions can result in extreme engine damage or personal injury.
- Never drop or violently strike the bottle. Doing so may result in an explosive bottle failure.
- Never change the pressure settings of the safety relief valve on the nitrous bottle valve. Increasing the safety relief valve pressure settings may create an explosive bottle hazard.
- Nitrous bottle valves should always be closed when the system is not being used.
- Notify the supplier of any condition that might have permitted any foreign matter to enter the valve or bottle.
- Keep the valves closed on all empty bottles to prevent accidental contamination.
- After storage, open the nitrous bottle valve for an instant to clear the opening of any possible dust or dirt.
- It is important that all threads on the valves and solenoids are properly mated. Never force connections that do not fit properly.

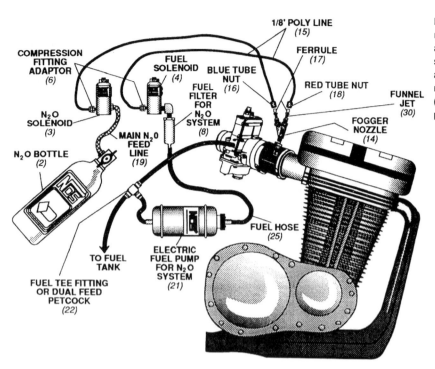

Fogger-type nitrous systems are now very common on motorcycles, but the system is similar or identical to automotive nitrous system, with the exception of the small bottle size, the smaller metering jet(s) (usually!), and the requirement for an auxiliary fuel pump in most cases when the bike fuel system is gravity-fed (though kits *have* been designed for gravity-fuel fuel pressure). *NOS*

It is wise to start with good raw material when building a nitrous powerplant, and modern factory-turbo engines like this Solstice turbo Ecotec almost always have super-duty parts you'll want for running moderate-to-extreme amounts of nitrous boost: forged pistons and rods, steel crank, 4- or 6-bolt mains, and good head gaskets. In many cases modern direct-injection gasoline engines can be manipulated into providing enrichment fuel through the stock direct injectors via increased system fuel pressure under factory computer control. *GM*

Engine Health. A nitrous kit will only magnify symptoms of a sick or worn engine. The engine you start with should not only be running but in very good health, lest the stresses of nitrous boost bring its swift downfall.

These days, with extremely good motor oils, port fuel injection under computer control, and unleaded fuel, engines can last an extremely long time without significant wear. Nevertheless, if a candidate engine for a nitrous conversion has more than 30,000 miles, you should verify the health of all internal engine systems, including cylinder head and valves, pistons and rings, cylinder bores, and the crankshaft assembly. Good health means excellent compression that's close to the ideal specification, and it means cylinder leakdown that's less than 6 percent. Anything less than 10 percent leakdown is usually considered acceptable on a factory engine, but not so for a turbo conversion or or nitrous installation.

Since an engine can have decent compression but poor leakdown, you need to test both. Both tests involve installing special gauged fittings in the spark plug holes; the compression test measures accumulated pressure as the engine cranks with the ignition disconnected, while the leakdown test involves sequentially moving each piston to top dead center on the compression stroke, and adding compressed air while observing two gauges that display the difference between the source pressure and pressure in the cylinder after any leaking effects are factored in. Any competent hobbyist can perform compression and leakdown tests, and many repair shops will perform such tests for a reasonable price (usually in the $50 to $100 range).

If you're worried about internal engine wear, there are special labs that can analyze motor oil for unusual amounts

found in the normal-charged version of the engine, more so the heavier the vehicle—forged pistons, stronger rods, moly rings, improved head gaskets, engine oil coolers, and so on.

BEFORE THE INSTALLATION . . .

Before proceeding with a nitrous installation, it is critical to evaluate the engine and vehicle platform from all points of view.

Aluminum rapidly loses strength as it is heated, which is why this Solstice Turbo piston is cooled from the underside with oil-squirting jets fed directly from the main block oil gallery.

	Upgraded Ignition	Premium Fuel	Race Fuel	Colder Plugs	Reduced Plug Gap	Fuel System Upgrade	Dedicated Fuel Pump	Open Plenum Intake	Forged Pistons**	Aftermarket Con Rods	Forged or Billet Crank***	Ignition Retard
SNIPER	○	●	○	○	○	◐	○	○	○	○	○	●
TOP SHOT	○	●	○	◐	◐	◐	○	○	◐	○	○	●
POWERSHOT	○	●	○	○	◐	○	○	○	◐	○	○	●
SUPER POWERSHOT	○	●	○	◐	◐	◐	○	○	◐	○	○	●
CHEATER	●	●	◐	◐	●	●	◐	●	●	◐	◐	●
BIG SHOT	●	N/A	●	●	●	●	●	●	●	●	●	●
PRO PLATE	●	N/A	●	●	●	●	●	●	●	●	●	●
DOUBLE CROSS	●	N/A	●	●	●	●	●	●	●	●	●	●
ANNULAR DISCHARGE	●	N/A	●	●	●	●	●	●	●	●	●	●
SPORTSMAN FOGGER	●	●	●	●	●	●	●	○	●	◐	●	●
PROSHOT FOGGER	●	N/A	●	●	●	●	●	●	●	●	●	●
PROSHOT TWIN FOGGER	●	N/A	●	●	●	●	●	●	●	●	●	●
PRO RACE FOGGER	●	N/A	●	●	●	●	●	●	●	●	●	●
OEM EFI	○	●	○	○	◐	◐	○	N/A	○	○	○	●
***HI-PERF OEM EFI**	●	●	◐	◐	◐	●	○	N/A	●	●	●	●
***NOSzle™ OEM EFI**	○	●	○	●	○	○	○	○	◐	○	○	○
***NOSzle™ RACING EFI**	◐	●	●	●	●	●	●	○	●	◐	●	●
POWERFOGGER™ EFI	○	●	○	◐	○	○	○	○	○	○	○	○

○ NOT NECESSARY
◐ RECOMMENDED
● MANDATORY

*Kit produces more than 40% of engine's rated horsepower ** After 140 HP nitrous or more *** After 200 HP of nitrous or more

NOS designed this chart to graphically illustrate engine preparation and tuning requirements to obtain best results with various NOS nitrous systems. Note that many NOS systems are approved to work with virtually any stock engine. And certain upgrades are recommended, but not essential. The more powerful systems require a true high performance engine with forged aluminum pistons, forged steel or aluminum rods, and a forged steel crankshaft. Due to high cylinder pressures, NOS advises equipping such a powerplant with heavy-duty cylinder head and main studs. Most of the more powerful kits listed require an aftermarket fuel pump, and NOS also recommends installing an ignition with nitrous-retard capabilities. *NOS*

of various metals without even opening the engine. Street nitrous does not by itself require super-stock oil pressure or volume, but the engine oil pressure should meet stock specifications—the testing of which, these days, usually means attaching a test gauge in place of the stock oil pressure light sending unit, since very few vehicles have enumerated oil pressure gauges anymore.

It is surprisingly difficult to do a truly great engine rebuild, which is why a known-healthy used factory stock motor without too many miles can be preferable to a rebuilt engine. It's also why a factory performance crate motor—typically available with a selection of boost-ready super-duty internal parts—is probably better than what you can build yourself, even if you know what you're doing. Engineering experts at GM specifically claim that even wizard aftermarket engine builders cannot equal factory quality—and they have evidence to back this up. For example, factory engine-building robots deploy DC electric gang drivers and "torque to turn" controls these days to simultaneously tighten all the head fasteners on an engine at once to the correct torque, for perfectly even clamping force and improved head-block sealing that GM says is beyond the capability of ordinary pro engine builders. Factory-machined cylinders, these days, were probably bored and honed with a sophisticated stress plate torqued in place on the block to simulate the block-warping stress head fasteners impart to the block to make sure that cylinder machining will produce bores that are stretched perfectly round when it matters—when the head is torqued in place. The trouble is, the cylinder head itself will warp when torqued in place (and not necessarily with perfect linearity), meaning the perfect

stress place should not simply be as rigid as possible. Except with very common performance engines, it can be difficult for aftermarket machine shops to build or obtain stress plates that accurately simulate cylinder head give-and-take on clamp-down, resulting in less round cylinders and increased blow-by. Really round cylinders spell "power"—sometimes *a lot* of power—so make sure your kick-ass nitrous motor has them.

Difficult Engines. When it comes to the engine choice for a custom or semi-custom nitrous installation, some engines present special problems.

Vee or horizontally opposed flat configuration engines typically require longer, more complex direct-port nitrous plumbing where heat-soak and increased supply line volume can produce the type of sluggish, soft nitrous hit sometimes referred to as "nitrous lag."

The *"packed-full" complexity of almost any modern engine compartment* can make it a challenge to install nitrous injection without serious heat-soak problems.

Air-cooled engines tend to run hotter cylinder head temperatures than liquid-cooled engines (though cold cylinder temperatures can also be a problem in the case of snowmobile and aviation engines when uneven shock-cooling warps cylinder heads or barrels in the freezing temperatures of winter or high altitude if the operator throttles back too much during a fast descent and then subsequently compounds the problem with a sudden application of high power and rapid thermal loading). Overheated combustion chambers can quickly lead to detonation and pre-ignition, either of which can kill an engine in a matter of seconds. Obviously, though, Porsche created a supercar out of a turbocharged air-cooled flat-six 30 years ago when it released the 930, and many people have successfully installed power adders on air-cooled Porsche and VW powerplants. The first oxygen-injection was installed by NACA on an air-cooled aviation radial engine, and aircraft powerplants are routinely nitrous-injected in glamour-class air racing (though liquid-cooled Merlin and Griffin V-12s are much more common). It can be difficult or impossible for aftermarket tuners to upgrade air-cooled cylinder or head cooling, and it's worth noting that Porsche actually converted the cylinder heads of some super-high output air-cooled engines to liquid cooling for boosted applications. Eventually, Porsche phased out the old air-cooled flat-six. High-output air-cooled engines under heavy load will generally require

If you are hot rodding an engine hard with nitrous, you will probably want to replace the engine fasteners with upgrade parts. This 1MZ-FE Toyota V-6 already had six-bolt mains from the factory, but ARP main studs will keep the mains from working at radical power levels.

richer air-fuel mixtures than liquid-cooled engines to cool combustion, so the brake-specific fuel consumption of a boosted air-cooled powerplant tends to be higher. Beyond this, the oil temperature of air-cooled engines tends to be hotter than liquid-cooled powerplants even in non-boosted applications, making high-efficiency engine oil coolers critical when nitrous or turbocharging is involved.

Street engines with *high static or effective compression* ratios can be a challenge for a nitrous installation due to the increased likelihood of detonation.

Emission-compliant engines can be a challenge to juice. Obviously, to be street-legal, all late-model automotive engines and vehicles must comply with federal or state emissions requirements. Some states require a vehicle to pass a tailpipe sniff test on a rolling road, plus an under-hood inspection to verify that the original engine and emissions equipment is in place and that no untoward power-adders are present (though nitrous system removal is generally so easy that returning an engine to stock condition for testing is very viable). There are specified procedures to get aftermarket nitrous kits approved for legal street usage, but the expense of getting a vehicle through the Federal Test Procedure (FTP) is prohibitive for most individuals. The FTP was designed to force the professional performance aftermarket to demonstrate that exhaust and crankcase emissions are not degraded from stock by performance modifications in a rigorous procedure conducted at a special testing laboratory. The good news is that even in California, vehicles more than 30 years old are not required to pass emissions testing (nor are diesels, electric vehicles, hybrids, motorcycles, or heavy vehicles weighing more than 14,001 pounds fueled by natural gas)—hence, the popularity of *old* vehicles for hot rodding in California.

The newest late-model engines have increasingly been designed with engine management system (EMS) logic that

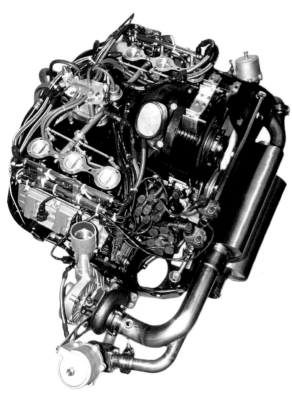

Air-cooled engines have much less thermal momentum than liquid-cooled powerplants and typically run 100 degrees hotter. Avoiding lean mixtures is even more critical than usual to prevent engine damage or even seizure. That said, this daily-driver Twin-turbo 3.6 liter Porsche 993 engine from Motorsport Design was successfully hot rodded to over 700 horsepower, and nitrous injection has been successfully implemented on *many* air-cooled VWs, Porsches, motorcycles, snowmobiles, and ATVs.

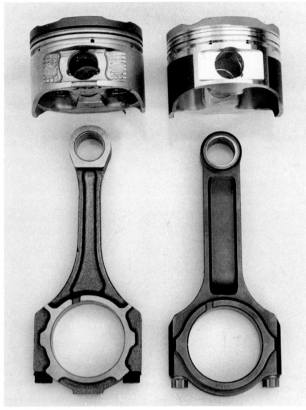

Modeling and simulation software have enabled modern automotive engineers to get very good at designing engine components that are just good enough to live forever. If you add more than 30 percent power, you are going to want forged pistons and rods, as seen here in this photo comparing stock Toyota 1MZ-FE 3.0L V-6 rods and pistons to custom Crower forged steel rods and Wiseco forged aluminum pistons. Keep in mind that aftermarket forged pistons vary widely in the amount of silicon in the alloy, with less silicon producing stronger pistons, and more silicon producing better thermal expansion characteristics.

from piston overexpansion. In this situation adequate fuel enrichment is critical.

Head-block sealing. As GM found out with the Ecotec racing project, sealing between the block and head must be beefed up or the head gaskets will definitely blow out at full-howl, high-boost. What is "full-howl, high-boost?" That depends on your engine. "Full-howl" definitely encompasses any time the engine knocks under boost, the pressure spikes of which will challenge *any* stock head-block sealing strategy, and quickly defeat even the best super-duty solutions.

There are several major aspects to head-block sealing, the most important being the strength of the fasteners holding down the head. If the head lifts under high combustion pressure, no gasket system can seal it. Beyond that, the integrity of the gasket material is important—solid-metal gaskets have much greater strength than organic gaskets with metal reinforcing. Unfortunately, copper and steel gaskets have a much greater tendency to leak water from the cooling jacket, and therefore require *extremely* flat deck surfaces, necessitating special head-milling techniques that eliminate even the normal machining marks left behind by a cylinder mill or belt-sanding device.

Sooner or later, if you pump up the power enough, you will probably need to O-ring the cylinders of a nitrous powerplant. O-ringing consists of machining a shallow groove into the fire-ring area of the block or head around each cylinder bore and then installing into the groove gapless machined-steel rings or steel wire (with the ends sanded flat using a special tool designed to produce a virtually nonexistent end gap). The correct O-ring is slightly tall for the groove and therefore bites hard into the head gasket when the head is torqued. In extremely high-output powerplants,

makes it difficult or impossible to modify the air-fuel ratio or ignition timing as required to accommodate performance modifications such as turbocharging without damaging the engine. In some cases EMS logic now encompasses *full-time* 100-percent closed-loop engine management in which O_2-sensor feedback gets factored into the injection air-fuel calculation under control of a target air-fuel ratio table. These days, there is a lot to be said for exclusively employing a very common performance engine as the basis of a power-adder project because much will be known regarding pushing the envelope in terms of power and longevity. In the case of performance cars like the Chevrolet Corvette, the engine management system has been hacked to the point that downloadable software like LS1edit can be used to modify essentially anything in the factory PCM (powertrain control module) calibration. For "off-highway" use, closed-loop air-fuel controls can be entirely deactivated.

Two-stroke engines can make power on nitrous, but it's tricky, since a stock 2-stroke is already at higher risk of seizing

You're going to want a powerful spark to ignite nitrous-fuel mixtures, so install a good coil along with the nitrous system. You may need to reduce the spark gap to get good ignition at full howl. *MSD*

Manual transmissions are usually okay until you go completely mental with the nitrous shot, but the stock clutch is usually one of the weakest components when you amp up the low-end torque tremendously, as is the case with almost any nitrous system. Figure on upgrading the clutch before you wipe out the stocker. If you are running an automatic transmission, you will probably want progressive nitrous to soften the initial hit, and you may want to momentarily halt nitrous boost during the actual shift. (There are electronic controllers that can do this.) GM Racing used this super-duty clutch pack in their record-setting Bonneville Cobalt with boosted Ecotec I4.

engine builders have sometimes used two concentric O-rings around each bore. Where adjacent cylinder sleeves are Siamesed very close together, the O-ring groove may form a "figure-8" around two cylinders, with a single long piece of wire sealing both bores. O-ringing serves the purpose of providing extremely high clamping pressure in the area of the wire in order to provide a very strong combustion chamber seal. Perhaps more importantly, by biting deeply into the gasket (and thus deforming it) in such a way as to provide a physical interlock between the O-ring and the gasket, the O-rings provide an immovable barrier that prevents the head gasket from pushing sideways and blowing out of the head-block interface.

If the head has never been off a factory performance engine that's old but healthy, the stock gasket will often be "glued" to both the block and head to the extent that a composition gasket tears apart before it detaches from either deck surface. The glued-on gasket and relatively strong head fasteners (factory turbo engines often have these) will usually prevent the head from lifting until the combustion pressures

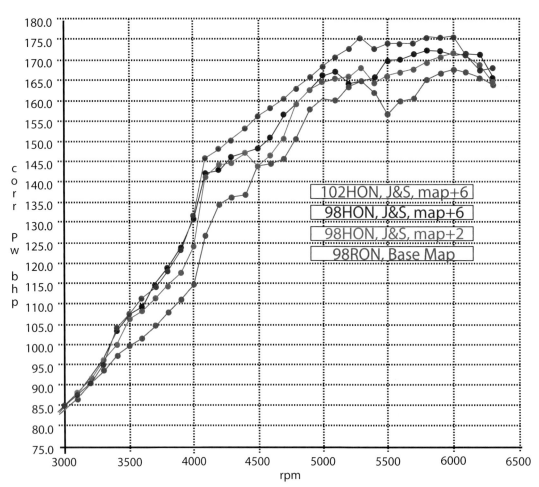

J&S Dynochart showing achievable knock-limited horsepower with 98 and 102 research octane (RON) gasoline, with the Safeguard knock sensor system providing insurance against knock damage that allows the engine calibration to be optimized for higher horsepower. *J&S*

INSTALLING NITROUS OXIDE INJECTION

Installing dual nitrous tanks in Lance Wester's Z06 Corvette. Each nitrous stage has it's own carbon-fiber tank with bottle heater system and remote-control bottle control valve.

are quite high (or until the engine starts knocking). However, once you've replaced the stock gasket, my experience is that without additional countermeasures (like better head bolts or studs) it will blow more easily the next time.

Compression Ratio. A higher compression ratio increases the thermal efficiency of combustion, and increases the expansion ratio as well, which is where thermal energy is converted into kinetic energy. Except for the fact that higher compression (and the hotter combustion) increases NOx emissions in the exhaust, more static compression is a good thing, giving an engine the crisp, torquey feel all driving enthusiasts enjoy. Unfortunately, higher static compression and the added combustion pressure of nitrous boost increase the likelihood of the charge mixture auto-igniting in an explosion before normal combustion smoothly burns its way through the air-fuel mixture. Detonation must be prevented at all cost using some combination of (1) higher octane fuel, (2) reduced combustion temperatures, (3) special engine management countermeasures such as fuel-cooling, retarded ignition timing, or water injection, (4) diminished maximum power boost, or (5) reduced static compression ratio via internal engine changes.

Twenty-five years ago, aftermarket turbo experts commonly used the rule of thumb that each 10 percent increase in torque (for example, from roughly 1 pound of turbo boost) raised an engine's octane number requirement (ONR) by one point. If an engine required 87-octane unleaded regular fuel in normal-charged stock form, the rule said 8-psi boost would require 95-octane leaded premium (which was gone from American street gasoline after the lead phase-out was complete in 1986). In those days, experts recommended 8.5:1 as a maximum static compression ratio for a power-adder engine, and many ran less than that,

which could result in sluggish performance before the boost kicked in. Keep in mind, those were still the bad old days of single-carb engines with ubiquitous fuel distribution problems and mechanical or hardwired electronic ignition timing advance curves. This all changed with the advent of (1) modern 4-valve pentroof combustion chambers, (2) smaller bore sizes requiring less flame travel during combustion, (3) port fuel injection, and (4) sophisticated computer-controlled engine management strategies, which together dramatically increased the amount of power boost that's feasible with the current 91- to 94-octane premium pump gasoline. I have personally boosted a 10.5:1 4-valve turbo-conversion engine running on 93-octane fuel to double the stock horsepower using aftermarket engine management, illustrating that large amounts of overfueling and ignition retard can be extremely effective in fighting detonation, though cylinder wall-washing from excessive enrichment fuel ultimately can have its own negative effect on engine longevity.

Alcohol fuels can be very effective in fighting detonation with their high octane and evaporative intercooling effects, and super-high-output modern competition powerplants such as GM Racing's Ecotec have used oxygenated fuels to deliver spectacular wins in both drag-race and Bonneville competition. It is fairly common to equip high-boost street nitrous powerplants with a small auxiliary fuel tank, allowing a nitrous system to inject ultra-high-octane racing gasoline or methanol as the supplemental nitrous boost enrichment fuel.

When you can't run super-high octane fuel, and none of the other anti-knock countermeasures mentioned above are sufficient, there is no choice but to lower compression. The right way to lower compression is to install new pistons in which the crown is lowered to increase the combustion chamber volume. Piston manufacturers like Wiseco, JE, Venolia, and others can punch a few numbers in a computer and build you custom pistons designed to achieve the exact

A nitrous bottle mounting bracket from Nitrous Outlet. *Nitrous Outlet*

Solenoid-forward fogger-type direct-port nitrous system components. The individual-cylinder metal hardlines must be bent and routed to form a functional and aesthetic nitrous and fuel supply system that is not subject to excessive heat soak. *Edelbrock*

compression ratio you want on your engine, with its particular bore and stroke (which, of course, may no longer be stock if the engine has ever been overbored). Some people have machined pockets one-by-one in stock pistons to reduce the compression, or even machined out the combustion chambers to add to the clearance volume. This is probably not the best idea, because you are weakening the piston crown or combustion chamber, which was probably the thickness it was for a reason. In some cases that might make a difference. New custom pistons can be surprisingly affordable—in the case of some luxury performance cars, significantly less than factory stock pistons. (If you absolutely can't afford replacement pistons, you are probably in over your head with a high-boost nitrous installation, in which case it is wise to heed the advice of NOS, which is to limit boost on stock engines to a maximum nitrous shot of 40 to 50 percent stock power). If the stock pistons have very thick crowns, or you only need to remove a tiny bit of compression, machining outside of the squish ring (see below) can be viable if you know what you're doing.

Another questionable procedure is installing thicker-than-stock head gaskets. When you are buying copper head gaskets, the manufacturer will ask you what thickness you want, and it might be tempting to go for thicker gaskets as the solution to lowering compression. The trouble is, a thicker head gasket can be very problematic. Thicker gaskets will cause problems by adversely changing the geometry of the head-block interface on the intake manifold of a V engine. A thicker gasket can subtly alter cam timing on an overhead-cam engine. Worst of all it could degrade the "squish" effect in the combustion chambers, which can actually be a greater pro-knock factor than a little more compression.

All modern overhead-valve and overhead-cam engine pistons and combustion chambers are designed with a flat squish ring around the periphery of the combustion chamber and piston such that when pistons are at top dead center, the two areas are virtually touching. The squish ring squeezes charge mixture toward the center of the combustion chamber as a piston nears top dead center, violently churning the burning air-fuel mixture in a way that greatly decreases the likelihood of any homogeneous "end gas" pockets remaining unburned late in the combustion process that could explode as combustion temperatures and pressures increase in the process of normal combustion. It is critical that any compression-lowering strategy not mess with the squish ring. Adverse changes to the squish ring could result from thicker head gaskets, machined stock pistons, shorter-than-stock connecting rods, relocated wrist pins, or pistons that are shorter than stock. Don't do it.

Intake Manifold. Vendors selling wet nitrous kits with very high nitrous and supplemental fuel delivery commonly recommend running an open plenum (single-plane) intake manifold to flow large amounts of nitrous oxide and fuel with the least possible degradation of air flow. Intake manifolds with individual runners for each carburetor butterfly should not be used for large-dose wet kits. Although single-fogger wet nitrous kits can work on multi-port EFI engines, due to possible severe distribution problems it is never a great idea to run fuel mixtures through a dry manifold that was not designed to handle wet charge mixtures.

Cylinder Head Preparation. The head itself is one of the last areas that could need attention on a serious nitrous project. If you are only trying to boost an engine's power and torque as hard as you can with stock engine internals, you almost definitely do not need to change anything about the cylinder head that affects airflow. Nitrous boost alone will do the job up to the limits of the weakest engine parts. Even with improved pistons and maybe better rods, if the goal is to push the power envelope as far as possible within the mechanical limits of a super-stock street engine, you do not need to modify the cylinder head beyond installing sodium-filled or other super-duty exhaust valves. In fact, many nitrous installations retain the stock valves and live for a long time. On the other hand, GM installs sodium-filled valves in the

260-horse Pontiac Solstice, which is boosted 100 horsepower above the normal-charged base engine. If you want factory reliability, know that GM is not spending the money for better exhaust valves for no reason. What can I say?

But if you are trying to make astronomical levels of horsepower, you will need to have the engine making *a lot* of torque with high efficiency at very high rpm. All the standard head flow tricks will work on a nitrous engine to this end, including porting and polishing the runners, increasing the valve size, running more cam lift and duration, and installing the strong valve springs required to keep the valves from floating at super-stock rpm. In the case of nitrous injection, volumetric efficiency is affected by the uniquely high ratio of combustion products to reactants, which makes it vitally important to improve the powerplant's exhaust efficiency. Nitrous combustion proceeds with uniquely high flame speeds, which means exhaust efficiency can be improved by installing large exhaust valves along with an exhaust cam that opens the exhaust valves unusually early.

When you custom-build a direct-port nitrous system with steel hard-pipes and compression fittings, you're going to be cutting and bending—carefully!—very small pipes with a pipe-cutter like this. *Nitrous Outlet*

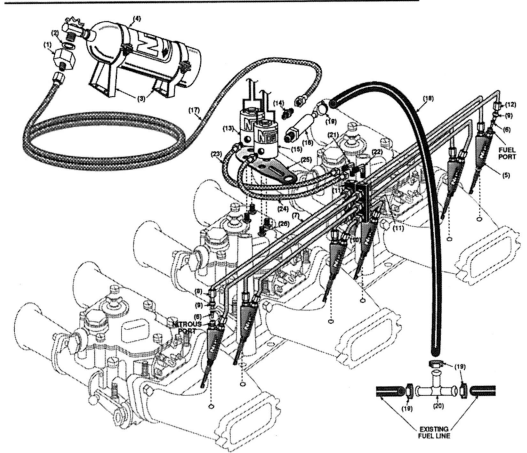

Direct-port nitrous systems with fogger nozzles or nitrous nozzles require drilling and tapping the intake manifold in multiple locations to install the nozzles. The best way to do this is to remove the manifold and work with a drill press to get the geometry of the nozzles perfectly in line with each other for best appearance and correct aim. In a pinch you can grease the drill bit and tap and drill with the manifold on the engine, but there is always a risk that metal debris not caught in the grease or vacuumed from the intake will be sucked into the engine later on startup. *NOS*

Block Preparation. If you are working with a strong iron-block powerplant with a closed block deck or a strong modern closed-deck alloy performance block, you probably won't need to modify the block unless you are significantly increasing the redline (in which case, the typical super-duty screamer tricks of block girdles, super-duty main studs, cross-bolted main caps, and so forth will be required). If you want to work with a lightweight non-turbo powerplant with an open deck, you should choose an engine that has already been heavily hot rodded by experts, or you will have your own private R&D project. Honda engine builders know that some open-deck engines are subject to core-shift if you lean on them too hard, and there are off-the-shelf parts available to convert some blocks to a closed deck. The time to figure this out is before the block is damaged in the first place, because once the cylinders begin to move around, they won't want to stop, and the block is a write-off. Four- or six-fastener main caps are less apt to "work" or "walk" in high-output nitrous conversions than two-bolt mains, and main studs are better than main bolts because all threads are always fully engaged, allowing the highest possible torque loads. Head studs reduce the likelihood of the cylinder head lifting or moving and the head gasket blowing, and it is common practice in maximum-effort engine projects like GM's drag-race Ecotec to machine the block and head for oversized head studs.

GM's Ecotec could not be successfully converted to a closed deck, but it didn't need that anyway. GM Racing did eventually bore out the open deck and press massive steel cylinder sleeves into the floor of the block above the crank

Installing threaded nitrous nozzles into the plastic intake manifolds increasingly found on new engines presents a challenge, since you cannot usually just drill and tap the plastic. One common approach is to epoxy nozzle bosses into the plastic and thread the nozzles into the bosses, which is the approach taken by HP Engineering of Houston, Texas, on this Corvette Z06 manifold.

An alternative approach to drilling the manifold for direct-port nozzles is a special adaptor-nozzle like the NOS NOSzle that installs underneath port-EFI electronic injectors, and thus requires no drilling or machining (except possibly to relocate the stock fuel rails to work with the relocated fuel injectors). *NOS*

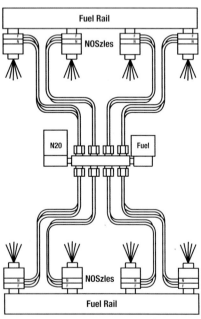

As shown in the V-8 flow diagram, NOS NOSzles normally connect to direct-port nitrous and fuel distribution manifold(s) using flexible plastic or braided-steel hoses rather than rigid steel pipes, which is also true of competing-brand adaptor-nozzles that install under the electronic fuel injectors. *NOS*

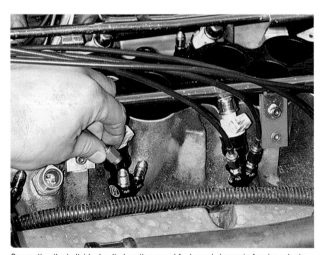

Connecting the individual-cylinder nitrous and fuel supply hoses to fogging adaptor-nozzles that install without machining under the stock electronic fuel injectors. Note that the stock fuel rail on this engine has been relocated upward with metal plates as seen at the right. *Nitrous Express*

DRY NITROUS, TIME, AND RPM

Since nitrous injection is usually designed to occur at a steady rate per time, the amount of nitrous arriving in a given cylinder varies with engine speed according to the time available in a complete power cycle, during which injected nitrous gas is building up in the air intake system and enriching the oxygen content of the air that will be ingested in the next intake stroke. Ideally, supplemental boost enrichment fuel per power stroke should similarly be automatically modified according to the time available for nitrous delivery to each power stroke, meaning according to engine speed.

Electronic fuel injection, however, delivers one or two injector squirts of a specific length per power stroke, according to the engine's torque curve and actual loading, and the amount of fuel injected is not directly affected by time available per power stroke unless the injectors reach 100 percent duty cycle (which should never be allowed to happen). Of course, time has an indirect effect on injection pulsewidth since engine volumetric efficiency (cylinder filling) will be affected by engine speed and throttle angle. But since nitrous is normally only injected at wide-open-throttle, engine loading is not a factor on injection pulsewidth during nitrous boost and is thus not a consideration in determining ideal supplemental enrichment fuel delivery.

With the delivery of nitrous steady over time, increasing engine rpm slices the constant flow rate of nitrous into smaller and smaller amounts actually delivered per combustion event. Meanwhile, full-throttle fuel-injection pulsewidth increases with rpm as the engine approaches peak-torque rpm, then declines as the torque curve noses over as rpm approaches peak horsepower and beyond. The fuel enrichment software logic of a nitrous-capable aftermarket EMS software logic should factor in time available for nitrous injection in computing the required increase in injector pulsewidth to fuel the nitrous. If this is not done, the air-fuel mixture will become increasingly rich as engine speed increases due to the fall-off in time available for nitrous (oxygen) induction. To some extent this is a good thing, since thermal loading is more of a factor at higher total levels of horsepower and more fuel-cooling is usually required to fight knock, but over-enrichment *can* become dysfunctional, particularly above peak power. That said, the spread between air-fuel ratios producing rich and lean best torque is fairly wide for gasoline, and the acceptable air-fuel ratio range gets even wider on the rich end if you're willing to tolerate suboptimal power increases and a certain amount of cylinder wall washing for the (usually) brief duration of nitrous boost. For practical purposes, if combustion gets a little richer than ideal as a nitrous run proceeds, that's okay given the cost advantages of a simple mechanical dry nitrous system. In the real world of street nitrous systems for street cars with stock engines and stock redlines in a very price-elastic marketplace, increasingly rich air-fuel ratios are a fact of life where the priority is to deliver a bunch of dirt-cheap power rather than wring-out every last horsepower.

when it was 800-horsepower time, pouring epoxy around the bases to add strength. Re-sleeving has become the modern (but expensive!) solution for strengthening open-deck blocks, and not just for 1,200-horse superfreaks, but for semi-pro racers and "Fast and Furious" street freaks making four-cylinder power in the 500-plus-horse range. At this time of writing, superfreak cars from pro-racer performance specialists like engine wizard and supertuner Bob Norwood were building engines in which the block water jacket was completely filled with epoxy and cement for short-duration drag racing, although others, like the GM Racing team, had tried and abandoned the practice in some engines.

Stock cast-iron crankshafts are prone to break, and even original-equipment forged cranks can bend, twist, or crack in super-high-output nitrous applications. If you are using a common performance engine, you can probably find off-the-shelf aftermarket forged cranks that will work with high-output nitrous situations. Otherwise, you'll need to have an outfit like Crower build a custom forged/billet crankshaft.

Nitrous pistons and rings. Most stock pistons and rods will work fine to about 140 to 150 percent of stock power (though, of course, no *automaker* would *ever* sell a 6- to 7-psi turbocharged engine of similar power boost without better pistons and rods). Beyond that, it's anyone's guess on a particular engine, but cast pistons are very prone to failure at elevated cylinder temperatures and pressures, and standard stock-type forged or powder-metal connecting rods

tend to buckle under the highly compressive loads generated with large doses of nitrous. Unless you have GM's ability to waste blocks to find out when the pistons and rods fail, you'll need to plan on upgrading to aftermarket forged pistons and aftermarket forged steel or aluminum rods as you push a nitrous installation into the realm above a 40- to 50-percent horsepower shot. GM Racing found out the hard way when the original normal-charged Ecotec destroyed its rods with simultaneous compression fractures at twice stock power on nitrous.

Factory turbo engines typically have similar headroom to pump up the power and torque without immediately killing the stock (upgrade) rods and pistons, and you can certainly figure a 50 percent torque increase is possible—particularly when the power boost comes from constant nitrous injection, which provides the biggest power boost at lower rpm, precisely when the turbo is likely to be delivering very modest boost. In my own experience, a 2.0-liter MR2 Turbo magazine project car—good for 200 horsepower and 200 lb-ft torque at the stock 7.5-psi boost—survived hundreds of dyno pulls and many long, hard trips around Texas and the United States with the stock rods and pistons and boost pumped up enough to make at least 300 lb-ft of torque. Cranking up the boost on an MR2 to 15 psi (a full atmosphere) is the point at which you are running out of grace to live much longer with the stock rods and pistons. When it still had stock rods but JE forged stroker pistons, my MR2 Turbo project car survived many scores of dyno runs in the 400- to 550-horsepower range, two to three times stock power range.

Fuel supply adaptors that connect to a stock EFI fuel rail without welding or machining (for example, by attaching to the fuel pressure test port or other connectors) can really save time and money. This NX unit is designed for GM and Chrysler engines, and adaptors for early and late 4.6 Ford engines are also common. A common alternative is to cut the fuel supply line upstream of a return-type fuel pressure regulator for installation of a Y-fitting, or modify a banjo bolt in the fuel supply system (typically at the fuel filter) for some type of hose barb or NPT connector. *Nitrous Express*

Fuel Calculation in Gallons per Hour

Pounds per hour (fuel)	= Horsepower / 2
Gallons per hour	= Pounds per hour / 6
Safe fuel	= Gallons per hour * 1.15
Example: Engine makes 600 horsepower	
Pounds per hour	= Horsepower / 2 = 600 / 2 = 300
Gallons per hour	= Pounds per hour / 6 = 300 / 6 = 50
Safe fuel	= Gallons per hour * 1.15 = 50 * 1.15 = 57.5 (gallons per hour)

It is critical that fuel supply pump and plumbing have the capacity to supply the horsepower requirements for all-motor *and* nitrous-boost requirements without any pressure drop. Calculate the pounds or gallons per hour requirement using these formulae.

Ignition System. Factory ignition systems are very likely to misfire at high rpm under heavy loading with a lot of extra nitrous and fuel in the combustion chambers. Most nitrous vendors recommend upgrading to a powerful aftermarket racing ignition system for all nitrous applications, because serious loads of nitrous require a spark with the ability to jump at least 20 mm (.878")—though, obviously, spark plug gaps are never that large. There are spark strength test devices available that find the limits of an ignition system by allowing the tester to increase a test gap while cranking the engine until the spark can no longer jump the gap. Many stock engines now specify spark gap of .030 to .050, but performance tuners commonly decrease the gap on high-output turbo and nitrous engines down to .020 or even lower if the ignition system misfires at high boost.

Transmission. If a manual transmission vehicle will be exposed to severe operating conditions, including drag strip use, the standard clutch should be replaced with a high-performance unit. An automatic transmission bound for competition use should be upgraded with super-duty parts that can survive a huge torque boost without catastrophic failure. Street automatics will last a lot longer if the nitrous can be cut out during the shift using electronic or electrical means.

INSTALLING NITROUS OXIDE INJECTION

You'll need to mount the nitrous bottle, install the nitrous-injection devices, mount and connect solenoids and regulators, route and connect the nitrous delivery plumbing, route and connect supplemental fuel plumbing for wet and direct-port systems, install wiring and switches, and possibly upgrade certain aspects of the stock engine management system (such as ignition) on a nitrous conversion.

MOUNTING THE BOTTLE

To prevent significant changes in bottle pressure that could impact nitrous mass flow or cause the tank pressure relief system to vent the entire contents of the bottle, always mount the bottle away from heat sources, such as the engine compartment or exhaust system, and away from windows that expose the bottle to direct sunlight.

Ideally, the bottle should be environmentally separated from the driver's compartment. Because hatchback cockpits are not isolated from the luggage compartment by a firewall, the standard safety pressure relief cap on a nitrous bottle should be upgraded with the installation of an aluminum blow-down tube or -8 neoprene-lined braided hose that is routed to the exterior of the vehicle.

Before mounting a nitrous bottle in a racing vehicle intended for use in sanctioned events, check with the sanctioning association for any applicable rules. Most associations require the bottle to be mounted within the confines of the safety roll cage with the safety pressure relief cap vented outside the driver's compartment.

Bottle orientation. Bottle orientation is critical to ensure that the system always delivers liquid nitrous during hard acceleration or cornering. If there is a pickup tube installed inside the tank, it is important to understand how it and the bottle valve are clocked in relation to each other to ensure that the tube draws liquid nitrous from the very bottom of the tank. Various brands of nitrous bottles are assembled so that the pickup tube offset is reliably opposite the bottle label, the bottle valve discharge, or the handle. When using a bottle equipped with a pickup tube, the bottle must always be mounted so the valve end is higher and the pickup tube is "under water" at the opposite end.

The most efficient bottle orientation is the lean-over position with the valve toward the front of the vehicle, which allows the greatest amount of liquid to be used before the pickup tube begins to deliver gaseous nitrous oxide. Whenever a bottle is mounted in a lean-over position, it must be oriented so that the pickup is guaranteed to be at the lowest point.

If the bottle is mounted vertically, the pickup tube must be offset toward the rear of the vehicle, where the liquid N_2O will slosh during acceleration when the bottle is nearly empty.

A bottle that will be mounted upside-down must be ordered without a pickup tube, or have the pickup tube removed (after emptying the bottle of all nitrous and pressure!).

If the bottle has to be mounted sideways (parallel to the rear axle of the vehicle), the tank should be oriented so the pickup tube offset is approximately 45 degrees rear of straight down so the tank will expel liquid during acceleration (bearing in mind that cornering G-forces from turns in the direction of the pickup tube will tend to slosh liquid nitrous *away* from the pickup tube, causing a dramatic reduction in nitrous mass flow as the tank begins to deliver gaseous nitrous oxide to the engine).

Bottle installation. The trick when bolting down a nitrous tank is to loosely assemble the bottle in its brackets with the bottle nut adaptor, washer, and supply line tightly connected, thus allowing an installer to ascertain before drilling holes whether a proposed location for the bottle assembly provides easy access to the bottle valve, hose connection, and bracket clamp bolts for easy bottle changes. In difficult situations, you may discover that a different tank, mount, bottle valve, or nut adaptor makes more sense. When you have found a location that works in all respects, use the bottle bracket holes as a template to mark hole locations for the brackets and to route the plumbing from the bottle valve and blow-down. Drill and mount the brackets. Tighten the bracket clamps. Done.

INSTALLING SPRAY NOZZLES

If you are installing a single nitrous spray nozzle or nitrous-fuel fogger nozzle, you will be mounting it at the entrance to the inlet side of the throttle body or farther upstream in the air intake *as per the instructions that come with the kit.*

Find a suitable location for a side-spray injection nozzle in the inlet side of the throttle body; if you do not wish to drill and tap the throttle body, many nitrous vendors offer a special adaptor fitting for installing the injection nozzle in the upstream plastic or metal air inlet ducting. Check for interference between the spray nozzle and nearby components. Make sure the hood does not contact the nozzle (or supply hoses) when closed. When drilling, it is critical to keep metal or plastic debris from contaminating the engine and causing severe damage. It is best to remove the throttle body and precisely drill it in a drill press, after which the throttle body can be cleaned with solvent or soapy water and blown dry with high-pressure air. Alternately, if you are very careful, you may be able to stuff a rag in the throttle body and drill the injection nozzle hole with the throttle body installed on the manifold.

A side-spray injection nozzle should be installed in a hole drilled perpendicular to the throttle body centerline in such a way that the installed nozzle will not interfere with the

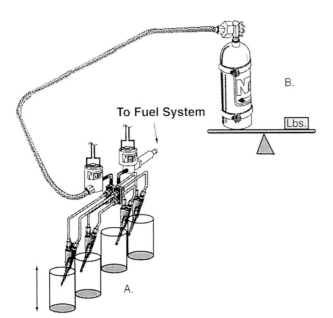

When you have calculated fuel-supply requirements using mathematic models and when all the hardware is installed, flow-test the actual pumping capacity of the system as shown in this diagram and described in the text of this book. The trick is to run the fuel (*not* nitrous) system as full pressure for a fixed length of time and measure the volume of fuel that can be pumped without pressure drop. *NOS*

Direct-port fuel and nitrous rail and connector fittings are designed for hose-type individual-port distribution rather than steel hard-pipes. *Nitrous Express*

action of the throttle plate. In some cases, nitrous vendors have recommended drilling into the throttle body *through* the inlet duct and clamp, after which the duct and clamp can be drilled out with a slightly larger drill bit so that the duct and clamp will easily slip over the inlet end of the injection nozzle after it's installed. Before that can happen, however, the throttle body hole must be tapped with NPT threads (again, best done with the throttle body off the engine and securely clamped in place in a drill press or mill to make sure the tap is aligned precisely in the drilled hole).

Make sure a side-spray nozzle discharges toward the engine by drawing a mark aligned with the nozzle discharge on the exterior that will enable you to know when the nozzle is correctly aligned. It is never a good idea to mount supplemental enrichment fuel injectors or nitrous-fuel foggers in such a way that the fuel spray has to travel uphill to get in the engine, because fuel may drop out of the air stream and puddle in the manifold, entering the engine at irregular intervals. This is particularly important when installing wet or direct nitrous on a dry EFI manifold that has intake runners that run uphill on the way to the engine. My old EFI turbo-conversion Jaguar XKE project used an XJ-6 EFI manifold with runners that bent sharply downhill as the runners moved away from the engine to achieve the required length in a limited engine compartment. Predictably, an early additional injector controller with dual supplemental injectors upstream of the throttle body performed poorly compared to fueling the engine with upgrade primary injectors and aftermarket EMS due to the long uphill pathway for supplemental enrichment fuel introduced upstream of the throttle body.

SOLENOID AND REGULATOR MOUNTING AND CONNECTIONS

The critical point when installing dual primary/secondary pressure-regulated dry nitrous solenoids or a set of wet

Nitrous supply tanks are typically self-pressurized to 750-1,070 psi, and most nitrous system builders still supply aircraft-quality braided steel supply hoses. Nitrous hoses are power-crimped by machine and cannot typically be user-modified to remove unneeded length, so you might have to have one custom-built to your required length if you want to optimize the performance of the initial nitrous hit by eliminating slack in the hose that worsens the heat-soak effect. *Nitrous Express*

nitrous fuel and nitrous solenoids is to make sure that parts are installed in the correct flow direction. On a dry nitrous system with a dedicated pressure regulator feeding conditioned nitrous pressure to the EFI fuel pressure regulator reference port to jack up fuel rail pressure during nitrous boost, install the nitrous regulator assembly in a location that minimizes its distance from the fuel pressure regulator. Make sure that the nitrous regulator bypass jet is sized correctly so that boost fuel pressure is correct and so that conditioned nitrous pressure in the fuel pressure regulator diaphragm bleeds down quickly when nitrous boost ends. Small metal hard lines or (small!) braided-steel Teflon hose will have slightly better response than expandable vacuum hose in getting dry system fuel pressure up to the point where the secondary nitrous regulator opens and boost begins. All vacuum hoses require robust hose clamps. Commercial nitrous kits will include brackets for mounting the solenoids. Solenoids and plumbing should always be installed in a location away from hot engine and exhaust components where radiator fans or road-draft will not continuously bathe the solenoids in heated air. A relatively cool location with cold-air draft is ideal. In difficult situations, you may need to insulate the solenoids and plumbing components and construct composite heat shields with insulation material sandwiched between sheet aluminum or steel. Such techniques will make a huge difference in preventing nitrous or fuel vaporization

Dual-stage direct-port nitrous and fuel distribution network on a Z06 Corvette. Getting steel hard-pipes to line up perfectly can be a challenge if you do it yourself, but most nitrous suppliers offer expert fabrication if you ship them your intake manifold. Note the difference between the braided-steel and braided-nylon supply hoses for nitrous and supplemental fuel.

and foaming as well as fuel and nitrous density reductions from thermal expansion.

Nitrous kits typically supply a prefabricated short supply line that connects the nitrous solenoid to the injection nozzle, which limits the mounting options for the solenoid to a spherical area within the radius of the short supply hose—unless you replace or extend the line with a union and second AN hose. (AN stands for "Army Navy." Braided-stainless hoses are usually specified in AN sizes, for example, AN -4, or "dash four.") United Kingdom nitrous expert Trevor Langfield of Wizards of NOS recommends placing the solenoid in the following locations, in order of preference: between the windshield and engine bay; behind a headlamp; the front grille; or in front of the inner wing area. Locations specifically not recommended are hot areas at the rear of the engine, on the firewall, or on the rear of the inner wing. Again, if there is no other choice, then you'll want to build heat shields to prevent excessive heat soak into the solenoids.

Once a nitrous or fuel solenoid is mounted in place (see next section), connect and tighten the supply line from the tank. Blow out the discharge line with air, then connect the line loosely to the solenoid outlet port. Insert the fuel or nitrous jet in the injection device, attach the other end of the solenoid discharge line. Tighten—but do not over-tighten—both ends. With the solenoids installed, pressurize the line to the solenoid and check for leaks by spraying soapy water on the lines and connectors, and looking for bubbles. Done.

NITROUS SUPPLY LINE MOUNTING

Many people will want to use braided-stainless Teflon-core hoses to transport fuel and nitrous from the tanks to the engine. Braided-stainless hoses are usually specified as AN sizes, for example, AN -4. AN sizes originally referred to the outside diameter in 16ths of an inch of rigid thin-wall metal tubing used by the aerospace industry in aircraft or spacecraft, meaning that AN -4 metal tubing had a diameter of 4/16 inch, or 0.25 inches. The meaning of the AN -4 rating for braided steel or nylon hose is that the hose has a flow rate equivalent to that of the old thin-wall metal tubing with a quarter-inch outside diameter. This rating says nothing directly about the outside or inside diameter of braided-stainless hose, which may require a different inside diameter than metal tubing to deliver the same fluid flow rate, given differences in friction, with the outside diameter an indirect function of the pressure capacity of the hose. Anodized-aluminum AN connector fittings now have a standard SAE thread size for each dash number. AN and mil-spec (military specification) fittings use a 37-degree cone angle and are thus incompatible with industrial JIC-spec connectors, which call for a 45-degree angle cone. Aeroquip and Earl's Performance Plumbing are two well-known suppliers of AN hoses and fittings. Obviously, the flow capacity of a given size AN plumbing is dependent on the pressure.

Determine the routing for your braided-stainless or nylon nitrous (and fuel, if applicable) feed lines. It often works well to follow the route of the stock fuel supply line along the underside of the vehicle and into the engine bay. Ensure the path is clear of exhaust system, suspension, steering, wheels, electrical lines and components, tires, and anything else that might move or get hot. Braided-steel and nylon hoses will kink if forced through a tight-radius curve that is outside the specs of the hose or if the hose is twisted more than a little.

Engine and vehicles and everything on them vibrate and "work." Make sure to route nitrous or fuel fluid delivery lines and connectors where they will not abrade anything or be abraded by sharp edges. In some cases it may make sense to encase nylon and braided-steel hoses in some kind of soft spiral-wrap or even run the hose through aluminum conduit to protect softer materials from the abrasive effect of vibrating braided-stainless sheathing.

Tape off the ends of the nitrous supply line to keep out debris. If you are going to insulate the line—especially with a thermal sleeve—now is a good time. Race shops or even Home Depot can provide flexible thermal sleeving, insulated aluminum tape, side-slit cylindrical tubing of the type designed to provide a thermal barrier around hot water pipes, or other types of insulation that can be effective in providing a thermal barrier around pipes and hoses. If it is necessary to support the nitrous supply line under the vehicle, use Tinnerman padded tube clamps or nylon tie-wraps. Take a look at how they do it on a big-bucks pro-race vehicle. If you are interested in how engineers route and support fluid lines when failure would cause death and destruction, drive to the local airport and talk an airframe and powerplant mechanic into showing you the inside of an engine cowling. Aircraft fasteners are expensive but designed to survive forever in a high-vibration environment.

Feed the main nitrous supply line along the proposed route, and when you've got it right, remove the tape from the ends. Attach the line to the nitrous bottle valve adapter, if necessary installing an optional AN 45- or 90-degree fitting to keep things neat and workable. Purge the nitrous supply line as follows: Wrap the end of the nitrous line with a rag and hold securely. Point the opening away from people. Have a helper briefly crack open the bottle valve.

To prevent debris from plugging tiny nitrous metering orifices, it is critical that you install one or more nitrous debris filters and that the filter not be a bottleneck that produces a pressure drop that causes liquid nitrous to vaporize or foam in the supply line, interfering with accurate mass-flow metering. *Nitrous Outlet*

Attach the nitrous supply line to the nitrous solenoid inlet port, if necessary using an optional AN angle-fitting. Any junctions with pipe threads should be carefully sealed with Teflon paste (*never* tape, which can extrude sliced-off threads during tightening that can block tiny jets and nozzles downstream).

Place the correct jet in the injection fixture inlet, then affix and tighten connectors on the supply line between the solenoid outlet and the injection fixture inlet.

INSTALLING SPACER PLATES AND FUEL SYSTEMS

A fuel system should be capable of supplying at least 0.10 gallons of fuel per hour per horsepower at the design pressure of the fuel system under worst conditions. For carbureted engines, this could be as low as 5 to 10 psi, though it is often a good idea to convert carbureted vehicles to a high-pressure return fuel loop with pinch regulator to supply wet nitrous and direct-port nitrous fuel requirements, with loop pressure regulated down into a spur line supplying the carburetor. Keep in mind that the flow of many fuel pumps is rated at 0 psi, and will be much lower at 5, 10, 20, 40 or 80 psi.

Install injector plate. Remove the air-intake system ducting from the carburetor or throttle body. Disconnect the throttle linkage. In the case of a carbureted engine, disconnect the fuel line. Loosen the nuts, remove the carburetor or throttle body, then loosen the studs by installing and jamming together two or more nuts on a stud, then turn out the studs with a wrench on the deepest of the jammed nuts. Install the new extended studs from the nitrous kit using jammed nuts or nuts bottomed out on the stud. Install the injector plate with the correct side toward the engine, then reinstall the carb or throttle body and tighten the nuts.

Install fuel supply plumbing. Assuming you have verified that the fuel pump can deliver sufficient fuel at the required working pressure, a simple supplemental fuel system can be fabricated by installing a tee fitting in the fuel line upstream of the carburetor or fuel rail. Another option is to machine a threaded hole in a fuel-supply banjo bolt (see the section of this chapter on mounting a fuel pressure sensor) and mount it in a hole machined in the fuel rail, or the fuel pressure test port on a fuel rail, or other fuel supply component. Other options include fabricating a completely auxiliary nitrous fuel supply system with its own electric fuel pump running independently to the main fuel tank, or even installing a small auxiliary fuel tank in or near the engine compartment with its own fuel pump that provides an independent source of ultra-high-octane race fuel for nitrous fuel enrichment.

Whatever the choice, exercise caution in depressurizing the fuel system and if the engine is hot, use extreme care undertaking modifications to the fuel system, which will inevitably result in some leakage of liquid fuel or fumes. When constructing new fuel system plumbing, coat any pipe threads with Teflon paste (again, *not* Teflon tape). As mentioned elsewhere in this book, you may want to convert the main fuel system from a dead-head carb system to an EFI-type fuel loop with high-pressure electric fuel pump, pinch regulator, and fuel tank return line, the advantage being that high pressure fuel supply systems can get away with smaller

S40 (.040 Wall)

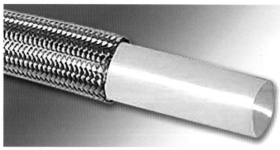

S40 Series hose is reinforced with 304 stainless steel wire. All sizes are extruded from virgin PTFE and have a minimum wall thickness of .040" resulting in 33% more PTFE than other manufacturers. The additional tubing thickness provides an improved bend radius, greater kink resistance and decreased gas permeation.

Temperature Range: -65F to + 450F

* Z Indicates Double Braiding

Installation guide for S40 series hose.

Dash Size	Hose ID	Hose OD	Working Pressure @ 72F	Min. Burst Pressure @ 72F	Min. Bend Radius	Wt. Per Ft. LBS
-03	.125	.250	3500	14000	1.00	0.051
-04	.187	.320	3000	12000	1.50	0.081
-05	.250	.375	3000	12000	2.00	0.082
-06	.312	.435	2500	10000	3.50	0.117
-08	.406	.565	2000	8000	4.50	0.155
-10	.500	.656	1750	7000	5.00	0.181
-12	.625	.780	1500	6000	6.00	0.240
-16	.875	1.05	1000	4000	9.00	0.380
-16Z*	.875	1.10	1250	5000	7.30	0.557
-20Z*	1.125	1.35	1000	4000	11.00	0.682

diameter plumbing and small fluctuations in fuel pressure are much less significant as a percentage of total fuel flow.

Whatever the source, route a quality fuel line of appropriate pressure capacity toward the injector plate *by way of a dead-head fuel pressure regulator* that conditions fuel to the required pressure that's compatible with the fuel and nitrous jetting. Obviously, a 40-psi EFI fuel system regulated down to 35 psi for a direct-port or (wet) plate nitrous system requires different fuel jetting to achieve a target fuel mass flow than a carbureted fuel system regulated to 5 psi at the injector plate.

PLUMBING DIRECT-PORT NOZZLES AND LINES

Most direct-port systems are identical to a wet plate system as far as the solenoids. The added complexity of the direct-port system comes in the extensive plumbing to connect the solenoids to individual injection nozzles in each intake runner. The modern trend has been to inject both fuel and nitrous from individual-runner monojet fogger nozzles.

There is usually a certain amount of latitude regarding where to install individual-runner injection nozzles (nitrous, fuel, or nitrous-fuel). Accepted modern practice is to install fuel and nitrous nozzles that are not integrated together in the runners close to the plenum to reduce reversion resulting from high-speed nitrous or nitrous-fuel bouncing off the intake valves when closed and ricocheting back out into the manifold plenum and so there is as much runner length as possible for nitrous and supplemental fuel to mix well with each other and intake air before entering the cylinders. This, of course, may be compromised by the need to route individual supply lines around myriad obstacles such as electronic fuel injectors, preferrably in a way that

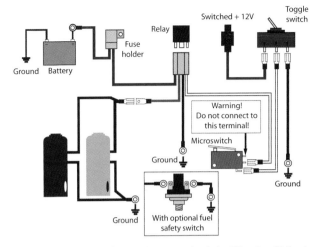

Wiring diagram for a plate nitrous system on a carbureted or TBI engine. *Edelbrock*

looks good. In cases in which fuel and nitrous spray from integrated monojet nozzles, installing the nozzles close to the intake valve can improve performance by getting more liquid nitrous in the cylinders, thus improving air volumetric efficiency by reducing the volume of air displaced by gasified nitrous oxide.

You'll almost definitely want to remove the intake manifold before drilling the manifold for direct-port nozzles, but if you are very meticulous, you might be able to get away with drilling the manifold on the engine. This is usually an unwise move because of the potential for getting metal debris in the engine and due to the increased difficulty of drilling really precise holes with a hand drill. If you are determined to drill the manifold on the engine, pack rags in the manifold runners and grease up the drill bit and pipe tap to help trap metal filings in the grease rather than letting them fly into the intake runners. You might consider turning the engine so that intake valves are closed on the next runner to be drilled, and then vacuum metal filings out of the port with a flexible tube attached to a strong vacuum cleaner, followed by a strong blast of air pressure, followed by additional vacuuming. I wouldn't do it on my own engine unless the manifold was impossibly difficult to remove and the layout was exceptionally well designed in terms of facilitating countermeasures to keep metal out of the engine.

Some modern intake manifolds are plastic, and many nitrous installers working with them have encountered difficulty with nitrous nozzles working loose. The usual trick is to drill and epoxy adapters into the plastic and then screw the nozzles into the adaptors. Make sure that the epoxy or glue will work with the exact type of plastic used for the intake.

You may want to use a drill press or other means to be sure that the nozzles will all be aligned at precisely the same angle. Use a straight edge to mark a common plane through

There are a million prefabricated fittings to make designing and installing nitrous injection systems easy. This aluminum Y-fitting makes it simple to supply two nitrous stages from one tank, or two fuel stages from one fuel pump. *Nitrous Express*

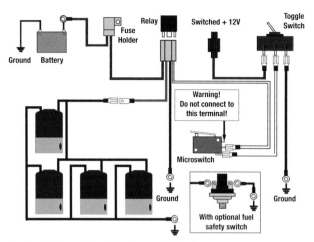

Direct-port nitrous system wiring diagram. *Edelbrock*

the runners that delineates the distance of the nozzles from the cylinder head, and then mark and punch the intersection with the centerline of each runner. Drill each hole at an angle that aims fluid spray directly down the center of the runners, and then run a tapered pipe tap through the hole with high precision to the correct depth so the nozzle achieves a good interference fit at the specified installed height for the particular type of nozzle that puts the nozzle deep enough into the runner to keep spray from bouncing off the walls at close range. You may want to use a drill press or mill to guide the tap to achieve high quality machining results, which in the ideal case would start the threads for all holes at the same clocked position so that all nozzles would have the same orientation at an equal installed height. Many people with limited experience using a drill or pipe tap are not capable of doing really first-rate drill-and-machine work. Be honest: If this describes you, get help or pull the manifold and have a nitrous vendor or machine shop do the dirty work. When the nozzles are in place, use a straightedge to make sure they are at equal installed height. Most nitrous vendors offer a service that allows you to ship them an intake manifold for installation of nozzles, hard lines, distribution blocks, and solenoids.

Plumbing fuel or nitrous connections from the individual intake runners to a distribution manifold is much easier if you use nylon hoses rather than stainless steel hard lines because there's no bending involved and nylon hose cuts with a scalpel or single-edge razor blade. One-by-one, carefully route a piece of nylon hose from each injector to a port on the distribution manifold, then cut to length. Slide the compression pieces onto the ends of the hose, and fasten the hose to the injection nozzle and distribution manifold port. Tighten. Route the main braided steel or nylon supply hose from the distribution manifold to the output port on the solenoid and tighten. Done.

Routing, bending, and cutting steel hard lines is much trickier, and the results will look ratty if things don't line up

quite right even if everything is perfectly functional. The critical trick is to study the layout of direct-port nitrous assemblies or photos of assemblies you like, and mock up the lines with pieces of coat hanger wire or brake line. Let me repeat: Mock up the assembly with heavy wire, brake lines, or something similar, and do not cut corners (so to speak). The other trick is to employ a lot of thinking, a lot of patience, and an artistic sense of style.

You'll need to first figure out what is workable, decide on a tentative location for the distribution manifolds, and make sure the nozzles will be in a location you *know* will work so you do not end up having to weld or epoxy closed nozzle holes in a wrong location that couldn't be plumbed properly or interfered with something critical. There will probably be inconvenient constraints. On a V powerplant, mock up the direct-port assembly starting on the throttle-linkage side of the engine so you're working around the linkage from the beginning, and make sure the linkage clears the hard pipes at all throttle positions. You'll need to form pipe bends of a specified radius that leave enough straight piping after the final bend close to the end to form the required compression or flare connection; keep in mind that each bend and flare will consume a certain amount of piping, and that there is a minimum workable bend radius with any particular type of piping. It is easier to grind or cut a pipe a little shorter than to start over from scratch with new tubing if it's too short, so installers commonly mark the tube or tube bender with a reference line and then add 0.5- to 0.75-inch extra tubing. The reference mark for the first bend coming out of a flare or compression connection should normally be a minimum of 1.0 inch from the end of the tubing, with the bend starting at the mark and moving away from the end of the tubing, leaving a full inch of straight tubing before curvature begins. Within the above constraints, keep the hard pipes as short as possible to reduce nitrous lag, and try to keep the pipes relatively equal in length.

The nozzle and distribution manifolds are critical reference points for everything else, so put a lot of thought into finding the ideal location that looks good and doesn't interfere with the throttle linkage, TPS sensor, engine cover, or anything else that moves. And, of course, keep the routing away from anything especially hot. You'll need to single-flare

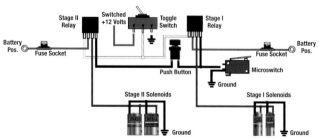

Dual-stage nitrous system wiring diagram. *Edelbrock*

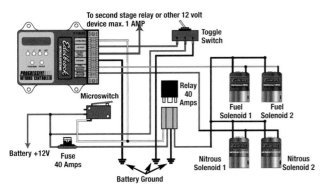

To second stage relay or other 12 volt device max. 1 AMP

Toggle Switch

Microswitch

Relay 40 Amps

Fuel Solenoid 1

Fuel Solenoid 2

Battery +12V

Fuse 40 Amps

Nitrous Solenoid 1

Nitrous Solenoid 2

Battery Ground

Progressive Nitrous Controller wiring diagram for pulse width–modulated progressive nitrous control. *Edelbrock*

or double-flare the tubing ends *after* installing the required ferrule and compression nut or sleeve fitting and B-nut as the particular connection demands. Double-flare connections consume more pipe length, so make allowances.

When fabricating the actual hard pipes to a rectangular distribution manifold located near the center cylinders of an engine or a vee bank, begin by building two *nitrous* tubes (*not* fuel) that originate at the two closest injection nozzles on adjacent runners and crisscross at the distribution manifold from opposite directions, connecting to the bottom inside ports on the opposite sides of the distribution manifold. Holding up the distribution manifold as a guide next to the crisscrossed tubes at a location that is aesthetically pleasing (usually centered), mark each tube so when it cut it will insert properly into the correct port in the manifold to the correct depth. In general, the use of geometrically complex modern distribution manifolds with improved flow (rather than rectangular distribution blocks) will not allow opposing lines to be at a 180-degree angle to each other. This situation requires somewhat more sophisticated methods of line-cutting, but the principle is to get the two lines at the correct angle with the manifold, hold up the manifold at the chosen location, mark the lines, cut, install the connection fittings, flare the ends (if required), and install the two pipes tightened just enough to prevent movement. This is the time to make any required (hopefully minor) adjustments to the distribution manifold location to avoid interference or improve the aesthetics by using the tubing bender to adjust bends in the two completed lines. With this out of the way, proceed to the build additional lines in a logical order that completes the pipes connecting to the hardest-to-reach distribution manifold ports first.

As always, cheap tools are false economy because they break or produce poor results; buy or borrow a really good professional-quality flare tool and a professional bending tool with reference marks for factoring in tubing lost to bends. Tools that meet mil-spec standards are always a good idea. Avoid repeatedly tightening flare or compression fittings during the fabrication and installation process, which can

gall or distort metal pipes and fittings and cause leaks. Some fittings should be cleaned and sealed with fresh Teflon paste each time they are assembled. Many people recommend cutting hard lines with a band-saw or hack saw and de-burring with a drill bit rather than using a pipe cutter, which will tend to compress the inside diameter of tubing in a way that produces a slight bottleneck.

INSTALLING NITROUS ELECTRICAL SYSTEMS

At a minimum, all nitrous systems require enough battery power to operate at least one nitrous solenoid and two or more triggering switches. Verify that there is enough power available to drive an aftermarket high-power ignition system, a boost-retard or aftermarket knock sensor system, additional or upgrade fuel pump, relays (they consume some power too), and any other auxiliary devices requiring power that were not original equipment. Ideally the vehicle's alternator should have enough capacity that nitrous boost does not drain the battery.

Always disconnect the battery before working on the electrical system.

Unless you already have extensive experience wiring, read up on the principles and tricks of building good wiring systems. Even if you have wiring experience, newer, better methods, tricks, and components come along on a regular basis. Good tools and good components are critical to building highly reliable wiring systems. Most nitrous systems come with everything you need for the wiring, and good instructions, though you may decide to upgrade to race or even mil-spec wiring standards

Wiring problems are the cause of many if not most problems with nitrous control systems. It is essential that there be robust connections. Contrary to popular belief, the ultimate connections are not soldered, but involve crimped *metal* connectors. It is thus critical to have the right crimping tool, and these are not cheap. This industrial-strength crimping tool from MSD ignition is equipped, however, with interchangeable crimping jaws, allowing it to be used to correctly crimp almost anything from cable-TV coax to 20-gauge butt connectors. *MSD*

Install pressure switch. Many dry nitrous systems use a fuel pressure safety switch to disarm the main nitrous solenoid until fuel rail pressure reaches a threshold level sufficient to provide adequate nitrous fuel enrichment through the primary electronic fuel injectors. A fuel pressure switch of this type installs at a convenient point in the main fuel loop upstream of the return-type EFI fuel pressure regulator, preferably downstream of the fuel filter (which could lower fuel pressure if partially plugged). Possible sources for reference fuel rail pressure are the fuel pressure test port in the fuel rail, a custom port drilled and machined in the fuel rail, a custom port drilled or welded to a fuel banjo fitting at the entrance or exit to the fuel filter or fuel rail, or a tee fitting inserted into a high-pressure rubber fuel line upstream of the fuel rail.

Some nitrous kits provide a custom extension tube that installs in the fuel rail test port (usually in place of the Schrader fitting (which relocates to the end of the tube) and provides a port for installing the pressure switch. An EFI fuel loop may be pressurized as high as 40 or 50 psi, so be careful when removing the fuel rail test port fitting or otherwise opening the fuel loop. Fuel sprayed onto hot engine components could start a fire. Always allow the engine to cool before performing this operation.

Installing nitrous injection in a motorcycle, watercraft, snowmobile, or ATV is very similar to installing automotive nitrous injection—except for the fact that there are typically very severe vehicle space constraints, more exposure to weather or a harsh marine or winter environment, and greater visibility for beautiful—or not so beautiful!—fabricated wiring, supply systems, and related components. *NOS*

If the engine does not have a fuel rail test port, the fuel system may be equipped with one or more banjo fittings. Examine the diameter of the banjo bolt shank. To use this fitting to mount the fuel pressure switch, the banjo bolt typically must be sufficiently large to drill and tap a 1/4-inch hole through the centerline of the fitting. If this is not possible, it may be feasible to drill a smaller hole and weld or braise a coupling with 1/4-inch female threads to the banjo bolt in such a way that the banjo bolt can still be tightened with a wrench or socket.

Install throttle switch. Many nitrous systems trigger boost using a full-throttle switch. If the engine has EFI, the easiest type of full-throttle switch to install taps into the signal from the EFI throttle position sensor (TPS) wiring, closing the trigger circuit at a configurable voltage or electrical frequency. Tap into the TPS wires and connect them to the switch, hold the throttle at an appropriate position at or near full throttle, and rotate the switch until the circuit closes. Done.

In other cases, you may need to install a mechanical microswitch on the throttle body or carburetor that triggers nitrous boost at wide open throttle. Most nitrous kits supply a "universal" bracket to which the micro-switch may be mounted in a variety of positions, with the bracket itself bendable to suit the application. It is critical that the micro-switch not interfere with normal throttle linkage operation because any binding or dragging could create a potentially dangerous stuck-throttle condition.

Mount the microswitch bracket on the throttle body or intake manifold, and bolt the switch to the bracket. Set up the micro-switch to trigger at full throttle by adjusting position until the actuation arm of the switch "clicks" just

Installing a nitrous-capable aftermarket engine management system in a common performance street vehicle can be almost plug-and-play, when the EMS is equipped with an adapter that plugs into the stock wiring harness. Or it can be mighty complex, as is the case with this custom Motec wiring harness in the process of construction at Norwood Autocraft in Dallas, designed to handle a boosted EFI Chevy small-block in a later-model Jaguar sedan.

as the throttle linkage reaches wide-open throttle against the throttle stop. Verify that the accelerator pedal positively closes the micro-switch by listening for the click as an assistant slowly presses the accelerator pedal to the floor, or, even better, connect a continuity tester across the micro-switch and verify that the meter "beeps" as the throttle reaches the fully open position.

Install relay and switches. Install the arming switch in the vehicle interior, within easy reach of the driver. Install the main arming relay with wiring harness attached in the engine compartment, and attach the input wire directly to the battery (+) terminal or (if the battery is not in the engine compartment) to a thick heavy-gauge wire that is directly connected to the battery (the hot-side starter connection, for example). Wire the relay output to the solenoids; there is normally no specified polarity, so either solenoid connection is usually okay. Connect the remaining solenoid wire to ground. Connect one side of the main relay triggering circuit to ground through the full-throttle switch (the other terminal of which must be grounded), and connect the other side of the relay trigger circuit to a switched 12-volt power source through the heavy-duty arming switch (which may have its own built-in relay). In some cases the relay triggering circuit may require not only that the full-throttle switch be closed, but that fuel or oil pressure switches are closed by threshold safe pressures. Reconnect the battery. Done.

Install upgrade fuel pump. The easiest way to upgrade fuel delivery is to install an auxiliary in-line fuel pump that

Individual-line nitrous debris filters can be deployed to keep debris from clogging the extra-tiny metering jets of a direct-port nitrous system. *Nitrous Outlet*

acts as a booster pump for the main in-tank fuel pump (see sidebar for information about testing fuel pump capacity). Find a safe place to mount the auxiliary fuel pump away from anything really hot—ideally somewhere near the stock fuel line routing. It may be tempting to use rubber fuel line, but in my experience hose clamps on rubber line are very prone to developing leaks if the auxiliary fuel pump is located in a place where fuel drains out of the pump and line when the vehicle is not in use. Preferably the auxiliary pump would be installed down low where fuel will not drain out of the pump, and would be connected to the fuel tank and engine with braided-steel hoses equipped with power-crimped AN connectors that attach directly to the auxiliary fuel pump.

The simplest way to wire an auxiliary inline fuel pump is to tap into the power supply for the primary in-tank fuel pump, but it is usually not necessary to run the auxiliary pump all the time, in which case you might want to drive the auxiliary pump from the nitrous solenoid circuit so the pump only operates when the engine is boosting. It is vital not to degrade electrical power to either fuel pump or the nitrous solenoid circuit, so drive the auxiliary fuel pump with a relay connected to a robust source of battery power (via a fused link of appropriate resistance) with heavy gauge wire, and trigger the relay from the main fuel or solenoid circuit.

INSTALLING A BOOST-RETARD BOX

If you run more than a 25- to 30-percent power boost, you will need robust fuel enrichment plus very-high-octane fuel or ignition retard during nitrous boost, or all of the above. If the nitrous installation knocks with the best fuel you are willing or able to supply the powerplant, you will need to retard ignition timing during boost, which is easily accomplished with a few keystrokes on a nitrous-capable aftermarket EMS, but can be difficult or impossible with factory electronic or traditional old-school mechanical engine management controls. Retarding global static ignition timing is a simple matter on carbureted and first generation digital EFI

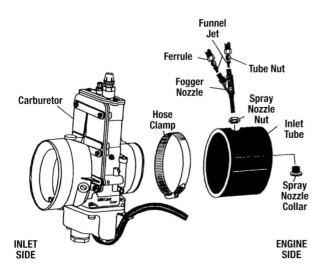

Carburetor

Funnel Jet

Ferrule

Fogger Nozzle

Tube Nut

Spray Nozzle Nut

Hose Clamp

Inlet Tube

Spray Nozzle Collar

INLET SIDE

ENGINE SIDE

Installing fogger-type nitrous nozzles in a motorcycle type engine is exactly like installing nozzles in a car or truck intake, but keep in mind that the nozzles are typically installed *downstream* of an individual-cylinder carburetor as seen in this drawing. High-pressure nitrous has occasionally been installed upstream of a carburetor—and a nitrous blast through a boost venturi can result in fuel enrichment in and of itself—but this is not something to try unless you really know what you are doing, or are following explicit instruction in a proven nitrous kit. *NOS*

Here's the engine compartment of Lance Wester's Z06 "Psycho Nitrous 'Vette" following installation of 350-horsepower worth of nitrous that arrives in a quad-solenoid direct-port nitrous layout that allows the driver to stage nitrous as small stage, large stage, and both stages. The engine compartment is equipped with a small front-mounted auxiliary tank of 108 octane race gas with independent fuel pump and G-Force assist, rpm window switch, and boost-retard ignition box.

powerplants, but doing this will hurt the efficiency and torque of the engine during non-boosted conditions. Spark timing is not adjustable at all on most late model EFI engines unless you can hack the calibration tables, and even then special boost timing is impossible. Fortunately, there are a variety of electronic boost-retard devices available that will selectively retard ignition timing during nitrous or turbo boost or if any of the cylinders begin to experience detonation.

In chassis dyno testing I found knock-sensor-based retard boxes like the J&S Safeguard effective at eliminating detonation using tactics that are least detrimental to engine performance because they are capable of limiting ignition retard to circumstances when detonation would actually damage the engine. The control algorithms maximize power while protecting the engine by retarding *only the cylinders that are actually knocking*. Newer versions of J&S Knock Sensor Systems provided start and rate controls that allow tuners to optimize the retard curve for the particular application. In addition, the Safeguard provided a switched retard function that triggers ignition retard on the basis of a nitrous switch or a manual toggle switch (in case you fill up with low-octane fuel). The Safeguard was capable of being triggered by a factory knock sensor or an optional user-installed Bosch knock sensor. The newest Safeguards were designed to work with distributor ignitions, waste-spark direct ignition, or coil-on-plug individual-cylinder direct-fire ignitions.

The Safeguard, which was installed in the passenger compartment, installed as follows on a coil-on-plug direct-fire EMS:

1. Locate the (individual) coil driver signals on the factory onboard computer. Using taps provided in the kit, splice the Safeguard control wires to the coil driver signal wires. Firing order is not critical unless you care to visibly identify the specific knocking cylinders. In this case you'll need to order the "Knock-Finder" option, in which case you will wire the coils to the control wires in order, 1 through X. LED 1 will then relate to cylinder 1, LED 2 will relate to cylinder 2, and so on, making it easy to know which cylinders are knocking.

2. Wire a switched 12-volt source to the Safeguard (coil positive is ideal, since 12-volt is present during cranking as well as run).

3. Wire a good chassis ground (*not* sheet metal) to the Safeguard.

4. Install the knock sensor on the engine block. Run the two-wire knock sensor cable through the firewall to the Safeguard, crimp connector pins onto the wires (polarity does not matter), and insert the pins into the rear of the connector body. Plug the connector into the knock sensor.

5. Connect the Safeguard to a source of manifold pressure with the 1/8-inch nylon tubing.

6. If you are using nitrous oxide and want automatic deterministic retard, connect the Safeguard's "Aux" wire to the nitrous solenoid circuit. When nitrous solenoid opens, the Safeguard will automatically retard timing either 2 or 4 degrees, depending on the position of a configuration dip switch. (If nitrous is disarmed but you want to run lower octane fuel, a manual toggle switch and relay can be wired to command automatic retard).

7. After start and self check, the display LED shows the amount of knock retard. When there is no knock retard, the LED will be off. When knock retard occurs, the LED brightness will increase in proportion to the amount of knock retard (and the optional bar graph display will progressively light more LEDs with each 2-degree increment of retard). The unit will not detect knock unless rpm is above 1,750 rpm and manifold pressure drops below 5 inches of vacuum.

Test the knock sensor as follows:

- Set the dip switches to command maximum retard on all cylinders at once in case of detonation, thus making it easier to hear if ignition retard is occurring.
- Temporarily unplug and cap off the source of manifold vacuum, which forces the Safeguard's onboard MAP sensor to detect 0 psi pressure, thus enabling knock retard.
- Set the sensitivity control to maximum, start the engine and hold the rpm to at least 2,000.
- Tap rapidly on the knock sensor with a screwdriver to simulate knock.
- You should be able to hear the engine slow down and see the timing retard with your timing light. The monitor LED on the front panel should simultaneously

glow dimly, increasing in brightness with increasing knock retard. If you have the Safeguard knock/retard bar graph display, you can also see the exact amount of retard.

- Assuming the Safeguard unit is working properly, set the dip switches to return the unit to individual-cylinder retard mode, and 10-degree maximum retard. Reconnect the source of manifold pressure. Set the sensitivity control to mid-range.

Adjust Safeguard sensitivity as follows:

- Keep in mind that a common mistake is to set the sensitivity control to maximum. This will usually cause the unit to over-retard due to engine noise.
- Begin by setting sensitivity to mid-range and road-testing the vehicle.
- Run the vehicle up to highway cruising speed.
- To ensure that the Safeguard is armed, find a slight hill, and load the engine to 0 vacuum. This should avoid knock, but arm the unit. Increase the sensitivity until the unit just starts to retard due to engine noise. This is easiest to do if you have the optional knock retard monitor.
- If you don't have a monitor, the monitor LED on the front panel will glow dimly, increasing in brightness with increasing knock retard.
- Give the unit only as much sensitivity as it takes to make the ping go away.

Observe the monitor LED when setting the boost retard. Adjust the boost retard so that knock retard is kept at a minimum. If the engine is equipped with a turbo or supercharger, adjust the boost retard start and rate, which calibrate the minimum manifold pressure for onset of automatic boost retard and the rate of retard per psi increase in manifold pressure. At full counter-clockwise, the boost retard start knob begins automatic retard at 0 psi, and at fully clockwise, automatic boost retard begins at 10 psi. At full counter-clockwise the boost retard rate is 0 degrees per psi, and 2 degrees per psi at full clockwise.

Obviously, manifold-pressure-based boost retard is not a factor on nitrous engines without any type of air-supercharging, in which case automatic nitrous retard will remove timing when required.

INSTALLING A PROGRESSIVE NITROUS CONTROLLER

This can be as simple as mounting the controller box in a convenient place and connecting power, ground, input trigger, and solenoid driver output. On the other hand, some progressive nitrous capabilities are more complex, providing ignition retard, knock control, multi-stage, rpm window, cranking ignition delay, additional (electronic) injector controller, and powerful fuel interceptor capabilities. There is much more information about interceptors and piggybacks in my book *How to Tune and Modify Engine Management Systems*, also available from Motorbooks.

Once a progressive controller is installed, you'll have to configure (program) the controller to determine start duty cycle, build-up time to full power, and in some cases such parameters as initial delay, final duty cycle, run timer, and burn-out proceedure.

TYPICAL NITROUS POST-INSTALLATION CHECKLIST

- Verify nitrous or fuel jetting sizes.
- Change fuel filter.
- Purge nitrous line of any debris.
- Verify nitrous-off fuel-rail pressure (typically 39 psi with vacuum reference hose disconnected).
- Ensure a pressure gauge is in place to verify fuel pressure rise during nitrous injection.
- New spark plugs should be installed one to two heat ranges colder.
- Orient the nitrous tank per instructions so G-forces don't interrupt the flow of liquid nitrous on hard acceleration.
- Retard static spark timing as per instructions if applicable.
- Optional low-rpm limit switch prevents nitrous engagement at too-low rpm.
- Perform a compression test/leak down on the engine (before and after).
- Flow-test fuel injectors for uniformity and high-flow rate.
- Use unleaded race gas only in the fuel tank (at least initially, then 92+ only on the street).
- Inspect the stock ignition system (install new plugs, wires, distributor cap, and rotor).

- Upgrade the coil, plugs, and wires (always a good idea on power-modified engines).
- What happens if the tank vents from over-pressure (will the car fill with nitrous-plus and maybe suffocate you, cause you to crash, or hurl from sulfur dioxide inhalation)?
- Are the anti-knock countermeasures in place (e.g., J&S Safeguard Knock Sensor or other boosted-conditions timing retard device)?
- Does fuel pump provide sufficient volume?
- Is the nitrous tank pressure OK?
- Is a fire extinguisher on hand?
- Is the nitrous system armed?
- Any chance nitrous has been released into the intake manifold during shutdown? (This can cause a huge explosion on startup.)
- Make sure the engine is above 2,500 rpm before the full-throttle nitrous run begins.
- Use the smallest nitrous-shot as a starting place.
- Is the clutch up to the job (depending on the tires)?
- Is the nitrous nozzle perpendicular to the throttle and centered in the air intake or throttlebody?
- Do you have an extra car available, just in case you smoke the engine?
- Do you have a change of underwear available (in case you don't)?

Chapter 6
Tuning and Optimizing Nitrous Injection

They don't make nitrous engines like they used to, and this definitely impacts the difficulty of the tuning task. The earliest applications for nitrous oxide on World War II piston-engine combat aircraft were designed to boost power temporarily in order to improve climb performance, top speed, and service ceiling during emergency conditions—providing what amounted to a piston-engine "afterburner." In this type of application, the engine operates at a relatively constant speed as it struggles to lift a heavy weight at maximum speed against the force of gravity or air resistance, and maximum performance is truly a function of continuous raw horsepower—continuous but temporary. Like a jet engine on afterburner, the maximum duration of warbird power boost was typically measured in tens of seconds or, at most, a few minutes. And after a half-hour or so of nitrous boost, mechanics rebuilt the engine.

In modern times, there are limited twenty-first-century nitrous applications comparable to a nitrous-sprayed piston-engine spy plane clawing for altitude or a nitrous-injected pursuit plane dog-fighting early Nazi jets. Constant raw power is the key to success only in certain performance niches like glamour-class air racing, land-speed-record trials, tractor-pulling, sand dune climbing, as well as certain marine applications where a burst of horsepower at the right time can be important (drug runners, anyone?). In every other application—including drag racing, circle-track racing, hill climbs, sprinting, slalom racing, and rallying—acceleration is critical. In most modern nitrous applications the engine is required to produce hard acceleration for brief periods across a wide dynamic range of engine rpm and vehicle speed.

So the question these days is rarely how much peak power the engine can achieve in a narrow speed range, or even how fast the vehicle goes, but how *fast it goes fast*—with drag racing as the primordial example. Acceleration racing is a particularly challenging application for nitrous oxide injection because everything is changing in such a huge hurry, and nitrous injection can be dynamically unstable and difficult or impossible to control precisely due to changing environmental factors: As they used to say, everything depends on everything else, and nothing is certain. A lot of things must happen in order to go fast *fast*, but whether you're on the track or street, a sudden uncontrollable burst of ass-kicking power that smokes the tires, turns the car sideways, and tears up the transmission is worse than useless.

Bob Norwood and crew preparing to race the T&T Celica dragger at Redline 1/8th-mile drag strip near Rockwall, Texas, east of Dallas-Fort Worth. All engine management is from a (nitrous-capable!) Motec M880 engine management system, configurable and tunable via laptop computer. Power comes from a gigantic Garret GT-45 turbo, but Norwood, who did some of the original automotive nitrous research in the 1960s and early 1970s, has employed intermittent progressive nitrous injection to eliminate turbo lag.

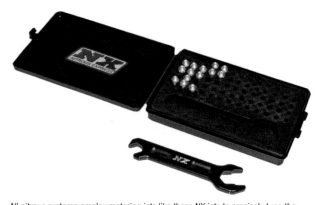

All nitrous systems employ metering jets like these NX jets to precisely tune the nitrous-fuel ratio and determine the size of the horsepower boost. Unfortunately, nitrous pressure, temperature, and density also have a large effect on fluid mass flow through the jets. *Nitrous Express*

INSTALLING, BREAKING, AND DYNO-TESTING WET AND DRY-EFI NITROUS KITS ON A 1.6-LITER HONDA CRX SI

When I was young and stupid I had this Honda CRX Si magazine project car, ready to yank and bank, looking bad with new paint, ready to stop in a hurry with Stillen upgrade brakes and suspension, all ready for air-supercharging with an Alamo Autosports turbo kit. The project was ultimately a turbo build-up, but I had this NOS 50-horse *PowerFogger* "wet-kit" nitrous system, still shiny brand-new and shrink-wrapped to the original cardboard, ready and willing to make horsepower at a moment's notice.

Tests on the Alamo Autosports Dynojet chassis dynamometer revealed that the 1.6 Honda engine was indeed healthy, with less than 6 percent cylinder leak down and *driving-wheel* power at 96.9 horsepower (as good as it gets on a stock 1989 CRX Si, which had 108 advertised horsepower at the crankshaft). On the road, Honda's bone-stock 9:1 compression 1.6-liter 16-valve single overhead cam (SOHC) port-EFI engine was great fun in the lightweight 2,100-pound car. With no hot-rodding modifications the car responded smartly when you punched it, and the engine sounded great.

Nitrous injection has a reputation as the fastest, cheapest path to unmanning bigger engines and faster cars, but it also has a reputation as a loose cannon. In this case, however, I knew people who'd used this type of kit on the 1.6 Honda with good results. And the whole thing bolts on in a few hours. It seemed almost irresponsible not to hang that nitrous kit on the Project CRX at some stage for a head-to-head turbo-nitrous comparison. On a 1989 CRX, a 50-shot nitrous kit would add 50 percent more peak power, and blast torque to the stratosphere at lower rpm where nitrous' effect on instantaneous twisting force is even more dramatic.

The thing to keep in mind is that fogger nitrous systems spew wet "fog" into the intake charge from a single nozzle a short distance upstream of the throttle (NOS recommends a straight shot of 6 to 12 inches, though the Honda air inlet makes a 90-degree turn several inches from the throttlebody) that mixes nitrous and fuel by blasting 900-psi nitrous liquid directly at the 40-psi fuel at close range. This is truly single-point nitrous injection, and you have to hope the air, fuel, and nitrous stay nicely mixed all the way past the throttle and through the intake manifold plenum and runners, such that each cylinder gets the

Here's the NOS fogger system we tried first on the 1.6L Honda CRX project: Simple NOS 5130 wet fogger kit for EFI applications. *NOS*

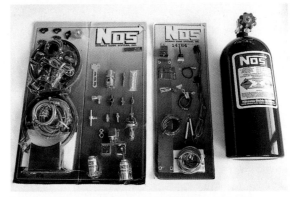

And here's the NOS 5122 Dry kit that worked best for us on the CRX. Supplemental enrichment fuel comes from the stock electronic injectors when the NOS kit applied regulated nitrous pressure to the stock pressure regulator reference port to jack up fuel pressure by 30-40 psi.

proper dose of nitrous, gasoline, and air in one well-mixed homogenous cloud of vapor.

The trouble is, gasolines, nitrous, and air have different fluid dynamics and they don't corner equally well in a twisting, turning manifold, which is why "wet" carbureted manifolds are designed with special dams, ribs, cross-sections and gentle turns to distribute air-fuel charge as evenly as possible among the cylinders and to keep wet gasoline from dropping out of the air and condensing in the manifold. In fact, except on race engines, wet manifolds are commonly heated to improve vaporization and keep the gasoline suspended in air—which, of course, decreases volumetric efficiency, particularly at lower engine speeds. Modern dry EFI manifolds like the one on the CRX are optimized with inertial and resonation tuning effects to cram the maximum amount of air in the cylinders—with no consideration given to keeping gasoline suspended in air as is the case with wet carb or throttlebody-injection manifolds. EFI manifolds are designed to get the maximum equal air charge to all cylinders, but distributing gasoline evenly to the cylinders requires port fuel injectors.

According to NOS and Alamo Autosports, plenty of people had run fogger systems on EFI 1.6-liter Hondas with good results, sometimes with nitrous jets up to an 80-shot. I'd been planning to write—in theory—about how you have to be careful with nitrous, how too much nitrous or too little gasoline can toast your engine in a matter of two or three seconds, and how nitrous can literally explode the intake or crankcase. How Dallas supertuner Bob Norwood once destroyed a twin-turbo Ferrari Testarossa intake plenum and engine cover using nitrous when seemingly unrelated wiring caused a nitrous system solenoid to malfunction. As it turned out, none of that was necessary.

What happened is we made a single awesome nitrous run with the fogger kit. I pulled the CRX onto the Dynojet and made a benchmark dyno pull at stock power with the nitrous disabled. Then brought the engine back up to 2,500, put the hammer down hard to 100 percent, and as the engine revved through three grand, flicked a dash-mounted arming switch to bring the nitrous on-line. The D16A6 engine let out a low-pitched growl like a PCP-hyped Frankenstein clearing his throat, gained super powers, and spun up the two 1,200-pound Dynojet rollers in a mad, nitrous-enhanced dash to the redline, and when I dumped the throttle, reverted instantly back to its mild-mannered secret identity as a 1.6-liter Honda economy car. We graciously accepted the applause of

The first thing when installing a nitrous kit is to find a place to mount the nitrous tank. We installed ours right behind the driver's seat in front of the luggage compartment where the valve can easily be actuated from the driver's seat.

You need an arming switch to disable nitrous boost when you're all about peace and love. We installed this trick NOS switch with (red) flip-up safety cover in a convenient place near the key.

the onlookers and drove (fast) to the local saloon for beers where pretty young barmaids hung leis around our necks and kissed us on the lips.

Unfortunately, that didn't happen. The instant the CRX's roar fell back to an idle, it was clear something was very wrong. The car was missing and stumbling like a zombie, hitting on maybe half the cylinders. Following that one nitrous run, the CRX was left with approximately enough guts to labor off the dyno under its own power and limp across the lot into an empty parking spot where it immediately stalled into a deep coma. The crowd of onlookers stood by in the sudden stillness, letting out half-hearted rebel yells and farting noises. OK, that didn't happen either, but it should've.

As expected, testing revealed the 1.6 engine's two center holes had zero compression. We hoped the problem was something easy—a blown head gasket, maybe. Forensic analysis by yours truly on a marathon Saturday night cylinder-head R&R session revealed that three of the Honda's eight exhaust valves looked as if someone had attacked them with an oxyacetylene cutting torch. In the space of a few late-night hours at Alamo Autosports, I removed, disassembled, and resurfaced the

head, replaced and lapped the bad valves, made sure everything else (pistons, and so on) looked to be in good shape, then cleaned and block-sanded the deck surface of the block, reinstalled the head, and buttoned up the engine. The whole sorry episode was such a perfect lesson in what *not* to do that I should probably claim we did it on purpose.

In any case, we fired up the newly repaired engine at about 2 a.m. Sunday morning. None of us looked too good by this time, but I must've been living right, or something: The engine fired up immediately and ran like a top. A new dynorun proved the 1.6 had exactly as much power as before we'd flame-torched three of the four exhaust valves on the two center cylinders. Things could've been much worse: melted or cracked pistons, broken ring lands, squeezed or broken rings, and flame-torched valves. Clearly there'd been a relative lack of gasoline or an overabundance of nitrous in the center cylinders. In this kind of situation, likely causes include a weak fuel pump (resulting in fuel rail pressure drop) or insufficient straight-line distance between the fogger nozzle and the throttle plate that results in insufficient nitrous-fuel mixing before the charge hits the throttle plate—sending freezing-cold boiling nitrous and

Here's the Honda CRX with NOS Fogger wet nitrous kit installed. Note the long braided-steel lines snaking around from the solenoids on the passenger-side firewall to the fogger nozzle a short distance upstream of the throttle body. This is a 40-horse nitrous boost on a 110-horse engine. A 14-foot braided steel nitrous supply line travels under the car to the engine compartment and upward to the nitrous solenoid. The nitrous fuel supply is tapped off a Y-fitting in the high-pressure rubber EFI fuel line downstream of the fuel filter on the firewall. No muss, no fuss.

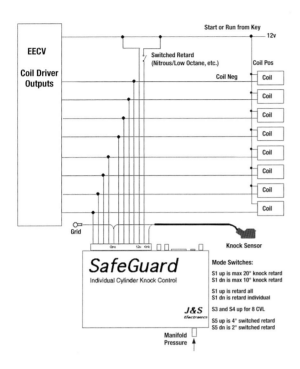

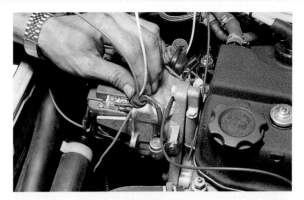

When we installed the dry nitrous system, we decided to get smart and install a J&S SafeGuard individual-cylinder knock sensor system which would listen for spark knock in the various cylinders and retard timing exclusively on the subset of cylinders that are typically actually detonating. Here's the wiring diagram for the Safeguard.

Installing the Safeguard knock sensor system required opening the distributor/coil unit to intercept the coil-driver signal so that the Safeguard could introduce a delay in spark timing on a stroke-by-stroke basis.

fuel droplets dodging past the throttle and careening through the dry intake manifold in such a way that the nitrous and fuel *never* fully mix. The Honda's two center holes had clearly received a relative surplus of nitrous that burned the available gasoline and then, with nothing else to do, burned up three exhaust valves where they'd been preheated from previous combustion cycles.

Single-nozzle nitrous systems for naturally aspirated EFI cars like the CRX can work well, but nozzle location is critical and the wrong location can nuke an engine. When fogger systems don't work right, the problem is virtually always enrichment fuel starvation at one or more cylinders. The fluid dynamics of freezing-cold vaporizing nitrous and raw gasoline entering through a fogger nozzle in the air intake, mixing, then blasting around the throttle plate and into the howling winds of a long-runner EFI manifold can obviously be problematic in a manifold not specifically designed to handle liquid.

At this point, we acquired a 50-shot NOS #5122 dry EFI kit—a highly fail-safe type of universal kit for four- to six-cylinder engines with port EFI. Like the fogger system, the dry kit still injected nitrous a short distance upstream of the CRX's throttle body (optionally *in* the throttle body), in a steady stream, independent of engine speed. But the new kit provided enrichment fuel by artificially jacking up fuel pressure in the injector rail. In this architecture, when the system is armed, a full-throttle micro-switch activates a relay that sends 12-volt power to a primary nitrous solenoid located at the end of the main nitrous supply line. The primary solenoid delivers nitrous oxide to (1) a secondary nitrous solenoid and (2) a regulator that steps down tank pressure to 60 to 70 psi, which is applied to the fuel pressure regulator diaphragm through a T-fitting inserted in the manifold pressure reference line.

The Safeguard dash display illuminates LEDs to indicate when the unit is actually retarding timing. The unit can also display air-fuel ratio if connected to an O_2 sensor.

A bypass jet (or check valve) limits the rate at which nitrous pressure can escape backwards through the stock manifold pressure reference line into the intake manifold. The size of the bypass bleed jet thus fine-tunes nitrous pressure to the fuel regulator diaphragm, which, in turn, raises fuel pressure to the injectors during nitrous boost by a calibrated amount. The result is a substantial gain in fuel pressure during nitrous boost, from the stock CRX Honda's normal 36-psi maximum to a design pressure in the 60- to 70-psi range. Each fuel injector squirt now provides enough additional gasoline to combust the additional oxygen that will be supplied by the nitrous. When rail pressure reaches 50 psi,

The NOS 5122 dry nitrous system uses two nitrous solenoids and a nitrous pressure regulator to provide nitrous oxide injection and fuel enrichment. The first solenoid is activated when full throttle triggers start of boost. This solenoid delivers reduced nitrous pressure through the pressure regulator to the reference port in the fuel pressure regulator, causing fuel pressure to begin increasing. When fuel pressure climbs to a preset level, a pressure switch in the fuel rail activates the primary nitrous solenoid, which begins flowing nitrous oxide through a single-point nozzle located upstream of the throttle in the intake. If fuel pressure for any reason drops below the threshold pressure, the pressure switch automatically terminates nitrous injection.

To enhance the performance of the CRX's wimpy stock in-tank EFI fuel pump selected by Honda to fuel 109 crankshaft horsepower in the CRX, we installed this inline booster pump to handle the heavy lifting of delivering 150-200 horsepower worth of total fuel at 70-80 psi fuel pressure.

a NOS pressure switch installed in the fuel rail or supply line grounds and opens the secondary nitrous solenoid, delivering nitrous oxide to a fan spray nozzle in the engine intake. If fuel pressure ever drops below the threshold of 50 psi, the fuel pressure switch immediately cuts off nitrous flow by de-energizing the primary nitrous solenoid, preventing lean-mixture engine damage.

When might rail pressure drop? This should never be able to happen, because the fuel pump capacity should exceed the maximum requirement of the engine at peak horsepower and fuel pressure under worst conditions. Worst conditions includes maximum all-motor fuel injection (factoring in power modifications to the engine that increase breathing capability and fuel requirements), maximum supplemental fuel for the nitrous horsepower shot, and air-density fuel corrections in cold weather or low elevation. What's more, fuel pumps can lose efficiency due to aging, and battery voltage can drop, reducing the pumping capacity of the fuel pump. There could be a minor—almost invisible—fuel leak that is the final factor that pushes the total fuel requirement beyond what the fuel pump can deliver, causing rail pressure to drop.

A dry EFI kit, like the NOS 5122, only puts nitrous into the manifold plenum, not fuel. Injected nitrous liquid immediately begins to vaporize, making additional "free" power available from the VE improvements of a denser air charge. Nitrous vapor is heavier than air but it behaves much like air in the manifold, hitching a ride into the cylinders and enriching the oxygen content of the intake charge by up to 10 percent. By the time the nitrous reaches the intake valve, it has warmed up enough that it has little detrimental effect on gasoline vaporization. When nitrous is heated to 560 degrees F in the combustion chamber, the oxygen and nitrous molecules break apart and the oxygen becomes available for combustion.

Having been burned (literally!) once, when we installed the NOS dry EFI nitrous system on the Honda, I acquired two auxiliary devices to increase the safety margin of the system. One was an NOS 550-horsepower, in-line high-pressure electric fuel pump. The other was a first-generation J&S SafeGuard individual cylinder knock-retard computer. The NOS pump can be installed in line anywhere upstream of

Here's the NOS dry EFI kit we installed on the CRX on NOS recommendation after the wet fogger nitrous kit toasted three exhaust valves in a dyno pull. With fuel delivered from the stock electronic injectors, fuel distribution is guaranteed accurate, assuming the fuel injectors are in good shape. Have them flow-tested if there is any doubt. Single-point nitrous injection requires careful placement for good distribution, but the task is made easier by the fact that some of the nitrous liquid immediately vaporizes in the intake. The NOS dry kit gave us zero trouble, but keep in mind that it is difficult or impossible for most dry nitrous systems to achieve consistent oxygen-fuel ratios across the rpm range when the nitrous remains constant but the fuel pressure increases that provide fuel enrichment act on injection pulse width that does change across the rpm range in concert with engine volumetric efficiency.

the fuel rail, but Alamo prefers to see it installed downstream of the fuel filter. We installed it in the Honda's engine compartment and wired it to an automotive relay such that it only ran when the nitrous system was armed by turning on the dash-mounted switch. In this situation it is wise to verify that any auxiliary inline fuel pump does not interfere with the stock EFI fuel pump functionality when the auxiliary pump is off.

The SafeGuard easily wired into the stock Honda ignition, providing the ability to remove up to 20 degrees of timing in 2-degree increments from any cylinder found to be knocking by a knock sensor that bolted into the block or intake manifold. The knock threshold for any particular cylinder can depend on a lot of factors, and rarely will all cylinders on an engine begin knocking at once. The great thing about

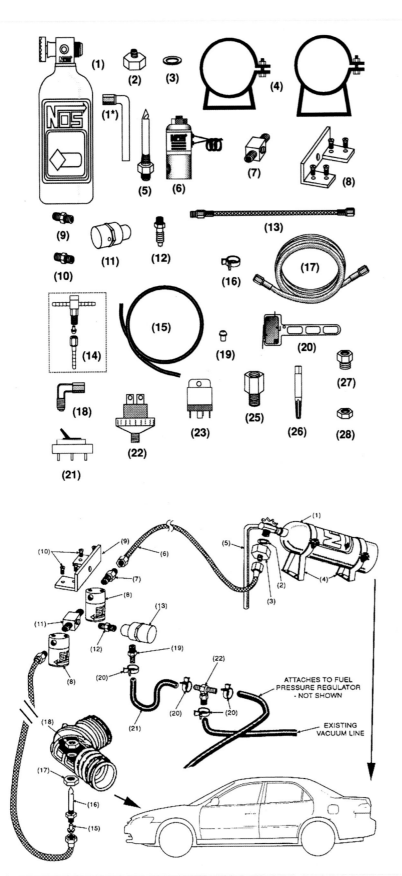

NOS 5122 Kit Components legend

Item	Description	Qty
1	Bottle 10 lb.	1
2	Bottle Valve Adapter (4 AN)	1
3	Bottle Valve Washer	1
4	Bottle Bracket Set	1
(5)	Fan Spray Nozzle (Blue)	1
6	Nitrous Solenoid	2
7	Nitrous Solenoid Tee	1
8	Solenoid Mounting Bracket	1
9	4 AN Nitrous Filter Fitting	1
(10)	1/8" NPT Male × 1/8" NPT Male Nipple	1
11	Nitrous Pressure Regulator	1
12	1/8" NPT × 3/16" Hose Barb	1
13	3 AN Hose ml 1/8" NPT Male Fitting	1
14	Vacuum Hose Pressure Tee	1
(15)	Vacuum Hose	1
16	Ratcheting Hose Clamps	5
17	Main N20 Feed Line 4 AN 14 ft.	1
18	4 AN × 4 AN 90° Fitting (optional)	1
19	Flare Jet	1
(20)	Microswitch Bracket	1
21	8-32 × 5/16 Phil Pan Screw	4
22	Fuel Pressure Safety Switch	1
23	Wiring Relay-30 AMP	1
24	Harness for Wiring Relay	1
(25)	G.M. Schrader Tube	1
26	1/16" NPT Tap	1
27	Nozzle Mounting Collar	1
28	Nozzle Mounting Nut	1
29	1/8 NPT Female Coupler	1
(30)	Adapter-4AN ml × 1/16 NPT ml	1
31	14 Gauge Blue Wire	1
32	16 Gauge Red Wire	1
33	14 Gauge Green Wire	1
(34)	Cap Plug	1
(35)	Relay Supplement Wiring	1
	Open Spade Terminal	2
	Ring Terminal	2
	Ring Terminal	1
	Blue Male Spade Connector	1
	Green Male Spade Connector	2
	Ring Terminal	1
(36)	Basic Wire Pack	1
	Rocker Switch	1
	15 amp Fuse	1
	Microswitch	1
	Screws	2
	Nuts	2
	Ring Terminal	3
	Blue Female Spade Connector	7
	Blue Male Spade Connector	1
	Scotch Lock	1

the SafeGuard was that it was designed to listen for knock, identify the cylinders knocking, and retard ignition timing on only the troublemakers rather than retarding all cylinders at once like most contemporary factory knock sensor systems. This strategy maintains higher power and lower coolant-jacket temperatures, while protecting the engine from damage.

NOS specified that a 50-shot Honda EFI nitrous system is workable with stock timing and premium street fuel, but the Safeguard was good insurance to kill knock before it could hurt the engine in case of unexpected nitrous combustion heat or pressure, or the wrong gasoline. The Safeguard was designed to remove timing from individual cylinders in 2-degree increments, the dash-mounted display illuminating the corresponding number of LEDs for the various cylinders, thus enabling a driver to be aware of when there *would've* been detonation without the Safeguard, and on how many cylinders. An adjustment screw provided sensitivity calibration to tune out normal engine sounds that might otherwise trigger unintended ignition retard. We never saw evidence of the Safeguard killing *nitrous* knock, but later in the CRX project, we did later occasionally see it eliminate detonation from too much turbo boost. The Safeguard package included an auxiliary wiring harness, processor module, indicator module, knock sensor, as well as power and ground leads. In the case of the CRX, which has a distributor ignition, the best method of supplying power to the module involved tapping into the low-voltage ignition wiring inside the CRX's integrated distributor/coil module. Ideally, the knock sensor should be mounted at the top-center of the block near the head, but we didn't find a convenient threaded hole, and instead mounted it near the driver's end of the block.

Honda CRX with turbocharger and NOS 5122 dry nitrous kit installed. After initial dyno testing with nitrous injection, a turbocharger conversion was installed, and the nitrous system converted to an intermittent hit used briefly to provide a burst of low-end torque and quick turbocharger spool-up controlled by a nitrous-capable Accel aftermarket engine management system.

Programming the CRX's Accel computer-controlled nitrous engine management system with a laptop computer.

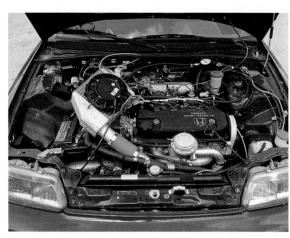

With the Accel EMS optimized, the next step was dyno-testing with an air-air intercooler installed. Nitrous liquid injection provides massive intercooling during nitrous boost, but with the turbo installed, nitrous injection would only happen for very fired periods. The dual-power-adder system approximately doubled stock horsepower from 97 front-wheel horsepower to over 200 on the Dynojet.

The bottom line is that *using, tuning, and optimizing modern nitrous injection to maximize acceleration is a cute trick.* We're used to modern street cars with computer-controlled engines that run flawlessly with clean exhaust emissions under all conditions, but in many ways nitrous injection is a throwback to earlier times when mechanical engine management systems were unpredictable and crude, and far less effective at precisely controlling an engine. Believe it or not, there was a time when engines would sometimes refuse to start at all because they were "flooded" or suffering from "vapor-lock." There was a time when people would give their carbureted Ferrari an "Italian tuneup," because redlining certain classic Italian sports cars as hard and long as possible could sometimes make the engine run better by burning carbon off the plugs. Tuning modern street vehicles with nitrous injection can be a matter of "2009, meet 1959."

TU-NING

Anyway, back to the future. You've installed a commercial nitrous kit or a do-it-yourself custom nitrous-injection system that looked good in theory. You've tightened that last screw, and your engine now has super powers. Yeeeeeeehah!!!

Well, no. Two nanoseconds after you tighten the last screw on the installation is not the time to fire up the engine

Big domestic V-8 competition engines have used nitrous to produce unbelievable horsepower. Three hundred horsepower is easy on a big-block Chevy V-8, and people have achieved more than 1,000 horsepower on big-block methanol dragsters. More to the point, how much additional power can a street Honda engine stand before it gives up and heads for that big dragstrip in the sky? Experts used to say you shouldn't add more than 30 to 50 percent more power to an engine unless you upgrade the engine's internals (particularly the pistons and rods). According to NOS, 50 horsepower was the maximum reliable horsepower you could use on a stock D16A6 Honda, though NOS admitted there were people out there driving "time-bomb" stock Hondas equipped with 60- or 80-horse port-injection NOS systems that are still living. These systems are logically similar to our 50 system, but with larger nitrous jetting, recalibrated nitrous pressure to the Honda fuel pressure regulator for increased fueling, and individual nitrous lines running to each intake runner with separate injection nozzles for each cylinder.

The NOS EFI nitrous system was advertised to deliver 50 crankshaft horsepower. Testing on the Alamo Autosports Dynojet chassis dyno revealed a gain in peak power of 38 horsepower at the wheels, increasing power from 96 to 134 horsepower with the nitrous active—a 40 percent power boost. Considering that the car's 108 advertised crankshaft horsepower translated to 96 wheel horsepower on a chassis dyno—an 11 percent drivetrain and rolling resistance loss—134 nitrous wheel horsepower translates to about 151 crankshaft horsepower, an actual gain of approximately 43 horsepower. This was clearly a conservative rich calibration that could have made more power if the fuel pressure was brought down a little to lean out the oxygen-fuel ratio, but we stuck with the NOS factory calibration and moved on.

The really great thing about nitrous injection is that the entire horsepower boost (and additional torque) was available instantly at 2,500 rpm (the lowest activation rpm recommended by NOS), with the power boost continuing all the way to redline. With the car strapped hard to the Dynojet where tire slip is virtually impossible no matter what the torque boost, we were worried about clutch slip, but that never occurred until later in the project when we were adding as much as 100 horsepower with turbo boost.

NOS 5122 Tuning

Configuration	N_2O Jetting	Fuel Quality	Ignition Timing	Plugs
05122NOS	.032"	92+ Octane	Stock	Stock
05120NOS	.036"	92+ Octane	Stock	Stock
05175NOS	.045"	92+ Octane	Stock	Stock

Tuning the CRX with NOS 5122 dry EFI nitrous installed.

Testing the nitrous, turbo conversion, and Accel engine management on the Alamo Autosports Dynojet chassis dynamometer.

It wasn't long before the stock clutch was toast, so we installed this aftermarket clutch designed for smooth performance street use rather than all-out drag launches.

and flog it immediately to full howl for an Italian tuneup. No one who can spell I.Q. does this with a virgin spray motor.

The trick with nitrous is to start with the smallest viable horsepower shot and *tune* the package of engine, nitrous system, and vehicle to work well together. This is not the time to be impatient or lazy, and it's not the time to tell yourself, hey, NOS engineers designed the kit, and that's good enough for me. The priority at the company that sold you the nitrous kit or components is not to optimize your vehicle's performance but to keep the nitrous kit from destroying your engine—or at least to avoid the perception that it was their fault the nitrous kit burned down your engine. It is not their problem if you run it forever dead rich, washing down the cylinder walls with gasoline and polluting the earth with black smoke until the engine is old before its time. Nitrous kits are designed to be as tolerant as possible of wrong timing, wrong air-fuel-nitrous mixtures, wrong fuel, wrong tires, wrong transmissions, wrong suspensions, wrong wiring, wrong fuel pumps, and every other depressing thought you can imagine. There are almost always ways to squeeze more performance out of a nitrous engine and vehicle on up to and beyond meltdown. The Zen of successful hot rodding and racing is to think of that last tightened screw not as the end of the installation, but as an important milestone in an interesting ongoing science project.

Post-installation is a great time to take a break, have a beer, get some sleep. There is a very good chance you have made some mistakes that could be dangerous to you and your engine—or at least your wallet. The next step is to think again.

THINK AGAIN BEFORE STARTING

Primary State of Tune. It is a fool's errand to attempt running nitrous if the engine was not running all that great without nitrous. I am constantly amazed what hot rodders are willing to put up with from modified engines. If there is the slightest doubt about the quality of the calibration, take the vehicle to a dyno shop with a well-maintained wideband lambda meter, and log some full-power dyno runs while

NX 38 jet. The ratio of the sizes of the nitrous and fuel jets depends largely on fuel and nitrous pressure. *Nitrous Express*

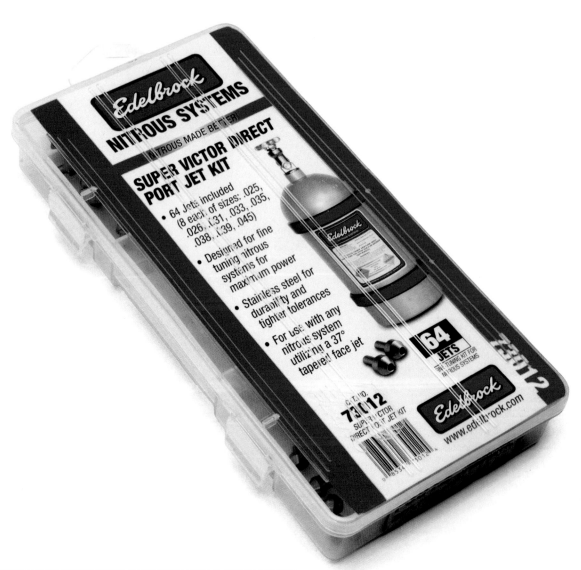

Super Victor direct port V-8 direct-port jet kit with eight groups of eight jets. *Edelbrock*

TUNING AND OPTIMIZING NITROUS INJECTION

140

NITROUS OXIDE & FUEL JET SIZES

Nitrous Jet Size In Millimeters 1 mm = 0.03936 inch	Approx Power increase with 800 psi Nitrous Oxide pressure	Fuel Jet (mm) for a 3 BAR or 45 psi (above manifold) fuel injected	Fuel Jet (mm) for a separate fuel pump & regulator set to 10 psi pressure	Fuel Jet (mm) for a fuel pump & regulator that also feeds carburetors at 3 psi	Motorcycles that use gravity feed from tank No Fuel pump needed	FLOW RATE - Time to fill a 1 Pint container with fuel. (+ / - 5%)
0.30	6.3 bhp		0.30	0.40		1,031 sec
0.35	8.6 bhp	Too small for reliability & practicality	0.35	0.50		755 sec
0.40	11.2 bhp		0.40	0.55		580 sec
0.45	14.2 bhp	0.300	0.45	0.60		457 sec
0.50	17.5 bhp	0.325	0.50	0.70		317 sec
0.55	21.2 bhp	0.350	0.55	0.75		309 sec
0.60	25.2 bhp	0.400	0.60	0.80	*1.50	260 sec
0.65	29.5 bhp	0.450	0.65	0.90	*1.70	216 sec
0.70	34.3 bhp	0.475	0.70	0.95	*1.90	191 sec
0.75	39.4 bhp	0.500	0.75	1.00	*2.10	162 sec
0.80	44.8 bhp	0.525	0.80	1.10	*2.10 / no jet	144 sec
0.85	50.6 bhp	0.550	0.85	1.15		130 sec
0.90	56.7 bhp	0.600	0.90	1.20		114 sec
0.95	63.2 bhp	0.625	0.95	1.30		103 sec
1.00	70.0 bhp	0.675	1.00	1.35		92 sec
1.05	77.1 bhp	0.700	1.05	1.40		84 sec
1.10	84.7 bhp	0.725	1.10	1.50		77 sec
1.15	92.5 bhp	0.775	1.15	1.55		71 sec
1.20	100.2 bhp	0.800	1.20	1.60		65 sec
1.25	109.3 bhp	0.825	1.25	1.70		59 sec
1.30	118.3 bhp	0.875	1.30	1.75		55 sec
1.35	127.5 bhp	0.900	1.35	1.80		51 sec
1.40	137.4 bhp	0.950	1.40	1.90		47 sec
1.50	157.5 bhp	1.000	1.50	2.00		41 sec
1.60	179.2 bhp	1.075	1.60	2.15		36 sec
1.70	202.3 bhp	1.150	1.70	2.30		32 sec
1.80	226.8 bhp	1.200	1.80			29 sec
1.90	252.7 bhp	1.275	1.90	Larger Solenoid		26 sec
2.00	280.0 bhp	1.350	2.00			23 sec

Calculated nitrous sizes for various horsepower and various fuel pressures. *www.nitrousinfo.com*

Most fuel pressure regulators are equipped to adjust fuel pressure (and, therefore, the oxygen-fuel ratio) by adjusting pre-load against the regulator diaphragm spring. Many nitrous tuners commonly fine-tune the oxygen-fuel ratio not by changing jets, but by adjusting fuel pressure. This is a standard EFI return-type fuel pressure regulator designed to vary fuel pressure according to a manifold pressure reference signal. Some dry nitrous kits hijack the reference signal during nitrous boost by feeding regulated nitrous pressure to the fuel pressure regulator (with an adjustable bleed determining how much nitrous pressure is bypassed), causing fuel pressure and fuel delivery to spike and increase fuel delivery per injector squirt. *MSD*

recording air-fuel ratio. If there is a way to do it, road- or track-test the vehicle while datalogging the air-fuel ratio, and analyze the plausibility of the engine's state of tune under a variety of realistic conditions before turning on the nitrous.

Nitrous Jetting. If you have no previous experience with nitrous oxide injection, you should definitely rethink the size of the nitrous jetting before taking the vehicle on its virgin nitrous voyage. Start with the smallest jetting recommended by the manufacturer as feasible, even if that means acquiring smaller jets than the original equipment supplied with a kit. You won't regret it. Start small or very small with the nitrous system. A 25-horse shot may seem ridiculously small, but it is a great shakeout jetting on a street car because it is fairly difficult to break anything with only 25 horsepower. Start small, shake things out, tune, calibrate, optimize, try again, take notes, live, and learn. These days, many nitrous kits arrive with a variety of jets, but if yours didn't, buy a jetting kit or a selection of metering jets that will take you all the way from mild to wild with ample ability to tune the oxygen-fuel ratio along the way.

One excellent reason to resist going nuts with the initial nitrous jetting is to keep from killing your stock transmission or clutch. A nitrous powerplant delivers tremendous torque at the lower end of the nitrous rpm range as the fixed nitrous and fuel flow is divided among a relatively small number of power strokes. The shock loading of a massive low-end nitrous

torque hit can kill an automatic transmission or clutch in one hard drag run. You should definitely investigate the known torque and power limitations of the clutch or auto trans, and compare this to the projected peak torque that will be generated at various rpm breakpoints during nitrous boost. Keep in mind that the extreme low-end torque jolt from a hard-hitting nitrous shot is much more likely to wreck a clutch or automatic transmission than torque applied to a drivetrain steadily. Automatic transmissions are especially vulnerable to failure while shifting, which is why some supercharger systems are rigged to foil boost during the shift.

Edelbrock Flow Tool Jet Selection Chart

Jets Size	X4 Jets	X8 Jets	Jet Size	X4 Jets	X8 Jets
14	28	40	15	30	42
16	32	45	17	34	48
18	36	51	19	38	54
20	40	57	21	42	59
22	44	62	23	46	65
24	48	68	25	50	71
26	52	74	27	54	76
28	56	79	29	58	82
30	60	85	31	62	88
32	64	91	33	66	93
34	68	96	35	70	99
36	72	102	37	74	105
38	76	107	39	78	110
40	80	113	41	82	116
42	84	119	43	86	
44	88		45	90	
46	92		47	94	
48	96		49	98	
50	100		51	102	
52	104		53	106	
54	108		55	110	
56	112		57	114	
58	116		59	118	

A Flow Tool enables a tuner to adjust fuel pressure while simulating the effect of fuel usage on fuel pressure. The Flow Tool must have a jet installed with the same total area as the fuel flow area of all nitrous jets. *Edelbrock*

Fuel Temperature. The specific gravity of gasoline is lower in hot weather due to thermal expansion, meaning a cubic centimeter of gasoline will have less mass. This can change the oxygen-fuel ratio if fuel and air temperature are not the same or in the absence of an effective air temperature compensation strategy. Make sure that the supplemental fuel for nitrous enrichment is correct for actual weather conditions.

Fuel Octane. Make sure the tank is fueled with fresh gasoline of the highest possible octane. On a street car with a moderate power boost, unleaded racing gas is good insurance when calibrating a nitrous system. On higher-output engines with

Direct-port nitrous fuel-side pressure regulator. Note Allen-head adjustment bolt with jam nut. Properly adjusting fuel pressure requires a Flow Tool.

high static or effective compression ratio and a lot of boost, you might even want to acquire some leaded racing gasoline, some of which is available with octane approaching 119 to 120 (keeping in mind that it is illegal for stree use and will damage oxygen sensors rather quickly). If you have planned ahead, the vehicle fuel tank was nearly empty before the nitrous installation, in which case it may be possible to remove the drain plug from the tank and drain the small amount of remaining fuel into an auxiliary gas can. Another option is to temporarily reconfigure the fuel system plumbing to deliver the fuel to an auxiliary gas can—or even the fuel tank of another vehicle—and pump the fuel tank empty with the electric fuel pump. There is not much else to do with drained gasoline except burn it in a vehicle, but really old gasoline can knock ferociously even in low-compression grocery-getter engines, so dilute old gasoline with large amounts of fresh gasoline to prevent trouble.

Nitrous Tank Pressure and Temperature. As this book has pointed out at great length, the temperature and pressure of the nitrous tank can have an important impact on nitrous oxide mass flow during boost. When you are calibrating and troubleshooting a freshly installed nitrous system, it is a great idea to control the temperature of the nitrous tank and plumbing to eliminate pressure, temperature, and density variables. If you are not willing or able to install pressure or temperature normalization equipment (bottle heaters, external pressurization systems, and so on), there are still worthwhile steps you can take to remove uncertainty from tuning and thus make the process more scientific. What you definitely do *not* want to do is begin the tuning process on a cold morning with a cold-soaked nitrous tank (and cold-soaked gasoline),

Bypass-type fuel pressure regulator internal structure.

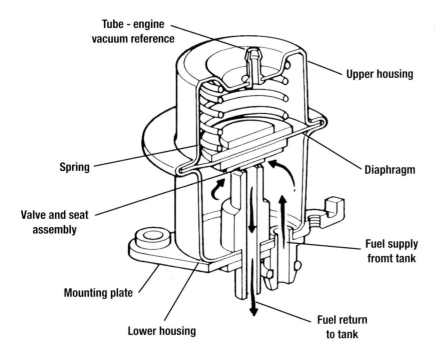

Tube - engine vacuum reference

Upper housing

Spring

Diaphragm

Valve and seat assembly

Fuel supply fromt tank

Mounting plate

Lower housing

Fuel return to tank

and then resume later when the vehicle has sat in the sun for hours and the tank is heat-soaked to near or beyond the critical temperature. What you might want to do is remove the tank and store it overnight indoors in a climate-controlled situation. Pay attention to the weather, and do your test-and-tune sessions at a particular time of day.

Fuel Pressure. Many racers and hot rodders recalibrate the nitrous-fuel ratio on an ongoing basis not by re-jetting the nitrous or enrichment fuel but by calibrating enrichment fuel pressure with an adjustable fuel pressure regulator. On wet nitrous systems with a low-pressure (carbureted) fuel system or a totally independent nitrous fuel supply, it is a simple matter to install (or calibrate) an adjustable fuel pressure regulator to increase or decrease pressure to the fuel solenoid. It's acceptable to enrich fuel delivery by raising pressure, but leaning out the nitrous-fuel ratio

should be handled by reducing the size of the fuel jetting so fuel pressure stays above a certain minimum that prevents unavoidable fuel pressure resonation and spikes from producing significant variations in fuel mass flow. To use fuel pressure as a tuning tool, wet nitrous systems fed from a high-pressure return fuel system of the type used on EFI engines will need an adjustable regulator installed between the main fuel loop and the nitrous solenoid with the initial pressure (and compatible fuel jetting) set at a pressure lower than the fuel loop that allows sufficient headroom to move fuel pressure to the nitrous solenoid either up or down as required to calibrate the oxygen-fuel ratio.

Pressure-regulated dry nitrous systems already calibrate fuel enrichment delivery by increasing fuel pressure to the EFI system during nitrous boost, but this is usually done by delivering regulated nitrous tank pressure to the diaphragm reference port on the stock return-type fuel pressure regulator during boost. On this type of dry nitrous system, the adjustment of the nitrous pressure regulator or the associated adjustable nitrous bypass bleed accomplishes the same thing as an adjustable fuel pressure regulator on a wet system i.e., calibrating fuel delivery during nitrous boost.

Progressive Controls. In some cases a constant-flow nitrous kit will hit too hard. A proportional nitrous controller or nitrous-capable aftermarket EMS enables you to fade in the nitrous and fuel hit gradually using solenoid pulsewidth modulation techniques in order to (1) improve traction, (2) reduce the possibility of engine damage, and (3) protect clutch, automatic transmission, or other drivetrain components from shock damage and premature failure (particularly during the initial stages of the tuning process, when you don't know how fast and hard the nitrous will hit and may not be experienced controlling the vehicle and engine). Some basic progressive controllers simply increase the nitrous or fuel solenoid duty cycle gradually from an initial (configurable) value to 100 percent over a configurable period of seconds or tenths of seconds, while others implement more sophisticated tricks that, for example, change the progression to a configurable maximum-duty cycle according to the gear, rpm, manifold pressure, and so on. You may want to consider installing a progressive controller (or activating progressive controls on a nitrous-capable aftermarket EMS) before using and calibrating the nitrous system.

Nitrous Purge. In some cases it may be difficult to get the nitrous system to hit hard enough. A nitrous purge system hardens the hit by reducing or eliminating nitrous vapor or foam from the initial hit, which increases the immediate nitrous mass flow. A purge system removes uncertainty from the calibration process by allowing you to cool the nitrous supply lines and purge nitrous vapor and heat-soaked nitrous liquid from the nitrous plumbing immediately before triggering boost. This tends to increase

Regulator Settings for NOS	Holley #	Test Jet
	73	.079
Regulators should be set	74	.081
to a flowing fuel pressure.	75	.083
	76	.084
Use a test jet and flow fuel into any container.	77	.086
Use the following formula to determine	78	.089
which jet should be used:	79	.091
	80	.093
Flow Tool Jet Size = SQR	81	.093
[Jet Size² * Number Nozzles]	82	.093
	83	.094
(SQR means take the square root of the quantity.)	84	.099
	85	.100
This is equal to the TEST JET size in thousandths	86	.101
of an inch. Use the table at right	87	.103
for cross-referencing jet sizes.	88	.104
	89	.104
	90	.104
	91	.105
Example:	92	.105
	93	.105
Eight #32 jets are equal to one #91 test jet.	94	.108
	95	.118
	96	.118
32 × 32 = 1024 × 8 jets = 8192.	97	.125
	98	.125
The square root of this number is 90.509.	99	.125
	100	.128
Round it off to 91 and you're there!		

Regulator settings and formulae for Flow Tool jets that approximate various NOS (Holley) fuel jets. *NOS*

Flow Tool Jet Size = $\mathrm{SQR}\ [\text{Jet Size}^2 * \text{Number Nozzles}]$

Flow Tool for setting nitrous fuel pressure under flowing conditions. *Nitrous Express*

Tri-turbo Jaguar with progressive nitrous under 100-percent computer control. All fuel requirements are included in the basic fuel calculation and supplied by two electronic injectors per cylinder on the 4.2L inline six.

the forcefulness of the nitrous hit, but, more important, increases the *repeatability* of the hit so you can depend on events unfolding in a more predictable manner as you trigger boost and evaluate system performance. Purge kits are easy to install, so you might want to consider having one in place from the beginning to make tuning less problematic.

Ignition. Your engine's ignition system will have a harder time firing through the denser air-nitrous-fuel mixture during nitrous boost. Nitrous refrigeration effects that increase charge air density will raise the effective compression ratio of the engine. You can sometimes piss away a fair amount of boost power with weak spark before you can hear actual missing. A high-power aftermarket ignition system is a really good idea for any nitrous system making more than about 25 horsepower. A stronger ignition would typically include upgraded coils and improved high-tension leads (whether true plug wires or the shorter wires of a coil-on-plug direct ignition), an ignition amplifier (which might include capacitive-discharge or multi-spark capabilities), and spark plugs gapped as recommended for the new ignition. Otherwise, you should replace the spark plugs and stock plug wires and make sure that they are routed (if applicable) an inch or so from each other and nearby metal engine components (even if the rerouting doesn't look as good as a tight, parallel array of wires in close proximity to each other). At a minimum you should make sure that existing plug wires and plugs are dead-clean by cleaning with solvent, then re-gap the plugs to .030 or less. If you have doubts about your ignition, there are spark strength testers capable of measuring the power of the spark at the end of the plug wires. Any nitrous system with 50 horsepower or more should run colder plugs (more on this subject in the tuning section of this chapter) to prevent the possibility of the spark plug becoming a glow plug and causing surface ignition.

Timing Controls. Many modest-shot nitrous kits on newer vehicles are designed to get away with stock ignition timing during boost, with no retard required, but the overriding reason for this is a pragmatic one: Ignition timing is not adjustable on late-model (EFI) engines. It's expedient to build

nitrous kits that are workable with stock timing, particularly since the street nitrous market is very price elastic, and no one wants to bundle in—i.e., give away!—the electronic interceptors required to retard timing during nitrous boost on late-model engines.

But stock timing is almost definitely not ideal for any amount of nitrous boost that's enough to be worth doing, with most experts suggesting you should figure on 1 degree of retard per 25 horsepower nitrous boost. Some people have the misconception that maximum power is obtained by running as much timing advance as an engine can tolerate without detonation, but this is wrong. That "low-boost" 50-horse shot Honda dry nitrous kit would probably make better torque or power with at least 2 degrees less timing advance during boost because cylinder pressure is peaking a little too early to maximize torque. What's more, if timing is over-advanced, you need large amounts of fuel in the combustion chambers to kill knock. There is a very good chance that a nitrous kit without timing controls on an engine without adjustable timing is throwing a lot of extra coolant fuel in the engine, which compounds the performance loss from too much nitrous-on timing advance.

In any case, fuel octane and quality can change, as can the octane number requirement (ONR) of the engine, especially if you re-jet the fuel or nitrous (or even along with the *weather*). I firmly believe in the use of boost-retard strategies coupled with individual-cylinder knock control systems. It is just good insurance. Even if boost retard and knock control systems are not required at initial power settings, there is a

Edelbrock Pro-Flo add-on EFI and closed-loop electronic engine management for Chevrolet Small-Block. This is what it takes to provide basic all-motor fuel injection. *Edelbrock*

high likelihood you will not stay with the initial settings. And if your engine is running on the ragged edge of detonation, these devices will enable you to run nitrous boost even if you cannot get fuel with as much an octane as you're used to (if you live in Texas, you're used to 93 octane premium, but the best they've got if you drive to California is 91), or if anything changes that pushes up the ONR of the powerplant during nitrous boost above the octane of available fuel.

PRE-START TESTING

Test Fuel Pump. If you haven't tested fuel pump capacity, now is the time. You are looking to verify that the fuel pump can maintain the required pressure and fuel flow for primary non-boosted fuel requirements *and* for supplemental nitrous enrichment requirements *under worst conditions* (at highest working fuel pressure, with battery/charging system stressed to the maximum with all other electrical appliances running, at peak normal-charged horsepower at low elevation and high barometric pressure).

Follow this test procedure for wet or direct-port nitrous systems:

1. Disconnect electric power from the nitrous solenoid.
2. Close the nitrous bottle control valve.
3. Disconnect the fuel solenoid output pipe from the injection device or fuel distribution manifold.
4. Attach a test nozzle (such as an extra nitrous enrichment fuel nozzle) containing a test fuel

Fuel table for computer-controlled engine management. Note that this system approximates the entire range of all-motor engine conditions for engine speeds ranging from 200 to 6,200 rpms, and for engine loading ranging from 13.44 to 101.57 kPa. Fuel delivery can be changed with a variety of functions from this laptop user interface, the simplest being to retype entries in the table. After reading the look-up fuel value in the basic table, the computer modifies the basic calculation according to factors like coolant temperature, whether nitrous injection is turned on, and the particular nitrous jet size. *Accel*

enrichment jet that's slightly larger than the combined metering capacity of all enrichment jets in the nitrous system to provide a margin of error above the maximum total fuel flow (horsepower!) you need to verify the fuel pump and plumbing can deliver. Alternatively, the actual injection nozzle on a single-point system could be temporarily removed from the manifold and used for the test with the replacement test jet (in this case you'll need to plug the manifold where the nozzle was installed).

5. Run the hose and test nozzle to a large catch bottle.

6. Attach an accurate fuel pressure gauge to the pressurized section of the fuel delivery system using a tee fitting and a long enough hose that the gauge can be routed out of the engine compartment (often through the soft rubber gasket at the rear edge of the hood) and taped to the windshield of the car where it can be read while driving.

7. With the vehicle stopped and the engine running, trigger the nitrous system for a precise period of time that exceeds the expected maximum time of a single episode of nitrous boost.

8. Measure the amount of supplemental fuel pumped during the test and then dispose of the fuel by pouring it back into the fuel tank.

9. Mount the catch bottle in a safe location in the engine compartment, and attach the enrichment fuel solenoid output pipe securely to the bottle.

10. Road-test the car with an assistant monitoring the fuel pressure gauge, repeating the test at wide-open throttle (WOT) for precisely the same length of time as the previous test.

11. Any pressure drop during the test that is larger than 5 to 10 percent (2 to 4 psi on a 40-psi EFI fuel-loop; 1/4 to 1/2 psi on a 5-psi carbureted fuel supply) is a strong indication that the fuel pump is not up to the task of maintaining the required fuel pressure. The fuel pump will have to be upgraded or augmented with an auxiliary pump.

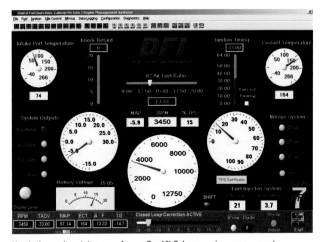

Here's the engine status page from a Gen VII Calmap engine management system, showing 3,450 rpms at 15 percent throttle, and an air-fuel ratio of 13.33. During nitrous boost, air-fuel readout is really showing the air-fuel ratio that would provide residual exhaust gas oxygen equivalent to the air-fuel-nitrous mixture actually going into the engine. *Accel*

12. Compare the volume of fuel in the catch bottle with the results from the previous static test. If the volume pumped is greater than or equal to the previous test and pressure during the test did not drop, the fuel pump and supply system should be adequate for the current nitrous enrichment fuel jetting.

13. If the fuel pump and plumbing are not adequate, try measuring fuel pressure at the pump and then at the engine to make sure that the plumbing is not introducing excessive pressure drop when fuel demands are high. Assuming the plumbing is not a bottleneck, you'll need to upgrade the fuel pump, or install an auxiliary in-line fuel pump, or install a Boost-A-Pump device to jack up voltage to the existing fuel pump to increase the pumping capacity.

Alternatively, to test fuel delivery capacity on EFI engines with return-type fuel loops follow this procedure:

1. Divert the fuel tank return line flow into a measuring container.

2. Hold the fuel pressure regulator reference port at the maximum achievable manifold absolute pressure (atmospheric pressure on all-motor engines; maximum manifold pressure on turbocharged engines—which will require some sort of hand pump or regulated pressure source).

3. Start the engine and turn on all electrical appliances to create a worst-case drain on the the battery and alternator, which could potentially reduce electrical power available to run the fuel pump at maximum performance.

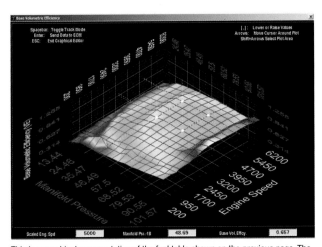

This is a graphical representation of the fuel table shown on the previous page. The shape of the "map" can be changed by selecting various breakpoints and raising or lowering the graph with arrow or similar keystrokes—which adjusts the values in the data table. *Accel*

4. Measure the volume of fuel pumped in a minute or a precise fraction of a minute. This is a measurement of the maximum amount of fuel that can be supplied by the fuel pump at the required pressure.

5. Calculate the total horsepower (including wasted "coolant fuel") that can be supplied, assuming a worst-case rate of brake-specific fuel consumption (consult chart or formula in this book) to satisfy all boosted and non-boosted requirements. This test does not require the vehicle to be moving.

There are purpose-built fuel flow meters commonly used by Pro Modified drag racers (running 527-inch blown-alcohol V-8s or 820-cubic-inch V-8s running gasoline and nitrous that delivers as much as 2,500 horsepower used to calibrate an adjustable fuel pressure regulator in order to deliver a specified amount of fuel. Basically, you install a jet in the fuel flow tool that has a metering area (flow rate) equal to that of the combined flow jets in the nitrous fuel enrichment subsystem. A flow tool calibrates the nitrous fuel enrichment subsystem by changing fuel pressure as an alternative to changing the size of fuel or nitrous jets (see tuning section of this chapter).

Test the nitrous electrical control subsystem. Compare the actual nitrous wiring system to the wiring schematic that came with the kit or that you designed before fabricating a custom wiring system. You did use color-coded wiring and draw a schematic, right? If you didn't, do it now. Trust me, you will not remember the details down the line when a relay or something fails—and you're debugging the system and find yourself in the odd position of having to reverse-engineer your own work. Make sure the wiring is correct. Make sure any and all fuses are healthy. Verify that any wires connected to chassis, engine, or battery ground are very well grounded (poor grounding is responsible for many electrical problems on modified vehicles).

With the vehicle's battery disconnected, use a voltmeter, continuity tester, or test light to verify that all nitrous circuitry operates as expected. Turning on the arming switch should complete a circuit that delivers power (or ground, depending on how it's wired) to the main nitrous system relay (in the case of computer-controlled dry nitrous, the arming switch may alternatively or additionally deliver power to a nitrous-on input pin of the EMS). The full-throttle switch should be closed at full throttle and the full-throttle circuit should deliver power (or ground, as the case may be) to the *trigger* circuit on the main nitrous relay. If you are using a TPS-activated full-throttle switch, the TPS will need to be energized for this test, so the main EMS will need to be on.

With the battery reconnected, turning on the ignition switch should deliver power to the input circuit of the main nitrous relay (usually via an additional relay that delivers power directly from the battery when the ignition circuit triggers the relay). The nitrous main relay should audibly close and deliver power to the output circuit when the trigger circuit has both power and ground. You may have other in-series switches in the arming circuit such as an oil pressure switch that disarms the system if the engine stalls. Test and make

Here's the laptop interface to a Honda del Sol turbo with the Hondata programmable conversion. In some cases it is a fairly simple project to convert a stock EMS so it can be recalibrated for power-adder modifications (in this case by adding a replaceable PROM chip and user-interface software, and utilizing a PROM-emulator for tuning). Some conversions provide add-on capabilities like the ability to partially integrate nitrous injection with basic engine management. This photo shows the Hondata fuel table screen.

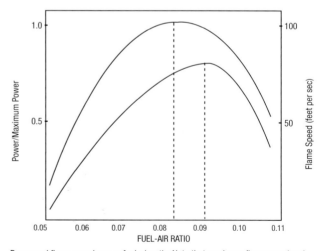

Power and flame speed versus fuel-air ratio. Note that maximum flame speed and maximum power occur at disparate fuel-air ratios. There is a range of fuel-air ratios that produce best torque, but the best-torque ratio narrows at higher engine speeds due to changes in flame speed that impact the ability of combustion to complete in the available time.

Lambda Calculations

Fuel Curve		Input—Red Only	
	Gasoline	Eth-E85	Methanol
Engine Air/Fuel Ratio Target	12.8	7.9	5.7
Engine Oxygen/Fuel Ratio	2.69	2.80	3.39
Engine Horsepower	700	700	700
Fuel Curve			
Nitrous-Fuel Target Ratio	6.00	4.00	3.00
Nitrous Oxide/Fuel Ratio	2.16	2.49	3.16
Comb. Oxygen/Fuel Ratio	2.55	2.72	3.33
Fuel Ratio: Example	5.0-5.5 Rich	3.3-3.8 Rich	2.0-2.5 Rich
	5.5-6.0 Safe	3.8-4.2 Safe	2.5-3.0 Safe
	6.0-6.5 Lean	4.2-4.7 Lean	3.0-3.5 Lean
New Lambda w/Nitrous	0.825738	0.782407	0.865005
Equivalent Air/Fuel Ratio	12.13835	7.745832	5.596582

Air-Fuel Ratio

	Gasoline	E-85 Ethanol	Methanol	LPG	Diesel
Lambda					
0.70	10.3	6.9	4.6	10.9	10.2
0.75	11.0	7.4	4.9	11.6	10.9
0.80	11.8	7.8	5.2	12.4	11.6
0.85	12.5	8.3	5.5	13.2	12.3
0.90	13.2	8.8	5.9	14.0	13.1
0.95	14.0	9.3	6.2	14.7	13.8
1.00	14.7	9.8	6.5	15.5	14.5

You can no longer talk meaningfully about the air-fuel ratio during nitrous boost, because there's nitrous in there, too, and the operative factor becomes the *oxygen-fuel* ratio. A common shorthand that avoids having to talk about ratios is Lambda, which is essentially the ratio of the current mixture versus a stoichiometric or chemically-perfect ratio in which all fuel and oxygen are consumed in combustion. Lambda is meaningful for various fuels and oxidizers as shown in this chart. O_2-*Technology*

sure everything is functional. With fuel and nitrous disabled, you should be able to hear the nitrous and fuel solenoids snap open when the nitrous system goes active, and the test meter should verify that battery power is arriving at the solenoids as it should.

Verify Fuel Flow Subsystem. With the engine stopped and the nitrous bottle control valve closed, verify that fuel flows from the fuel solenoid (if installed) when the nitrous system is armed and activated. Defeat any disarm protections that

may be in place to keep the nitrous system from triggering when the engine is stopped, open the throttle wide, and verify that fuel flows through the fuel solenoid and out the injection nozzles (ideally through a flow tool equipped with a metering orifice equal in flow area to the total flow area of all nitrous subsystem fuel jets). Direct the fuel *into a safe container* and dispose of it safely. On direct-port systems, you'll probably want to disconnect the fuel supply hose from the fuel distribution manifold, attach a professional flow tool or homemade flow device and verify that fuel is flowing out

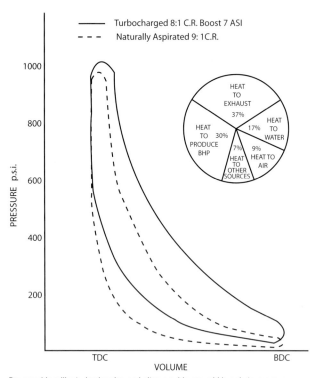

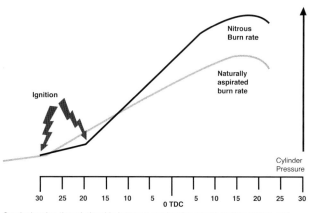

Graph showing the relationship between combustion speed, ignition timing, and cylinder pressure. Nitrous-on ignition should occur later because combustion accelerates faster to peak cylinder pressure. Ignition may have to occur even later than this if the engine-fuel combination cannot tolerate full cylinder pressure without detonating, which will cause the downward movement of the piston after top dead center to dissipate peak pressure.

Power-adders like turbocharging and nitrous oxide can add hugely to *average* cylinder pressure without greatly increasing *maximum* cylinder pressure as shown in this chart, which also graphs the disposition of heat loss to various destinations. Achieving maximum cylinder pressure can only occur with a fuel of high-enough octane rating that ignition can be timed so that peak combustion pressure occurs at about 15 degrees after top dead center. The higher flame speed of nitrous combustion and the greater tendency to detonation usually requires modifying ignition timing during nitrous boost to optimize horsepower.

of the fuel solenoid. Verify that the fuel flow stops as it should when the throttle closes or the nitrous system is disarmed.

In the case of a pressure-regulated dry nitrous system, you'll need to install a fuel pressure gauge in the fuel rail and verify that fuel rail pressure increases when the nitrous system attempts to activate. Install a gauge in the rail test port (if there is one), or stop and fabricate a permanent fuel rail pressure gauge (a *great* idea under any circumstance), ideally with an electrical dash display so you can monitor fuel pressure while driving. On this type of nitrous system, the nitrous bottle valve must be open in order to unleash a spring-loaded series of events that raise fuel pressure and trigger nitrous injection. To prevent nitrous oxide from being injected into a stopped engine, disconnect the wiring from the *secondary* nitrous solenoid or remove the nitrous injectors from the engine. Do *not* simply disconnect the nitrous supply line from the distribution manifold or injector because nitrous may free-flow out of the secondard nitrous solenoid discharge line without ever properly building pressure at the nitrous pressure regulator downstream of the primary nitrous solenoid. Nitrous pressure is needed to raise reference pressure at

the fuel pressure regulator diaphragm in order to increase EFI fuel rail pressure, so you're going to want at least a makeshift nitrous flow tool on the secondary nitrous solenoid discharge.

You will need to jumper the fuel pump so it runs continuously during the test, and defeat any systems that normally prevent the nitrous system from being active when the engine is stopped or stalled. You will probably see about 40-psi fuel pressure when the fuel pump is running with atmospheric pressure delivered to the fuel pressure regulator reference port. With the nitrous bottle open, the system armed, and the secondary nitrous solenoid electrics *disconnected*, open the throttle wide. The primary nitrous solenoid should snap open, delivering nitrous through an auxiliary nitrous pressure regulator to the fuel pressure regulator reference port, causing fuel pressure to shoot up to 70-plus psi. With a continuity meter on the fuel rail pressure switch (NOS), you should see the switch close as rail pressure approaches the threshold minimum boost fuel pressure (55 psi is common on NOS dry systems), which normally opens the secondary nitrous solenoid (disabled for this test), delivering nitrous oxide to the engine.

In the case of a computer-controlled dry nitrous system, you will not be able to visually verify supplemental boost fuel enrichment, because the system delivers enrichment by way of the nitrous-capable aftermarket EMS extending base all-motor fuel-injection pulsewidth. The tuner will, however, be able to monitor engine and EMS status in real time with a laptop computer, making it simple to note changes in the nitrous subsystem status and fuel injection pulsewidth. You can test the fuel enrichment on this type of system on the street or dyno as follows: Disable the nitrous delivery system (by closing the nitrous bottle valve), and disable any safety systems that automatically disarm the system if the bottle valve is closed or there is zero nitrous pressure at the nitrous solenoid. With the nitrous system armed, bring the engine to full throttle, and verify that injection pulsewidth increases and the engine goes dysfunctionally rich, losing power and making black smoke.

Verify Nitrous Flow. With a nitrous injector disconnected from the engine (or the solenoid-discharge hose), held firmly and aimed into an open space or rage away from yourself and any other human being, activate the nitrous system. You should see a visible blast of frigid nitrous fog when the system triggers. The nitrous plume should immediately stop when the throttle closes or the nitrous system disarms.

Check Nitrous and Fuel Filters. Inspect the nitrous filter for debris, which could introduce a pressure drop and changes in nitrous mass flow and produce refrigeration effects. Clean or replace the filter. Inspect or replace any fuel filters between the fuel tank and any part of the primary or enrichment fuel systems. If you have any doubt about when the fuel filter was last replaced, do it now. This is cheap insurance.

Test the Knock Sensor or Boost-Retard System. Assuming you have installed some kind of system to retard ignition timing during nitrous boost, if you have not already done so, this is the time to verify that it is working.

In the case of a knock-sensor system like the J&S SafeGuard, start by setting the system to command maximum retard on all cylinders at once in case of detonation, thus making it easier to hear if ignition retard is occurring. Adjust the knock sensitivity to maximum. Defeat any controls that prevent the knock control system from working at idle under zero load (for example, disconnect the manifold pressure reference hose if the knock control system requires zero vacuum before it will allow knock control). Start the engine and hold the rpm to at least 2,000. Tap rapidly on the knock sensor with a screwdriver to simulate knock. You should be able to hear the engine slow down and see the timing retard with a timing light, or the knock control box may have a visible indication that it has detected knock and retarded timing. Assuming the test is positive, return the knock-control system to the recommended initial settings, and follow the recommended road-test sensitivity adjustment procedure before activating the nitrous system.

You may have a boost-retard device that's designed to automatically retard ignition timing under certain conditions whether or not the engine is actually detonating. You'll want to test the device to make sure it does retard timing by jumpering positive voltage or ground to the correct lead that is used to sense when nitrous boost is active. The engine should slow and a timing light should reveal that timing has, indeed, retarded (usually 1 or 2 degrees per 50 horsepower of nitrous boost). It is possible that you could have a boost-retard interceptor that retards timing during nitrous boost according to engine rpm or loading. Follow the instructions for test procedures, or call customer support at the supplier.

CALCULATING JET DIAMETER FOR FLOW TOOL

To set a nitrous system fuel enrichment flow with a flow tool you will need to install a jet in the flow tool that has the same metering area as the combined area of all fuel jets on the nitrous system. But what size jet will do? If the nitrous system only has one fuel jet, that's easy, the same size fuel jet goes in the flow tool. If the nitrous system is running direct-port fogger-type nozzles with one per cylinder, you'll need to do a tiny bit of math. Let's say that the direct-port fogger-type nozzles are equipped with .025-inch diameter jets. We need to start by calculating the area of each jet and then add them together.

$$Area = \pi \times radius^2$$

where

π = 3.141592654 . . . [to infinity]
radius = diameter / 2

Therefore, the area of each fogger jet is

$$area = 3.141592654 \times (.025 / 2)^2$$
$$= 0.000490874$$

Therefore, the total area of the fogger jets on a V-8 engine is

$$8 \times 0.000490874 = 0.003926991$$

The diameter of a single jet with the same area is

$$diameter = 2 \times (SQR\ [area / \pi])$$

where

SQR = [take the square root of the quantity]
π = 3.141592654 . . . [to infinity]
radius = diameter / 2

Therefore,

$$diameter = 2 \times (SQR\ [.003926991 \times 3.141592654])$$
$$= 0.070710689$$
$$\approx 0.071$$

The rounding error in this case is (0.071 - 0.070710689) / 0.070710689 = 0.004091475 (which is less than a half of 1 percent).

Actually, depending on the pressure, a single jet of equal area will flow slightly more fuel than eight individual jets due to reduced friction (the combined circumference of the individual jets is greater than the single jet).

If you change the size of the fogger jets, you will have to recalculate the flow tool jet size and install a different jet in order to dial in precise fuel pressure that yields the target flow rate.

TUTORIAL ON SELECTING AND READING SPARK PLUGS

TUNING AND OPTIMIZING NITROUS INJECTION

To select the right spark plugs and get the final word on what is going on in the combustion chambers of an engine, you need to read the plugs—even if you have individual-cylinder EGT probes and a wideband lambda meter. The rest is hearsay. Plug-reading is especially important with nitrous engines due to the enhanced heat and combustion speed of nitrous boost. Unless you are a plug-reading "engine whisperer" with psychic powers, you cannot read a plug by glancing at it casually with the naked eye. You need a good magnifying glass with plenty of natural light or a plug-reading tool with built-in color-corrected light source.

Heat range. Spark plugs live in an environment in which combustion temperatures can easily reach over 1,500 degrees, but fortunately, this is soon followed by a cooling cycle in which fresh intake charge cools the plug and combustion chamber. Spark plugs absorb a tremendous amount of heat. To some extent this is good, because to function for a long time, a spark plug has to stay hot enough to burn off oil and carbon deposits that would eventually short-circuit the spark. Staying clean and functional requires that the plug operate at a minimum of 700 degrees F. On the other hand, spark plugs must not get too hot. An overheated white-hot spark plug can begin to act as a glow plug that initiates premature surface ignition in advance of the scheduled spark event, triggering a runaway cycle of skyrocketing temperature rise, detonation, more preignition, more heat, and so on that burns down a boosting engine in a matter of seconds. The threshold temperature for preignition depends on the auto-ignition qualities of the fuel components, but surface ignition of gasoline can begin at temperatures below 500 degrees F. There are other less severe upper thermal limits for plug operation. At 1,100 degrees, micro quantities of sulfur in the fuel will begin to erode spark plug electrodes. The plating burns off at 1,600 to 1,800 degrees F, and standard nickel-alloy plug electrodes begin to oxidize. To be safe, it is important that plug temperatures stay between 700 and 1,000 degrees F.

Unfortunately, achieving relatively homoeothermic temperatures in the exposed spark plug components is not trivial, which is why there are so many spark plug designs. Spark-ignition engines vary tremendously, and the conditions under which a particular design of

engine operates can also vary tremendously. Hot-rodding modifications like turbo conversions or nitrous injection have a large effect on the thermal loading of the engine and its combustion chambers. Ignition timing, horsepower output, coolant temperature, mixture strength, and heat of vaporization of the particular fuel or oxidizer (like nitrous oxide!) have an important impact on how hot spark plugs will run. All engines require spark plugs with design-appropriate thermal characteristics.

Depending on the geometry of the combustion chamber and intake ports, spark plugs are air-cooled to some degree by the intake charge and flame-heated by combustion. Once the spark plug location has been fixed in the cylinder head design, the thermal loading of the plug is determined. At this point, the question is, how efficiently can a plug shed heat from the center electrode, ground strap electrode, and plug nose? For a given amount of thermal loading, the main factor impacting plug operating temperature is the length of the pathway through the plug that transfers heat from the sizzling-hot center electrode and ground strap through the threads and plug washer into the cylinder head, where most spark plugs are effectively water-cooled from passages that route coolant in close proximity to the spark plug threads, meaning that in addition to everything else, plug temperature will be impacted by coolant temperature.

The design thermal transfer efficiency, i.e., heat range, of a particular spark plug design is set by varying the length of the thermal transfer pathway from the center electrode tip into the head. A spark plug with a short insulator nose tends to run colder because there is a short, efficient thermal transfer pathway out of the hot end of the plug. The same basic plug with a longer insulator nose will operate at a higher temperature for a given amount of combustion heat because heat is forced to flow deeper into the plug before it can escape into the cylinder head. In either case, it is the engine that heats and cools the plug, never the reverse. Ideally, neither plug should run any hotter or colder than the other in a particular engine application because the plug and engine characteristics should be matched to ensure that temperature remains in the same safe and functional 700- to 1,000-degree range.

Unfortunately, some high-performance powerplants have a dynamic operating range so large that the engine makes essentially impossible demands on the thermal transfer characteristics of the plug, heating or cooling it out of the acceptable temperature range under some circumstances. The need to stabilize the cylinder head and plug temperature for improved performance, emissions, and maintenance intervals is one of the reasons manufacturers like VW and Porsche and an increasing number of ultra-high-performance motorcycle builders, have moved to water-cooled architecture. The demands on the heat range of a spark plug almost always get worse when the engine is modified to make more power because there is intermittently much more combustion heat that must be dissipated through the original equipment systems. Overly cold plugs designed to stay cool at full howl will load up if there is a lot of idling or low-speed operation. Hotter plugs that stay clean idling and pass emissions with no worries will overheat and erode if the engine is run hard a lot at high boost. Since the consequences of overheating a plug are worse, engine manufacturers tend to recommend plugs that run a bit on the cold side as a countermeasure against maniac drivers and worst-case conditions. This, of course, is not optimal if the engine is operated conservatively in a mild environment.

How do you know if the plugs are running too cold or overheating? The plugs will tell you their story if you remove them and read what they have to say. Plug-reading is a black art for many people—including many competent hot rodders and amateur racers

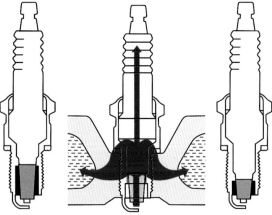

Spark plugs require a "heat range" appropriate to the conditions such that the plugs remain hot enough to keep from loading up with fuel soot at idle, such that the plug stays clean and cool enough at full power that the plug is not damaged when operating at a good state of tune. The heat range of the plug is largely determined by the length of the pathway from the hot end of the plug, through the central core, and into the cooling jacket of the engine.

There are many different types of spark plugs.

of some success—who consequently haven't the slightest idea how hot the plugs in their engine are actually running. Most people install the plugs recommended by the engine manufacturer or builder, and hope for the best. Hot rodders—particularly hot rodders spraying their engines with *nitrous oxide*—tend to assume the engine automatically needs colder plugs along with the power-adder installation, which is not always the case.

How do you get colder plugs, assuming that's what you need? Most plug manufacturers offer a number of heat ranges for many designs of spark plug, with a numbering scheme that lets you know if plugs are hotter or colder or the same as where you started. So you ask the dealer for plugs for the year and model engine "one range colder." And the parts guy tells you if there is such a thing and hands you the plugs. (And you trust him, right?) In some cases you might have to jump brands to find the heat range you need. In some cases there is nothing colder or hotter than what you already have. In a worst case you might decide to modify the spark plugs or even machine the cylinder heads to accept spark plugs of a heat range and design that will work for your custom application.

Changing plug brands can be problematic if you're already running plugs of a non-stock heat range, since the numbering scheme for a given brand tells you the heat range of a particular plug relative to the other heat ranges offered within the brand, but not necessarily how much colder or hotter the plug will run in absolute terms. Two ranges of change in a particular brand *could* be about as cold or hot as one range of another brand, or somewhere in the middle. This could work to your advantage if you need something just a bit colder or hotter than what you have in one particular brand. Try out the equivalent in another brand, and read the plugs. As soon as you move away from the stock heat range plug for a particular engine, you cannot assume anything beyond the fact that the plug will certainly run relatively hotter or colder than the next number in the coding scheme. There is no good way to know unless someone you trust already knows.

Some spark plug designs, by the way, have more flexible thermal characteristics than others. In some cases the thermal range of a plug can be extended by changing the design. Projected-nose plugs use an architecture in which the electrodes and insulator nose project farther into the combustion chamber, which reduces the distance flame fronts must travel to the farthest recesses of the combustion chamber. This increases efficiency and the likelihood normal combustion will complete before detonation can occur. Because projected-nose plug components extend farther into the combustion chamber where combustion gases are quenched least by proximity to the piston crown or cylinder head, depending on airflow and turbulence in the combustion chamber the plug is both more effectively heated during combustion and more effectively air-cooled (or nitrous-cooled!) during the intake stroke—particularly when the plug is centrally located where it experiences the full cooling force of the intake air blast in a hemi-head or four-valve pentroof engine. The result is that this type of spark plug is relatively more resistant to both fouling at idle and overheating at full power. Project-nose plugs could interfere with some types of pop-up high-compression pistons.

Spark plug designers have also tried more or less the opposite approach to a projected-nose design. Surface-fire plugs send a spark across the gap between the center electrode and the cylindrical plug nose that bends inward from the metal shell to form a circular flange around the center electrode, with only the tip of the center electrode peeking out of an insulator almost flush with the tip. The thermal transfer properties of this type of plug are so favorable that surface-fire plugs operate at essentially the same temperature as the walls of the combustion chamber, and the plug is thus virtually unable to overheat and produce surface ignition. Unfortunately, because the architecture produces a spark at the periphery of the combustion chamber, combustion is rather inefficient and surface-fire plugs require a powerful ignition.

Jacketing an ordinary thick, blunt nickel-iron center electrode in platinum, gold-palladium, or silver alloy can improve the robustness of the electrode sufficiently that the electrical properties can be improved by whittling the electrode down to a fine, sharp wire that sheds electrons much more readily at lower voltage than a standard electrode. Platinum plugs throw a spark more easily, but can be problematic on power-adder engines where the high thermal loading produced by improved specific power or excessive spark advance can overheat the fine-wire electrodes before there is any other evidence of overheating. If this happens, the best case would be that the electrode melts and the cylinder begins to miss. Some experts have recommended against installing platinum plugs on boosted powerplants.

If a boosted engine requires colder plugs to prevent plug overheating at peak power to the extent that fouling is then a problem at idle, the ability of the ignition to fire moderately-fouled plugs may be improved by installing auxiliary-gap spark plugs. Whereas a conventional plug that is slightly fouled might misfire if deposits on the insulator are constantly bleeding off rising electrical potential from the coil through the deposits to the extent that there is never enough power accumulation for a spark to leap the gap, an auxiliary-gap plug's secondary air gap acts like a switch to isolate the coil from the spark plug until sufficient energy has built up to overcome the resistance of the auxiliary gap and successfully leap both it and then the smaller spark plug gap. Air-gap plugs have sometimes been marketed to drivers trying to keep their oil-burning beaters from constantly fouling plugs with oil deposits, but auxiliary-gap plugs to some extent mimic the fast voltage rise qualities of a capacitive discharge ignition, and they work especially well on engines equipped with high-power ignitions.

Misconceptions. There are a number of commonly held misconceptions about spark plugs, heat ranges, and spark timing that commonly result in tuning mistakes and can actually be dangerous.

The first is that hotter plugs will make the engine run hotter. Plugs are heated by the engine, not vice versa, and the only time overheated plugs will make the engine run hotter is if the combustion chamber is already so hot that white-hot plugs are the straw that breaks the camel's back to instigate runaway preignition.

Another misconception is that colder plugs are an effective anti-detonation countermeasure that will allow you to run more spark advance. Detonation, which is the serial killer of an unimaginable number of pistons, occurs when entire pockets of unburned charge explode all at once rather than being consumed sequentially as the flame fronts burn through the charge mixture all the way to the end like a fire burning through a field of dry grass. Detonation produces a tremendous but short-lived premature spike of cylinder overpressure and a large amount of heat. This is quite different from surface-ignition touching off the charge mixture too early at one place, though it's true that the heat of preignition can result in overheated charge that does detonate. The temperature of the plug electrode or ground strap is not capable by itself of causing entire areas of unburned charge to auto-ignite.

The goal of running as much spark advance as possible is a corollary of the misconception that all engines make more and more power as you add spark advance until the engine knocks, at which point you back off a bit and figure that's as good as it gets. A consequence of this type of thinking can be that tuners end up dumping huge, suboptimal amounts of fuel or water injection into an engine in order to run excessive timing advance, resulting in overly rich oxygen-fuel mixtures that are, by themselves, suboptimal in terms of delivering maximum torque. For one thing, depending on the fuel, not all engines are knock-limited. Furthermore, if an engine *is* knock-limited that does not mean that it is necessarily running suboptimal spark advance to fight knock. Excessive spark advance that results in early peak cylinder pressures not only does not achieve peak power but is a tremendously effective pro-knock factor that is usually, at this stage of the game, fought by pouring in the fuel—which further reduces torque.

Reading plugs. In any case, you've got whatever plugs you have, and now you want to know what the plugs can tell you about combustion temperature, air-fuel ratio, spark timing, and, most of all, whether the engine may be experiencing detonation that is difficult or impossible to hear over all the other noise. Here's the trick: Remove a

spark plug, let it cool for 17.5 seconds, and then hold it firmly against your forehead so you can *feel the force, Luke* (Bubba, Fred, whoever you are) in your deepest of souls. Feel the engine talk to you. *Just* kidding. The way you read plugs is to run a set of new plugs on the engine at a particular speed and loading, and then abruptly kill the engine so that the archeological evidence you are evaluating when you examine the plug is not corrupted by newer evidence from more recent operations. The trick to reading plugs is to remove *all* the plugs, devise some other way of keeping them in order so you know which hole each came from, then examine them carefully one by one in good light with a good magnifying glass or a good otoscope (that thing doctors use to look in your ears) for forensic evidence of combustion problems.

There are three kinds of forensic evidence found on a spark plug. The first is the fuel film of carbon soot left behind—or not left behind where the plug was hot enough to burn it off—on plug surfaces when mixtures are rich of stoichiometric and there is not enough oxygen to fully burn every bit of fuel. A second type of forensic evidence is the color of the plating on the plug's metal surface, which changes with temperature. Spark plug plating changes color if the temperature gets hot enough to anneal or to oxidize the plating, and some racing plug manufacturers intentionally plate spark plugs with alloys of precious metals like cadmium or zinc that change color in an obvious way at a temperature corresponding to the correct operating temperature of the combustion chamber. The color change migrates from the hottest portions of the plug nose and electrodes toward cooler areas as the temperature increases enough to anneal or oxidize more and more of the ground strap, plug nose, and into the topmost threads of the plug body. The third type of forensic evidence is the removal or deposition of metal on the surfaces of the plug. The type of fuel—gasoline, propane, alcohol, nitro, and so on—will impact combustion evidence left on the plugs.

The first thing you're looking for is any evidence of abnormal combustion, specifically detonation. Detonation occurs when cylinder pressure and temperature rise sufficiently in the *unburned* portions of the combustion chamber that explosions ensue across entire pockets of air-fuel mixture before normal combustion has had a chance to burn smoothly and progressively through the entire oxygen-fuel mass. Normal combustion begins when a spark jumping the gap between the spark plug center electrode and ground strap heats oxygen-fuel mixture above

These images show NGK spark plugs provided by Don Burton, who competes in Super Street Outlaw in the NMRA. *NGK*

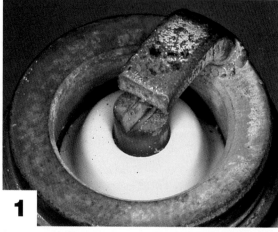

Just lean enough. Perfect for hot weather. Slight timing problem noticeable at the tip of the ground strap.

2

Just lean enough like #1 but with 5 degrees more timing. The engine will run stronger with more timing advance.

3

Rich fuel film noticeable at the bottom of the ceramic. Slight timing problem. Will run well in good air.

4

One degree more timing than #2. This plug is just lean enough to make more power and is probably as good as it gets for the engine.

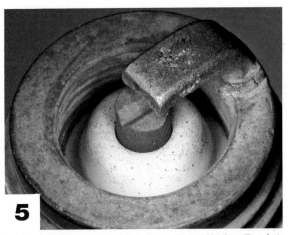

5

This plug is hot from too much timing advance. This combination will run fast but is hard on the rings. Some evidence of preignition.

6

This plug is also too hot. Note the brown tint on the ceramic. Definitely too much timing.

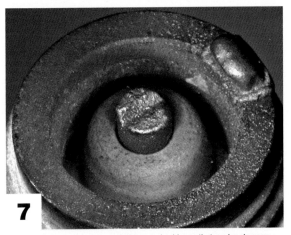

7

The plug shows way too much timing—and evidence that engine damage may already be occurring, such as a pinched ring or lifting ring land. Time to take 4 degrees out of that cylinder and begin tuning over again.

the auto-ignition temperature of the fuel. At first there is a tiny bubble of flame in the immediate vicinity of the spark plug tip, but the ball of flaming fuel and oxygen quickly expands and accelerates to speeds as high as 150 feet per second, depending on how well the oxygen and fuel are mixed, how much surplus oxygen there is, the amount and speed of combustion chamber turbulence and tumble, and the temperature and pressure of the unburned charge gases beyond the expanding ball of flames. Automotive engineers go to a great deal of trouble to design combustion chambers with advantageous swirl, because swirl accelerates normal combustion. Fast combustion means there is less opportunity for detonation to occur before there's nothing left to burn. As combustion proceeds, flame speed accelerates as the surface area of the flame ball expands and as the unburned charge heats from thermal radiation and the adiabatic heat of increasing pressure. In all-motor engines with optimal timing, the flame ball will have consumed most of the charge by the time the piston is at top dead center, and 100 percent in time for peak cylinder pressure at 15 degrees after TDC. Engines boosted with turbochargers make most of their power boost due not to much higher peak cylinder pressures, but to vastly higher *average* pressure in the early part of the power stroke when the piston is moving away from the head. The improved combustion speed of nitrous combustion and the advantageous products-to-reactants ratio increases both the peak cylinder pressure and the average pressure.

When the spark plug heat range is correct, reading the plugs will tell you what's happening in an engine and specifically when the spark advance and oxygen-fuel ratio are where the engine needs them to be for optimal performance. Unless you are an experienced plug-reading wizard, do not even try to read old spark plugs, which will have a coating of fuel (and possibly oil) deposits that obscure the forensic evidence that can be found on a plug that has been run hard for only a few minutes. Install new plugs, and get a few minutes of hard-running time on them. Get the heat range warm enough that the plugs can tell you their story. Until a plug is running hot enough to keep the insulator clean, it is difficult to know much else besides the fact that the heat range is too cold. The heat range of a new or fresh spark plug is correct when the plug is running hot enough to keep the insulator nose entirely clean, but cool enough that the electrodes show no signs of severe overheating.

A spark plug's center electrode has the highest sensitivity to overheating from high-combustion temperatures as well as from too much timing advance, but overheating can affect the ground strap electrode and the insulator as well. When the electrodes are getting too hot, the edges will be rounded by erosion or melting, but it's the subtleties that distinguish the fallout of too much ignition advance from the principle evidence of overheating. If it's mainly or exclusively the center electrode that shows evidence of overheating, then the timing is definitely too advanced and you'll want to back out timing 2 to 3 degrees at a time until the whole plug is running cooler, allowing a film of fuel deposits to begin forming on the insulator from the insulator nose outward toward the tip of the center electrode. If the tip of the ground strap electrode also shows signs of overheating, there may be too much timing advance, but you know for sure that combustion is too hot. Overheating can also affect the insulator, the surface of which usually starts out new with a chalky white appearance. Overheating may turn the original smooth white surface of the ceramic granular and porous. In other cases, overheating can actually melt the porcelain's glass component (the rest is mostly clay and Mullite or Porcelainite), which may have a melting point as low as 1,500 degrees, glazing the surface to a shiny texture.

Ignition timing has a direct impact on combustion chamber heat, with earlier timing producing more chamber heat and lower exhaust gas temperatures as combustion completes sooner and more heat stays in the engine. Later timing lowers combustion chamber temperatures as fuel is still burning much later in the power stroke (and even into the exhaust stroke on some engines!), with much more heat lost into the exhaust. Timing will have a direct impact on the color of the ground strap electrode and the first few threads of the plug. You are looking for the location of a blue line on the ground strap electrode, which indicates the farthest extent from the tip where the surface has reached annealing temperature. Blued chrome exhaust headers or the blue line on steel in the vicinity of arc or gas welding illustrates the same thing. The longer and hotter the welding process, the farther the blue moves from the point of heating. The more combustion heat you pour into an engine, the farther the blue line migrates from the tip of the electrode.

Plate coloring is easiest to see on a spark plug with a gold-colored ground strap like an NGK. In some cases you might want to clean the plug with brake cleaner to remove fuel soot if that is an issue. One nice thing about reading the plating on plugs is that cleaning off the soot following a marathon of heavy loading will not contaminate the evidence as it does when analyzing fuel soot. The flip side of this is that the plating color is evidence of the hottest the plug has ever been, so you will not see evidence of cooler running when retarding the timing or enriching the mixture until you change the plugs—yet another reason to tune from retarded to advanced and rich to lean.

When timing is over-retarded, after a hard run, the ground strap will still appear gold or possibly light gray with a few bubbles. As you advance timing and combustion heats up, the ground strap and the end threads begin to turn a darker gray. As the grayness extends and darkens with increasing advance and temperature, you'll eventually begin to see a blue band appear around the ground strap and then move along the electrode toward the weld where the ground strap attached to the plug nose. Ideally, the blue line should end up just beyond the sharp bend in the ground strap closest to the weld. If you continue to advance the timing or other factors increase the heating, the blue line will migrate to the weld and disappear and rainbow greens and blues will show up on the strap. Beyond that, more advance will begin melting the strap starting at the tip, at which point the engine will be detonating and in mortal danger.

When plug-reading shows that timing is getting close to optimal, you should be increasing timing in small increments of 1 or even 1/2 degree at a time. On most engines it's unlikely that all cylinders are running equally hot, so that a blue line in the perfect place on the ground strap on one cylinder means that other cylinders may be running hotter or colder (or both). Once most of the cylinders are close to the ideal temperature, this would be the time to calibrate the timing of individual cylinders if your EMS provides this capability.

The fuel film that forms on a plug's center electrode when the plug is running cool enough can be a valuable informant when it comes to making subtle corrections to ignition timing. Even if a spark plug is two or three heat ranges too cold, when timing is too advanced (as is the typical case) but within a few degrees of correct, the film of fuel deposits will end abruptly part way along the center electrode a couple of millimeters from the tip where localized thermal loading from the excessive timing continues to burn away deposits. When timing is retarded back to the correct ignition advance, fuel film will expand outward on the electrode to within a hair of the tip. If ignition timing is excessively retarded, the only electrode surface area clear of fuel film will be localized spots where the electrical discharge blasts holes in the film (commonly found in a curved pathway off to one side of the electrode where combustion turbulence has blown the spark off center).

This asynchronous spark blush is distinct from the sharp symmetrical heat ring produced when timing is too advanced.

When timing is finally optimal, it may be necessary to revisit plug heat range before giving attention to evaluating what the plugs have to say about oxygen-fuel ratio. If you make global changes to spark timing by pulling advance to suit lower-octane fuels or match the higher flame-speed of nitrous or turbocharged combustion, there will be a tendency for plugs to load up during non-boosted operations. You may want to consider trying warmer plugs to clean up the insulator in advance of calibrating the optimal fuel ratio.

If you add timing on a dynamometer until peak power begins to fall off, and the porcelain insulator looks healthy but there is no color on the ground strap electrode, then the plug itself is too cold. If you see color on the ground strap and the insulator is perfectly clean and white, then the plug heat range is too hot.

Higher-octane racing gasoline may burn more slowly than lower octane fuel, which will require adding timing if you change over to higher-octane fuel.

When calibrating the oxygen-fuel ratio of a competition engine, it is wise to work from a maximum ignition advance *known* to work well for your particular engine configuration. This procedure is safe and will allow you to limit power by retarding the timing without having to make drastic changes to the oxygen-fuel calibration. When optimizing charge oxygen-fuel ratios, keep in mind that fuel soot is black because it is mainly carbon. Varying thicknesses of fuel film may appear gray or tan on the white porcelain insulator, but color has nothing to do with this aspect of plug reading. Fuel soot is the residue of incomplete combustion when there is insufficient oxygen present to burn every bit of fuel, leaving behind a visible film of carbon on the spark plug. When it comes to fuel soot, the location is what's revealing. If an engine is running rich with cold plugs, there will be soot all over the insulator. However, when the mixture is too rich but the plug is running hot enough to prevent fouling, you will not find fuel soot on the insulator nose because it is too hot there for soot to collect.

The forensic data is hidden more deeply. The place to look for evidence of mixture strength on an engine with the correct heat range plug is farther away from the combustion fire, deep inside the plug body where the insulator joins its shell and things are much cooler. If there's too little oxygen for complete combustion, there will be a ring of soot on the insulator here. Since the insulator grows progressively hotter closer to the nose, the thickness of the soot ring provides a gauge of mixture strength. For example, a soot ring even a millimeter thick on an all-motor engine tells you two things: The mixture is safe but too rich to deliver maximum power. On non-boosted engines, peak power occurs when the mixture is just enough richer than stoichiometric to leave a trace of carbon soot at the base of the insulator, or in some cases on some fuels, none at all. On the other hand, high-output boosted engines running on street premium require much richer mixture as an anti-detonation countermeasure, with power optimized by pouring in the fuel in order to run more nitrous or higher manifold pressure without knocking. If a boosted engine is not knock-limited on the available fuel, the engine will typically make more and more power as you lean the mixture until something melts.

If you are having a tough time reading the plugs, you may want to get a second opinion from the exhaust. If the engine has been run for a while at heavy load (*not* idling for extensive periods with a big cam, cold plugs, and over-rich mixtures), remove the headers and look inside the pipes. They should be medium to dark gray or tan. If they are black, the mixture is rich. If they are white or light gray, you are running lean.

The circular flat nose of the plug at the end of the threads should appear dark gray or flat black with no soot. Soot in this area could mean that the plug is loose enough that fuel, air, and combustion gases are blowing and sucking past the plug threads.

Tuning in a lean direction from dead-safe mixtures almost always makes some power, but leaner mixtures are increasingly likely to detonate and thus are increasingly dangerous. It is therefore critical that spark advance always be squared away safely before pushing the mixture envelope (or adding boost). Keep in mind that you're still not finished with timing, because changing the air-fuel-nitrous ratio will affect combustion flame speed as follows: Rich mixtures burn slowly and are easy to ignite; lean mixtures burn fast and are hard to ignite. When the oxygen-fuel mixture looks good, you will still want to revisit timing. If you leaned out the boost mixture on a mild nitrous engine and were running stock all-motor timing, it is more likely than ever that timing is over-advanced when the nitrous is on, so there may be a little power available if you can pull a little timing. If the timing was really conservative, you may then possibly want to add a little advance if there is no sign of detonation and a reliable way—that is, a dynamometer—to know if advancing the timing a bit actually improved torque or not. But knock is so deadly so fast on a boosted engine that it doesn't usually pay to push the envelope with timing unless you are *very* good. Nitrous engines, in particular, do not want a lot of timing, because the combustion is so fast. Not only will excessive timing amp up the possibilities for detonation, but it is suboptimal in delivering maximum power. This is something to think about when you see a nitrous kit that provides no way to remove timing advance on an EFI engine with no timing adjustment. If timing was correct before nitrous, it is almost definitely too advanced with nitrous in the picture. That boost-retard interceptor will not only keep the engine safe, but it can actually improve power and may enable the addition of even more power by leaning out the mixture a little.

Assuming you have a magnifying glass, the spark plugs will warn you if there has been even mild detonation. Mild detonation shows up on a plug with a magnifying lens in the form of black specks peppered onto the insulator nose, and possibly tiny aluminum balls concentrated around the tip of the center electrode. You should immediately stop tuning and make sure nothing is wrong that is unrelated to the engine management calibration that is temporarily increasing the octane number requirement of the engine (like the cooling system is overheated and the cylinder head temp is unexpectedly high for reasons unrelated to the timing advance or mixture strength). Otherwise, cool off combustion by pulling a little timing or adding a little fuel, or both. If you hold the plug up to the sun or a strong light and you see tiny diamonds twinkling on the porcelain, detonation is more serious. In the case of severe detonation, the shock wave and heat will blast enough aluminum off the piston crown to spray-paint the spark plugs gray. Grayed spark plugs are a bad omen that the engine is in mortal danger or has already gone over to the Other Side. Brave tuners have proven some super-high-output screamers will continue to make power as the mixture and timing are optimized all the way into *mild* detonation, but boosted engines should never be tuned to the extent that there is any microscopic aluminum whatsoever misting onto the sharp edges of the plug center electrode. Peppering on the insulator with aluminum specks on the electrode can be a death knell or a reprieve telling you to stop what you are doing before you burn down the engine.

The bottom line is that even if you have a wideband lambda meter and a dyno, only the spark plugs are present when the mystery of boosted combustion unfolds in a nitrous powerplant, and the data they provide is tremendously valuable if you know how to read it. Spark plugs are the nitrous tuner's friend.

Check Spark Plugs. Make sure that the plugs are in excellent condition with the gap set as recommended for the ignition. If you haven't done it already, you will be installing new plugs when it is time to read the plugs to assess the combustion quality during nitrous boost with respect to oxygen-fuel ratio and ignition timing.

AFTER-START TESTING

"Static" Test of Nitrous Powerplant. This is not a widely accepted practice. United Kingdom nitrous vendor Wizards of NOS (WON) recommends static-testing WON nitrous kits (though *not* other brands of kits!) with the vehicle stopped and the engine running at normal operating temperature while configured with (1) 25-horse nitrous jetting, (2) a relatively long nitrous solenoid discharge line, and (3) solenoid-resident metering jets (conducive to a *soooooft* nitrous hit). That said, non-WON nitrous systems of identical or similar morphology should behave more or less the same.

The idea is to verify that the initial nitrous-fuel ratio delivered by the nitrous system is approximately correct or correct it before boosting the engine at full power. The procedure is to hold the engine unloaded steady at one-third redline and then activate the nitrous system by having a helper manually close the full-throttle micro-switch—which should cause the engine to advance quickly to near redline and emit some black smoke. Releasing the full-throttle micro-switch should immediately return the engine to one-third redline rpm.

If rpm only increases by a few hundred with lots of black smoke, you could lean out the fuel jet a little before road-testing the vehicle with full-load nitrous boost. Nitrous systems on knock-limited engines running street premium gasoline would rarely be running leaner than the nitrous-air-fuel ratio that produces rich best torque (RBT), though some tuners with access to really high octane gasoline or alcohol could optimize peak *horsepower* using slightly leaner nitrous mixtures than what produces maximum peak torque, particularly on really high-revving engines.

If rpm revs sharply through the redline, this could indicate the nitrous-fuel mixture is lean. Lean mixtures might indicate that the fuel pump lacks the capacity to maintain required pressure and flow during nitrous boost—or it might simply indicate that the recommended default fuel jetting or rate of gain in fuel pressure does not properly match the nitrous jetting on the particular engine.

The WON static test procedure is dependent on running no more than a 25 nitrous shot and a soft hit to negate the possibility of severe lean backfire and lean engine damage as the nitrous hits the unloaded engine. WON does not recommend using the procedure with hard-hitting large nitrous hits and non-WON nitrous kits, which will, in any event, rev too fast to provide useful nitrous-fuel feedback. In the case where static testing works as it should with a 25-horse shot, the rich-lean jetting information gleaned from the test is then scalable to larger nitrous shots.

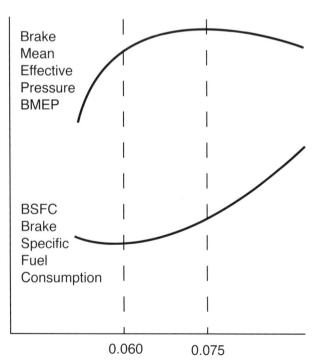
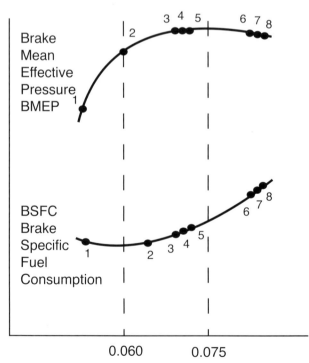

Relationship between Brake Mean Effective Cylinder Pressure and Brake Specific Fuel Consumption as the fuel-air ration changes.

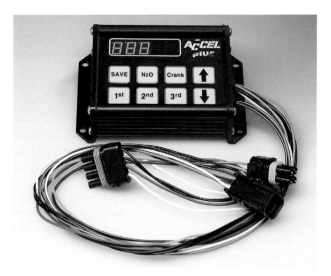

Accel Plus Timing Retard Module was designed to allow nitrous tuners to optimize ignition timing during both all-motor and nitrous-on conditions. Trying to handle both situations with one timing curve is a poor compromise. *Accel*

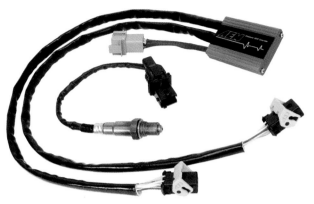

AEM Wideband UEGO (universal exhaust gas oxygen) Controller was designed to allow aftermarket engine management systems or other electronic controllers access to very accurate oxygen-fuel data at very high speeds. The trick with tuning nitrous engines is to get the air-fuel calibration as perfect as possible on the motor, and then tune the nitrous-fuel ratio during boost. Never attempt to use nitrous fueling to correct problems with the basic air-fuel calculation. Or at least never do it unless you are intentionally over-fueling the all-motor calibration so that a nitrous-only hidden nitrous system can kick in and make power by burning the surplus fuel. *AEM*

Alternatives to static-testing a nitrous installation to validate the default nitrous-fuel ratio involve testing a vehicle on an inertial chassis dynamometer or test track while measuring and logging the air-fuel ratio using a high-quality wideband lambda meter that deduces total air-nitrous-fuel ratio based on micro changes in exhaust gas oxygen. Most tuners consider inertial chassis dynos to be superior to water-brake or eddy-current designs for this type of testing because brake dynos are less forgiving than inertial chassis dynos like the standard Dynojet 248 and can easily result in engine damage during nitrous boost unless the operator is very experienced in loading nitrous powerplants.

Full-power Test and Tune. Again, your engine needs an excellent all-motor state of tune before you even consider attempting to tune on the bottle. This may seem like a tautology but for an engine to have an excellent state of tune, it must be tune-able—meaning, first of all, that the engine must not burn oil, must not be leaking water internally, and must be mechanically sound. The cooling system must be working properly, and the engine management systems and any sensors and actuators must work correctly.

Keep in mind that tuning will be affected by the **architecture of the combustion chambers**, with hemispherical, wedge, pentroof, and rotary combustion chambers all having unique airflow and combustion characteristics. The **distance from the spark plug** to the farthest point in the combustion chamber will affect ignition timing and maximum safe boost, with combustion completing faster with less likelihood of knock when the plugs are centrally located. The **displacement of the engine** will have an effect on combustion, with

larger engines more detonation-prone due to the fact that it takes longer for combustion to burn its way through a large combustion chamber than a smaller one.

Compression ratio is important, because higher compression leads to the higher cylinder pressure and higher heat that makes engines accelerate hard. High compression increases combustion speed by packing inducted charge more densely into a smaller space, but the higher cylinder pressure and heat make it more likely the engine will detonate. Even without air-supercharging, the refrigeration effects of nitrous will change the **effective compression ratio** of the powerplant during boost by increasing the density of inducted air as it flows toward the cylinders. The same is true when manifold pressure increases from air-supercharging. For these reasons, when you are tuning a modified engine, you are finding your way in the dark with both hands and a flashlight because it is a science project rather than a cookbook.

As well, the nitrous system must start with a safe nitrous-fuel calibration designed and recommended by the engineers who designed the nitrous kit for your application. This initial calibration (which some people refer to as a "jet map") is designed to be safe for nearly all applications. Which, unfortunately, means the default calibration almost definitely makes sub-optimal power and torque in most applications and that the efficiency at delivering power per weight of fuel is probably not very good. The standard calibration may not be very efficient at delivering horsepower per pound of nitrous oxide.

Whether or not you will be using progressive PWM metering to feather in the nitrous and fuel, exotic progressive tuning (beyond just feathering in the nitrous/fuel hit) should be attempted *after* you've got the system working well at low levels of power boost in constant-flow mode. The initial

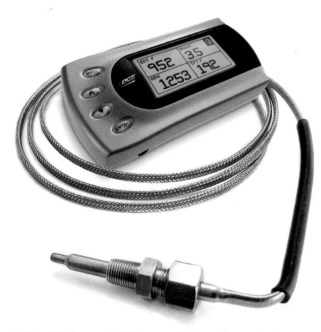

An Exhaust Gas Temperature (EGT) gauge and display provides warning of dangerously hot combustion. *Edge Products*

nitrous and fuel metering (jet size, and so on) should be set for the nitrous installation/kit and specific vehicle according to the recommendations of experienced technical support personnel. That is, don't mess around with using the variable orifices to limit *maximum nitrous flow* in various circumstances until the plugs, timing, and mixture strength at wide-open flow (jetted for the lowest possible power boost) are squared away under constant-flow conditions. Progressive controls add electrical, mechanical, chemical, and tuning complexity to the situation. There are more things to go wrong using progressive controls. The same is true for multi-stage nitrous. Tune one stage at a time until everything is right, and then tune the combined stages together, in no case assuming that if the various stages work well alone you've automatically got the combined hit tuned properly.

Fuel and nitrous pressure must meet specifications of the default nitrous-fuel calibration.

Initial ignition timing should be at the recommended default for the kit at its lowest horsepower jetting. Most people recommend making sure that initial boost ignition timing is retarded from the all-motor calibration 1 degree per 25 horsepower nitrous shot across the rpm range during boost. When you've got the air-nitrous-fuel ratio dialed in, you can revisit timing for further optimization in various subsets of the range of speed and loading, followed by more nitrous-fuel work, and so on until everything is perfect.

The correct procedure is to start with the minimum nitrous shot and work upward from there. *Never* start with a large power increase when tuning a virgin nitrous system.

You're going to run the engine hard to load up the spark plugs, chop the ignition, and allow everything to stop, at which point you'll remove *all* sparkplugs to evaluate what is happening in the combustion chambers (see sidebar on plug reading on page 150), after which you may conclude you want or need to modify the nitrous-fuel ratio.

Particularly when tuning, unless you really know what you're doing, do not use nitrous boost under circumstances where the engine could not accelerate freely without nitrous boost, such as climbing a steep hill in a high gear at low rpm or braked to full load on a torque-cell dynamometer. Ideally, you should test and tune a virgin nitrous system on an inertial chassis dynamometer where acceleration is *always* possible, *not* a brake dyno of the type that provides only continuous loading (even if it's in tiny steps during a *simulated* acceleration run). It is much easier to operate inertial dynos without problems, because little or no expertise is needed to operate the dyno. The dyno pull on an inertial chassis dyno unfolds quickly (and the weight and configuration of various inertial dynos vary such that they are appropriate to car, truck, motorcycle, snowmobile, and other applications), so there is less time for thermal loading to melt things, break parts, or detonate the engine to pieces.

There are other obvious advantages to using a rolling road—i.e., inertial chassis dynamometer—for "road-testing" a virgin nitrous installation: no traffic, no cops, little or no danger, totally controlled conditions with fire extinguishers, fans, and so forth. You can stand beside the engine and keep an eye out for leaks or other visible problems on the virgin nitrous run. When you chop the power and cut the engine to read the plugs, you're already stopped, even if the wheels and dyno rollers are still freewheeling. It is much easier to attach test equipment like a wideband lambda

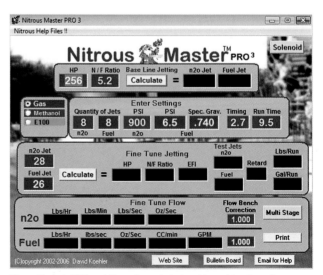

Nitrous Master's PRO³ modeling software is designed to model various nitrous tuning situations and predict the effect of changing various nitrous system tuning parameters on horsepower. *Koehler Injection*

meter or a data recorder to a stopped vehicle on a dyno. Keep in mind that the chassis dyno may have inertia that's different from the sum total of your engine, drivetrain, and vehicle (many Dynojet 248 chassis dynamometers, for example, have rollers with 3,200 pounds of inertia), which

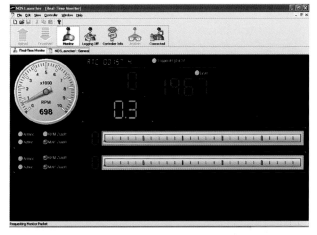

NOS Launcher progressive nitrous controller Real-time Monitor laptop display screen. Note that the screen shows the engine is running at 700 rpms. MAP cutoff is in effect for Stage 1 and Stage 2, and rpm cutoff is in effect for Stage 2. Stage 1 is not currently armed. *NOS*

could influence the ideal size and ratio of nitrous shot and supplemental fuel.

Unfortunately, dyno time normally costs money.

The next best place for initial testing is a test track, but tracks aren't normally free either.

If you are going to road-test a nitrous installation on an actual road, you need a long, straight, flat stretch of track in a deserted rural area where you will not be arrested or crash into civilians if something goes wrong. If you have any doubts, post observers with cellphones so they can warn you if someone is coming (so no one gets hurt, right?). You should not have to drive at insane speeds to get the job done, though you will, hopefully, be guilty of "displays of speed."

I recommend less-experienced tuners debug virgin street nitrous or turbo powerplants with unleaded racing gasoline as added insurance against engine damage from knock or surface ignition. On higher-horse shot street kits with more potential for engine damage, it makes sense for anyone to start with race gas. Of course not all racing gasoline is the same. There are unleaded racing fuels available with fairly high octane—in the range of 105 or better—but you don't need this much octane for a system that's intended to run on street premium, and really high octane unleaded racing gasolines can have unintended consequences for tuning: Most 105-plus octane unleaded gasolines are a blend of aromatic hydrocarbons with

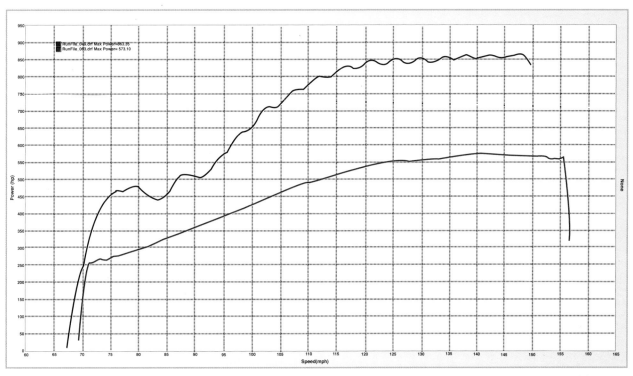

Dyno tuning is invaluable if not essential for optimizing a nitrous system. This horsepower graph indicates the Spray-Z06 powerplant is probably not reaching its full potential yet is in the 80-100 mph range. The next step would be to datalog lambda information from a wideband O_2 sensor, or abort the test at 85 mph, kill the engine, and read the plugs. You'd want to ascertain not only oxygen-fuel information, but whether there appeared to be suboptimal timing in the region.

a significant amount of oxygenated alcohol or ether, so the air-nitrous-fuel proportions required to achieve stoichiometric combustion can diverge from the ordinary premium street gasoline you may be planning to run after the system has been debugged with race fuel. The specific gravity (density) of super-high-octane unleaded versus street premium could also be different enough to require different air-nitrous-fuel ratios.

Unless you are running a very radical nitrous shot (which you shouldn't be at this stage on a new installation), you will find that one of the several racing gasolines with octane in the 100 to 101 range will do the job in providing much better resistance to knock during debug operations compared to street premium. If race fuel or avgas is not an option, you might want to add something to boost the octane of street premium. Pure toluene (114 octane, available at some hardware stores in 1- or 5-gallon cans for use as a solvent) can be blended with street gasolines as an octane booster, with the combined octane increasing according to the average of the two octanes weighted according to the proportions used. The octane of a brew of 10 percent toluene and 90 percent 93 octane street premium is $(0.1 \times 114) + (0.9 \times 93) = 95.1$

To perform low-budget test-and-tune operations on the road, you'll need, at a minimum, an assistant, a stopwatch, a sparkplug wrench, a magnifier to help with plug reading, and a log in which to record your data as you make changes (*very* important). If the timing on your vehicle is adjustable, bring a good timing light. A G-Tech or other accelerometer-based on-the-go "dyno" is an extremely useful tool and much better than a stopwatch for evaluating the effect of tuning changes. They are affordable for most people who have the money for substantive hot rodding projects. Ideally, you've got someone on the scene who is experienced in reading spark plugs. It is a good idea to have one or two complete sets of extra spark plugs in case you load any to the point that they are too fouled to fire well or if the plugs get too loaded to permit accurate reading. If there is any doubt about the heat range of plug to run, bring all ranges of plugs you *might* need.

A precision wideband lambda meter can be invaluable, particularly because the forensic evidence of certain types of timing problems versus fuel problems on the spark plugs can be subtle. Also valuable is Datalogging equipment to monitor and log (1) lambda, (2) individual-cylinder exhaust gas temperature (EGT), (3) rpm, (4) manifold pressure, (5) intake air temperature, and (6) all other engine sensor statuses. The more test equipment you have the better. In fact, data recorders are almost essential to producing a truly superlative state of tune. Wideband oxygen sensors and individual-cylinder EGT probes are great, though they are indirect evidence about what is happening in the cylinders, since things are happening so fast in a boosting nitrous powerplant and the measurement takes place downstream in the headers or exhaust system. Wideband air-fuel ratio meters (particularly combined with other logged engine data) will enable you to see if the oxygen-fuel ratio is changing significantly in unintended ways during a full-throttle run so you can enact countermeasures.

You'll need to read the plugs (see sidebar) to optimize the tune of a nitrous engine. Racers and engineers with all the test gear in the world still read spark plugs for first-hand feedback on combustion conditions in a particular cylinder. Unless you've got radically expensive in-cylinder pressure transducers, high-speed cameras, and other exotic scientific tools, the plugs are the only first-hand witness to what's happening in the combustion chambers of your engine. Fortunately, there is at least one plug per cylinder, which provides plenty of data upon which to base tuning decisions. To fully appreciate the subtleties of the archeological evidence provided by spark plug reading for the most accurate tuning decisions, you'll need strong light and a high-quality magnifying glass. An otoscope—the tool doctors use to

Nano External-Pressurization Nitrous Dyno Results

	BASELINE	NANO	GAIN
CONFIGURATION: 175 SHOT			
Intake Air Temp Deg	100.2	98.7	
Vapor Pressure (In. Hg)	.46	.47	
Barometric Pressure	29.37	29.34	
Correction Factor (SAE)	1.04	1.04	
Air/Fuel ratio Avg.	11.6	11.3	
Horsepower	579.2	604.5	25.3
Average Horsepower	559.3	587.5	28.2
Torque	661.4	708.7	47.3
Average Torque	546.0	573.5	27.4
CONFIGURATION: 300 SHOT			
Intake Air Temp Deg	111.2	100.3	
Vapor Pressure (In. Hg)	.32	.29	
Barometric Pressure	30.19	29.52	
Correction Factor (SAE)	1.01	1.03	
Air/Fuel ratio Avg.	11.4	11.3	
Horsepower	714.3	761.8	47.5

Data comparing nitrous pulls with and without NANO external pressurization installed on a nitrous powerplant running 175- and 300-horsepower nitrous shots. The ability of the NANO system to maintain nitrous tank pressure and eliminate intank refrigeration effects as the pulls unfold results in gains of 27.5 and 47.5 horsepower, respectively.

Dyno-tuning a boosted Ferrari F50 on a Dynojet 248 chassis dynamometer.

look in your ears—provides light and magnification in a single convenient package. You can buy an otoscope from Amazon.com, Target, Staples, and various other sites on the Internet. Using an otoscope may feel awkward at first, but you'll figure it out with a little practice.

Strap the vehicle to an inertial chassis dynamometer, or take it to a test track or a remote untraveled road. Make sure that the engine is warm, and then prepare to make full-throttle pulls in third or fourth gear across the range of the nitrous powerband with the nitrous disabled.

Never make a nitrous pull through the redline, particularly if the engine will hit a rev-limiter, which could cause an explosion or engine damage if the rev-limiter begins randomly dropping out spark or primary injected fuel on various cylinders in a way that could produce lean mixtures while the engine is still receiving strong nitrous boost or instigate backfires into the intake that explode large amounts of nitrous and enrichment fuel. If for any reason you back off the throttle during a nitrous pull (during initial tuning or way down the line when you are, say, an experienced nitrous dragger), *do not get back in the gas* even if you are in the middle of a race because it could produce the same type of explosive effect.

HERE IS THE TEST AND TUNE PROCEDURE:

1. With the nitrous tank valve closed and the nitrous system *disarmed*, accelerate in third or fourth gear at wide open throttle from a speed above the minimum nitrous-activation rpm through the rpm range—say from 30 to 70 miles per hour—measuring the time it takes for the vehicle to accelerate if you are not on a dyno or using a G-Tech. When you reach the target speed or rpm, simultaneously release the throttle and depress the clutch (if applicable), kill the engine, and coast to a stop. To get an accurate reading at the track, have the car towed back to the pits because running the engine will immediately change the plugs' forensic record of full-throttle combustion. If towing isn't possible, drive the car as briefly as possible before reading the plugs.

2. Write down everything you observed during the test run. Remove *all* the spark plugs for evaluation. If you don't have a lot of experience reading plugs, good color photos of various types of plug conditions can be very useful as a comparison. If you have a good camera and know what you're doing, you might want to photograph each plug up close with a macro lens. Obviously, at this stage, without nitrous, the plugs should all look normal. Write down everything you observe about every spark plug.

3. Reinstall the plugs in their original position, open the nitrous bottle valve, and rerun the acceleration test with the nitrous armed and engaged, again timing the length of the run (or, much better, logging power and torque data with the dyno or G-Tech). If the nitrous is working correctly, the car should accelerate smoothly and sound and feel louder and stronger, depending on the weight of the vehicle and the size of the nitrous shot.

How To Find The Right Nitrous Jet

Nitrous jet	at 900-925 psi	16	20	22	28	32	36	40	43
Fuel required	lb/hr	60-72	92-110	112-135	122-147	151-181	197-236	233-280	246-295
	4	19-21	26-29	30-32	31-34	34-38	N/A	N/A	N/A
	6	17-19	21-23	21-25	23-26	26-29	30-32	34-38	35-39
	8	16-17	19-21	21-23	22-24	24-26	27-31	31-35	32-36
	10	14-16	18-20	20-21	21-22	22-25	26-29	28-33	29-34
	20	13-14	15-17	17-19	18-19	20-22	22-23	23-26	24-26
	30	N/A	14-16	16-17	17-18	18-21	20-22	21-23	22-24
Fuel jet @ psi	40	N/A	13-15	15-16	16-17	17-19	19-21	21-22	21-22
	50	N/A	N/A	14-16	15-17	17-18	18-20	20-22	21-22
	60	N/A	N/A	14-16	14-17	16-17	17-18	19-21	20-22
	70	N/A	N/A	14-15	14-15	15-17	17-18	18-20	19-21
	80	N/A	N/A	N/A	14-15	15-17	17-18	18-19	18-20
	90	N/A	N/A	N/A	N/A	14-16	17-18	18-19	18-20

If you hear spark knock or anything else that sounds ominous, *immediately* get out of the throttle (and *don't* get back in it until you have stopped to evaluate and correct the problem). As before, when you hit the target speed, immediately kill the engine, coast down, and read the plugs.

4. Regardless of how the engine "feels" on nitrous, the acceleration time or dyno numbers should prove that the vehicle is accelerating faster when boosted. Obviously, a dyno or G-Tech graph that overlays before and after runs should reflect a significant power increase across the board with the nitrous active that's consistent with the advertised horsepower shot. Keep in mind, however, that there is a difference between horsepower measured at the crankshaft and horsepower measured at the wheels (there is less at the wheels due to friction and rolling resistance). If there is no change in the before and after runs, then the nitrous system is probably failing to trigger, and needs debugging. If the vehicle is *slower* when you trigger nitrous boost with excessive black smoke, you are probably getting supplemental fuel without any nitrous (Is the bottle valve closed? Is the tank *empty*?). Or perhaps the nitrous-fuel ratio is grossly rich (if everything is installed correctly and sensibly—in other words, the nitrous line is not routed against the exhaust header or something equally crazy—and you've got the default recommended nitrous and fuel jetting, this should not

be able to happen). You'll know more in a moment when you read the plugs.

5. Remove and read the spark plugs. If the nitrous system was alive and making power, the plugs will ideally be the same color as they were after the normal (non-boosted) run, or perhaps a bit darker. If there is evidence of lean mixtures, overheating, or detonation, it is critical to correct the situation immediately before boosting the engine again to avoid damaging it. Write down everything. If the plugs are black and sooty or very sooty, then you will definitely need to tune the system to improve power and eliminate future engine wear from overly rich mixtures washing lubrication off the cylinder walls. When you've finally established the proper nitrous-fuel ratio, it may be scalable to *slightly* larger nitrous horsepower shots, though significantly larger power increases will certainly require additional fuel coolant on knock-limited engines, meaning richer air-fuel-nitrous mixtures. If and when you jack up the nitrous to a significantly larger horsepower shot, you should start over at the default settings and jetting and tune from there.

Keep in mind that weak spark can produce the same symptoms as excessively rich air-fuel-nitrous mixtures: black fuel smoke and reduced performance. Conversely, the mixture strength will affect how much electrical power is required to spark through the charge (mixtures rich with fuel and nitrous require a hotter spark). If you are trying to find power by leaning out the enrichment fuel on a nitrous-fuel calibration suspected of being rich, read the plugs. If pulling a little fuel doesn't seem to help, instead of robotically pulling *more* fuel, suspect weak spark, and see if narrowing the spark gap down as low as .020 or less helps. If it does, upgrade the ignition, and then return to the default nitrous-fuel metering before proceeding with the test-and-tune process.

6. Recalibrate the air-nitrous-fuel ratio. A common method of calibrating the oxygen-fuel ratio during nitrous boost is to adjust the enrichment fuel pressure. If the plugs reveal that combustion is too rich, reduce the fuel pressure. If combustion is lean, increase the fuel pressure. Keep in mind that reducing fuel pressure on low-pressure nitrous fuel systems (found on carbureted engines, certain throttle body injection [TBI] engines, and some types of wet EFI nitrous kits) is problematic because unavoidable fuel pressure variations during highly dynamic operating conditions become more and more significant as a percentage. The alternative is re-calibrating the fuel or nitrous delivery by changing fuel or nitrous jets or pressure-regulated dry nitrous bypass jets. Or, in the case of computer-controlled dry nitrous, using a laptop computer to deliver a bit less fuel in the appropriate rpm and loading range.

Some experts recommend adjusting nitrous to correct oxygen-fuel ratio problems, leaving the fuel delivery constant. It is a fact, though, that adding nitrous will tend to result in the horsepower creeping higher, which is not a good thing on a powerplant that is operating near the ragged edge. Other nitrous experts recommend that you should *never* tune by changing the nitrous delivery, except when jumping to a bigger horsepower shot. Still others recommend choosing the conservative approach, in other words, *reduce* the nitrous metering if the combustion mixture is lean, *reduce* the fuel metering if the combustion mixture is rich. The advantage of this last strategy is that tuning changes can never outrun the fuel supply system, causing pressure to drop.

Never re-jet in either direction more than two sizes at a time on a single-jet plate kit or one jet size on a nitrous system with multiple jets (where the effect of changing jet size is multiplied by the number of cylinders). If you *are* tuning with fuel pressure changes (preferably from a lean condition richer), make *small* changes: On a low-pressure system, change pressure in steps of 0.125 (1/8) psi; on a high-pressure system, change pressure in steps of 0.5 psi. If you have a low-pressure fuel supply system, strongly consider converting to a return-type high-pressure fuel loop, which will improve

How To Calculate Horsepower From Nitrous Jetting

Nitrous jet (900-950 psi)	Fuel jet (Gasoline)	Horsepower			
		HP / JET	HP × 4	HP × 6	HP × 8
14	18	6	24	36	48
16	20	9	36	54	72
18	22	12	48	72	96
20	24	15	60	90	120
22	26	17	78	102	136
24	28	20	80	120	160
26	30	25	100	150	200
28	32	30	120	180	240
30	34	34	136	204	272
32	36	38	152	228	304
34	38	40	160	240	320
36	40	45	180	270	360
40	44	50	200	300	400
42	46	60	240	360	480

the consistency and repeatability of fuel delivery by minimizing adverse resonation and pressure-spike effects as boost starts and stops and the pressure regulator works to control fuel pressure.

If, for safety reasons, you have been testing with racing gasoline that you do not plan to run when the test-and-tune or shakeout process is over, keep in mind that sooner or later you are going to have to reduce the octane of the fuel. Really good gasoline can help you find the optimal state of tune for the powerplant when maximum power is not knock-limited. But many nitrous kits of respectable power boost probably cannot achieve maximum power on high-performance street engines with street gasoline. This is one more reason why it is critical to log every change you make. It is a judgment call as to when it's time to get real with the fuel, but keep in mind that if you optimize tuning with 100-octane unleaded race gas, you may need anti-knock countermeasures if you switch to 93 octane street premium. Once you have a handle on the ideal air-fuel-nitrous ratio with race gas at the target power setting, you may or may not decide to change to street gasoline before optimizing the timing. And you could end up needing richer oxygen-fuel ratios to help fight detonation. Do *not* optimize tuning with race gas and then abruptly switch to street premium.

7. Make another acceleration pull and read the plugs. If you started with the recommended default nitrous jetting, yet it appears you need to make drastic changes in jetting, stop and think, because something is wrong. The fuel or nitrous pressure might be way off, or you're running out of fuel or nitrous, or the contents of the nitrous tank have overheated past 97.7 degrees F and converted into a gas-like supercritical fluid, or the fuel or nitrous filter is blocked, or the spark is weak, or the timing is way wrong, or something else is out of whack that has to be fixed before pushing on. Unless you really know what you're doing (and even if you do), consult an expert before you push forward. Don't be afraid to get a second or third opinion if you question the wisdom of the first expert. It's your engine. Think, investigate, fix the problem, return to the default jetting, and begin the test regime again. In general, if you change anything on the vehicle that could influence the performance (replace nitrous components or plumbing, install an adjustable fuel pressure regulator, change the primary fuel injectors, etc., etc., etc.), fall back to the default low-power nitrous (and fuel enrichment) test jetting, retune if necessary, and then verify or recalibrate the high-power nitrous-fuel delivery accordingly.

8. Optimize timing. To be safe, the rule of thumb is that the higher flame speed of nitrous combustion requires 1 degree less timing advance per 25-horse shot. That's usually the recommendation unless, as I've discussed,

a low-power low-cost nitrous kit must get by on the cheap with stock timing. OK, you've tuned the oxygen-fuel ratio until it's nuts-on. Revisit the timing. One degree of timing retard per 25-horsepower boost is a safe, conservative anti-knock countermeasure that should be enough for any nitrous engine running an appropriate octane fuel, but it may well be more than you need, and there may be power gains available from advancing timing a bit. Keep in mind that excessively retarded timing that puts peak cylinder pressure after the optimal 15 degrees after top dead center is wasting thermal energy into the exhaust as fuel continues to burn deep into the expansion cycle when the piston is moving away from the cylinder head at very high speed.

Advance timing in small steps, listening for knock and measuring power and torque gains with the stopwatch, G-Tech or inertial chassis dyno. Never advance timing more than a degree or two at a time. Some advanced race engines running very good gasoline have reportedly optimized power with as little as 8 to 9 total degrees of nitrous-on timing retard for a 350-horse shot of nitrous, which is less than 0.25 degrees timing retard per 25 horsepower boost. This, however, is very unusual, and is not going to happen on a street engine running street premium fuel. You should hold off on advancing boost timing retard until you are very familiar with the nitrous kit and how the engine behaves on boost.

9. Make sure your parts can take the horsepower! I can't tell you how many times I've seen people throw a 350-horse shot kit on their stock engine and then wonder why they're breaking parts. Stock rods and pistons may handle a 30 to 50 percent power increase for short bursts if nothing is detonating, but modern engines are less over-built because modern modeling software gives engineers a much better idea about when parts will fail. Modern engines already have much better specific power than older engines anyway, and they have less mechanical headroom for horsepower increases.

Do not assume the optimal oxygen-fuel ratios from lower power settings are scalable to higher power levels. As the power increases, the tendency to knock will increase, requiring that you retard timing and add coolant fuel. Plan to re-tune from scratch starting from the recommended default fuel and nitrous settings for each nitrous shot increase.

Before you pump it up to the next horsepower setting, measure the power gains you already have on a dyno or by calculating the average power based on acceleration results. Compare the results of boosted and non-boosted runs, preferably on a dyno. Are the power gains during boost what they should be? Does power jump by the predicted

DEBUGGING VIRGIN NITROUS SYSTEMS

Zero or Very Little Power Boost
- Bottle valve is turned off
- Nitrous tank is dispensing low-density nitrous vapor instead of liquid because the nitrous is above 97.7 degrees F or the tank is oriented in such a way that the discharge is blowing vapor from the gas bubble rather than purging liquid
- Unrealistic expectations: A small nitrous shot may not feel like much at higher rpm on a high-output engine
- The air-fuel-nitrous ratio is excessively rich
- The nitrous kit is mal-installed as follows:
  - The full-throttle switch doesn't close at full throttle, or doesn't stay on
  - Leaking fittings in the nitrous supply plumbing
  - Insufficient electrical power supply to nitrous solenoids
  - Bad electrical connection or relay fails to activate some or all of the nitrous system
  - Improper fuel source—i.e., return segment of EFI fuel loop—fails to pressurize enrichment fuel system
  - The nitrous supply line is exposed to excessive heat, vaporizing the liquid flow
- Weak or delayed spark

Nitrous Lag (Hits too Slow)
- Rich bog because
  - The pressure drop through the long nitrous supply line allows nitrous to vaporize before reaching the engine
  - The pressure drop through a large bore line allows nitrous to vaporize before reaching the engine
  - Excessive supply-line heat soak vaporizes some or all of the nitrous before reaching the engine
  - A pressure drop *and* heat soak vaporize the nitrous before reaching the engine
  - The self-pressurized nitrous tank loses temperature and pressure during high usage

Engine Stalls When Nitrous Triggers
- Bottle valve is turned off, tank is empty, or tank orientation is discharging nitrous vapor
- Nitrous filter or metering jet is blocked
- Fuel solenoid is triggering, nitrous solenoid not triggering

Engine Misfires During Nitrous Boost
- Inadequate spark for nitrous ignition due to lack of super-duty components:
  - Inadequate coil power
  - Excessive spark plug gaps
  - Spark plugs leaking voltage through deposits
  - Voltage leak or high resistance in original equipment resistor-type plug leads
  - Voltage leak from distributor cap or excessive resistance in corroded electrodes

- Voltage leak, corroded electrode, or high resistance in resistor-type rotor
- Upgrade coil voltage escaping due to lack of other super-duty components:

Malfunction Indicator ("Check Engine") Light On
- Engine sensor out of range due to
  - Exhaust gas oxygen (EGO) sensor detects excessively rich mixture during nitrous boost
  - Intake air temperature (IAT) sensor overcooled by evaporating nitrous in intake system

Detonation
- Fuel octane too low
- Ignition timing too advanced/no boost retard capability
- Lean air-fuel-nitrous mixture
- Cylinder head temperature too high (cooling system over-stressed)
- Intake air temperature too hot
- Too large nitrous shot
- Too much turbo boost and nitrous shot
- Spark plugs overheating and causing surface ignition
- Carbon on combustion chambers or exhaust valves causing surface ignition
- Suboptimal plug design for application
- Compression ratio too high
- Fuel pump cannot maintain enough pressure during boost

Too Little Power or Performance
- Weak spark
- Suboptimal spark advance
- Suboptimal air-fuel-nitrous ratio
- Engine is detonating
- Fuel pump cannot maintain enough pressure during boost
- Advanced factory engine management system is thwarting optimal nitrous state of tune
- Slipping clutch or automatic transmission
- Slipping tires!
- Progressive controller set at a too low duty cycle
- Engine is receiving nitrous vapor rather than liquid
- Pumping efficiency of the exhaust valves and exhaust cam is too low
- Exhaust system too restrictive for high products-to-reactants ratio of power boost
- Engine is not healthy
- Horsepower shot is too small (too little nitrous, too little supplemental fuel)

Nitrous Hits Too Hard
- Nitrous solenoid too close to injectors
- Horsepower shot too large for vehicle
- Multiple nitrous stages required
- Progressive controller required

---

amount (correcting for differences between crankshaft and wheel horsepower) when the boost hits, and do the boosted and non-boosted horsepower graphs parallel each other to the end of the run? Check in with the kit vendor's product support at the nitrous kit builder. Do they agree you're where you should be? If not, the boost tuning is probably not as good as you think, and there is more work to do at the current power shot before moving up. Keep a record of *everything* that happens, every change you make, every setting, every result. All of this is valuable information you can reference later on when you are tuning the kit or talking to someone good about tuning it.

Chapter 7
Extreme, Special, and Advanced Nitrous Issues

For the purpose of this discussion, "extreme" refers to any automotive nitrous system that boosts power by more than 250-300 horsepower or 50 percent. Given the power-to-weight ratio of motorcycles, snowmobiles, and watercraft, any of these vehicles with a nitrous system has to be considered extreme. Nobody installs nitrous on a turbo diesel engine unless it is already boosted to within an inch of its life with a lot of turbo boost and all the air-surplus is being burned by overfueling, so all nitrous diesels also have to be considered "extreme." Similarly, given the mandatory conservative nature of aviation power-boosting, and the requirement of FAA approval of any modifications to normal category aircraft, most aircraft with add-on boosting systems are licensed in the "experimental" category, and the powerplant is almost certain to be installed in a homebuilt kit plane or air racer—making the small number of such aircraft by definition "extreme." In all, an interesting group of people-movers....

The Norwood Max-4 engine runs three plugs per chamber, which is helpful in reducing the likelihood of detonation running on nitromethane, methanol, and intermittent nitrous injection. Lighting the fires in three places at once helps to ensure that normal combustion completes before there is time for detonation.

Radical nitrous systems these days usually include at least a 15-pound nitrous tank, AN-6 or AN-8 Teflon-core braided-stainless supply lines, oversize solenoids that may open with CO_2 pressure rather than electromagnetism, and a purpose-built high-flow bottle control valve—all designed to make sure that the supply plumbing area is never narrower closer to the tank end and that the critical supply bottleneck is always the metering jets rather than anything else. The newest 400 to 750-horse plate nitrous systems often employ tricks like peripheral annular orifice injection, which eliminates aerodynamic restrictions caused by air colliding with spray bar pipes, while simultaneously providing better mixture distribution and a bigger power shot without the tradeoff of diminished airflow.

Since the key to making a massive nitrous shot work well depends on the ability to accurately deliver and distribute fuel to match the nitrous flow, aftermarket researchers have invented some innovative designs to improve on the traditional over-under spray bar spacer-plate system used on 4-barrel carbureted V-8s that had traditionally been limited to providing a power boost in the 100- to 250-horsepower range. Innovations include:

- *Bottle Blown* four-hole plate with same-side nitrous and fuel feed to equalize spray bar pressure, equipped with multiple discharge orifices custom-drilled for the individual application
- *HVH's Super Sucker* plates integrated HVH's own expertise with performance-improving carb spacers and the plate-nitrous expertise of Nitrous Express to deliver a dual side-mount spray bar architecture
- *Nitrous Express* patented a billet plate system designed to eliminate the restriction of fragile spray bars, complete with custom-bent stainless steel supply lines
- *Nitrous Express* two-stage billet plate with injection orifices machined directly into the billet plate provided as much as 750 horsepower boost.
- *Nitrous Pro-Flow* two-stage plate with 88-hole spray bar delivered a 360-degree spray pattern to the intake manifold, complete with direct-purge solenoids on the plate, and replaceable burst panels.
- *Nitrous Supply/Edelbrock* plate system with crisscross spray bars, each fed simultaneously from both ends to eliminate pressure drop along the bar

This turbocharged Japanese Domestic Market 3-rotor Wankel engine makes a great drag motor in a heavily-modified RX-7—especially with a single nitrous fogger nozzle to hit the engine with a burst of low-end torque that kills turbo lag.

Juiced drag-race sled from Mad Max Racing. At the time of this writing, wheel-equipped snowmobile draggers with more than 400 horsepower easily ran in the 8's at speeds of nearly 170 mph. *Wizards of NOS*

- *Nitrous Works Magnum "X"* arrived capable of delivering 550 horsepower using two-stage spray bar injection delivered from a relatively thin 1-inch spacer plate.
- *Speedtech's* diffuser system was designed to deliver a radial 360-degree fog of nitrous and fuel emanating from a conical fixture located in the *center* of a four-hole spacer plate—an architecture intended to increase airspeed and facilitate improved carb signaling.
- *Zex* billet plate system eliminated restrictive spraybars entirely in favor of an annular-orifice injection system delivering nitrous from 12 points around the periphery of the plate, with the added benefit of a self-chilling plate architecture.

In general, many performance engines respond well to a carefully designed 2-inch-thick open spacer plate installed between the carburetor and manifold, which in some cases can add more than 10 lb-ft torque across the rpm range *independent of nitrous boost*. If there is enough hood clearance, the all-motor performance of a thinner nitrous plate might be improved by adding a second spacer underneath.

Solenoids for all nitrous applications are specially designed with relatively large internal passeges and orifices, and a flow path least conducive to causing a pressure drop and nitrous phase change. Due to the high pressures and the possibility of large changes in nitrous temperature and very cold operating conditions, nitrous solenoids are built with special seals. Perhaps surprisingly, Neoprene, which seals best, is the way to go for street applications, where preventing leaks is paramount. For hard-core racing, Teflon seals are more rugged, especially for progressive PWM pulsing. Given the potentially catastrophic implications of a nitrous solenoid failing to close, common racing practice is to install backup solenoids (which are *not* pulsed, and therefore live an easier, longer life), which will positively stop nitrous flow if the primary solenoid fails. Common race practice is to install timers or counters or otherwise accumulate usage data on a solenoid, and replace the solenoid after a suitable interval before it fails. Mean time-to-failure specifications provide guidance as when a solenoid must be replaced to reduce the possibility of failure to negligible. Nonetheless, all competition progressive systems should have backup solenoids that will positively stop nitrous and supplemental fuel flow to avert disaster in the event a pulsed solenoid seizes open.

To improve the launch on traction-limited cars and suppress engine shock, extreme nitrous vehicles almost always require a method of **softening the initial nitrous hit**. In some cases that's just a matter of delaying full nitrous activation after launch (and transbrake release) until a certain time has passed, or the engine has gained some rpm, or the vehicle has reached a certain gear—or some amount of all three. The usual tactics consist of (1) a delay controller or other trigger switch controlled by an adjustable timer, (2) a staged nitrous system with a modest primary nitrous shot, (3) a progressive controller that fades in full nitrous and fuel flow by pulsing the solenoids rapidly open and closed (beginning at a configurable frequency and increasing to full power), (4) softening the hit with timing retard and fuel enrichment, or (5) a nitrous-capable aftermarket engine management system that delays, pulses, or stages nitrous activation according to sophisticated, configurable table-driven internal logic based on a variety of engine and drivetrain sensors. The trick is to hit the

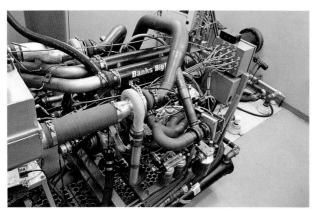

Competition Banks Power "Big Hoss" turbo-diesel. Yes, people have run nitrous with propane supplemental fuel, but the "normal" thing is to increase diesel injection with electronic means and dump in the nitrous to burn it. Oxygen-fuel ratios are not critical on diesel engines, which actually run cooler when there is a large surplus of air. *Banks Power*

The Wild 773-inch Ford Hemi drag motor controls multiple stages of wet and direct-port nitrous with gas-actuated solenoids to keep down the battery drain.

car with as much power as it can stand without breaking parts and smoking the tires, keeping in mind that improvements in acceleration and speed early in a drag run when the vehicle is moving slowly have disproportionately more effect on elapsed time than improvements when the car is moving faster.

Many racers and sanctioning bodies have resisted switching over to **progressive** and **computer-controlled** nitrous architectures. Some nitrous tuners have avoided progressive nitrous control because it is assumed to be hard on the solenoids, while others have complained that pulsing in the nitrous boost can result in transient over-rich mixtures with some control algorithms. Progressive evangelists make the point that PWM techniques are so effective in softening the nitrous hit to precisely the required degree that it can be difficult or impossible to detect when the boost hits. They point out that progressive control strategies work great to fine-tune optimal traction while keeping the front wheels of the vehicle on the ground. Progressive control strategies are very effective in preventing detonation that would otherwise occur if a huge constant-flow nitrous shot hit all at once in such a way as to drive the low-rpm nitrous-air ratio to insane levels that knock cylinder pressure and torque through the roof.

Progressive or not, a number of nitrous tuners recommend limiting nitrous to 500 horsepower in a single hit, beyond which a **multi-stage** control system should be used to choreograph-in various power stages, each with independent solenoids and fluid supply systems. As of this writing, some Pro Modified nitrous racers were running 7-stage nitrous systems. These systems bring in successive stages of nitrous as fast as the car can handle them, without eviscerating traction or lifting the front end. Keep in mind that different nitrous stages can have different distribution eccentricities. Experienced nitrous tuners agree that you cannot simply tune each stage independently and then let her rip, assuming that the combined air-fuel-nitrous ratio and timing advance curve will be viable.

Tuning multiple stages of nitrous can be problematic, but some people have avoided the issue on manual transmission cars with a lot of traction by activating big nitrous with a switch triggered by clutch rather than throttle action just before full clutch release to eliminate nitrous lag, then handling traction problems by adjusting a slipper clutch—or fine-tuning the violence of the initial hit on a transbrake car with ignition timing and a delay box.

Virtually all electronic nitrous controllers are capable of narrowing the low- and high-rpm ranges during which nitrous boost is permissible. If not, any extreme nitrous system—particularly on a manual-shift vehicle—must be protected with an **rpm window switch**. A window switch wired into the arming circuit disarms nitrous triggering below a configurable low-rpm threshold to prevent detonation and above redline to prevent earth-shaking nitrous-on rev-limiter backfires, allowing a driver to power-shift with confidence.

It is impossible to stress the vital importance of the **nitrous fuel supply system** on extreme nitrous powerplants. An accurate, repeatable, and robust fuel system is God. Anything that can be done to improve the fuel system is worth considering.

Huge, high-flow, high-pressure fuel pumps capable of supplying tremendous fuel requirements with a single unit have eliminated the need for multiple fuel pumps. Various nitrous tuners have their own theories regarding the utility of running independent fuel supply systems. Some value the fact that a single larger fuel pump reduces the complexity of the fuel and electrical systems and draws less power than two independent pumps. Others insist that independent pumps and supply systems provide redundancy and make it easier to troubleshoot nitrous system problems.

The flow rate of a fuel pump depends on the head of pressure the pump encounters when pumping, with flow inversely proportional to pressure. Flow will change with pressure variation, and vice versa. In order to make sure that the fuel pump is up to the job under all circumstances, some nitrous drag racers have recommended installing a pump capable of meeting the worst-case engine fuel requirements at *three times* the required pressure at the fuel pump discharge in order to deal with the effect of high-G accleration inertia on moving fuel. When it comes to flow rate, one rule of thumb is that a 140-gallon/hour (gph) pump is good up to a 240-horsepower boost, a 300-gph pump is good to 450 horses, and a nitrous shot in excess of 450 requires a dedicated 500-gph pump.

A number of advanced nitrous tuners advocate using an **EFI-type high-pressure fuel loop** with return-type regulator for supplemental enrichment fuel. This approach is easier on the fuel pump than deadhead regulation and less susceptible to hammering and resonation effects. The high-pressure approach provides better fuel atomization, compatibility with forced-induction manifold pressures, smaller fuel mass-flow fluctuations from equal-size fluctuations in fuel delivery pressure or manifold pressure, and an increased ability to create subtle micro-changes in fuel delivery based on practical pressure adjustments of measurable size to supplemental nitrous fuel pressure. The downside is that most prepackaged competition nitrous systems are calibrated for low-pressure fuel systems, and thus require re-jetting for high-pressure fuel supply. The decreased diameter of EFI-pressure individual-port nitrous fuel jets mandates the highest standards of fuel filtering to keep debris out of the jets.

Extreme nitrous system with direct-port or plate architecture are almost universally equipped with an **independent adjustable fuel-pressure regulator** for the nitrous fuel supply that installs in parallel with the primary fuel supply to the carburetor or EFI fuel rail. Tuners commonly fine-tune the nitrous-fuel mixture by recalibrating supplemental enrichment fuel pressure. The price of a fuel pressure regulator is not always well correlated with the quality, but whatever regulator you buy, it is important to verify that the pressure does not creep away from the adjusted

number you calibrated. To avoid high or low pressure spikes when the nitrous fuel system suddenly has to overcome inertia to accelerate motionless fuel to the required peak flow rate on a conventional wet nitrous system, some nitrous tuners advocate installing an auxiliary return line metered by a .025- to.030-inch nitrous fuel jet upstream of the deadhead regulator to keep fuel moving in the supply line when nitrous boost is inactive by returning a percentage of fuel to the main fuel tank or fuel cell.

When you adjust the fuel pressure on a hard-core nitrous engine, make sure to do it while the fuel is flowing at the actual rate required during boost. You'll want to use a properly jetted flow tool as described in Chapter 6.

Because the fuel side of a nitrous system runs at much lower pressure than the nitrous side, some racers install a small auxiliary fuel tank at the front of the vehicle with its own independent fuel pump, allowing inertial force to augment rather than diminish pumping capacity, helping to minimize fuel lag.

Aside from detonation and overloaded mechanical parts, **nitrous and fuel distribution problems** in the intake manifold are often the constraining factor on how much nitrous boost an engine can tolerate. Distribution problems are the leading cause of engine damage or failure in plate racing engines, and a great nitrous system can be fatally compromised by a poor manifold design. A dual-plane manifold's divergent plenum floor heights, center divider, and unequal-length runners make it very difficult for a plate injection system to achieve optimal spray pattern distribution with large amounts of nitrous; the intake manifold on a super-high-output wet nitrous engine must be a single-plane, square-flange race unit with runners as equal in length as possible. That said, it can sometimes be challenging to achieve really good distribution with plate nitrous systems installed on single-carb intake manifolds, and some people have remedied distribution problems by installing a divider plate in single-plane open plenum manifolds (usually at the expense of some top-end performance).

This Harley spray bike runs dual NOS nitrous tanks, one on each side of the rear wheel.

Nitrous pressure gauge on a Harley spray bike. Unfortunately, nitrous pressure gauges indicate nothing about how full the nitrous tank is until all the liquid nitrous has been used.

Intake manifold and throttle selection issues are obviously not unique to nitrous injection. Suffice it to say that **nitrous injection adds a lot of flexibility**: Non-boosted low-speed torque and responsiveness become less critical on competition nitrous powerplants if the nitrous system can be designed to impact low-rpm performance, thus eliminating the need for *any* high-rpm all-motor compromises in selecting the intake manifold, carb, or throttle body for pure maximum horsepower. On the other hand, an extreme street vehicle that runs most of the time in unboosted mode might better be designed with an induction system and throttle airflow that optimizes unboosted low-end *launch power* at the expense of some top end, leaving it up to the nitrous system to deliver serious peak power at the high end when required. Sophisticated progressive nitrous controllers allow you to accomplish either, leaving it to the engine builder to decide where in the rpm band to optimize all-motor performance.

If you are running carburetion, the only way to have real control on an individual-cylinder basis is if there is a separate carb throat for each cylinder, which potentially allows a tuner to provide EFI-type individual cylinder air-fuel trim. Keep in mind that running individual-port fogger-type nitrous injection *will not guarantee perfect distribution* if the **nitrous and fuel distribution manifolds** do not deliver equal flow to all the individual-cylinder plumbing, nor does direct-port architecture ensure that nitrous and supplemental fuel will be well-mixed with each other and the primary air-fuel mixture, or even that the quality of the mixing will be the same in the various cylinders. Nitrous spray and fuel spray should violently intersect for best mixing—whether you've got individual-port, centralized nozzle, or plate injection.

Most nitrous tuners seem to agree that **the primary fuel system should be optimized** for all-motor operation without concern for potential changes in available intake system volume and charge air density resulting when injected refrigerated nitrous and enrichment fuel materially impact the space available for the normal air-fuel charge. Most tuners also ignore the possible impact of the above on the metering signal to a carburetor or to EFI engine air flow sensors. A small minority of nitrous tuners have attempted to optimize

power across the rpm range on their radical competition nitrous powerplant by **recalibrating the primary air-fuel system**, thereby grievously sacrificing the ability of such a carbureted engine to function *without* nitrous boost.

Nitrous racers run nothing but the **highest octane leaded racing gasoline** they can afford—a fuel like VP Racing Fuels' *C16*, with motor octane of 117 for engines with compression ratio up to 17:1; VP *NO_2*, with motor octane of 120-plus and unusually low specific gravity; VP *C23*, the "ultimate" fuel for nitrous, with motor octane of 120-plus; or *Q16*, a highly oxygenated gasoline for all extreme applications that sanction it, which significantly expands the range of oxygen-fuel ratio acceptability and requires a 4 to 6 percent increase in fuel flow while delivering 3 to 5 percent more power than standard gasoline. The shelf life of such extreme fuels is often reduced compared to lower octane fuels because radical gasolines deteriorate faster and are highly susceptible to damage from sunlight and UV radiation. It may be tempting to think it will work well and save money to run a nitrous engine on whatever octane fuel the powerplant needs without nitrous, reserving the really high octane stuff exclusively for spraying through the the supplemental nitrous fuel supply during boost. Keep in mind, though, that independent fuel supplies are a distinction that goes away once the fuel disappears down the engine's gullet, with the final octane rating of two varieties of fuel averaging together in the combustion mixture.

Where fuel octane is limited—or even when it's not—trying *burning water*. OK, you're not really *burning* the water, but **water or fluid injection** can work well instead of gross fuel enrichment to fight detonation by cooling down combustion, which may permit more optimal ignition timing and improved power. When NACA tried out water injection on nitrous engines in experiments on supercharged combat aircraft during World War II, it was highly effective at combating detonation. The biggest risk with injecting pure water into a boosting nitrous powerplant is that the refrigeration effect of boiling liquid nitrous will freeze pure water into ice crystals; NACA's experiments involved injecting nitrous vapor warmed to room temperature—conditions under which such freezing was not a problem. An alternative

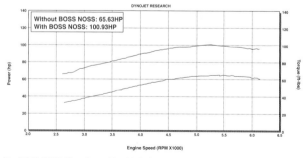

The BOSS NOSS bike nitrous kit adds 35 horsepower across the range of this dyno pull, nearly a 100 percent gain at 2,700 rpms.

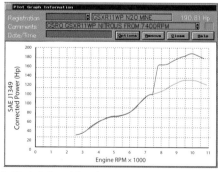

The effect of a 50-shot nitrous kit on the power curve of a Suzuki GSXR superbike.

NANA drag boat on nitrous. "This boat hauls arse 0-60 faster than most sports cars."

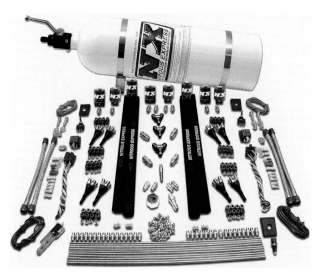
Dual-stage fogger-type direct-port V-8 nitrous kit. Drill once, two stages. Note that many direct-port V-8 nitrous kits run solenoids for each Vee bank and each stage. *Nitrous Express*

to water injection where it's legal is injecting methanol, ethanol, or a mixture of alcohol and water. Replacing some fuel enrichment with water or alcohol injection can greatly reduce the risk of ring lifting resulting from the super-rich mixtures that would otherwise be required to fight detonation in the absence of fluid injection.

Competition nitrous systems with multiple stages will **gobble electric power** to run multiple high-amp nitrous solenoids, fuel solenoids, purge solenoids, nitrous controllers and delay boxes, serious fuel pumps, switches and relays, powerful ignitions, and transbrake-release solenoids. Some drag racers run a full charging electrical system with alternator, dual 16-volt race batteries (or multiple lightweight turbojet air-restart batteries), but an increasing number have taken to reducing electrical requirements by running CO_2 gas-actuated solenoids controlled by low-power electrical pilot solenoids available from outfits like Combo-F10.

Low-amp micro-switches, delay boxes, or progressive controllers make it mandatory to switch power-hungry solenoids with robust **electric relays**.

Top-quality wiring is critical on any race vehicle, but especially when you're managing as much electrical junk as a radical nitrous racer. Substandard wiring is the endemic cause of many damaged engines and other catastrophic problems, and must be avoided at all cost. Unfortunately, good wiring can be highly technical and involve techniques and tricks that are not intuitive, which is the reason some manufacturers of high-end aftermarket engine management systems sell their systems exclusively with factory-manufactured custom wiring harnesses built to the buyer's specification. Many people erroneously believe that the ultimate step up from plastic butt connectors is soldering electrical joints and insulating them with heat-shrink tubing. It is true that the plastic-covered butt connectors you find at consumer auto parts stores are junk, but soldering is not the best way to go for serious wiring that must never fail despite harsh racing conditions and frequent component R&R. The heat of soldering has an unfortunate tendency to make the individual strands of

flexible wiring brittle, which can produce serious reliability problems when there is a lot of vibration and wire movement. The ultimate trick is to use heat-shrink-covered high-quality metal connectors crimped by a high-quality (expensive!) application-specific crimping tool. The wiring will remain supple and, done right, the wires themselves will tear before high-quality crimp connectors fail. Whatever components and tricks are used, it is critical to verify that the ground pathway back to the negative side of the battery is fully as robust as the power side of the circuit, so smart nitrous tuners are fanatics about ground integrity.

The enriched oxygen content of a nitrous-air-fuel charge mixture provides advantages over normal air-fuel mixtures when it comes to **charge-gas ignition**. A super-dense nitrous mixture will actually ignite more readily than ordinary all-motor charge mixtures, and combustion will accelerate faster. That said, the combustion chamber of a boosting nitrous powerplant is packed with 20, 30, 50, 100 (whatever it is) percent additional fuel, thicker nitrous-chilled air, and a dense mist of nitrous droplets and compressed vapor. Despite the improved ignitability of nitrous-enriched charge, throwing a miniature lightning bolt across a spark gap filled with all that stuff **requires a powerful, high-amp ignition** and, typically, spark plug gap reduced into the .025 to .030 range or below. Without exception, competition nitrous powerplants should run a fully digital ignition that permits adjusting global timing in any increment as well as setting individual-cylinder trim. Most competition ignition boxes are designed to interface seamlessly with delay timers and other nitrous control subsystems.

Overheated **spark plugs** are a serious risk on nitrous powerplants. When it comes to spark plugs, plan on going at least one heat range colder for each 100-horse shot of boost

FLUID INJECTION

Injecting water or alcohol—or better still, a 50-50 fluid mixture of water and methanol—will cool charge air with the latent heat of vaporization of the injection fluid as it boils, which can be very effective in fighting detonation. Water injection combustion cooling is not usually considered to be a power-adder in and of itself, since the injection fluid vapor displaces a certain amount of air, which will negate some or all of the increase in charge density. Alcohol injection, of course, does add horsepower to a gasoline-fueled powerplant because alcohol has a better specific energy than gasoline (meaning a given amount of oxygen can produce more energy burning alcohol at stoichiometric mixtures than gasoline), which is why it may not be legal in competition. Windshield-washer fluid—containing water and methanol—makes a great injection fluid, or you can make your own brew from water and methanol, ethanol, or iso-propanol alcohol, all of which love combining with water (too much, in fact, in the case of water-contaminated fuel systems).

Fluid injection originated as a critical anti-knock countermeasure for World War II piston-engine combat aircraft engaged in maximum-performance climb maneuvers, and it moved into mainstream automotive use when Oldsmobile used "Turbo Rocket Fluid" injection to fight detonation in the early-1960s high-compression factory-turbocharged Olds Jetfire. Fluid injection was a common anti-knock countermeasure for carbureted turbo engines in the 1970s and early 1980s, but it fell out of favor when electronic injection and programmable aftermarket engine management systems allowed tuners to conquer detonation with fuel, timing, and intercoolers. Fluid injection has made something of a comeback in recent years, particularly as California reduced the octane of street premium fuel, because it combines well with most other anti-knock countermeasures to lower the octane number requirement (ONR) of an engine. As tuners have pushed "streetable" turbo performance to ridiculous levels, fluid injection has once again become a valuable tool to consider in heat and knock control.

Water injection is much better than it used to be. Aftermarket companies have released products in recent years (with names like "Aqua-Mist") that don't simply piss liquid into the intake charge using modified windshield-washer systems but actually deliver high-pressure 50-plus-psi injection under electronic control, thereby providing accurate quantities of injection fluid and the excellent atomization required to maximize the cooling effect by producing tiny drops of injection fluid with a very large surface area. A modern fluid-injection system precisely injects water or injection fluid in a ratio that's typically 10 to 25 percent of the engine fuel requirement.

Some older racers and turbo specialists hate water injection, which they remember as being unreliable from the old days when it had to function with electric or mechanical controls rather than computer logic controlling the system as is now the case. There is nothing as effective as a knocked-to-death expensive performance engine to sour you on unreliable water injection. But the problems of electro-mechanical fluid injection are about as relevant to modern engines as the problems of magneto ignitions and carburetors in this day and age when a million complex electro-mechanical emissions control systems routinely function with high reliability under factory computer control, and modern aftermarket programmable engine management systems have the capability to manage water injection as reliably as any other complex engine system.

Fluid injection *is* effective in preventing spark knock in gasoline engines, and some fluid-injection venders claim it is effective in lowering EGT in diesel engines, thus permitting facilitating overfueling diesel engines for more power without flaming the engine (though GM Research did not find EGT reductions when fluid injection was studied). But since fluid injection fights knock by lowering combustion temperatures in a spark-ignition powerplant (and GM study confirmed that it does do that with high effectiveness), it is unclear why fluid injection would *not* reduce EGT in a diesel.

One of the biggest problems with fluid injection is that the required amount of fluid is quite small, requiring a small orifice that can easily become blocked with dirt or corrosion. That is not much different from electronic fuel injection, which also must be protected with in-line fuel filters and fine screens upstream of each injector. Another problem is that you have to keep the reservoir filled with injection fluid or water. Either way, if you're depending on fluid injection and it stops, unless you've got

above a 100-horse baseline nitrous system, and know that it is common for nitrous engines to require spark plugs that are two to three heat ranges colder. Avoid platinum plugs with their delicate fine-wire center electrodes, which tend to break off at the first hint of detonation. Some experts recommend avoiding extended- or projected-nose plugs due to the increased risk of detonation on boosted engines. Avoid resister-type spark plugs. Steer clear of split-electrode or other gimmick spark plugs. Extreme nitrous engines have run well with purpose-built racing plugs from Champion, Autolite, and NGK. In general, copper-core plugs with copper-alloy electrodes tend to be more forgiving of variations in operating temperature, and will tolerate higher temperatures without the center electrode overheating. If spark plugs are overheating, a temporary fix is to reduce combustion temperatures by increasing fuel enrichment during nitrous boost, but keep in mind that prepackaged nitrous systems are already calibrated rich out of the box, and additional fuel enrichment required to fight knock will inevitably reduce power.

In some cases the center electrode will run cool enough but the ground-strap electrode is still overheating, and a colder plug might not help. You may need a plug with a shorter ground strap, meaning the length of the electrode from the weld to the tip. In this case, projected-nose plugs could actually help, due to the fact that the ground-strap is typically shorter and has a short, straight electrode that runs directly from the weld toward the center electrode. Some people have had good luck modifying the ground strap electrode on standard plugs by cutting it shorter and bending it more directly toward the center electrode. Some extreme nitrous engines with plug overheating and surface ignition or detonation problems have had good luck with "retracted-nose" or even "surface-fire" plugs, in which the center electrode essentially fires directly to the plug casing from a well formed below the bottom threads where the lip of the casing bends inwards to form a circular anode that essentially runs at cylinder head temperature. The main problem is that lighting off the charge from inside a hole introduces combustion inefficiencies and requires a very powerful ignition. Some nitrous tuners have found a functioning automatic knock sensor ignition-retard system, the engine will begin knocking the next time you hit the gas and make real boost. Fluid injection permits more timing advance and more boost without knock, but produces diminishing returns in power gain as injection fluid displaces charge oxygen in increasing amounts and eventually begins to cause misfiring in spark-ignition engines. True, fluid injection is one more thing to go wrong, one more complex system that must be maintained and kept full and worried about. But there is actually no reason that fluid injection can't be as reliable and robust as fuel injection (particularly if you're willing to spend the money to build a robust fail-safe fluid-injection system). Fluid injection can be made to work, and alcohol or alcohol/water injection is ultimately one more thing in the racer's bag of tricks for managing heat in a turbocharged powerplant.

GM Research studied the impact of water introduction on the combustion process via injection into the intake air. Testing examined anti-knock characteristics of water, minimum advance for best torque (MBT) spark requirements, engine power and efficiency, volumetric efficiency, lean operating limits, smoke, exhaust gas temperature, engine cooling requirements, drivability, and exhaust emissions. The studies ignored engine durability, lubricant degradation, catalyst deterioration, and long-term deposit accumulation.

The studies found:

- Water has definite anti-knock characteristics. Adding water at a mass flow rate of up to 40 percent fuel weight increased the research octane linearly by roughly 10 numbers, from 90 to 100. Motor octane increased in a linear fashion from 82 to 87 at 20 percent water (due to the heat of vaporization of the water, it was not possible to obtain a motor octane number with a 40-weight water addition).
- Alternatively, without increasing fuel octane, a 40 percent water addition allowed the knock-limited engine compression ratios to be safely increased one full ratio (in the testing, from 8:1 to 9:1), which increased engine power and efficiency. This increased engine efficiency approximately 3 percent. Other than this, the effects of water injection on engine efficiency (reduced compression workload due to water's heat of vaporization reducing gas pressure by lowering temperature; reduced peak combustion pressure, which decreased the work done during the combustion cycle) essentially balanced each other out.
- MBT increases with water injection. Forty percent water increased MBT requirements by 5 to 15 degrees, due to water addition slowing down the combustion process.
- The addition of water to inlet charge had little or no effect on thermal efficiency, volumetric efficiency, lean operating limits, smoke, exhaust gas temperature (EGT), and engine cooling requirements. Water addition to the engine slightly reduced the coolant system load.
- Exhaust emissions were affected, with oxides of nitrogen decreasing by up to 40 percent with 40 percent water, while hydrocarbon emissions increased about 50 percent with direct manifold water injection—and this in spite of the fact that GM determined that water was not decreasing the efficiency of the catalytic converter. Carbon monoxide emissions essentially stayed the same.

In conclusion, scientists testing water injection concluded that water injection offers tuners the following:

1. The ability to use lower octane fuels safely without detonation in an otherwise unchanged engine
2. The ability to increase compression or turbo boost without engine octane requirements increasing, with the benefits of increased power or efficiency
3. Reduced oxides of nitrogen, by lowering combustion temperatures (like EGR)
4. HC emissions are increased with water injection but can be reduced to acceptable levels with other technology.
5. Water injection tends to contaminate the lubrication system (which can reportedly be eliminated by direct injection of water into the cylinder near the end of compression).
6. Water injection may corrode internal engine surfaces.
7. In cold climates, injection water freeze protection can be achieved by the addition of methanol.

that big old traditional full-bodied 13/16-inch spark plugs resist overheating better than the smaller plugs in modern applications (especially "shorty" plugs, which may be easier to remove but have less porcelain on the back of the plug). This approach requires drilling and machining the cylinder heads to handle the 13/16th threads, which will move the threads closer to the coolant jacket.

When it comes to **tuning** an extreme nitrous system, the **tweak-able parameters** include nitrous metering, nitrous density, nitrous temperature, nitrous pressure, fuel metering, fuel density, fuel temperature, fuel pressure, solenoid-to-injector distance, and ignition timing. Once upon a time it was common to tune the length of the solenoid-out plumbing to soften or harden the initial hit by carrying an assortment of hose lengths. However, hose-tuning can throw off the factory calibration of a prepackaged nitrous system. Most racers now work with fixed-length plumbing that's as short as possible, strive to normalize nitrous pressure and temperature, and tune with fuel pressure, nitrous and fuel jetting, and ignition advance.

There's no such thing as too big a nitrous tank. A big tank has more thermal momentum, which means there is less temperature and pressure drop during sustained boosting because there is more mass to donate heat for boiling liquid nitrous to maintain vapor pressure. A really huge tank that is *somewhat underfilled*, however, will experience a smaller pressure drop when the system begins spraying, because there is a larger high-pressure gas bubble in the tank that will not be greatly depressurized the moment you spray a little nitrous liquid out of the tank. Many nitrous racers have a rule of thumb that says that a nitrous tank is fully effective at delivering "sweet" nitrous in a continuous burst only while it remains above two-thirds full. The smaller percentage of nitrous used, the better. The ideal competition nitrous tank is less than half full yet contains at least three times the nitrous you'll use to race—well, except the thing weighs more and takes up more room.

There are a number of common misconceptions regarding **nitrous tank pressure**. One is that the more nitrous pressure you start with, the more you'll have at the end of a run. Another is that you need a lot of initial nitrous pressure to keep nitrous liquid from "flashing into a gas" if pressure gets too low. It is *absolutely a myth* that a tank of nitrous oxide will "flash from liquid to gas" if pressure drops below, say, 760 to 780 psi. This can only happen when the tank is nearly empty and the temperature is fairly warm such that *every bit of liquid nitrous boils* before the tank can reestablish equilibrium vapor pressure. As long as there is any significant amount of nitrous in the tank, the liquid will "flash" into a gas (also known as "boiling") only until the process has generated sufficient vapor pressure to restore gas-liquid equilibrium. Until all the nitrous liquid is gone, at ordinary working temperatures, nitrous oxide *cannot not* create its own extremely high vapor pressure, the exact dimension of which is an exclusive function of *temperature*.

Besides totally depleting the liquid in a nitrous tank, the ways to have a material impact on nitrous tank pressure are to (1) change the temperature of the tank with external means, (2) boost bottle pressure with external nitrogen pressurization that's *higher* than the vapor pressure of the nitrous at the working temperature, (3) spray nitrous out of the tank at a high enough mass flow rate that the nitrous liquid remaining in the particular type and size of tank simply *cannot boil fast enough* to maintain equilibrium vapor pressure, or (4) cause the nitrous tank to significantly self-cool by expelling nitrous out of the tank at a fast enough rate that thermal transfer from the environment is too slow to supply all the heat required for vaporization. Unfortunately, it doesn't take very much nitrous mass flow to outstrip the ability of boiling nitrous to maintain full vapor pressure or for the refrigeration effects to vastly surpass the heating capacity of the environment around the nitrous tank (including, say, a 400-watt bottle heater, as described in detail in the architecture chapter of this book).

One problem with running **a lot of nitrous tank pressure** at the beginning of a run is that this can defeat the goal of delivering a relatively stable nitrous mass flow throughout the run so as to make sure the engine delivers optimal power in the top end of a drag run where you can use

Diesel nitrous kit. Pour in the nitrous and amp up the injection pressure. More power. *Nitrous Express*

as much horsepower as possible. Temperature-based pressure and density effects should theoretically cancel out each other within a few percent when it comes to nitrous mass flow, but there can be important temperature gradients and even thermoclines within a tank that can have an unexpected adverse impact on mass flow in an environment that is *not* in equilibrium. For example, the nitrous vapor and liquid may not be at the same temperature, and the boiling liquid surface may vary in temperature from other portions of the liquid. Many experienced nitrous tuners have observed that running higher initial pressure seems to *amplify the eventual pressure drop* in a nitrous tank as a run proceeds, presumably by blowing disproportionate amounts of liquid nitrous out of the tank early in the run that results in accelerated liquid nitrous depletion followed by rapid vapor pressure drop and self-refrigeration to the extent that 1,070-psi maximum liquid start-pressure might transmogrify into 600 psi at the end of the pull, whereas a 950-psi start-pressure would actually maintain pressure as high as 750 psi at the end.

This, of course, ignores the effect of temperature-based nitrous density increases on nitrous mass flow. An unfortunate fact of life is that the faster you blow nitrous liquid out of the tank, the faster liquid nitrous still in the tank has to boil to produce vapor pressure—subject to unfortunate in-tank refrigeration effects that reduce the pressure of existing nitrous vapor and slow the rate at which cooling nitrous can boil *faster than temperature reductions produce a positive impact on mass flow by increasing the density of the liquid nitrous*. The lesson is that if you need more acceleration early on, you may want to do it with alternate means besides jacked-up nitrous tank temperature—which is precisely why racers might want to install progressive controls or deliver additional stages of nitrous injection fed by independent tanks—perhaps sized in such a way that the initial stages of nitrous deplete themselves and quit operation as bigger stages come online, with successive stages *replacing* earlier stages rather than augmenting them like a multi-stage rocket.

You know that neither of these radical diesel drag trucks is running nitrous injection, because nitrous could turn all that incompletely-combusted diesel smoke into horsepower. *Edge*

But there is a simpler alternative: external tank pressurization combined with a controlled start temperature. External pressurization is the only truly effective means of normalizing nitrous mass flow on a hard-boosting mobile nitrous powerplant. If rules permit it, and you can handle a little extra weight, consider running a **nitrous tank with external pressurization** and climate-control equipment to normalize the initial density of the liquid nitrous in advance. A small auxiliary tank of ultra-high-pressure nitrogen or air regulated down to, say, 1,100 psi feeding into the nitrous bottle through a special port in the bottle valve would guarantee that all nitrous in the tank remains in liquid phase throughout boost, that there is no self-cooling that takes place in the tank to maintain vapor pressure, and that nitrous tank pressure is guaranteed to remain constant on up to the critical temperature of 97.7 degrees F.

But what is the "correct" nitrous bottle pressure? There is no magic number any more than there is a "right" fuel pressure—well, other than the "never-exceed" critical point of 97.7 degrees F and 1,072 psi—above which nitrous oxide exists as a gas-like fluid that has substantially lost its refrigeration powers and is substantially less dense than nitrous liquid at 70, 80, or even 90 degrees F. As it turns out, 950 psi is a good number because most nitrous kit suppliers calibrate their nitrous-fuel maps at 950 psi (88 degrees F). As we've discussed, nitrous pressure is absolutely not going to remain at 950 during a hard nitrous run on self-pressurized nitrous systems. Some external pressurization systems have experienced problems with liquid nitrous aeration above 1,050-psi external pressurization, and external system pressure regulators typically experience an instant pressure

A Piranha direct-port kit installed on an LS-6 V-8 intake manifold, complete with fogger-type injection nozzles capable of delivering up to 50 horsepower per nozzle for a total of 300 V-8 horsepower, 500 V-10 horsepower. *Nitrous Express*

drop at activation, so 1,040 psi dropping to 940 psi is typical.

When there's nitrous involved, you're not just tuning the air-fuel ratio, you're really tuning the air-fuel-nitrous mix, or more precisely, the **oxygen-fuel ratio**. If you have a meter with a wideband oxygen sensor, you'll be tuning maximum power to an oxygen-fuel ratio number that's rich of the chemically perfect or *stoichiometric* ratio where 100 percent of the oxygen and fuel are consumed in combustion. The ratio of the actual oxygen/fuel ratio to the stoichiometric oxygen/fuel ratio is referred to as lambda, which is, of course, 1.0 when the ratio *is* stoichiometric. Most nitrous tuners recommend trying for .78 to .85 lambda on a gasoline-fueled nitrous powerplant, which produces residual exhaust gas oxygen identical to *air*-gasoline ratios in the range of 11.5 to 12.5:1. Very modest nitrous boost typically requires a lambda number identical to what the powerplant needs running all-motor, with the magic number moving progressively richer to something like .78 lambda or richer in the 450- to 500-horse shot range, where significant amounts of surplus fuel are being used to cool combustion.

Some tuners advocate adjusting lambda according to the percentage of nitrous-based oxygen enrichment. A 400-horse shot of nitrous in a 5.0-liter engine represents a smaller percentage of the combustion-chamber charge mass than that of a 500-horse shot in a 10.0-liter engine. And the fire chemistry will be significantly harsher in the smaller powerplant. The big motor could be satisfied with .78 lambda, while the smaller powerplant might need *.68 lambda* or alcohol injection to keep combustion under control.

The following equation can be used to predict a reasonable safe starting lambda:

$$\text{Lambda} = ([(\text{engine HP/total HP}) \times 13] + [(\text{nitrous HP/total HP}) \times 7])/\text{stoich}$$

NX's DF500 bottle control valve is capable of flowing 2,000 horsepower worth of nitrous though a .625-inch pickup tube and delivering it to the supply line through a .500 orifice. Keep in mind this kind of outflow is likely to deliver a fairly large pressure drop with significant refrigeration effects inside the tank that will adversely impact nitrous mass flow as nitrous boost continues. *Nitrous Express*

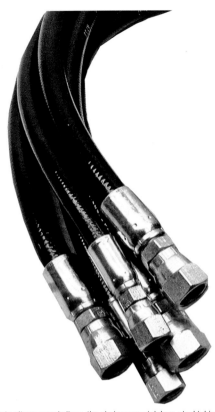

When it comes to nitrous supply lines, the choices are stainless-steel tubing, aircraft braided-steel-Teflon hose, high-pressure nylon hose, or reinforced rubber "Race Hose," touted to have improved insulation capabilities and improved flow compared to the alternatives.

Some nitrous tuners caution that although wideband exhaust gas oxygen sensors/meters are highly valuable tuning tools, the accuracy of the tool declines with increases in the nitrous/air ratio, making it critical—as always—to supplement this data by reading *all* of the spark plugs to get first-hand forensic data about actual combustion conditions.

Many nitrous racers use **fuel pressure adjustments** to fine-tune lambda. In the case of low-pressure (5 to 7 psi) fuel systems, relatively minor changes in pressure can have a large effect on mass fuel delivery. High-pressure EFI (40-psi) return fuel systems are much less sensitive to pressure changes, and pressure-regulated dry nitrous systems (70 to 80 psi) even less so. It is acceptable to *increase* enrichment fuel by adjusting pressure upward on low-pressure wet or direct-port systems (in 1/2 psi, 1/4 psi, or even 1/8 psi increments), but the nitrous-fuel ratio should be *leaned* by reducing the size of the fuel jetting.

There seems to be no consensus among nitrous experts regarding the utility of tuning with jetting changes versus pressure changes, but some sanctioning groups have regulated fuel orifice size, which can leave fuel-pressure adjustments as the only method of tuning lambda. When re-jetting nitrous or supplemental fuel delivery, keep in mind that the vastly higher system pressure on the nitrous side means that changing fuel jets on a wet or direct-port nitrous system will have a vastly

In which

Lambda = The ratio of the actual oxidizer-fuel ratio to the stoichiometric ratio of the fuel

Engine HP = Crankshaft horsepower available without nitrous boost

Total HP = Crankshaft horsepower available with nitrous boost

Nitrous HP = Crankshaft horsepower gain from nitrous boost (nitrous "shot")

Stoich = The stoichiometric (chemically perfect) oxidizer-fuel ratio in which all fuel and oxygen are consumed (14.65, in the case of most gasolines and air)

Assume engine horsepower is 400, nitrous horsepower is 200, and total horsepower is 600.

$$\text{Lambda} = ([(\text{engine HP/total HP}) \times 13] + [(\text{nitrous HP/total HP}) \times 7])/\text{stoich}$$
$$= ([(400/600) \times 13] + [(200/600) \times 7])/14.65$$
$$= 11/14.65$$
$$= .75$$

NX Iceman "Super Shark" nitrous solenoid will easily flow a 1,000-shot of nitrous. *Nitrous Express*

'99 Corvette LS1 engine with CO_2-actuated direct-port nitrous injection. *Combo-Flo*

greater effect on the oxygen-fuel ratio than changing nitrous jets. (See Chapter 6 for more information.)

Optimal **ignition timing advance** is affected by a large number of parameters, from fuel octane and nitrous shot size to non-engine considerations like vehicle weight, clutch, torque convertor, and gearing, but the increased flame speed of nitrous combustion virtually guarantees that a boosting engine requires reduced timing advance to fight detonation and optimize power. Discussions of nitrous timing tend to focus on global timing retard ("pull 1.5 to 2 degrees timing during nitrous boost for each 50 horsepower gained"), but simply yanking timing across the board by the same amount is almost definitely not going to optimize most of the torque curve the way a timing curve customized for nitrous boost would.

Keep in mind that optimal timing advance when an engine is not knock-limited is highly correlated with max torque delivery, and that the optimized torque curve of a boosting nitrous powerplant is often *radically* different from the optimal all-motor timing curve. In fact, the difference between a timing curve that is fully nitrous-optimized versus the all-motor timing curve globally cranked downward to remove spark advance can be a 30 percent change in average horsepower on the basis of timing alone. In fact, it is generally the engines that require the most aggressive timing *advance* during all-motor operation that require the most *retard* during boost. Some engines that make peak unboosted power with 38 to 45 degrees of timing advance and optimal oxygen-fuel ratios might achieve best power on a 150-horse shot of nitrous using 23 to 25 degrees of advance—which is 13 to 22 degrees of retard and massively more than the rule-of-thumb of 1 to 2 degrees retard required per 50 horses of boost. Meanwhile, running the maximum amount of timing that is possible during boost without detonation will quite likely not deliver optimal torque and power. What's more, though reduced

timing advance is a highly effective tool in fighting knock, it is often the case that an engine would run better and safer with a bit less nitrous and just enough timing than pouring in the torque with too much nitrous and then taking it back with aggressively retarded timing.

An engine produces maximum cylinder pressure at peak torque, though peak torque will not normally occur at the same rpm during nitrous boost (it will virtually always occur at lower rpm). Higher cylinder pressure increases the likelihood of detonation, so most wild nitrous engines do well with a few *extra* degrees of timing retard right around nitrous peak torque.

Fuel, air, nitrous, and cooling system effectiveness will probably not be distributed perfectly evenly amongst the cylinders in many nitrous engines, which will consequently run a little hotter in certain cylinders. In addition to modifying the shape of the global torque curve at peak torque while on the juice, most nitrous powerplants will make a little more power and run a little safer if you optimize torque by adjusting timing and mixtures strength on an **individual-cylinder basis** before finalizing global timing at peak power. Keep in mind that a single degree of timing change can make a large difference in torque on a nitrous powerplant. As always, start conservative, and advance timing in small increments, preferably on a dynamometer where you'll see immediately if adding timing stops adding torque before the engine becomes knock-limited.

A 500-horse shot of nitrous could require pulling 10 or more degrees of timing using an electronic interceptor, which can cause problems with **rotor phasing** on engines with distributors if the ignition fires with the rotor too far from the contact in the distributor cap. If you're retarding timing more than about 8 degrees with electronic means, you should probably think about installing a crank trigger so that the rotor can be phased correctly. Obviously, computer-controlled nitrous engines with direct-fire ignition have the advantage when it comes to sophisticated timing changes.

Extreme nitrous motors encounter interesting **failure effects**. Head gaskets live a *hard* life on big-horse shot nitrous

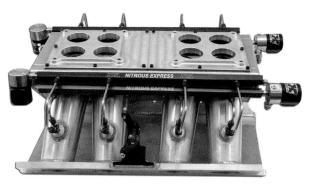

Competition's direct-port nitrous system delivers massive power on individual-runner dual-quad carbureted powerplant. *Nitrous Express*

powerplants as a consequence of high cylinder pressures and thermal loading, made worse in many cases by a certain amount of detonation from lean mixtures or over-advanced timing during tuning or ragged-edge operating conditions. Even without detonation, the higher pressure of nitrous combustion can cause head-lifting—and, subsequently, blown head gaskets. Any nitrous powerplant with much more than about a 50 percent power boost may need to have the heads removed for installation of improved head fasteners (preferably studs) and installation of wire O-rings in the block surface.

Head gaskets blow for a reason, and if you treat the problem exclusively with improved sealing techniques and fail to treat the underlying problem (lean-mixture detonation, inadequate head fasteners, whatever it is), it is almost certain to reoccur. Or something worse happens—like burned pistons.

Piston failures on boosted engines often occur due to lean mixtures, and most people rightly understand that richer mixtures generally run cooler and safer. If you find you have burned a hole through the crown of a piston, the problem is certain to be overheating from a dearth of fuel; if all the fuel is burned up and there's nothing else left for the remaining overheated, nitrous-enriched air to attack, it will start to burn the pistons.

On the other hand, over-rich mixtures can literally be too much of a good thing: Pistons in **extreme nitrous engines can be destroyed by excessive fuel**. How this works is that a surplus of nitrous-refrigerated liquid fuel enters the combustion chambers and fails to vaporize in time to prevent liquid fuel from flooding off the pistons and leaking past the top rings. Fuel build-up between the rings and in the grooves continues until high pressure and heat finally light off the fuel. Rich-fuel detonation can warp the ring lands upward ("ring lifting") and burn a channel through the rings into the piston skirt. Some racers recommend making sure the top ring gaps are 180 degrees apart, as well as changing to a fuel with a distillation curve light enough to ensure that less

Claimed as "the most powerful plate system in the universe," the NX Titan delivers a nitrous shot ranging from 100 to 750 horsepower.

ProStar's EFI series MagnaFuel electric gear drive fuel pump can deliver up to 2,500 horsepower worth of gasoline to a nitrous powerplant. *MagnaFuel*

fuel remains liquid on the piston surfaces. Some nitrous racers have overcome ring lifting problems by increasing the surface area of the intake ports, the intake side of the combustion chambers, and the fine grooves that encircle the top ring land by roughening the surfaces with a coarse grit to help fuel vaporization, particularly in problem areas where the intake valves and seats are sharply demarcated. Depending on the method of injecting fuel, it is possible to imagine situations where it would be beneficial to heat the fuel or intentionally inject warmer nitrous to reduce the powerful refrigeration effect when liquid nitrous vaporizes (colder liquid nitrous steals much more heat when it evaporates than liquid nitrous near the critical temperature of 97.7 degrees F).

When it comes to using competition-type nitrous systems, there are a number of **activation mistakes** that commonly cause trouble. In every case these can be eliminated with strict procedures or, even better, engineered out of existence with technology.

If you are adding nitrous so you can use it for part of a drag pass—if and when you need it—then you may want to install a **push-button trigger**, preferably mounted on the steering wheel when the nitrous is engaged. Racers who want a full pass of nitrous usually will want a **throttle switch**. To keep from accidentally zinging an unloaded engine way through the redline with the button before the rev-limiter can react if you miss a shift, or from fire-balling the manifold into the next county by powering hard into the rpm-limiter when you're spraying, you need to **junk the rev-limiter or install rpm window switches** that disengage nitrous boost when the engine is within striking range of redline. The best thing is an ignition with built-in window switches (or a nitrous-capable standalone engine management system!).

It is critical that no nitrous system should remain engaged and spewing fuel and nitrous **when the engine is stalled or stopped**. Some people have made the mistake of arming the nitrous system at the track before they have finished the burnout and staging is imminent. Why is this a mistake? Maybe the driver manages to kill the engine during the burnout. And maybe it takes putting the pedal to the metal to get the engine to start. And maybe they've got a full-throttle switch triggering the nitrous, so the whole time they're cranking, a big-horse shot nitrous system is juicing the engine full of nitrous and fuel. The moment the engine catches, huge fireball. It never makes sense to permit the nitrous system to be armed when the engine is stopped or stalled. Rpm window switches will usually do the trick, as will an oil pressure switch wired into the nitrous arming circuit and adjusted so the switch is open except when there's full engine-on oil pressure. Or simply have the procedure that you *never* arm the nitrous system until the engine is cleared out after the burnout and you're about to stage.

EXTREME NITROUS ENGINE BUILDING

The first trick is to **start with a block** that can handle the power without flexing during high-stress operations—meaning the largest, heaviest, stiffest block that will work in the application. You need strong, thick cylinder walls, and reinforced main bearing webs with four or six fasteners holding down the main caps. Modern engines with structural oil pans, cross-bolted main caps, and interconnected mains with integral block girdling, are the best.

Never try to run big nitrous with a cast-iron crankshaft, which will crack. And keep in mind that running a high-rpm engine without a suitable vibration dampener can shorten the life of the crank greatly. Some people swear by high-tech silicon-filled viscous dampeners. A custom billet crank may seem expensive, but not when the alternative is a factory crank that takes out the engine when it goes.

For extreme nitrous, you want strong, **low- or zero-silicon forged pistons**, ideally with a flat-top crown. The downside of this type of super-strong forging is increased thermal expansion that necessitates wider skirt clearances, which may result in reduced stability against the cylinder

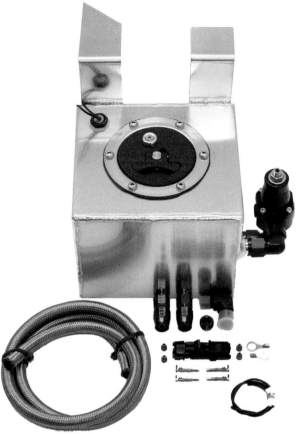

Auxiliary fuel tanks with a dedicated fuel pump delivers special enrichment race gasoline or alcohol for nitrous injection, and can be located in front of a drag-type vehicle where acceleration and inertial effects augment rather than fight the pumping ability of a fuel pump pushing fuel forward from the main tank, which is usually at the rear of the vehicle. *Nitrous Outlet*

Multi-stage mechanically driven pumping systems can be stacked to pump oil, scavenge dry-sump oiling systems, and supply massive quantities of fuel to a competition powerplant. *Banks Power*

walls, with increased blow-by and reduced peak power output under heavy loading. A compromise for fairly extreme street spray engines would be pistons manufactured from higher-silicon forgings with a slight oval shape to permit tighter skirt-cylinder clearances.

There are different theories about whether to coat pistons with a **ceramic thermal barrier**, and whether the bottoms of the pistons should be cooled with **oil jets** from gallery-resident oil-squirters or oil-squirting con rods. Keep in mind that the strength of aluminum decreases drastically with increasing temperature: Just 20 to 30 degrees of reduction in crown temperature can increase crown strength as much as 10 percent. So it is worth keeping nitrous pistons as cool as possible. The downside of coating pistons and combustion chambers is that there is some increased risk of detonation due to the increased combustion temperatures that result when less heat transfers out into the pistons, cylinder walls, and heads. The downside of oil-jet piston cooling is increased windage in the crankcase from the additional oil flying around, rod strength potentially compromised by long oil

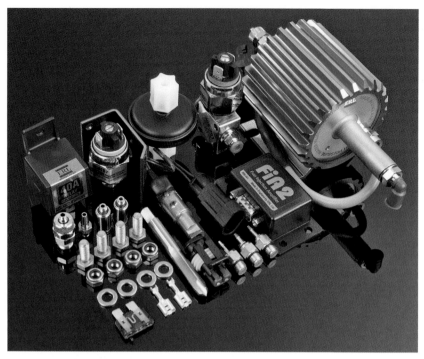

Aqua-Mist water-alcohol fluid injection systems bring modern electronic controls to charge cooling. Water injection can be extremely effective as a supplemental anti-knock countermeasure in high-power competition nitrous engines, or in circumstances where premium street gasoline is limited to 91 or 92 octane (in California, for example) and detonation is a serious problem. *Aqua-Mist*

"Maximizer" progressive nitrous controller. *Wizards of NOS*

channels angle-drilled into the con rods, and the possibility of reduced oil pressure.

In general, **failed connecting rods** usually result from tensile (stretch) overloading on the big-end bolts as the crankshaft yanks the pistons away from top dead center on the intake stroke at high engine speed—a consequence of extreme rpm rather than severe power loading. In the case of nitrous injection, the tremendous increase in torque usually means that achieving the required peak power does not require high engine speed, thus greatly diminishing the potential for tensile rod failure on nitrous applications. In some cases, however, extreme nitrous can actually cause rods to buckle and fail with a compression fracture. Nitrous loads that push power into the range of 200 percent of stock horsepower clearly necessitate not just improved fasteners but premium forged-steel connecting rods, which can be obtained off the

shelf for the most common performance engines, or acquired from custom component designers like Crower that have the ability to build individual sets of custom rods (as well as custom pistons and even custom super-duty steel crankshafts).

Obviously, the face-loading on **rod and main bearings** is higher with big nitrous, and there is a non-negligible chance that bearings will be hammered with at least some detonation pressure spikes in the tuning and racing process, so nitrous engines require the best premium rod and main bearings that are available. You may decide to run slightly more big-end bearing clearance within the maximum clearance recommended for normal race preparation, and then run higher oil pressure to build a thicker hydro-dynamic oil film between the bearings and crankshaft (believe it or not, a pressurized hydrodynamic oil film can resist deformation more than steel!). In extreme cases, you may decide to machine the crank to accept a wider-spec rod big-end, or deploy oversized welded crank journals or oversize journals on a custom crank to spread the rod loading over a larger surface.

Extreme nitrous pistons require **thicker ring lands** to prevent ultra-high combustion pressures—including detonation pressure spikes—from collapsing the top ring land, trapping the top ring, and destroying the ring's ability to seal with the cylinder wall or producing greatly increased friction leading to cylinder scoring and even seizure.

Hard-core nitrous pistons must be equipped with **exceptionally rigid wrist pins** and extremely robust pin bosses, regardless of any weight penalty over super-lightweight pins. In a worst case, flexing wrist pins can result in the pin towers tearing clean out of the pistons.

There are a number of theories regarding **the correct rings** for super-high-output nitrous powerplants. Slighter thicker-than-normal rings are a good idea, and high nitrous cylinder pressures behind the rings reduce the likelihood of ring flutter at high speeds, which is the usual justification for thin, light, fast-seating rings. Over the years, nitrous tuners have successfully campaigned pistons equipped with ceramic, moly, gapless, and stainless steel rings.

The benefit of **highly developed cylinder heads** is questionable on a big-nitrous powerplant unless you are truly building a "maximum effort" powerplant for competition. In this case, with nitrous providing all the required torque at lower engine speeds, the heads can be optimized for top-end horsepower. A purpose-built nitrous engine will not require the standard all-motor **intake to exhaust valve ratio** (in which intake typically flows 133 percent of exhaust), because a significant proportion of oxygen enters the combustion chambers as super-dense liquid nitrous oxide droplets, producing a higher-than-normal ratio of combustion products to reactants. Depending on the percentage of power made by nitrous injection and the efficiency of the nitrous system at intercooling intake air, a nitrous engine may do better if the exhaust flow increases to 85 percent of intake flow from the typical non-boosted 75 percent. In most conventional powerplants, increasing intake airflow is an order of magnitude more effective at improving power output than a comparable improvement in exhaust flow, but in the case of a nitrous motor, improving the exhaust flow can yield every bit as much benefit as increasing intake flow. Unfortunately, increasing valve size can be a zero-sum game in some engines, where larger exhaust valves essentially come at the expense of smaller intake valves. Of course, bare cylinder heads have more flexibility to accommodate larger exhaust valves (or undersized intake valves!) in some engine designs than others. In most cases it is not worth

A strong turbocharged powerplant is a far better starting place for a high-performance nitrous engine because the block and internals were designed for performance usage. This iron-block, aluminum head 2.0L Toyota 3S-GTE powerplant proved capable of being hot rodded to nearly 1,000 horsepower for Pikes Peak hillclimb competition.

sacrificing much intake flow to achieve the "correct" nitrous intake-exhaust flow balance. Nitrous powerplants do not need—and often cannot tolerate—as high static compression ratios as all-motor versions of the same powerplant. No need to go nuts removing combustion chamber material around the valves that could weaken the structure of the head and produce cracking or sealing problems.

With exhaust-side flow especially important on nitrous powerplants, very large headers can help in achieving maximum power, though it could be argued that extreme street vehicles should run headers and exhaust that are most efficient *without* nitrous—for maximum drivability and fuel efficiency. The more important boosted power is to the vehicle you're building, the larger the headers should be and the better flowing the exhaust system.

We've already touched on this, but **head sealing** will be a significant problem on many extreme nitrous motors. You will probably have to fit the block or heads—or both!—with wire O-rings, or, in some cases, interlocking multiple concentric **O-rings**—often combined with anneal-copper head gaskets, which can be custom-built in various thicknesses. The downside of **copper gaskets** is that they love to leak coolant, and many people—including yours truly—have had great success installing O-rings with *stock-type composition gaskets* on high-output power-adder engines. Some people swear by steel-shim head gaskets, which require special head and block surfacing but are not usually compatible with metal O-rings. The ultimate head sealing is nitrogen-filled Coopers rings, which install in a grove in the head or block deck and

Fuel and nitrous "pulseoids" are designed for pulse width–modulated nitrous systems, with effective duty-cycles that approach 10 and 90 percent before becoming effectively fully open or closed. *Wizards of NOS*

exert more and more sealing force as temperatures climb and expand the nitrogen.

Actually, the *definitive* **ultimate head sealing technique** is to weld the head to the block, or, even better, design the engine with cylinder barrels integral to the *heads* such that the head/cylinder subsystem bolts to the block as a unit and positively cannot leak unless the whole structure blows up. A well-known example is the old 4-banger turbo Offenhauser Indycar engine that dominated Indy for 50 years as recently as the late 1970s, making as much as 1,200 horsepower in turbocharged form.

Obviously, head gaskets cannot seal if pressure lifts the heads off the block, so super-duty **upgrade head fasteners** are mandatory on big-nitrous powerplants (which is a reason to begin with an engine that has more head fasteners, if you have a choice). If you push the power boost far enough, you will probably have to machine the block and heads to accept thicker than normal **head studs**, which exert higher clamping force than head bolts when installed correctly.

If an extreme nitrous powerplant can be equipped with extra-large exhaust valves, the additional exhaust volume and energy during nitrous boost might be handled optimally with stock valve timing. Where larger exhaust valves are not practical, additional exhaust flow and more power may be achievable by opening the **exhaust valves** a little earlier. Five degrees of exhaust valve advance may be enough for a low-speed engine, with 10 to 15 degrees of advance working better on high-speed engines. At the same time, low-end power may improve with slightly earlier exhaust valve closure. The combined effect is that the entire phasing of the exhaust cycle is shifted forward slightly into the power stroke. When the goal is to maximize valve flow, it pays to bang open the valves very quickly with an aggressively steep lobe ramp early in the flow cycle. For this, you need roller rockers and a roller cam.

At the same time, the intake side of a nitrous powerplant may not need as much duration. A cam that delivers peak torque at 4,000 rpm on the motor might actually be handling peak torque at *2,500* on the juice. The powerband of a nitrous engine is normally so robust down low that the powerplant need not be a high-rpm screamer, allowing intake duration to be reduced by 10 to 15 degrees to deliver optimal power 1,000 rpm slower. The nitrous equivalent of an all-motor engine that worked best with a race cam of 305 to 320 degrees of intake duration would thus work well on the juice with 290 to 305 degrees—though some nitrous tuners have intentionally run longer intake timing in order to fight low-end detonation with reduced cylinder pressure. Many nitrous tuners now take the view that low-end torque can be controlled more effectively by limiting low-end nitrous flow using progressive controls or by using electronic means to pull ignition advance when knock is a problem at low rpm on the juice.

JUICED SLEDS, WATERCRAFT, AND BIKES

The upside of installing nitrous on motorcycles, snowmobiles, small watercraft, and ATVs, is that it doesn't require very much horsepower boost to radically change the power-to-weight ratio of a light vehicle. A little nitrous will go a long way. There

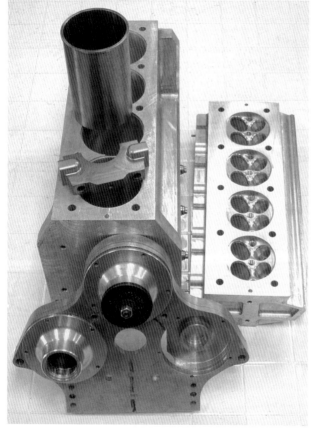

Bob Norwood's 325 CID Max-4 is derived from the Batten B4 overhead cam RAT Chevy competition powerplant. This solid-block (no coolant passages!) drag powerplant was designed to live a long time making 4,000 horsepower with twin-turbos, nitromethane, and nitrous-enhanced turbine spooling.

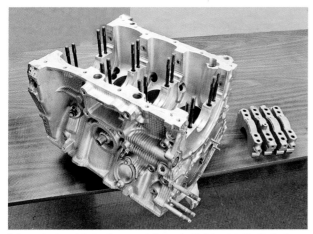

It does not get much better than a crankshaft embedded deeply in the block, six-bolt main caps with ARP studs and cross-bolts, and structure oil pan. This 1MZ-FE Toyota block was never released in a super-high-output version, but the design features are there in the block to survive a lot of turbocharging or nitrous injection.

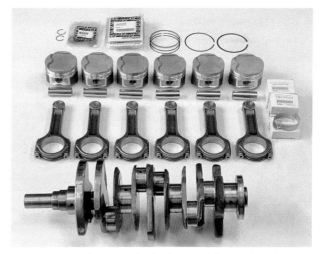

Almost any extreme nitrous powerplant is going to need all new reciprocating parts, and a billet crankshaft becomes a necessity as you approach 200-300 percent of stock power.

For any endurance powerplant with a lot of power boost, it is very important to protect the piston crown from heat-induced weakening. This GM Turbo Ecotec piston is equipped with ceramic thermal coating and piston-cooling oil squirters aimed at the undersides of the pistons. If adding block-resident oil squirters is impractical, you might want to machine channels through the con rods that shoot oil against the underside of the piston from its own connecting rod. *GM*

are also inherent advantages to boosting small engines. Small cylinders are less prone to detonation, mostly because the flame travel is shorter and smaller combustion chambers have less volume compared to surface area, and thus more quench and cooler combustion. So there is a greater likelihood normal combustion will complete before end gases can detonate. Small-displacement engines with multiple cylinders are as good as it gets as far as engine octane number requirement. Liquid-cooling has become more common on performance bikes, snowmobiles, and watercraft, with top-of-the-line powerplants representing Formula-One technology in a consumer vehicle and specific power as high as it gets on something *you* can get your hands on and drive. There are

significant advantages to liquid cooling, which has much greater thermal momentum than air-cooling. It is much easier to achieve even cooling among all liquid-cooled cylinders. Air-cooled engines tend to run much hotter than liquid-cooled powerplants and to gain or lose heat much faster.

Some snowmobiles and watercraft are equipped with two-stroke powerplants, which require oil in the charge mixture in order to provide in-cylinder lubrication. Most modern two-stroke engines are equipped with automatic oil-injection systems that eliminate the requirement of older two-strokes that oil be mixed with the gasoline, meaning the fuel tank contains only gasoline. However, unless you have disabled the stock oil-injection system and are premixing oil with the fuel, you will need to install an **auxiliary fuel tank** to supply supplemental fuel to the nitrous system that *has* had oil premixed into keep the engine adequately lubricated during nitrous boost.

By their nature, watercraft generally operate in temperate conditions where a human being is happy to get wet. Snowmobiles, on the other hand, operate almost exclusively in cold or very cold weather. The exception is snowmobile "asphalt racer" drag racing, an important venue for nitrous injection which originated when bored snowmobiles got tired of staring at their useless machines in warm weather, and began racing other snowmobiles on pavement, with wheels replacing the front skids and a special asphalt drag-race track replacing the snow track. At the time of this writing, some spray sleds were capable of 8.20 in the quarter at over 166 mph! In either case, watercraft and snowmobiles usually operate in an environment where cold air or cool water provides abundant cooling capacity. This is fortunate because performance 2-strokes are much more sensitive than 4-stroke powerplants to oxygen-fuel mixture problems that can rapidly cause out-of-control thermal loading leading to engine damage or even seizure. In practical terms this

If you run a lot of nitrous boost, you need good forged pistons with thermal coating and perhaps oil-squirter cooling, but you also need really good head-sealing. This will almost definitely mean installing wire O-rings in the block and perhaps annealed-copper head gaskets, which can be custom-built for a fairly reasonable price from a stock head gasket, in several thicknesses.

The leading cause of head gasket failures is detonation and high-power boost causing the heads to lift off the block. This extreme Offenhauser-based turbo Drake Indy engine was capable of making 1,200-plus horsepower and running for 500 miles. Designers solved head gasket sealing problems by eliminating the head gasket. The cylinder sleeves and support structure are part of the heads, with the whole thing bolting to the crankcase as a unit and overhead valves accessed from the cam cover and through the cylinder bores.

essentially mandates that 2-stroke engines run much richer mixtures than 4-stroke engines of similar power output. Of course, 2-strokes make a power stroke every revolution of the engine rather than every other, so they make much more power per cubic inch of displacement, but the brake specific fuel consumption is terrible. And it's even worse with nitrous, where supplemental enrichment requirements are piled on top of 2-stroke and air-cooled richness requirements.

And cold weather is not always a good thing for a nitrous system. Really cold intake air can cause detonation problems due to increased cylinder pressures. And then there's nitrous tank pressure. At 0F, the pressure in a snowmobile nitrous tank will be down to 283 psi, which has the effect of greatly increasing the density and refrigeration power of liquid nitrous oxide, but will also greatly diminish the volume of liquid nitrous pushed out of the tank per second. Many snowmobile nitrous kit designers supply a bottle heater with the kit, designed to keep the bottle temperature at 85F. A typical sled nitrous kit from NOS requires 12 amps of +12V power to run the nitrous system, and the charging/power supply system must be capable of supplying 150 watts of power for the nitrous system, and 270 watts if the bottle heating system is running during nitrous boost. NOS does not recommend installing the nitrous tank on the outside of the vehicle but rather inside the engine compartment of a snowmobile (but at least 6 inches from all exhaust components) so that engine heat will assist in keeping the tank warm. Mounting the tank in a tight engine compartment can be a challenge, particularly if you are also mounting an auxiliary fuel tank somewhere on the vehicle. The auxiliary fuel tank, of course, need not be kept warm, and can be mounted in the luggage compartment. Pressurizing supplemental enrichment fuel typically requires an add-on EFI-type high-pressure electric fuel pump.

Nitrous powerplants benefit from good breathing—but particularly on the exhaust side. In fact, the unusually high ratio of products to reactants in a nitrous engine calls for sacrificing intake valve area if necessary to gain exhaust flow, as discussed elsewhere in this chapter.

A typical NOS two-stroke sled nitrous kit for a 2-cylinder engine uses individual-cylinder fogger-type direct-port injection, with jetting supplied that allows the kit to be configured to provide a boost of 9, 12, 15, or 18 horsepower, with the 18-horse jetting requiring 100-plus octane fuel and the other settings requiring 92-plus octane gasoline. In fact, it is not uncommon to find 45-horse nitrous kits designed for use on EFI or carbureted sleds. These kits are designed to supply a 30 to 40 percent boost and power and torque from a tank containing 2.0 pounds of nitrous oxide, good for maybe a minute of boost before refill. Keep in mind that a 500-

cc 2-stroke sled might easily deliver 80 horsepower as stock, with power easily ranging to 150-plus in larger 2- or 4-stroke models, some of which are equipped with turbochargers. NOS recommends that forged pistons are required for the higher boost settings.

At the extreme end of off-snow snowmobile drag racing, championship winning power-adder class machines were likely to require 400 to 450 horsepower at this time of this writing from vastly hot rodded versions of 150-horse performance snowmobiles, with boost delivered by nitrous, turbochargers, or both.

Nitrous vendors have offered off-the-shelf drag-bike nitrous racing kits that deliver a 250-horse shot of nitrous boost for 2- or 4-cylinder 4-stroke bikes.

NITROUS WITH ADDITIONAL POWER-ADDERS

Nitrous injection works amazingly well with turbocharging because the strengths of each complement the weaknesses of the other. On one hand, the torque of a constant-flow nitrous powerplant gets stronger at lower rpm because the same flow of nitrous and supplemental fuel is distributed amongst fewer and fewer power strokes. At the same time, the constant flow of nitrous is dissipated among an increasing number of power strokes at high engine speed, diluting the effect of nitrous on engine torque per power stroke. On the other hand, turbochargers are totally ineffective below a threshold rpm, but they come on strong at higher engine speeds where there's more than enough turbine energy along with centrifugal compressor flow that, to a point, increases exponentially with increasing compressor rpm. But nitrous together with turbocharging it is a marriage made in heaven.

As discussed elsewhere in this book, the usual trick is to use a very modest 20- to 30-horsepower hit of nitrous for brief duration at low rpm to deliver an instantaneous 75 lb-ft torque boost that will significantly improve low-speed acceleration and provide a lightning-fast burst of exhaust energy to the turbo. The nitrous shot delivers its turbine-spooling exhaust energy and torque hit well below the normal turbo boost or lag threshold and then phases out as the manifold pressure rises and turbocharging is able to provide 100 percent of the required power boost at mid- and high-rpm using free compressed air. A simple manifold pressure switch wired into the nitrous arming circuit will disengage nitrous boost when engine torque has increased enough to provide a seamless transition into turbo-only boost. The good news is that while turbochargers usually must be fitted with restrictive turbine housings and small turbines to make any low-end boost, a dual power-adder engine that uses nitrous to deliver massive low-end torque at a time when exhaust energy is low can be equipped with a free-flowing turbine housing and larger turbine wheel that provide a massive improvement in high-rpm efficiency and power over restrictive turbines at zero performance cost. Given the very brief duration of this type of nitrous boost, a tank of nitrous lasts an order of magnitude longer in the role of a "wake up the turbo" power adder.

But there can also be a high-rpm role for nitrous on extreme street and competition engines that are up against the airflow limitations of a turbo compressor that works well to deliver excellent acceleration at lower speeds. The frosty burst from a nitrous hit can greatly improve intercooling on turbo units operating above their peak thermal efficiency. Nitrous—perhaps staged or modulated with progressive controls—can also be helpful to improve peak output from a turbo engine that could use a little more maximum power without the necessity for significant R&D that might be required to upgrade the compressor effectively and recalibrate

If you retard timing too much on engine equipped with distributor ignitions, the rotor will eventually misalign with the contacts on the distributor cap. The problem is best solved by installing a crank-trigger ignition or electronic engine management. *MSD*

Having the right spark plugs is critical in extreme nitrous engines. Ground-strap overheating is controlled in this NGK competition plug by reducing the length of the ground strap so that heat is quickly conducted into the plug body and into the cooling jacket of the cylinder block.

engine management. Computer controls could deploy nitrous at low RPM and then again at peak power.

Positive manifold pressure will have an impact on the pressure drop experienced by nitrous spray and supplemental fuel entering an intake manifold. As a percentage, this effect is negligible on the nitrous side, but as turbo boost increases, supplemental nitrous fuel delivered through a fogger nozzle or spraybar into, say, an extra atmosphere of pressure will definitely decrease. This could be a problem when a turbocharger is delivering very high manifold pressure: 40-psi nitrous system fuel pressure will deliver much more supplemental boost fuel at 2-psi manifold pressure than at 30-psi pressure. The answer is to regulate nitrous fuel pressure using a fuel pressure regulator that is referenced to manifold pressure in such a way that fuel pressure is always a fixed amount higher. This is precisely how modern engine management systems condition pressure to the fuel rail for electronic injectors, and it will occur automatically if you are using a nitrous-capable aftermarket EMS to deliver enrichment fuel through the primary fuel injectors but not with pressure-regulated dry nitrous.

Any extreme engine with nitrous and turbocharging will need to coordinate turbo boost control with nitrous injection to optimize acceleration and drivability. The optimal way to accomplish this is to have an aftermarket EMS manage turbo boost pressure using an electronic boost controller to manipulate the boost pressure reported to a turbocharger wastegate in order to open or not open the wastegate as

Yes, drag-race snowmobiles are equipped with tandem front wheels instead of skids, but that's not the end of it. Two-stroke nitrous motors may require special fuel systems. Unless you have disabled the stock oil-injection system and are pre-mixing oil with the fuel, you will need to install an **auxiliary fuel tank** to supply supplemental fuel to the nitrous system that *has* had oil pre-mixed with the fuel so that the engine will be adequately lubricated during nitrous boost. *Mad Max Racing*

required to deliver turbo boost under a variety of situations according to engine sensor data and internal boost control tables. The same EMS can provide progressive nitrous control, feathering in low-rpm nitrous as required, feather out nitrous as turbo boost reaches a threshold, and perhaps "overboosting" the turbo for a brief period in the transition from nitrous to air-supercharging.

ALCOHOL, NITRO, AND NITROUS

Some nitrous tuners have suggested that nitrous systems for small block V-8s, properly recalibrated, will deliver 50-80 more horsepower on methanol than on gasoline, and on a big block V-8, 80 to 100 more horsepower. In some ways, alcohol and nitrous are made for each other: Nitrous heats up combustion, while methanol and ethanol cool it down. Nitrous lowers the detonation threshold, while alcohol resists detonation very effectively. Methanol has a significantly higher specific energy per charge gas oxygen mass than gasoline, and methanol's rich flammability limits and ability to run well with rich mixtures tends to *multiply* the effect of the additional oxygen in nitrous-enriched charge air. Even at stoichiometric mixtures, methanol theoretically produces roughly 10 percent more power than gasoline on a given amount of inducted oxygen. Methanol's sensitivity to variations in the oxygen/fuel ratio is high, and its ability to resist knock diminishes rapidly with higher temperatures, but liquid nitrous injection tends to keep the charge mixture cool. Together, the chilling effects of nitrous expansion and methanol's high heat of vaporization (cooling by evaporation or boiling) can produce markedly improved engine VE by improving the density of the intake mixture. Interestingly, some experiments show that alcohol

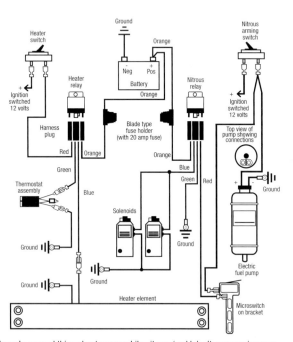

The only unusual thing about snowmobile nitrous (and I don't mean racing on a drag strip) is that the nitrous tank can get really cold to the point that it is difficult to maintain nitrous tank pressure. Note the default configuration of this NOS sled kit includes a nitrous tank heater. *NOS*

motors make more power with nitrous and *gasoline* injection, while gasoline engines make more power with nitrous and *alcohol* injection. The thinking is that straight alcohol-nitrous mixtures may be too cold to burn most effectively in a naturally aspirated motor, and that colder temperatures hinder the dissociation of nitrous into nitrogen and oxygen that makes power-boosting oxygen available for combustion. Given the lower stoichiometric oxygen-fuel ratios of ethanol and methanol, the fuel jets (and possibly the solenoids) of a nitrous system designed to deliver supplemental gasoline would have to be increased when injecting alcohol to deliver a flow rate that's 130 percent greater.

When you look at the length of the header plumbing between the exhaust ports and turbine inlet on this Norwood/Batten V-12, it is easy to see why a little nitrous injection can make a huge difference in improving off-the-line acceleration of some extreme street turbo vehicles.

Nitromethane's overwhelming advantage as a fuel is its large oxygen content and its high-energy nitrogen bonding, which allow huge amounts of fuel to be combusted by a given amount of air entering an engine. The specific energy—the energy released by whatever amount of fuel can be combusted by a fixed weight of air or oxygen—for nitromethane is high. Other than this, nitromethane is a terrible fuel, prone to detonation and in general very hard on an engine. Since nitrous exaggerates the weakness of a fuel, as expected, nitrous increases nitromethane's tendency to detonate. It's been done (see Sidebar "Quest for Power," on page 27), but look out.

But perhaps there is a better way. Although 500-inch Hemi powerplants with Roots blowers and nitro fueling currently own Top Fuel racing, turbocharged 132-cubic-inch Cosworth engines designed to last 500 miles have achieved 1,500 horsepower on alcohol. Extrapolating this power-per-cubic-inch result to the 500-plus cubes that are typical of Top Fuel drag engines, in theory, the potential exists to combine nitrous, alcohol, and turbocharging to build drag cars that launch well, due to the nitrous boost, and then quickly build 3,000 to 6,000 horsepower for the realm beyond 100 yards where dragsters begin to become power-limited. This approach of using the increased efficiency of large turbine and compressor turbochargers versus Roots superchargers combined with transient nitrous boost to provide a low-end kick and spool the turbos up fast has been used extremely effectively on street supercars.

Interestingly, when nitrous was banned from Top Fuel drag runs, some Fueler engine builders were injecting small amounts of nitrous at idle to help prevent plug fouling and produce a "cleaner" idle on nitro.

Garrett N° Turbo_029 Photo: WAKE UPP
Engine Boosting Systems Garrett VNT™ 25 (Variable Nozzle Turbine) Turbocharger

Variable-area turbine nozzle turbochargers are effective at improving the low-end performance of turbocharged powerplants, but extreme high-end power demands very large turbochargers. Progressive nitrous has the advantage that you can add whatever amount of low-end or mid-range torque that's required to explode off the line without damaging peak power. *Garret*

To be really fun to drive, a 1,200-horse street car like this twin-turbo Ferrari Testarossa needs plenty of low-end torque. Dallas racer and supercar-builder Bob Norwood installed nitrous to enhance the spooling capability of the 5.0L flat-12.

Chapter 8
The Rocket Science of Nitrous Oxide Injection

When NACA scientists decided to test nitrous oxide as a chemical supercharging agent during World War II, they were very careful to design an experimental system that would deliver perfectly consistent, repeatable results: The NACA apparatus injected a precisely metered adjustable mass flow of *gaseous* nitrous oxide preheated to an exact temperature into a similarly conditioned mass flow of air in a surge tank and fed the enriched air of known temperature, pressure, and oxygen content to the inlet of a constant-speed air-supercharged single-cylinder test engine connected to a water-brake engine dynamometer. The experiments proved that mixtures containing 10 or 20 percent nitrous could deliver 14 and 25 percent more knock-limited horsepower.

NACA scientists never actually experimented with liquid-nitrous injection, but they ran mathematical simulations showing that liquid nitrous had the potential to deliver even more power than gaseous injection because the refrigeration effect of boiling liquid nitrous offset air displaced by nitrous oxide (and fuel, in some cases) or even increased the mass airflow of the powerplant. And because refrigerated charge mixture lowered combustion temperatures and thus raised the detonation limits of the engine, permitting more chemical or air supercharging, or more efficient ignition timing.

NACA scientists were willing to live with injecting gaseous nitrous as 10 or 20 percent of intake air mass, and cooling combustion with fuel enrichment and water injection, but post-war racers and hot rodders had bigger things in mind—even if they were stuck using premium pump gas rather than 115- to 145-octane aviation gasoline. What NACA mathematicians dreamed—the godlike power of liquid nitrous oxide injection—hot rodders lived, opening up a huge can of thermodynamic worms.

In fact, scientific papers exploring subjects like "Liquefied Gas Self-Pressurization in a Catalyzed Nitrous Oxide Monopropellant Thruster" (for light satellite guidance) make it clear that the physics of liquid nitrous oxide injection actually *is* rocket science. When you look at the horrendous task of precisely predicting and controlling all aspects of liquid nitrous injection at very high boost levels in accelerating drag-race engines, you can see why the NACA scientists stuck to dyno-testing with nitrous vapor and left the liquid-injection to mathematicians.

As is true with any type of power-adder on a knock-limited powerplant, it is desirable to predict and control the total mass of charge-gas oxygen arriving in the combustion chambers of a nitrous powerplant with a high degree of precision, and critical to precisely manage the oxygen-fuel ratio during combustion to prevent engine damage resulting from detonation or combustion overheating. Unfortunately, this is not easy on an injection system that is dynamically self-pressurized by its own vapor to deliver a liquid stream that immediately self-refrigerates with so much power that the cooling effect is capable of materially impacting the induction temperature and volumetric efficiency of a super-high-output engine ingesting a roaring hurricane of hundreds or even thousands of cubic feet per minute of air, nitrous liquid and gas, and evaporating liquid and gaseous fuel.

NITROUS REFRIGERATION EFFECTS

Let's be very clear: *Warming up a nitrous tank reduces the density of the nitrous liquid inside AND reduces the cooling power of the liquid nitrous when it boils, whether inside the tank or in the intake air stream.*

NASA's Space Shuttle leaves Earth burning mono-methyl hydrazine rocket fuel with dinitrogen tetroxide, an oxygenated nitrogen compound similar to nitrous oxide but containing roughly twice the oxygen! *NASA*

Rocket science: NASA technicians working on the Space Shuttle's main engine systems. *NASA*

So how much does donating energy to vaporize liquid nitrous lower the temperature of 68 degrees F (20 degrees C) intake air?

Let's assume that we are dealing with an engine capable of breathing in 500 cfm of air, and assume that we are going to install a 100-horse shot nitrous kit. A 500-cfm engine is breathing in 14.1584 cubic meters per minute (m³/min) of air, i.e., .2359733 m³/sec. Since 68 degrees F (20 degrees C) air weighs 1.205 kg/m³, the mass airflow of the engine is

14.1584 m³/min × 1.205 kg/m³ = 17.06 kg/min
= .28433 kg/sec

Air, like all molecules, has a specific heat curve, which represents the amount of energy required at various temperatures to increase the temperature an additional amount. At atmospheric pressure, at temperatures ranging from -58 to 104 degrees F (-50 to 40 degrees C), the specific heat of air is 1.005 kJ/kg (per degree K).

A rule of thumb is that a typical 100-horse shot nitrous kit must be jetted to provide 6 pounds per minute of nitrous oxide, i.e., 0.1 pounds per second (actually, a really efficient system could potentially do it on 4 pounds per minute, as NACA testing showed in World War II). This translates to 2.72155 kg/min, or roughly 0.045359167 kg/sec.

At 68 degrees F (20 degrees C), the enthalpy of vaporization of nitrous oxide liquid is about 165 kJ/kg.

Thus, in one second, the engine ingests 0.28433 kg/sec of air mass, and 0.045359167 kg/sec of nitrous liquid mass, creating a charge mixture that's about 14 percent nitrous (assume, for a moment, that 0.28433 kg/sec is the actual amount of air, net of any displacement by nitrous or injected fuel). Vaporizing this mass of nitrous oxide requires the following amount of heat (per second):

165 kJ/kg [heat of vaporization] **× 0.045359167 kg/sec** [nitrous mass flow] **= 7.484262555 kJ/sec**

There are 0.28433 kilograms of air available per second to heat and vaporize the nitrous mass flow per second. Since the specific heat of air in the range of -58 degrees F to 104 degrees F is 1.005 kJ/kg, each degree of donated heat thus provides:

1.005 kJ/kg [specific heat of air] **× 0.28433 kg/sec** [mass air flow] **= 0.28575165 kJ/degree K** [air heat loss]

Thus, the air temperature drop required to boil all the nitrous oxide coming through each second is

7.484262555 kJ/sec [required heat for vaporization] **÷ 0.28575165 kJ/degree K** [energy available per degree F air drop) **= 26.19 degrees K** [total cooling effect on air required to boil nitrous]

The air temperature will drop 55.52 degrees F.

Of course, in reality the warm intake manifold will help intake charge air boil the nitrous (resulting in chilled metal or plastic rather than air), or, put another way, some of the cooling power of the nitrous liquid will be lost cooling the intake manifold and other internal engine components.

As discussed above, nitrous oxide has its own specific heat curve, which is critical to consider because some of the heat to vaporize nitrous oxide molecules will come from heat stored in other nearby nitrous molecules—for example, when liquid nitrous is vaporizing in a nitrous tank to create vapor pressure (self-pressurization), or when a droplet of nitrous is boiling as it flies through an intake system. As the nitrous content of the intake charge increases, this becomes more

Bob Norwood's propane-fueled twin-turbo Cadillac depends on nitrous injection to spool the turbo and amp up the top end. Note four giant air-propane mixers.

Direct-port Fogger V-8 nitrous kit from NOS. Like any traditional self-pressurized nitrous system, the mass flow of nitrous actually delivered to the engine will be a complex function affected by temperature, refrigeration effects, pressure drop, liquid nitrous thermal expansion, and other factors. *NOS*

and more significant. At 25 degrees C, the specific heat of nitrous oxide is .674 or .878 kJ/kg (depending on whether it's a constant volume or constant pressure situation), which is less than air's specific heat of 1.005 kJ/kg. However, some of the nitrous oxide liquid donates heat to vaporize neighboring nitrous molecules. And the required heat of vaporization of still-liquid nitrous molecules increases with temperature decreases as they are chilled more and more. Note that the energy required to vaporize nitrous at 68 degrees F, i.e., 20 degrees C (166 kJ/kg), is 192 times the energy required to heat nitrous 1 degree C at 20 degrees C (0.863 kJ/kg) if vapor pressure is preventing the nitrous from vaporizing. With a lower specific heat than air (remember, specific heat is the energy required to heat one degree when it is not vaporizing), nitrous oxide has a large potential potential to self-cool: As we shall see in a moment, nitrous will self-cool tremendously if nitrous oxide is forced to provide its own heat of vaporization when boiling in the tank to maintain vapor pressure.

In the real world, liquid nitrous will heat-soak significantly in the supply line on the way to the injector nozzle at the onset of nitrous injection when liquid nitrous is filling the supply line downstream of the solenoid valve or purging gas bubbles or nitrous foam out of a warm supply line upstream of the solenoid. Heat soak will raise the temperature of the liquid nitrous and reduce the refrigeration power available following injection into the air stream. As nitrous liquid heat-soaks warmer, the specific heat required to raise the temperature of nitrous one more degree increases slightly, helping slightly to moderate additional nitrous heat soak. If the heat soak is severe enough, nitrous liquid will

begin to vaporize, producing a far more substantial cooling effect on the line (if a nitrous line is cold or even frosted on the outside, you know there is liquid nitrous inside the line boiling into gas). The temperature of recently-boiled nitrous vapor will be at least temporarily higher than surrounding liquid nitrous in the line, since nitrous molecules gain heat when they vaporize, with nearby liquid donating heat.

Any bottleneck in the nitrous supply plumbing that causes an abrupt pressure drop has the potential to act like an A/C expansion valve, causing vapor bubbles to form in the liquid nitrous, a little like the bubbles in a foaming Coca-Cola. This foaming reduces the effective density of the liquid, but also self-cools the unboiled liquid, increasing its density. Any vaporization in the nitrous plumbing, of course, is likely to waste some of nitrous oxide's cooling capability chilling the supply line that would otherwise be available in the aftermath of injection. Density increases from nitrous self-cooling and density reductions from nitrous foaming combine to create a net effect that is temperature- and pressure-dependent and may cause the metering orifice to deliver a significantly unintended nitrous mass flow. Combined with consequent reductions in intake charge cooling that will increase engine volumetric efficiency, the net effect of supply line pressure drop is likely to be reduced horsepower due to reduced nitrous and air induction, coupled with suboptimal oxygen-fuel ratios at combustion time. In short, insulated supply lines are worthwhile in a heated environment.

As nitrous flow continues, supply line heat soak effects may completely disappear, with concomitant increases in nitrous mass flow, engine air VE, and, if uncorrected, increases in the oxygen-fuel ratio. Meanwhile, the core of a braided-steel nitrous supply line—even if it's Teflon—produces *friction* against the nitrous flow, which reportedly by itself produces a pressure drop of about 6.25 psi per foot of AN -4 line. Meaning even if there are no bottlenecks, depending on the temperature of nitrous liquid, the length of the line itself could reduce pressure enough that some foaming would occur—meaning the supply long would be too small for the length. That aside, bleeding or "purging" nitrous gas from the line at or near the injection nozzle immediately before nitrous boost initiation can markedly reduce surging and bogging from initial phase-change effects in the line.

The ideal nitrous system has insulated or even refrigerated steel supply lines. The reason is that when the on-off nitrous solenoid opens and 1,000-plus psi of nitrous surges through braided steel hose, the lines will, according to Butch Schrier, formerly of NOS, bulge or swell and temporarily increase in diameter from .295 to .307 inches, at which point the flow area has increased roughly 10 percent at working nitrous pressures. This, Schreir suggested, may produce pressure shock waves traveling through the lines with secondary effects on pressure drop and nitrous density as the supply line experiences a cyclical phase change. Steel pipe, on the other hand, resists expansion to much higher pressures.

EXTERNAL PRESSURIZATION EFFECTS

With an externally-pressurized nitrous tank, there will be no internal refrigeration because there is no boiling for self-pressurization. Meanwhile, unintended density changes due to environmental temperature changes and consequent thermal expansion or contraction of nitrous liquid within a tank can potentially be compensated for by adjusting the pressure regulator that determines that amount of external nitrogen or air pressure introduced into the nitrous tank. Because colder nitrous liquid is much more dense, pressure normalization would have to be adjusted to *reduce* pressure when the tank is colder. For example, assume a nitrous system has been calibrated to provide supplemental nitrous fuel based on nitrous delivery at 1,070 psia (external) tank pressure, and that it delivers 0.1 lb/sec of nitrous at 30 degrees C (86 degrees F)—at which point the density of nitrous liquid is 683 kg/m³. On a cooler 20 degrees C

(68 degrees F) day, the density of the liquid nitrous would be up to 783 kg/m³, which would increase nitrous mass flow by

783/683 = 14.64 percent

Therefore, the new nitrous mass flow is

0.1 × 1.1464 = .1146 lb/sec

In the absence of countermeasures, the engine will run lean at 68 degrees with 1,070 psi external pressurization.

Flow changes related to pressure can be computed using the formula

New Flow = SQR (New pressure/old pressure) × old flow

Plugging in the numbers to determine the pressure required to get the new nitrous mass flow at 68 degrees F back to the original 86 degrees F 0.1 lb/min mass flow:

0.1	**= SQR [new pressure/1,070] × .1146**
0.1/0.1146	**= SQR [new pressure /1,070]**
(.8726)²	**= New pressure /1,070**
.76143 × 1,070	**= New pressure**
New pressure	**= 814.73**

Which is above the 20 degrees C (68 degrees F) self-pressurization nitrous pressure of 757 psi.

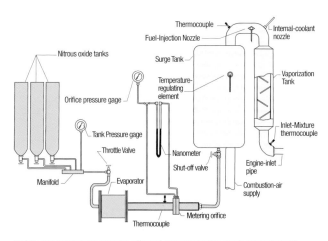

NACA's apparatus for testing the effect of nitrous injection on air-supercharged aircraft engine's during World War II was specifically designed to test only the effect of oxygen enrichment on power output by eliminating all parameters related to liquid nitrous temperature, phase change, density and so forth.

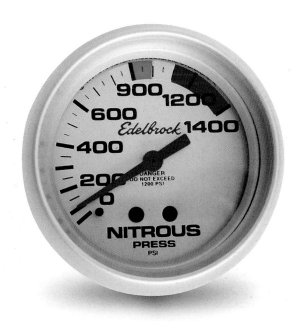

A nitrous pressure gauge is an indicator of vapor pressure in the nitrous tank, which is impacted mainly by temperature but also affected by temperature gradients through the tank and liquid therein, as well as the lag in achieving equilibrium pressure if nitrous cannot boil fast enough to maintain expected vapor pressure during heavy usage. *Edelbrock*

Working backwards, if the flow is .1 lb/sec at 814.73 psia absolute on a 20 degrees C day, then heating the tank up to 30 degrees C (86 degrees F) and raising the nitrogen pressurization back up to 1,070 gives:

New pressure = SQR(1,070/814.73) × .1
$$= 1.146 \times .1 = .1146$$

However, the density of the nitrous has decreased from 783 to 683:

683/783 = .872286
.872286 × .1146 = .1 lb/min

And we're back to the original flow, showing the effect of pressure compensation in action.

With external nitrogen or air pressurization keeping a nitrous tank above 1,070 psia, as long as temperature is below the critical temperature, 100 percent of the nitrous remains in liquid phase. When boost is active, heavier nitrous liquid is pushed out the pickup tube from the lowest point of the tank by a growing high-pressure gas bubble at the top until all nitrous oxide is exhausted, at which point the tank begins bleeding 1,070 psia nitrogen gas (or air, if it's air). In actual point of fact, some external pressurization systems seem to encounter problems with liquid nitrous becoming aerated at air pressures above 1,050 psi; NANO's system is thus normally calibrated to deliver a resting pressure of 1,040 psi and boost-on pressure of about 940 psi, meaning weather above 88 degrees F will cause nitrous vapor pressure to exceed the target tank pressure and the external pressurization system to lose control of the

tank pressure. The moment the nitrous liquid is gone, there will be a sudden severe reduction in engine performance with this type of system (worse if it's nitrogen instead of air pressurization) due to (1) the abrupt reduction in charge-gas oxygen due to the sudden reduction in nitrous mass flow, (2) oxygen-fuel ratios that are certainly now dysfunctionally rich (unless the engine management system is somehow able to detect the out-of-nitrous condition based on changes in exhaust gas oxygen, intake air temperature, or a calculated time-to-empty), and (3) reductions in engine air VE due to large reductions in charge cooling and air displaced by injected nitrogen once the nitrous oxide is depleted.

There are thermodynamic effects from external pressurization: Nitrous liquid is not compressible, but temperature reductions, as I've discussed, will cause the liquid to shrink. If there is gaseous nitrous oxide in the tank when nitrogen pressurization kicks in, compressing the gas into liquid will cause the temperature of the liquifying vapor to release heat into the surroundings due to the *heat of condensation*. The adiabatic heat of compression contributes to an increase in the temperature of the gas as it is compressed prior to liquification. As I've noted previously, nitrous oxide liquid density *decreases* with *increases* in temperature—*particularly near the critical point*, where liquid density drops by 35 percent between 86 and 97.7 degrees F due to thermal expansion. On the other hand, reducing the pressure of 4,500 psi nitrogen gas to 1,065-plus with a pressure regulator turns the lower-pressure nitrous oxide tank into an expansion chamber, causing the nitrogen gas to expand and cool (the lack of a phase change limits the cooling effect).

An externally pressurized nitrous system was patented many years ago, and there are commercially available systems

"Evil Twin" NANO external pressurization system for extreme nitrous systems. Two high-pressure tanks of nitrogen (or air) are regulated down to a selected resting pressure in the 1,000-1,100 psi range, in order to maintain constant pressure in the nitrous tank as liquid empties, and eliminate the refrigeration effects that are unavoidable when nitrous must boil in the tank to maintain equilibrium vapor pressure as a self-pressurized liquid nitrous tank empties.

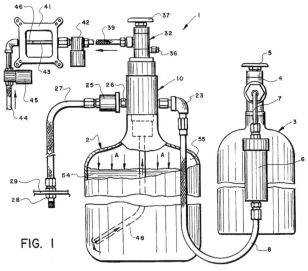

FIG. I

Nitrogen-assisted nitrous system patented by William M. Wheatley in May of 1984. Note that this system requires an overpressure relief valve to dump pressure in the nitrous tank in the event of overheating or should the nitrogen pressure regulator (#6) fail and empty full 4,500 psi nitrogen pressure into the lower-pressure aluminum nitrous tank.

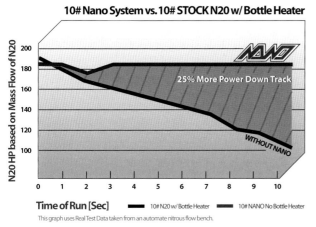

10# Nano System vs. 10# STOCK N20 w/ Bottle Heater

Y-axis: N20 HP based on Mass Flow of N20 — 200, 180, 160, 140, 120, 100

NANO

25% More Power Down Track

WITHOUT NANO

Time of Run [Sec] — 0 1 2 3 4 5 6 7 8 9 10

━━ 10# N20 w/ Bottle Heater   ━━ 10# NANO No Bottle Heater

This graph uses Real Test Data taken from an automate nitrous flow bench.

NANO graph indicating the benefit of external pressurization on nitrous mass flow as a nitrous drag run proceeds. *NANO*

External pressurization is not enough to fully normalize nitrous mass flow, since liquid nitrous density is significantly impacted by thermal expansion and contraction according to temperature. Given a little time, this bottle electric blanket will eventually achieve a semblance of equilibrium temperature throughout a nitrous tank and contents, but keep in mind that the tank will be constantly leaking heat into a cold environment. No onboard electrical bottle heater by itself has the power to maintain liquid nitrous temperature against the tremendously powerful refrigeration effect of nitrous boiling in the tank to maintain vapor pressure. *Edelbrock*

from outfits like NANO that deliver external nitrogen or air pressurization sufficient to maintain nitrous tank pressure when nitrous liquid is being removed from one tank at a rate of 500 or 800 horsepower.

Ultimately, one of the most important goals of a nitrous system is to achieve repeatable, reliable nitrous mass flow in order that the oxygen-fuel ratio can be optimized for best knock-limited horsepower and safe combustion temperatures. In this respect, an externally pressurized nitrous system combined with nitrous bottle preheating or nitrogen-pressure correction is as good as it gets.

SELF-PRESSURIZATION EFFECTS

Unfortunately, external pressurization systems can cost as much as the nitrous system itself, and may or may not be legal in all classes of racing that otherwise permit nitrous injection. Most nitrous systems are not externally pressurized because it is cheaper and simpler to allow nitrous oxide to self-pressurize, which it will do with high effectiveness at "room" temperature in automotive applications in temperate climates (motorcycles, snowmobiles, and cars with the tank stored in the trunk are a bit of a different story in a cold climate in the winter).

But nitrous self-pressurization introduces a host of variables that may affect nitrous mass-flow and the refrigeration effects of nitrous injection, to the extent that predicting the temperature and mass of nitrous and air available at the start of combustion with high precision is a nightmare: Everything depends on everything else, nothing is certain, and the performance of the nitrous system changes dynamically *as boost continues*. Under such circumstances, precision engine management is difficult or impossible, and many nitrous systems make do with safe oxygen-fuel mixtures that are grossly rich at least some of the time. NACA experimented using nitrous oxide *vapor* injection for chemical-supercharging World War II

piston-engine fighter aircraft, precisely because they wanted repeatable, predictable, and perfectly scientific results that would be difficult or impossible to obtain when dealing with the powerful refrigeration effects of boiling liquid nitrous.

NACA removed the guesswork from nitrous mass-flow by sourcing pressure-regulated gaseous nitrous oxide from giant tanks, heating it to a precise temperature, and precisely metering the conditioned nitrous gas into a mixing surge tank which the scientists also fed with a precise mass flow of conditioned air. The fighter aircraft boosting systems that resulted from Allied and Nazi research teams were designed to deliver a relatively modest power boost (300 horsepower on a 2,000-horse supercharged V-12), meaning that nitrous self-pressurization could not fail due to the refrigeration effect of nitrous boiling in the supply tank overtaking environmental heat-soak into the tank to the extent that self-pressurization failed to keep up with the engine's required nitrous oxide mass flow. On board an aircraft, of course, there is engine heat available to keep the nitrous tank from super-cooling. In modern times, the School of Aerospace, Tsinghua University, experimented using self-pressurized gaseous nitrous for small satellite propulsion, increasing pressure by catalyzing the gaseous nitrous oxide into the nitrogen and oxygen components to recover the heat of formation. One of the biggest challenges of in-tank self-pressurization on a nitrous delivery system dispensing vapor is dealing with the tremendous cooling effect of nitrous boiling exclusively in the tank, which will drastically lower the temperature and pressure of the tank.

300 watt electric nitrous bottle warmer. *Nitrous Outlet*

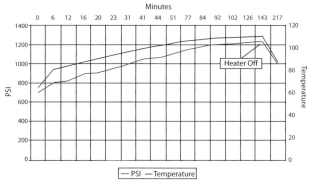

Bottle temperature and pressure over time when heated by a 400-watt electric bottle blanket from 68 degrees. Keep in mind that surpassing 97.7 degrees will cause all nitrous liquid to vaporize, and that the more you heat nitrous liquid, the less dense it is and the less refrigeration effect there will be when it boils in the intake system or combustion chambers of an engine.

NACA and Tsinghua nitrous self-pressurization experiments are precisely analogous to the situation of an old-fashioned steam railway locomotive that uses a boiler to provide steam to drive the pistons that move the train. Visualizing the situation with a steam engine can be helpful in understanding the physics of a nitrous delivery system. In a steam engine, water is placed in a closed boiling chamber in which the temperature of the container is maintained at a level sufficient that a continuing supply of steam can be bled out of the boiler to meet the needs of injecting high pressure steam into an engine (in the case of steam, directly into the cylinders to drive down the pistons). It may be helpful to consider that a nitrous tank is also a type of boiler. Systems delivering steam or gaseous nitrous oxide both require heat to boil liquid into gas, and in both cases the vaporizing molecules have a powerful cooling effect on the liquid as bubbles of vapor emerge from the pool of remaining liquid. In the case of the steam engine, water is heated above boiling temperature by thermal energy from a coal or oil fire. In the case of a nitrous tank, heat soaks into the liquid nitrous from the ambient environment which is far above the boiling point of nitrous oxide (well, or maybe from an electrical bottle heater!). The biggest difference between a steam boiler and a nitrous tank is that a nitrous tank is superheated from the get-go: A room-temperature environment will boil nitrous until the pressure is tremendously high (750 to 1,050 psi), whereas boiling water at sea level requires at least a 212 degrees F fire far above room temperature to get the job done and even more heat at the 300-psi working pressure of a typical steam engine. In either case, at the working pressure, vaporizing water or liquid nitrous consumes thermal energy voraciously to provide the required heat of vaporization. One system typically expels vapor from the boiler, the other liquid from the tank, but the power of a self-pressurized nitrous tank to deliver nitrous to an engine is perfectly analogous to the power of a steam boiler.

Now imagine that you begin to bleed off steam from a boiler filled with hot water and high-pressure steam to push the train down the tracks. There is a certain rate at which the boiler can generate steam, and this is a function of the available heat and the temperature and pressure of the liquid and steam in the boiler (*not* at the same temperature). Unless the fire can deliver the heat required for vaporization on a continuing basis, pressure in the boiler will drop, and a reduced mass of steam at a lower density and pressure will be expelled from the boiler to push the train. Keep in mind that if there is a lot of super-heated water in a boiler held in liquid form by steam pressure, there is a large potential to generate steam in a hurry as soon as pressure in the boiler begins to *drop*, though the phase change into steam requires a lot of energy, and will *rather quickly* consume heat stored in the water. On the other hand, if the volume of liquid in the boiler is reduced by boiling (and pushing the train), the thermal energy of the fire is applied against a smaller and smaller mass of water, exactly the way a stove burner will boil a small amount of water in a teakettle faster than if there's a *lot* of water being heated. Keep in mind that real-life steam engines harness the power of high-velocity pressurized steam to inject water from a partially pre-heated water jacket into the boiler in order to constantly recharge the water level and prevent the boiler from melting.

As Tsinghua discovered in nitrous satellite propulsion experiments, for a given metering-jet size, the viability of a self-pressurizing nitrous oxide satellite propulsion system depends on not attempting to boil nitrous at a faster rate than the heating capacity of the system (mostly the environment) minus the heat of vaporization. On one level, this is like saying that a steam engine with huge cylinders capable of gobbling a lot of steam of a certain pressure needs a boiler that can make more steam fast enough to keep the train running, though it is important to realize that vapor can be produced either by external energy heating water, or by boiler pressure dropping, which causes latent heat stored in the super-heated water to boil it into steam in the reduced pressure.

Nitrous systems make effective use of super-heating to an extreme degree: On an ordinary warm summer day, a tank of liquid nitrous oxide may be 215-plus degrees above its boiling point, and the latent heat will boil nitrous furiously the moment the pressure drops, particularly if the nitrous is also agitated heavily as it may be from high-G acceleration. In the case of boiling liquid with latent heat, you are using up the reservoir of heat to continue making vapor/steam without recharging the system with more energy (since the environment is below the boiling temp of water)—which is analogous to a car that is using electric power to run a huge stereo and a lot of fancy lights and all the normal stuff faster than the alternator can recharge the battery: Sooner or later there will not be enough power to run the ignition, fuel injection, and EMS, and the engine will stop. Once again, keep in mind that the heat required to vaporize a liquid becomes less and less as the temperature of the liquid approaches the critical temperature above which there can be no liquid phase, no matter what the pressure (the critical point is 97.7 degrees F at 72.79 atmospheres, in the case of nitrous oxide, and 705 degrees F at 217 atmospheres, in the case of water).

Tsinghua University loaded a 1-liter stainless steel tank with .95 kilograms (2.1 pounds) of nitrous oxide at 21 degrees C (70 degrees F), and began to bleed off nitrous gas from the top at a rate of .6 grams/sec (.02 ounces), a rate which started out at the instantaneous rate of 4 percent of the mass of the tank per minute. The experiment used a heated mass-flow sensor on the output to measure flow (and, as it turned out, *to help maintain the density of the gaseous nitrous mass flow even as the tank chilled itself through internal boiling to colder and colder temperatures*) in such a way that the mass flow of nitrous gas remained stable for approximately 16 minutes. In this situation, 100 percent of the boiling happened in the stainless tank. The sole source of heat was room-temperature air in

the lab surrounding the tank, and the scientists planned to test a number of different shapes of tanks with varying ratios of volume to surface area to evaluate the effect of the various parameters on self-pressurization and nitrous gas mass flow.

By the time the last of the nitrous oxide was gone from the tank when the experiment concluded nearly 50 minutes down the line, the lower part of the stainless tank had a thick coat of white frost where there had recently been liquid nitrous self-cooled to -80 degrees C (-112 degrees F)!

THE PHYSICS OF BOTTLE HEATING

A 400-watt nitrous bottle heater delivers the equivalent of .3794 Btus of energy per second, which is 0.536 horsepower at 100 percent efficiency. One Btu is the amount of energy required to heat a pound of water by 1 degree F (specific heat capacity of water can be expressed as 4.184 Joules/gram K).

Nitrous oxide's specific heat capacity is only 21 percent that of water, meaning that it requires only .21 Btus to heat a pound of nitrous (or aluminum, which is nearly the same) one degree. An aluminum tank that holds 15 pounds of nitrous oxide typically weighs 39 pounds when full, which is the total mass a bottle heater must cook when it is working.

If no heat is lost to the environment, it takes 196.56 Btus to heat 39 pounds of aluminum and nitrous by 24 degrees F (compared to 936 Btus to heat 39 pounds of water the same amount). A perfectly efficient 400-watt heater generating 0.3794 Btus per second would take 41 minutes and 7 seconds to heat the water from 68 to 92 degrees, but only 8 minutes and 36 seconds to heat the tank containing 15 pounds of nitrous the same amount. One real-world experiment found that it actually took a 400-watt heater an average of

A nitrous tank insulation blanket is designed to keep the warmth generated by an electric heater in the tank during cold weather, and to prevent solar heating from vaporizing nitrous liquid in warm, sunny weather. *Edelbrock*

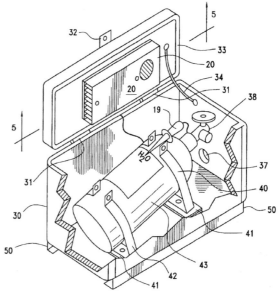

Onboard climate control housing for a nitrous tank uses a solid-state heat pump to warm or cool the tank as required by weather or intank boiling.

Here's what happens when there is a sudden removal of liquid nitrous from your nitrous tank to boost the engine:

- There is a sudden pressure drop in the tank (unless boiling can instantly replenish), which corresponds to the percentage increase in the ullage (gas bubble plume) per nitrous liquid volumetric out-flow rate (the percentage ullage increase is large at first, smaller later. For example, 1.0 cubic inch out of, say, 5.0 cubic inches of vapor is a much larger percentage than 1.0 cubic inch out of 1,728 cubic inches when the tank is virtually empty).
- If you remove a lot of nitrous very fast you'd expect a deeper pressure drop.
- A pressure drop from sudden removal of liquid nitrous causes boiling to begin.
- Boiling requires heat from the nitrous liquid or bottle (there is more initial stored heat in the larger initial mass of nitrous liquid and tank; later the liquid mass has much less energy because it is smaller and cooler. Due to specific heat increases at higher temperatures, as the temperature decreases, there's less available heat per degree temperature change.

- The rate of boiling of super-heated liquid is also influenced by pressure drop, which is instantaneously larger when the ullage is small versus big—meaning there's more furious boiling from a higher pressure drop from sudden removal of liquid.
- Donated heat for vaporization cools the remaining liquid during boiling.
- Cooler nitrous liquid has a higher density and smaller volume, and the loss in volume from cooling is greater near the critical point; thermal contraction from cooling helps to lower pressure, which tends to increase boiling at a given temperature
- Heat soaks from the tank (from the ambient environment or a bottle heater) into the nitrous liquid.
- Sudden removal of nitrous liquid reduces the liquid nitrous mass both from expulsion and from boiling to replace volume of expelled liquid
- Gaseous nitrous mass increases as sudden removal depletes the liquid and nitrous boils to maintain vapor pressure.
- Cooling increases the density of the liquid mass (it should be well-mixed).
- The nitrous vapor is warmer than the liquid during dynamic (boosting) conditions.

19 minutes to get the job done, the obvious conclusion being that the heater was only 45.26 percent efficient, losing more than half of its heat to the environment.

What happens when a 100-horse shot nitrous system with a bottle heater is actually *boosting*?

Assume:

- Initial temperature is 20 degrees C (68 degrees F)
- Initial pressure is 51.5 bar (751.7 psia)
- Initial mass-flow rate is 0.1 lb/sec of liquid nitrous (.045359 kg/sec)
- The tank is virtually full of 15 pounds of nitrous oxide liquid (6.80388 kg)
- Gas and liquid nitrous are at the same temperature.
- Initial liquid nitrous density is 783 kg/m³ at 751.7 psia = 0.783 kg/liter
- Initial gaseous nitrous density is 166 kg/m³ 751.7 psia = 0.166 kg/liter
- Specific heat of nitrous oxide in the temperature range is .674 to .878

1. In the first second, 0.0579 liter of liquid nitrous is expelled from the tank, creating a void that must be replaced with high-pressure vaporized nitrous gas (0.045 kg/sec mass flow constitutes a volume of 0.045 kg ÷ 0.783 kg/liter ≈ 0.0579 liters/sec).

2. If the temperature remains essentially constant within the 1-second time slice, sufficient liquid nitrous must boil to create and pressurize 0.0579 liters of nitrous gas to a density of 0.166 kg/liter (at 751.7 psi absolute). But there is a second-order effect: The actual nitrous liquid volume depletion per second will be a combination of the liquid nitrous expelled from the tank to boost the

engine *plus* the nitrous liquid that must vaporize to replace the volume of the nitrous liquid lost to maintain self-pressurization each second:

0.04536 kg (expelled) + 0.0096 kg (vaporized) ≈ .055 kg

This is the total liquid *mass* depletion (that must be replaced with vaporized nitrous each second).

3. The *volume* of depleted nitrous liquid mass per second is then:

0.055 kg ÷ .783 kg/liter ≈ .0702 liters
(up from **0.0579 liters**).

4. The corrected amount of vaporized nitrous required to fill this space is thus:

0.0702 liters/sec × .166 kg/liter nitrous gas
(20 degrees C and 751.7 psia) ≈ **0.0117 kg**
[up from **0.0096 kg**]

5. Over the course of 1 second, the cooling effect on the nitrous liquid (neglecting the thermal momentum of the metal tank itself) of the heat of vaporization of 0.01166 kg boiling nitrous at 20 degrees C is 161 kJ/kg, so:

0.0117 kg (mass of boiling nitrous) × **161 kJ/kg** heat of vaporization ≈ **1.876 kJ** total required heat per second ≈ 1,876 watts sec.

6. A 400-watt bottle heater working at *50 percent efficiency* lowers the net heating requirement to 1.676 kJ or 1,676 watts.

7. The specific heat of nitrous liquid (at 25 degrees C and 1 bar pressure) is 0.6745 or 0.878 kJ/kg .K, depending on whether or not it's a constant volume situation. This is the amount of energy required to increase the temperature of nitrous oxide liquid 1 degree K, which *becomes available in the form of donated energy if the temperature of liquid nitrous* drops *a degree.* Neglecting the metal tank as a heat source, the liquid nitrous mass available for heating is initially 6.80 kg.

8. Even with a large 400-watt bottle heater installed and generating heat, liquid nitrous must still donate some heat to vaporize the required portion of itself (0.0117 kg). The change in temperature dT ("delta-T") of liquid nitrous required to accomplish this is:

$$dT = \textbf{Required heat/(Specific heat × mass)}$$
[in the current second]
$$= \textbf{1.676 kJ/(0.6745 [specific heat, constant volume]}$$
$$\textbf{× 6.80 kg)}$$
$$= \textbf{1.676 / 4.5866}$$
$$\approx \textbf{0.3654 degrees C}$$

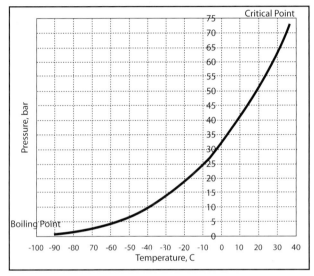

Saturated nitrous oxide vapor pressure as a function of temperature
Pressure versus temperature of equilibrium nitrous oxide liquid and vapor in a closed container. Below -128F (the boiling point of nitrous at normal atmospheric pressure), essentially 100 percent of the nitrous will be liquid; above the critical temperature of 97.7F, 100 percent of nitrous will be a gaslike "supercritical fluid."

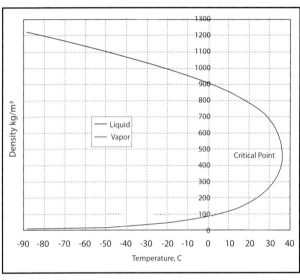

Nitrous oxide density as a function of temperature
This graph shows the density of the nitrous oxide liquid and vapor in a closed container as the temperature increases from -130F to 104F. Thermal expansion causes the density of nitrous liquid to *decrease* as temperature rises, while increasing pressure in the gas bubble causes the nitrous vapor to *increase* in density. Note that above the critical point of 97.7 degrees F, all nitrous oxide is a supercritical fluid with constant density.

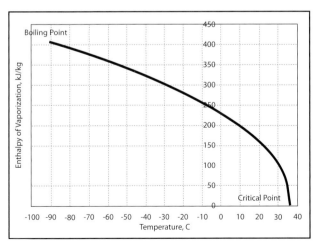

Vaporization heat as a function of temperature
Vaporization heat of nitrous oxide liquid versus temperature. It may seem obvious, but very warm ("superheated") nitrous liquid under high pressure requires little or no heat to vaporize when pressure no longer holds it in liquid phase, whereas very cold nitrous liquid must steal a great deal more heat to vaporize when a pressure drop permits this.

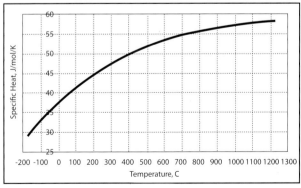

Specific heat as a function of temperature
The specific heat of nitrous oxide refers to the amount of heat required to raise the temperature one degree. The specific heat is higher at lower temperatures but does not vary a great deal in the narrow range near 25F within which nitrous oxide injection systems typically operate.

9. Factoring in the effect of the 400-watt heater, vaporizing 0.0117 kg nitrous liquid requires 1.676 kJ of heat from the 6.80 kg of nitrous liquid available in second one, which is capable of delivering at least 0.45866 kJ per degree near 20 degrees C. Therefore the total required number of degrees C temperature drop is .3654 *per second*, which is equivalent to roughly 0.66 degrees F.

10. If nitrous mass flow out of the tank could remain constant under these conditions for five consecutive seconds of nitrous boost, this would deplete the nitrous liquid by 5 × **.055 kg** ≈ **.2749 kg**, or approximately **0.61 lbs**. From this, you might assume that in five seconds the temperature would be down by 5 × 0.413 degrees C = 2.064 degrees C, or 5 × 0.743 degrees F ≈ 3.715 degrees F. The actual cooling effect, however, accelerates because there is less and less nitrous liquid left to provide heat for vaporization and the heat available in the remaining pool of liquid nitrous from each additional degree of temperature drop declines slightly as the temperature gets colder. Meanwhile, the heat *required* per second to vaporize the required mass of liquid nitrous into high-pressure gas *increases* as the temperature continues to drop.

One alternative to onboard bottle heaters is this powerful preheating oven which normalizes the temperature and pressure of nitrous tank in between runs in the pits of a drag strip. *Nitrous Outlet*

TEMPERATURE-BASED CHANGES TO FUEL DENSITY (THERMAL EXPANSION)

Like nitrous, fuel density changes with temperature (just not as much, and within a smaller temperature range). The easiest way to account for this is with a table. Keep in mind, though, that gasoline is not one thing but a stew of various hydrocarbons in the 5 to 8 carbon range, and the specifications of gasoline can vary a great deal. Higher octane fuels are usually a bit heavier, with slightly more energy per gallon, but the effect is the same: In general, gasoline density changes about 1 percent per 15 degrees F.

These changes are easier to visualize when graphed, which also allows you to extrapolate the effect of fuel temperatures hotter or colder than what are plotted here.

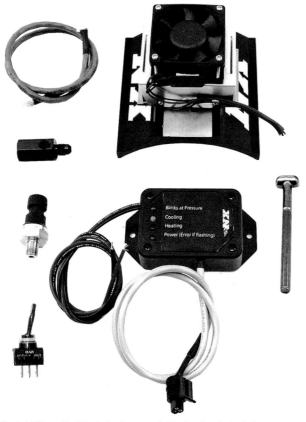

On-tank "Fire and Ice" heater/cooler uses a Peltier Junction electronic heat pump to normalize nitrous bottle pressure. *Nitrous Express*

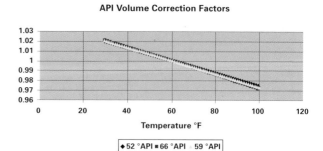

API Volume Correction Factors

◆ 52 °API ■ 66 °API △ 59 °API

Like nitrous oxide, the density of gasoline also changes as temperature changes cause thermal expansion and contraction. In general, each change of 10 degrees causes about a 1 percent change in density. This is why you get more gasoline for your money in wintertime, given that gasoline pumps do not correct for temperature changes in density in most of the United States but simply assume that gasoline is always at 60F. In Canada, where average temperatures are colder and not correcting would benefit the consumer rather than oil companies, gas stations do correct for temperature changes. Engine management systems usually correct for fuel density changes according to an air temperature correction table.

AIR FLOW REQUIREMENTS TO ACHIEVE A CERTAIN HORSEPOWER GOAL

This can be calculated using the following formula:

AF = HP × (AFR) × BSFC/60

where,
AF = Actual mass airflow in pounds per minute
HP = Target flywheel horsepower
A/F = Air/fuel ratio
BSFC = Brake specific fuel consumption in lb/HP × hr (divide by 60 to convert hours to minutes)

Assume the goal is 400 horsepower with an air/fuel ratio of 12.0 and use a BSFC of 0.55. Applying these numbers to the above formula:

AF = 400 × 12 × (0.55/60) = 44.0 lb/min of air.

THE THERMAL EFFECTIVENESS OF NITROUS-SPRAY INTERCOOLING

Total-loss nitrous is sometimes sprayed on the exterior of an air-air intercooler to dramatically increase its thermal effectiveness. Quantifying this is the same as for any other type of intercooling. Of course, the temperature of the cooling medium will be an average of the air temperature and mass and the boiling nitrous temperature and mass, which are affected by the size of the nitrous jets, the temperature of the nitrous in the nitrous tank and supply system, and the speed of the vehicle through air of a particular temperature. (For more information about the cooling effect of road draft air read my book *The Turbocharging Performance Handbook*, available from MBI Publishing, 2007.)

The *effectiveness* of a heat exchanger is a measure of how efficient it is at cooling a hot fluid down to the temperature of the cooling medium. If the hot pressurized air exiting a compressor discharge is 200 degrees F, and the nitrous spray and air used as the cooling medium in an air-air intercooler is at a combined temperature of 10 degrees F, an intercooler with 100 percent effectiveness would cool the hot charge air 100 percent of the way back down to 10 degrees F.

But let's say specifications indicate that a particular intercooler is 75 percent effective. How much will it cool 200 degrees F air, if the cooling medium is 10 degrees F nitrous spray and ambient air?

$$T_{drop} = TE \times (T_{charge} - T_{coolant})$$

where,
TE = Thermal effectiveness of a heat exchanger
T_{drop} = The actual temperature drop achieved through the heat exchanger
T_{charge} = Temperature of the hot pressurized charge air being cooled
$T_{coolant}$ = Temperature of the cooling medium (degrees F)

Gasoline Volume Correction

°F	VCF gasoline	in³/gal gasoline	VCF diesel	in³/gal diesel
115	0.9674	238.8	0.9734	237.3
110	0.9704	238.0	0.9758	236.7
105	0.9733	237.3	0.9782	236.1
100	0.9763	236.6	0.9806	235.6
95	0.9793	235.9	0.9830	235.0
90	0.9822	235.2	0.9855	234.4
85	0.9852	234.5	0.9879	233.8
80	0.9882	233.8	0.9903	233.3
75	0.9911	233.1	0.9927	232.7
70	0.9941	232.4	0.9952	232.1
65	0.9970	231.7	0.9976	231.6
60	1.0000	231.0	1.0000	231.0
55	1.0030	230.3	1.0024	230.4
50	1.0059	229.6	1.0048	229.9
45	1.0088	229.0	1.0073	229.3

U.S. Petroleum Gallon - Correction Factors to 60° F

Therefore,

$$\begin{aligned} T_{drop} &= TE \times (T_{charge} - T_{coolant}) \\ &= .75 \times (200 - 10) \\ &= 142.5F \end{aligned}$$

The temperature will drop 142.5 degrees F through the intercooler.

Actual intercooler-out temperature will thus be:

$$\begin{aligned} T_{IO} &= (T_{charge} - T_{drop}) \\ &= 200 - 142.5 \\ &= 57.5F \end{aligned}$$

Charge enters the engine with a 12.5 degrees F temperature drop over ambient 70 degrees F air.

HOW DO YOU COMPUTE THE EFFECT OF TEMPERATURE CHANGE ON AIR DENSITY? HOW MUCH WILL A PARTICULAR COOLING EFFECT INCREASE HORSEPOWER?

Assuming appropriate fuel delivery and engine management, any density increase from charge cooling will increase horsepower commensurate to the density changes resulting

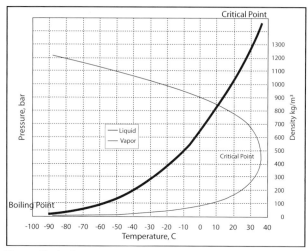

Nitrous oxide density versus pressure as the effect of temperature changes. Note that density and pressure change in opposite directions, tending to offset each other within a few percent, particularly in the 20-30C range where most nitrous systems do their work.

from the temperature drop. If intake air density increases 25 percent, power increases 25 percent.

It is easy to calculate changes in charge density resulting from the temperature drop of intercooling because the density change is a simple ratio of the before and after temperatures of the charge—converted to absolute temperature (degrees K).

Suppose you are cooling charge air that has been heated 250 degrees F above ambient temperature during turbocharging to about 28-psi boost with a .75 percent efficient compressor? Assume ambient compressor-inlet temperature is 70 degrees F. This means the turbocharged air is 320 degrees F leaving the compressor.

If an intercooler is capable of 60 percent thermal efficiency, it will cut the charge temperature increase by 60 percent of 250 degrees F, or 150 degrees F, so that the rise is

only 100 degrees instead of 250. This will produce important density changes.

Adding in the inlet temperature of 70 degrees, the non-intercooled air leaves the compressor at 70 + 250 = 320 degrees F, which converts to 780 degrees R absolute by adding 460. Now let's send the air through the intercooler. The charge air left the compressor at 780 degrees R but it departs the intercooler at 70 + 100 (new rise) + 460 = 630 degrees R. The ratio of these numbers is the key to the density change according to the following:

$$\Delta D = (T_1/T_2) - 1$$

Where,
ΔD = density change resulting from a temperature increase or decrease
T_1 = original temperature (degrees R) of air leaving the compressor
T_2 = new temperature (degrees R) of air leaving the intercooler

Plugging in the numbers,

$$\Delta D = (T_1/T_2) - 1$$
$$= (780/630) - 1$$
$$= .238$$

The density (and horsepower!) increase from intercooling is 23.8 percent.

Imagine if an intercooler could return the charge temperature all the way back down to 70F:

$$\Delta D = (780/530) - 1$$
$$= .471$$

Metal tubing for use as nitrous supply line or for venting nitrous overpressure out of a vehicle. Metal supply lines should be insulated to prevent heat soak from causing foaming or vaporization inside the line, which will tend to soften the initial hit and possibly produce a rich-bog until vapor and foam are expelled from the line.

Fuel pressure safety switches are used to disarm the nitrous system if fuel pressure drops below the threshold value, thus preventing dangerously lean air-nitrous-fuel ratios. *Nitrous Outlet*

This approaches a 50 percent power increase from cooling effect. No intercoolers are literally 100 percent efficient, but by using a very cold cooling medium (ice water, nitrous injection), some systems can certainly get temperature down to or below ambient air temperature.

CALCULATING JET DIAMETER FOR A NITROUS FLOW TOOL

To set nitrous system fuel enrichment flow you need to install a jet in the flow tool that has the same metering area as the combined area of all fuel jets on the nitrous system. But what size jet will do? If the nitrous system only has one fuel jet, that's easy—the same size fuel jet goes in the Flow Tool. If the nitrous system is running direct-port fogger nozzles with one per cylinder, you'll need to do a tiny bit of math. Let's say that the direct-port fogger nozzles are equipped with .025-inch-diameter jets. We need to start by calculating the area of each jet and then add them together.

Area = π × Radius²

where

π   = 3.141592654 . . .
Radius = Diameter/2

Therefore, the area of each fogger jet is:

Area = 3.141592654 × (.025/2)²
**   = 0.000490874**

Therefore, the total area of the fogger jets on a V-8 engine is

8 × 0.000490874 = 0.003926991

The diameter of a single jet with the same area is:

Diameter = 2 × (SQR [Area/π])

where

SQR = [take the square root of the quantity]
π   = 3.141592654 . . .
Radius = Diameter/2

Therefore,

Diameter = 2 × (SQR [.003926991 × 3.141592654])
**   = 0.070710689**
**   ≈ 0.071**

The rounding error in this case is **(0.071 - 0.070710689) / 0.070710689 = 0.004091475** (which is less than a half of 1 percent).

Actually, depending on the pressure, a single jet of equal area will flow slightly more fuel than eight individual jets due to reduced friction (the combined circumference of the individual jets is greater than the single jet).

If you change the size of the fogger jets, you will have to recalculate the flow tool jet size and install a different jet in order to dial in precise fuel pressure that yields the target flow rate.

BRAKE MEAN EFFECTIVE PRESSURE

Brake mean effective pressure (BMEP) is a function of torque and engine displacement as per the following formula:

BMEP = Torque × 150.8/displacement (CID)

Density of Air vs. Temperature

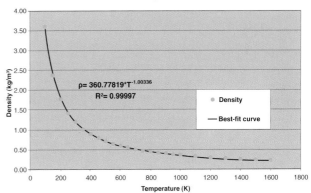

$$\rho = 360.77819 \cdot T^{-1.00336}$$
$$R^2 = 0.99997$$

Density of Air p vs. Temperature °C

Effect of Temperature

°F	°C	p in lb/ft³	p in kg/m³
14	−10	0.0837783	1.342
23	−5	0.0822176	1.317
32	0	0.0806569	1.292
41	+5	0.0792211	1.269
50	+10	0.0778477	1.247
59	+15	0.0764743	1.225
68	+20	0.0751633	1.204
77	+25	0.0739147	1.184
86	+30	0.0727286	1.165

Air density also changes with temperature (and altitude!), which is why virtually all engine management systems have barometric pressure sensors that enable air density change to be factored into the basic injection pulsewidth calculation.

... in which BMEP is a simple multiple of torque per cubic inch of displacement, and 150.8 represents 1.0 lb-ft per cubic inch of displacement in a 4-stroke engine.

In this example, a '91 MR2 turbo made 470 horsepower on a Dynojet chassis dynamometer on 118-octane leaded racing gasoline with highly effective total-loss intercooling.

Therefore,

BMEP = torque × 150.8/displacement (CID)
BMEP = 470 × 150.8/128.15
BMEP = 553.07

Reworking the formula allows torque to be computed from a known BMEP and engine displacement as follows:

Torque = displacement (CID) × BMEP/150.8

Assuming a maximum BMEP of 500 psi for a 2.1-liter turbo engine and the optimistic maximum BMEP of 500, the maximum "sustainable" torque for this powerplant is:

Torque = 128.15 × 500/150.8
Torque = 424.90 lb-ft

If this engine were run on methanol fuel instead of racing gasoline, then it could be boosted with air-supercharging or nitrous boost to BMEP of 700, then

Torque = 128.15 × 700/150.8
Torque = 594.86 lb-ft

Assuming that 90 percent of peak torque can be sustained to 6,250 rpm, maximum sustainable gasoline-fuel horsepower at peak BMEP can be calculated using the formula

HP = torque × rpm/5,250
HP = 382.41 × 6,250/5,250
HP = 455.25

With methanol,

HP = torque × rpm/5,250
HP = 535.37 × 6,250/5,250
HP = 637.35

If you re-cammed the engine to maintain 90 percent of this torque to 7,000 rpm (within the stock MR2 redline of 7,250 rpm)—382.41 lb-ft, then absolute peak "sustainable" power with turbocharging *or nitrous* can be calculated with gasoline using the formula

HP = torque × rpm/5,250
HP = 382.41 × 7,000/5,250
HP = 509.88

With methanol fuel,

HP = torque × rpm/5,250
HP = 535.37 × 7,000/5,250
HP = 713.83

Unquestionably, conventional gasoline engines can survive delivering 2.0 to 2.5 lb-ft torque (average MEP) per cubic inch from nitrous boost (305 lb-ft on a 2.0-liter engine), or 3.5 to 4.0 lb-ft with alcohol-gasoline fuel blends, and thoroughbred racing engines have definitively survived delivering 4.0 horsepower per cubic inch (about 244 horsepower per liter). For perspective, consider that a de-boosted version of GM Racing's turbocharged 2.0-liter Ecotec drag powerplant set several land speed records at Bonneville running at approximately 750 horsepower (6.15 horsepower per cubic inch), down from the 1,200 to 1,400 horsepower available at higher boost in short-duration drag racing (11.5 horsepower per cube!).

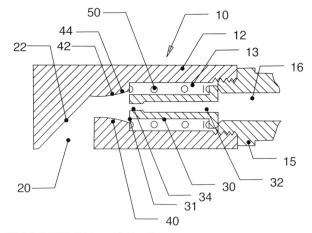

U.S. Patent 6938841 is for a variable-orifice nitrous injector, which is designed to correct nitrous delivery for pressure changes by choking nitrous flow as pressure increases in the supply line.

Normalizing the pressure of supplied nitrous oxide can seem like a great idea to eliminate mass flow changes from pressure drop during a nitrous run, but as discussed in detail in this book, the pressure drop in the nitrous regulator can cause foaming and refrigeration effects that change nitrous density, and the basic tank temperature and line heat-soak are not corrected by a regulator. *Zex*

Competition nitrous kit from Wizards of NOS in the United Kingdom. Note that the vehicle's electrical system must have the power to hold open 16 electrical solenoids. *WON*

One alternative to electrical solenoids for race vehicles without powerful alternator systems is the gas-actuated solenoid. *Combo-Flo*

On street engines where it is unacceptable for nitrous injection to compromise powerplant reliability, given the relatively rare occurrence of nitrous boost, 30 to 50 percent power increases are easily feasible with decent reliability, though this is more than the power-adding capability of many factory or aftermarket air-supercharged engines with strengthened internal engine components. A turbocharged long-block is great raw material for a nitrous motor, given its extra built-in strength to handle turbo boost—and overboost.

TORQUE VERSUS HORSEPOWER

The power-torque conversion formula is:

$$HP = (torque \times rpm)/5{,}250$$

5,250 is a number that lumps together several different conversion factors. It is based on something called radians per second, and is ultimately used to convert the distance aspect of torque (pound-*feet*) to the speed aspect of horsepower (@ *rpm*).

The purpose of the formula is to derive **Horsepower** from **Torque** at a specific engine speed. Conversely, torque can be derived from horsepower and engine speed as follows:

$$Torque = (HP \times 5{,}250)/rpm$$

INJECTOR FLOW AND PRESSURE

Pressure-regulated dry nitrous hijacks the stock EFI injection system to provide fuel enrichment through the primary electronic port injectors with the same excellent, precise fuel *distribution* expected from any modern engine with EFI. Unfortunately, the system has some intrinsic flaws. It provides relatively crude supplemental enrichment fueling *that is constant only in the most approximate sense*: Supplemental fuel ends up as a function not only of rail pressure but of changes in the stock fuel-injection pulsewidth, which varies according

Auxiliary fuel tank for supplying supplemental nitrous requirements. Note that if the tank is installed in the engine compartment (as is the usual case), heat soaking will change gasoline density about one percent per 10F temperature change. *Nitrous Outlet*

to the full-throttle volumetric efficiency curve of the stock, non-boosted engine in a way that will not necessarily correspond perfectly to the constant rate of nitrous injection under all conditions, meaning the nitrous-fuel ratio does not necessarily remain constant as the engine accelerates. What's more, the relatively low pressure ceiling on electronic injector operability (usually 70 to 85 psig max) means that pressure-based fuel enrichment offers only a modest amount of headroom to deliver supplemental nitrous enrichment fuel through the stock electronic injectors. For example, raising fuel pressure from 40 to 75 psi through an injector that was originally capable of 50 lb/min occurs as follows:

New flow = **square root of (new pressure/old pressure)**
            × old flow
         = **SQR (75/40) × 50 lb/min**
         = **68.47 lb/min**

The new flow rate, 68.47, is roughly 137 percent of the original 50 lb/min rate. Some of the fuel will be needed for combustion chamber cooling to fight detonation, but you could certainly figure that this method of providing supplemental fuel would support at least 25 to 30 percent more horsepower.

Another way to look at this begins with the observation that constant nitrous boost is a percentage of the peak horsepower capacity of the stock fuel injection system. Consider that a 40-horsepower boost on a 200-horse engine represents 20 percent additional horsepower, meaning that the flow rate through the injectors must increase by 20 percent during nitrous operations. Again, it's actually more, due to the need for combustion cooling on a nitrous powerplant, but let's keep it simple for now. If the rated stock fuel pressure is 39 psi, the stock horsepower 200, and the boost 40 horsepower, then the new fuel pressure required through the stock injectors to fuel the boost would be:

New pressure (psi) = old pressure × (old power + power boost)/old power)^2

= 39 × ((200 + 40)/200)^2

= 56.16 psi

With fuel pressure up from 39 to a little over 56 psi, the injectors will squirt out enough additional fuel for a 40-horse nitrous power boost. Now, let's assume you need at least 10 percent additional supplemental fuel for combustion cooling, increasing the effective fuel enrichment requirement from 40 horsepower worth of fuel to, say, 45 horsepower worth:

New pressure (psi) = (old pressure × (old power + power boost)/old power)^2)

= (39 × ((200 + 45)/200)^2)

= 58.52 psi

In this case, a 20 percent power boost requires about 59 psi fuel pressure to meet boost fuel requirements.

CALCULATING HORSEPOWER FROM QUARTER TIME AND VICE VERSA

To get a rough idea of the average horsepower required to achieve a particular speed in the quarter mile with a certain weight vehicle . . .

$$HP = (S/225)^{(1/.318)} \times W \; [\times C]$$

Where

HP = Horsepower
W = Weight (lbs)
S = Speed (mph)

Therefore

Horsepower = (Speed/225)$^{(1/.318)}$ × Weight

To calculate the achievable quarter speed with a particular weight vehicle with a known horsepower engine . . .

$$S = (HP/W)^{.318} \times 225 \; [\times C]$$

Where

HP = Horsepower
W = Weight (lbs)
S = Speed (mph)

Therefore

Speed = (horsepower/weight)$^{.318}$ × 225 [× correction]

There are a variety of assumptions in these two formulae that you could call "fudge factors." They are based on assumptions about the average horsepower produced across the power band for an all-motor engine of a specified peak power. Since nitrous engines produce a much higher average horsepower (area under the curve) than engines running only on the motor, nitrous engines require a correction factor. A suggested correction factor for nitrous-boosted engines is .8

Liquid Type	Metric		US	
	Low Density	High Density	Low Density	High Density
Crude Oil	below 610.5 kg/m³	above 1075 kg/m³	above 100 deg API	below 0 deg API
Gasoline*	below 653 kg/m³	above 770.5 kg/m³	above 85 deg API	below 52 deg API
Jet Fuel*	below 787.5 kg/m³	above 829 kg/m³	above 48 deg API	below 37 deg API
Diesel*	below 829 kg/m³	above 1075 kg/m³	above 40 deg API	below 0 deg API
LPG	below 495 kg/m³	above 610.5 kg/m³	above 155 deg API	below 100 deg API
Transition*	below 771 kg/m³	above 787 kg/m³	above 52 deg API	below 48 deg API

Liquid Type	Metric		US	
	Low Density	High Density	Low Density	High Density
Crude Oil	below 610.5 kg/m³	above 1075 kg/m³	above 100 deg API	below 0 deg API
Gasoline*	below 653 kg/m³	above 770.5 kg/m³	above 85 deg API	below 52 deg API
Jet Fuel*	below 787.5 kg/m³	above 829 kg/m³	above 48 deg API	below 37 deg API
Diesel*	below 829 kg/m³	above 1075 kg/m³	above 40 deg API	below 0 deg API
LPG	below 495 kg/m³	above 610.5 kg/m³	above 155 deg API	below 100 deg API
Transition*	below 771 kg/m³	above 787 kg/m³	above 52 deg API	below 48 deg API

API2540 Volume Correction Software enables the user to calculate the effect of temperature changes on fuel volume and density. This sort of thing is actually important for achieving maximum power in Land Speed Record and other motor racing at high altitudes or unusual temperatures.

NOS EFI System Jetting Map

	Fuel Jet at PSI				
N²O Jet	20 psi	30 psi	40 psi	50 psi	60 psi
24	19-21	18-20	17-19	16-17	16-17
26	19-21	18-20	18-20	17-18	16-17
28	20-22	19-21	18-20	17-18	17-18
30	21-23	19-21	19-21	18-19	17-18
32	22-24	20-22	19-21	19-20	18-19
34	22-25	21-23	20-22	19-20	18-19
36	24-26	22-24	21-23	20-22	19-21

EFI nitrous system jetting changes required at various fuel pressures. *NOS* (meaning that the required peak power of a nitrous engine to produce a certain speed in the quarter is only 80 percent that required of an all-motor powerplant).

HORSEPOWER AS A FUNCTION OF NITROUS JET SIZE AND VICE-VERSA

A rule of thumb calculation for the horsepower delivered by a particular jet size at 800 psi tank pressure is:

$$HP = (nitrous\ jet\ size)^2 \times 70$$

where

Nitrous jet size	= **diameter** (in mm; 1 millimeter = 0.03936 inches)
70	= **correction constant**
HP	= **brake horsepower** (@ 800 psig nitrous tank pressure)

Alternately, the formula for inches would be:

$$HP = (nitrous\ jet\ size)^2 \times 45184.33142$$

where

Nitrous jet size	= **diameter** (in inches)
45184.33142	= **correction constant**
HP	= **brake horsepower** (@ 800 psig nitrous tank pressure)

Reworking the formula, we calculate the Jet Size required to achieve a particular amount of power:

Nitrous jet size = SQR [HP/70]

Where

Nitrous jet size	= **jet diameter in millimeters**
SQR	= **square root of the [quantity]**

Or, using inches

Nitrous jet size = SQR [HP/45184.33142]

The fuel jets for a wet or direct-port nitrous system can be calculated as a function of the fuel pressure and nitrous jet size:

At 45 psi:
Fuel jet size = nitrous jet size [mm²] × **157**
  [= Nitrous jet diameter - 33%]

At 10 psi:
Fuel jet size = nitrous jet size [mm²] × **70**
  [= Nitrous jet diameter]

At 3 psi:
Fuel jet size = nitrous jet size [mm²] × **38.4**
  [Nitrous jet diameter + 35%]

A formula predicting the time in seconds to deliver 1 pint of fuel for a given power output is:

Time = 6,500/horsepower

where

6,500 = correction constant

Therefore, we get the following chart:

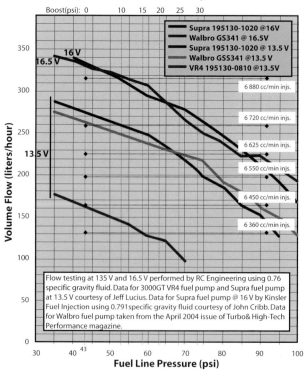

The volumetric pumping capacity of a fuel pump is directly related to the pressure, with higher pressure reducing the mass flow capability of the pump. A second factor in the pumping ability of an electric fuel pump is the power supply, with higher voltages increasing the pumping capacity. Yet another factor influencing the mass flow is temperature, with higher temperatures reducing the density of fuel and thus the total mass flow.

Chapter 9
Frequently Asked Questions

WHAT ARE THE ADVANTAGES OF NITROUS VERSUS OTHER PERFORMANCE OPTIONS?

Nitrous is dirt-cheap to buy and install compared to quality turbo and supercharger kits, and you pay for the juice as you need it. The horsepower per dollar ratio is as good as it gets if you don't use the boost too often, and the power boost can be as high as your engine can stand—which is why they use it in 2,500-horse Pro Mod draggers. Nitrous gives an engine super powers, but when you switch it off, your engine goes back to its secret identity as a mild-mannered grocery-getter with factory reliability that meets factory emissions standards.

WILL NITROUS DAMAGE MY ENGINE OR AFFECT THE RELIABILITY? CAN I BOLT A NITROUS KIT ONTO A STOCK ENGINE?

There is no question that any modifications that significantly increase engine power eat into the safety margin designed into the powerplant by factory automotive engineers, and this is certainly true of nitrous oxide injection. Many or even most nitrous engines could probably be damaged if driven by a determined driver. On the other hand, any engine will stand *some* additional power and thermal loading. Some engines with some nitrous kits with some drivers will live forever with complete reliability, and some engines with some nitrous systems and some drivers are a short-fuse bomb waiting to blow.

Lingenfelter LS1 with plate nitrous system. Note the auxiliary race-fuel tank.

It is critical to choose the correct nitrous shot for the application. A well-designed and -installed nitrous system with a conservative power boost on a healthy engine with excellent engine management can live a long, long time if operated sanely within the recommended operating envelope. As you increase the size of the power boost, you will need upgrade parts to maintain reliability or more careful operation to avoid engine damage. With sophisticated electronic control systems, it is possible to idiot-proof (or "crazy-proof") almost any nitrous system. In the longer run, adding significant power and using it a lot without upgrading internal engine parts will wear out the engine somewhat faster, but much less so with electronic engine management and fuel injection and a great factory (or aftermarket) calibration.

Industry-leader Nitrous Oxide Systems (NOS) recommends a maximum 40- to 60-horsepower boost on stock 4-cylinder engines with cast pistons and crank, 75 to 100 on a stock 6-cylinder with similar internals, less than 140 horsepower boost on stock small V-8s, and 125 to 200 horsepower on large V-8s over 7.0 liters with ordinary (non-super duty) internal parts.

CAN I ABUSE A NITROUS ENGINE AS MUCH AS I WANT?

That depends on your definition of "abuse." My definition does not include "driving it like you're mad at it." My definition of abuse is anything that is harmful to the engine, and obviously you can never do that. Most nitrous engines are not equipped with cooling and control systems capable of protecting a boosting nitrous powerplant from a maniac driver—which might be you, a parking valet, a friend, or the mechanic at the repair shop who always wanted to know exactly how fast a vehicle like yours could really go on nitrous and runs it all-out on the juice in hot weather until the engine overheats, begins to knock, and goes into melt-down. What else is harmful? Engaging the nitrous and lugging the engine at very low rpm, which can cause detonation and overstress mechanical parts. Triggering nitrous when the clutch pedal is depressed, which can zing the engine above the redline faster than you'd believe. Running through the rev-limiter with nitrous flowing, which could cause backfire explosions.

It is certainly possible to make nitrous engines idiot-proof, but most are not.

The author's tri-turbo 4.2L Jaguar XKE with computer-controlled progressive nitrous injection.

WHAT ENGINE AND VEHICLE UPGRADES ARE REQUIRED FOR A LARGER POWER BOOST?

You'll want to retard timing with anything much larger than 25 horsepower, which requires an electronic interceptor boost-retard device on most later-model EFI engines. Nitrous engines typically require cooler spark plugs with narrowed gap as the power climbs. At some point you will need an upgrade or additional fuel pump. Larger boost mandates replacing stock cast pistons with forged aluminum units. Unless you are running a nitrous-capable aftermarket engine management system on an engine with 4-valve pentroof heads, you will quickly run out of headroom for pumping up the volume unless you have access to 100-plus octane unleaded racing gasoline.

For boosting power much over 50 percent on modern engines, you'll want stronger connecting rods, a dedicated nitrous fuel supply system, and really high octane racing fuel above 110 octane (meaning oxygenated or leaded, in most cases).

At a minimum, you'll want to make sure the engine is up-to-date with all servicing such as valve clearance, optimize the ignition timing and fuel delivery (preferably on a chassis dynamometer), install new spark plugs of the heat range recommended by an expert, torque the head bolts to specs, and change the oil. I believe in fully synthetic multi-viscosity oil as good insurance for all power-adder applications.

HOW DOES NITROUS MAKE POWER?

Nitrous oxide is a chemical-supercharging agent that provides significant air enrichment by contributing a higher concentration of oxygen to the charge mixture. The oxygen is liberated during combustion as nitrous molecules reach 565 degrees F and split apart. The enriched air allows more fuel to be burned than would be possible if the engine were breathing ordinary air. Liquid nitrous

oxide also provides a tremendous refrigeration effect when it boils into vapor in the engine intake system, which helps cool combustion and improve air density to the degree that engine volumetric efficiency may be improved 10 percent even considering the air intake volume displaced by the nitrous oxide.

WILL NITROUS OXIDE INJECTION INCREASE CYLINDER PRESSURE AND TEMPERATURE?

That is the whole point: Cylinder pressure and temperature equal horsepower.

WHAT WILL NITROUS DO TO THE PERFORMANCE OF A VEHICLE?

Most modern nitrous kits are exclusively designed to improve acceleration (rather than top speed), and many commercial nitrous kits in many applications have improved quarter-mile drag times by 1 to 3 seconds and 10 to 15 mph. However, it is difficult or impossible to predict in advance how efficient a particular system will be at turning nitrous and supplemental fuel into horsepower in a particular application, and the hardness of the hit will affect acceleration, traction, and the ability of powertrain parts to survive boost without shock or thermal damage. Since most nitrous systems deliver constant flow, torque boost is much higher at lower rpm when the flow is allocated among fewer power strokes. Nitrous has a great reputation for delivering instant power, but it cannot

Pumping station for refilling nitrous tanks. You can do it with gravity (and cooling the recipient tank helps), but an electric pump makes commercial refills much faster. Note the scale for determining when the tank is full. "Full" does not mean truly full; ullage in the tank is required to allow thermal expansion without blowing out the overpressure burst disk and losing the contents of the tank. *Nitrous Express*

Arizona Speed and Marine built this gorgeous TPI F-body with nitrous injection from NOS.

generally be used below a threshold rpm without detonation or over-stressing mechanical parts, and "nitrous lag" may slow the rate of power buildup as the supply line is purged of nitrous vapor.

WHAT DOES NITROUS INJECTION COST?

The initial cost of the nitrous system hardware is modest. A basic dry-EFI or single-fogger nitrous system can be had for about $500. Direct-port nitrous hardware can be found for another $100, with individual-cylinder metal plumbing adding another $200 or so. NOSzle under-injector port nitrous adaptor/injectors could cost $100-plus each on top of the other direct-port hardware.

The truth, though, is that buying a nitrous system is a little like buying an ink-jet printer: It doesn't take long before the cost of the ink exceeds the cost of the printer. At this time, filling a completely empty 10-pound nitrous bottle could easily cost between 5 and 15 percent of the initial cost of the kit. In fact, a 100-horse shot of nitrous boost requires 4 pounds per minute of nitrous in the most efficient case, meaning a 25-horse shot requires 1 pound per minute of boost. Assuming a nitrous refill costs $2.25 a pound, an hour of 25-horse nitrous boost adds $135 to the operating cost. If you assume that a nitrous kit and support systems capable of providing constant boost costs $1,000 versus a low-pressure turbo kit that costs $4,000, and at this burn rate the breakeven point is 22 hours of nitrous boost.

HOW LONG WILL A FULL TANK OF NITROUS OXIDE LAST?

That depends on the size of the nitrous tank, the mass-flow rate of nitrous injection, and how often the boost is used. How big is the tank? Most cars, light trucks, and boats could fit a 30-, 40-, or 50-pound tank if the owner is willing to sacrifice the space. Many bikes, watercraft, and snowmobiles would have difficulty mounting more than a 2- to 5-pound

tank. Unfortunately, the mass flow rate is not perfectly even, even with a constant-flow nitrous architecture. Nitrous mass flow is a function of the nitrous phase (liquid, gas, or super-critical fluid), density (increases markedly at lower temperatures), and pressure (is it self-pressurized, which is temperature-dependent, or externally pressurized?). The only type of nitrous system capable of delivering perfectly even mass flow has a climate-controlled tank with external pressurization, and an insulated supply line. The rule of thumb, however, is that a 100-horse shot boost requires 4 to 6 pounds of nitrous per minute, depending on the efficiency of the system. This amounts to between .067 and .1 pounds per second, or a pound of nitrous every 10 to 15 seconds of boost. Dysfunctional nitrous-fuel mixtures can waste a lot of fuel and nitrous per horsepower of boost, whether rich or lean. How often will you put the hammer down with the nitrous armed? Probably a lot at first, when it's a new toy, and less later on, depending on the performance of the engine without nitrous. Some people burn up a tank of nitrous in a day or an evening; others might take six months between refills, more content to know the power is there than to actually use it.

Regarding actual numbers, according to NOS, a 125-hp PowerShot kit with a standard 10-lb.-capacity bottle "will usually offer up to seven to ten full quarter-mile passes." A 250-horse shot, says NOS, is usually good for 3 to 5 full quarter-mile passes, and more if nitrous is only used in second and third gears.

WHEN AND FOR HOW LONG CAN A NITROUS SYSTEM BE ACTIVE?

Most nitrous kits are not self-limiting when it comes to the length of the power boost, so a maniac throttle-jockey who keeps the pedal to the metal in high gear can theoretically

Throttle injection nitrous plate from Nitrous Outlet. Note the injection orifices in the upper perimeter of the throttle area. Nitrous suppliers have been ingenious in devising interesting ways to get nitrous into an engine, including all sorts of spacer plates, replacement MAFs, and much more. *Nitrous Outlet*

keep it on the juice until the nitrous tank is empty. Or the engine burns down. Whichever comes first. Many vehicles could not stand the thermal loading of constant nitrous injection for very long, because the cooling system could not handle the heat. But then many stock vehicles without power-adders would overheat if run at wide open throttle in warm weather for very long at maximum speed. Modern nitrous kits are almost exclusively designed for drag-style acceleration. Many kit-builders recommend limiting boost to less than 15 seconds at a time.

Most nitrous kits do not have anti-stupid countermeasures built into the system. So if you have a big nitrous kit on a heavy pickup pulling a 10,000-pound trailer up a steep hill, there is nothing to keep you from juicing the engine until it burns down. A similar situation occurs in a light vehicle lugging in top gear at very low rpm, when the torque boost per power stroke is huge. Most kit-builders recommend that nitrous boost should only be used to enhance acceleration under circumstances when the engine could "freely accelerate" *without* nitrous boost, and never to activate the system when the engine is under abnormally high loads. Never blow through the rev-limiter with nitrous boost active, since (1) the rev-limiter might not work right if the mechanism is to pull fuel, (2) a rev-limiter that pulls fuel might cause lean mixtures, and (3) a rev-limiter that drops out cylinders with ignition tricks might cause explosive backfiring.

ARE NITROUS OXIDE INJECTION KITS LEGAL IN ALL 50 STATES?

Potentially. The manufacturer of a device that significantly modifies an engine to add power must get an exemption order (EO), which requires strict testing to prove that the modifications do not increase exhaust emissions more than 10 percent above the factory standard. Larger nitrous suppliers like NOS have gone to the trouble and considerable expense to get an EO for certain of their most popular nitrous kits. Beyond emissions considerations, nitrous oxide is not specifically illegal in many states and countries.

Well, and then there's insurance. To make sure that your insurance covers you in case of an accident, you should be aware that it is probably written somewhere in the fine print of your policy that you are required to inform your insurance company of any power-adder modifications or, specifically, that the vehicle is not covered if it is modified. A nitrous kit could potentially be the basis of a denial of coverage in case the worst ever happens and you cause an accident. You may need to shop around to find an insurance company that will explicitly cover boosted vehicles. Expect to pay for the coverage, because there may be a correlation between installing a nitrous system and driving fast. You never know.

Nitrous does not burn, nor is it even an oxidizer until heated above 572 degrees F, but commercial vehicles carrying compressed gas like nitrous oxide are typically compelled to carry external warnings so first-responders will know about the danger of an enhanced fire or explosion following an accident. Although not mandated, some nitrous venders have recommended that a vehicle carry an external warning for nitrous oxide even if not mandated by law. There was a time when compressed gas cylinders were color-coded to aid in quick identification (hence, the light-blue color of NOS tanks), but you have probably already noticed that nitrous oxide tanks can now be any color (probably because light blue had essentially become an NOS branding).

IS IT NECESSARY TO RE-JET A CARB OR CHANGE THE PRIMARY EFI (NON-BOOSTED) CALIBRATION WHEN ADDING NITROUS INJECTION TO A VEHICLE?

Unless there are extensive modifications that would affect the basic volumetric efficiency of the engine, the great thing about nitrous is that it has zero effect when the boost is not active. You should not expect to have to make any modifications to the stock fuel calibration. Naturally, this does not apply if you have upgraded the primary fuel injectors so they will deliver more fuel for dry nitrous injection. Happily, some engine management systems on vehicles like the Corvette are designed with parameterized injector flow, meaning that it may be possible to hack the EMS and reconfigure injector size without having to provide an entire new fuel calibration table. For more information, read my book *How to Tune and Modify Engine Management Systems.*

IS NITROUS OXIDE FLAMMABLE?

No. Nitrous oxide itself does not burn but provides oxygen enrichment to the charge mixture when heated above 572 degrees F during combustion. Additional oxygen allows an engine to burn more fuel, increasing the horsepower output.

CXI built this gorgeous 1,000-horsepower nitrous C4 'Vette.

DOES NITROUS OXIDE CAUSE DETONATION?

It better not. Nitrous oxide boosts power by producing faster, higher-pressure combustion with more heat. Without countermeasures, this will unquestionably increase the octane number requirement (ONR) of the engine. An engine that was on the edge of knocking without nitrous injection will almost definitely knock during nitrous boost. High-power detonation under heavy load during chemical supercharging is deadly, and must be prevented at all cost. Commercial nitrous kits fight detonation with fuel enrichment and ignition retard, and by mandating higher octane gasoline. If you make a mistake and fuel the vehicle with ordinary gas, unless there is a knock-sensor ignition retard system installed, the engine will almost definitely knock, and must not have the nitrous boost activated until the vehicle is refueled with better gasoline.

WHERE CAN I GET MY NITROUS CYLINDER FILLED?

There are a number of options. Many nitrous system dealers offer a refilling service. Check online. Nitrous system manufacturers typically have a dealer referral service that will supply contact info for dealers within a configurable radius of your ZIP code or address. You will be paying retail speed-shop prices, and prices can vary considerably, in some cases based on the attitude of the customer. In some cases—depending on the climate and whether the refiller has a cryogenic pumping station—the refill time may be long enough that it is not practical to do it while you wait.

The other alternative is to rent a large donor tank and buy nitrous oxide in bulk from the distribution network of a national manufacturer such as AirGas or Air Products. You can probably even arrange to have it delivered. Obviously, it can be much more convenient to refill the onboard tank in your garage on your time. You can return for a refill whenever you want. You can sell it to your friends, at cost, if you choose, and there could be a price advantage to pooling demand to increase the volume discount. In fact, you may have to pay as little as 25 percent of retail, which adds up quickly if you are burning up a lot of nitrous, so shop around. Of course, an offsetting factor is that you'll be paying to rent the donor tank, which is similar to the cost of renting gas welding tanks, but this can add up if you rarely use much nitrous.

CAN I GET MORE POWER BY "CHIPPING" MY EFI NITROUS ENGINE WITH AN AFTERMARKET COMPUTER CHIP?

Almost definitely not, and you could damage the engine. *Don't do it.* Most modern stock automotive engines are already running at or very near the maximum state of tune from the factory, and the recalibration chips or re-flashes that manage to add a smidgeon of power somewhere in the rpm range often do it with very aggressive timing that increases the octane number requirement of the engine. This will greatly increase the likelihood of high-power detonation during boost, which

CXI C4 'Vette engine showing trick direct-port nitrous setup.

is deadly. You've got nitrous, so it's easy to get a little—or *a lot!*—more power by recalibrating the nitrous system.

Keep in mind that it is very important that nitrous boost be an offset to a great engine calibration, and a highly modified all-motor EFI engine *needs* to be recalibrated or "re-chipped" to run well and make maximum power, which could be considerably more than stock. A *nitrous* calibration from a blue-ribbon tuner that's targeted at your precise configuration on a modified EFI engine can be essential, since it will correct the primary stock calibration that manages the engine and pull some timing during boost.

HOW LONG DOES IT TAKE TO INSTALL A NITROUS KIT?

Many wet plate or dry nitrous kits are advertised to be installable in an average of three to six hours. Any nitrous system that requires removing the intake manifold for installation will obviously take longer, and custom-building direct-port hard lines can take *much* longer, especially if this is your first try at bending pipes. Any modifications to the stock fuel supply or engine management system like upgrading the fuel pump or ignition or installing a boost-retard interceptor will add time. Obviously, experienced mechanics with good tools who are very familiar with the vehicle and engine, or who have previous experience installing the nitrous kits or even *this* specific kit, will work much faster.

A nitrous system should be fairly easy to install, particularly in comparison to the immense work required to install turbo kits or substantial all-motor power upgrades. In the simplest case you'll be mounting a tank in the luggage area, routing a supply hose to the engine, installing a few small parts under the hood, connecting a few wires, and installing an injector or plate in the intake.

The author's mid-engine Lotus Europa, with turbo engine transplant and direct-port dry nitrous controlled by a nitrous-capable Accel engine management system.

DO I NEED TO UPGRADE THE INTAKE MANIFOLD FOR A PLATE-INJECTOR NITROUS SYSTEM?

Nitrous Oxide Systems, a division of Holley, which sells aftermarket performance manifolds, recommends that either a single- or dual-plane V-8 manifold will work fine in most cases. NOS recommends installing a single-plane manifold on nitrous engines with more than 200 horsepower boost due to the improved wet mixture distribution at high rpm.

ARE THERE ANY BENEFITS TO HEATING OR CHILLING A NITROUS BOTTLE?

Yes and no.

Chilling a nitrous bottle increases the density of the liquid nitrous and increases the refrigeration effect of boiling nitrous when it sprays into the intake manifold, both of which enable more fuel to be burned for more power. Unfortunately, chilling the nitrous tank automatically lowers bottle pressure on tanks that are self-pressurized (as most are), which can more than compensate for the improved density and intercooling effects of colder nitrous. Self-pressurized nitrous tanks spewing liquid nitrous into an engine experience a powerful self-cooling effect as nitrous boils in the tank to maintain vapor pressure.

Meanwhile, *heating* a nitrous tank increases the bottle pressure but reduces the density. These factors tend to cancel each other out within a few percent. However, if tank temperature should exceed 97.7 degrees F, 100 percent of the nitrous will change phase into a gas-like supercritical fluid, causing nitrous mass flow into an engine to plummet radically as the tank begins expelling the far-less-dense gas.

The best argument for bottle heating or cooling systems is that conditioning nitrous tank temperature on self-pressurized systems is highly effective in eliminating

variability in nitrous mass flow—at least until the boost starts. Once the boost starts, no practical onboard tank heater is powerful enough to keep up with the radical cooling effect of vaporizing nitrous.

Competition nitrous systems with external nitrogen or air pressurization systems combined *with climate-controlled tank heating-cooling system* negate the cooling effect of nitrous boiling in the tank and eliminate changes in mass flow from environmental temperature variations.

IS NITROUS INJECTION COMPATIBLE WITH AIR-SUPERCHARGING?

Very much so. Nitrous works especially well with turbocharging, in that nitrous is most effective at delivering torque at the low end of the powerband exactly when turbochargers are typically not spinning fast enough to make significant boost pressure. If nitrous is mainly used to spool up the turbo quickly and fill a hole in the torque curve, a modest amount of nitrous boost can be calibrated to come in at very low rpm. Both turbos and nitrous tend to increase the temperature of combustion due to increased charge oxygen and fuel density, but turbochargers have the additional liability that they inevitably heat the air as they compress it, in most cases requiring intercoolers to remove as much of the compression heat as possible. Nitrous, on the other hand, has a tremendous refrigeration effect as it sprays into charge air, especially welcome on Roots superchargers, which are typically incompatible with intercooling as installed on V-8 engines. The refrigeration effect of nitrous can be significant enough to increase manifold absolute boost pressure on a turbo engine.

DO MOST NITROUS KITS HAVE EVERYTHING YOU NEED TO MAKE IT WORK?

Yes and no.

Nitrous kits typically have everything you need to put nitrous and supplemental fuel in the engine, including the small stuff, and that very well may be everything you need on nitrous kits with a modest power boost. On the other hand, it is rather common for nitrous kits to require upgrades to the ignition system, colder spark plugs, a higher-capacity fuel pump, electronic ignition retard interceptor or knock-control system, and so forth. Really large horsepower increases typically require internal engine upgrades such as forged pistons. If the kit does not contain nitrous and fuel filters, these must be installed. There are many other extra-cost options, including bottle heaters and insulator blankets, progressive controllers, purge valves, remote-controlled electrical bottle valves, and so forth. Some people are religious about the utility of installing a wideband lambda meter that will warn you if the engine is seeing dangerously lean (or rich) oxygen-fuel ratios during nitrous boost. Others like to see a dash-mounted exhaust gas temperature gauge.

WILL NITROUS BOOST KILL AN ENGINE WITH HIGH MILEAGE?

That depends. Tests by oil companies on well-maintained engines with average usage running unleaded fuel, fully synthetic oil, and port fuel injection have seen insignificant wear at 200,000 miles. The efficiency of new engines may even increase in the first 20,000 to 30,000 miles as parts wear in and seal, and friction goes down. A sick or out-of-tune engine might be put over the edge with nitrous boost, but a well-used but fully healthy engine with low combustion chamber leak-down, good ring oil sealing, and reasonable combustion chamber carbon can certainly handle a moderate nitrous boost without difficulty. Anyone considering adding a nitrous-injection system to an engine should verify—insofar as is possible without a complete teardown—that the engine is healthy. The best way to accomplish this is with a leakdown test, in which various pistons are successively placed at top dead center with the tester installed in place of the spark plug—at which point compressed air is added to the combustion chamber and the rate of leakdown measured. Any leakdown higher than 6 percent is unacceptable. Excessive leakdown past the rings, intake valves, exhaust valves, or valve seals can typically be heard by listening through a hose inserted in the crankcase, intake manifold, exhaust manifold, or valve/cam cover—and the cause dealt with before exacerbating the problem with nitrous boost.

WILL INJECTION AFFECT MY CATALYST— AND VICE VERSA?

The fact that modern nitrous injection is normally limited to infrequent, short bursts of acceleration lasting no longer than 15 to 20 seconds means that unusually high exhaust gas temperatures or exhaust that's abnormally high or low in oxygen or hydrocarbon emissions are unlikely to damage a vehicle's catalytic converter very quickly. Nitrous oxide is a terrible greenhouse gas, but the fact that it dissociates at 572 degrees F means it's not going to make it through an engine intact. Excessive unburned hydrocarbons are definitely not good for a catalytic converter, so it is important that a cat-equipped vehicle be properly calibrated to avoid gratuitously wasting fuel and damaging the cat with soot or overheating. Large amounts of nitrous that require tremendous amounts of over-fueling to fight knock are not a good idea on cat-equipped vehicles.

The reactants-to-products ratio of nitrous combustion is unusually high, so anything that restricts exhaust flow will have an especially pernicious effect when nitrous is active. It is highly likely that the stock cat will reduce the efficiency of a nitrous system by requiring a little more nitrous to achieve the required horsepower. Companies like Random Technologies have a selection of high-flow cats designed to improve the exhaust restriction of engines modified with power-adders.

WILL A GIVEN SHOT NITROUS KIT WITH IDENTICAL JETTING DELIVER THE SAME PERFORMANCE INCREASE ON A STOCK VERSUS MODIFIED ENGINE?

In general, the nitrous kit should deliver the same horsepower increase in either application, meaning the percentage increase in power will be higher and more dramatic on the lower-output version of the engine. On the other hand, a high-output engine with a big cam might have *reduced* low-end torque compared to the stock engine, meaning that the massive low-end torque boost of nitrous could produce especially large percentage gains at lower rpm. The peak output of the stock and high-output engine with nitrous active will be additive, meaning the high-output engine will still make more total horsepower.

CAN PUMP GASOLINE BE USED FOR STREET-STRIP NITROUS APPLICATIONS?

Virtually all nitrous powerplants require at least 91 to 94 octane premium pump gasoline. The more octane you have, the more likely it is that the engine will be able to run at the most efficient ignition timing advance. Engines with very high compression or an unusually large nitrous shot may require 100-octane racing gasoline to avoid harshly rich mixtures and retarded ignition. Water or alcohol injection can increase the knock-limited power availability if you are unlucky enough to live in a state with 91 octane premium.

WHAT TYPE OF CAM IS OPTIMAL DURING NITROUS BOOST?

Nitrous engines need all the exhaust flow they can get, so cams with aggressive exhaust overlap and duration will make the most total horsepower while on the juice. On the other hand, it is dysfunctional to optimize the cam for

A built-up hemi-head Turbo Fuego engine replaces the stock Europa's S1 Renault powerplant, and nitrous-only direct-port NOS fan-spray nozzles make sure the turbocharger spools immediately.

boost conditions at the expense of non-boosted performance when the engine is running on the motor 99.9 percent of the time—particularly since adding a little more nitrous and fuel can easily make up the difference in most cases until stock exhaust flow becomes an insurmountable bottleneck above 200 percent stock power. The optimal upgrade cam is highly dependent on a vehicle's weight, gearing, and other factors, so before buying it is wise to consult with cam manufacturers or work the application through using a simulation program like Engine Analyzer Pro.

CAN I FIND A NITROUS KIT FOR MY LATE-MODEL EFI ENGINE?

Somebody makes a nitrous kit for almost any performance-oriented EFI engine, and there are "universal" kits that can be adapted for less common applications.

IS A DIRECT-PORT NITROUS SYSTEM BETTER THAN A PLATE SYSTEM?

Plate systems traditionally maxed out at 350 horsepower, and above that you went with direct-port nitrous. But there are now competition plate systems that provide an extremely radical power boost in the 400- to 600-horse range. Some dry-manifold engines and inline engines with long intake runners require individual-port fogger nitrous architecture to achieve adequate nitrous and supplemental fuel distribution—but that depends on having nitrous and fuel distribution manifolds (distribution blocks) that do more than look good in terms of achieving great fluid distribution. Direct-port nitrous is easier to hide (under the intake manifold), particularly on a V engine. Most plate nitrous systems can be converted to direct-port architecture.

Tsunami unlimited air-racer shows how far piston engines have come since NACA first investigated using nitrous oxide as an "piston-engine afterburner." Hot rod Merlin's are now pushing nearly 4,000 horsepower, but the dominant air racers for decades has been a juiced Grumman Bearcat with Wright 3350 radial engine.

CAN I RUN NITROUS ON MY MOTORCYCLE, WATERCRAFT, OR SNOWMOBILE?

Yes. There are numerous nitrous kits for light and non-automotive vehicles, including 2-strokes. Obviously, it may be difficult or impossible to carry a very big nitrous tank, but then you don't need very much boost to convert a superbike into a rocket-launcher. Forgetting about purpose-built drag bikes, I have heard of at least one spray bike in the Dallas, Texas, area capable of delivering 385 horsepower to the *wheels*, giving it perhaps the highest power-to-weight ratio of any "streetable" vehicle in history, equivalent to a Porsche Turbo with more than 2,300 horsepower!

WHAT IS THE BEST WAY TO MOUNT A NITROUS TANK?

The trick is to make sure the bottle always expels liquid nitrous rather than nitrous vapor—even when hard acceleration or cornering would tend to slosh the liquid nitrous away from the bottle valve or pickup tube. The best position is usually upside down with no pickup tube installed, tipped slightly toward the front of the vehicle. Since this position is impractical or impossible for automotive-sized tanks in most cars, the standard automotive mounting position for many kits is with the valve end up, at a 15-degree angle from horizontal, with the bottle control valve oriented in a specified direction such that a pickup tube drawing liquid nitrous from the bottom of the tank is always at the lowest point.

HOW CAN I KNOW HOW MUCH USEFUL NITROUS REMAINS IN THE TANK?

Pick it up and shake it. Just kidding. The most accurate way is to weigh the tank, subtract the empty weight, and then subtract 20 percent of the full nitrous capacity (since it is common for nitrous systems to begin surging when at or below 20 percent full). Some people like to say that for maximum performance in competition conditions, a self-pressurized nitrous tank only contains 30 percent "sweet" nitrous. That is, the nitrous mass flow begins to decline when the tank is less than 70 percent full due to robust self-cooling and reduced capability to maintain full vapor pressure in a timely fashion.

Obviously, weighing the tank works fine between drag runs, but it isn't going to happen out on the streets while driving. However, if you know the average, best, and worst time it takes for the tank to empty itself during boost, a nitrous timer will tell you how many seconds of boost are likely to remain in the tank. Unfortunately, due to temperature and vapor-pressure issues, time-to-empty is not a simple linear function, and may vary according to the weather and other factors. A few long episodes of nitrous boost will probably empty the tank more slowly than many short bursts. Progressive (pulsed) nitrous systems require even more complex algorithms to track nitrous consumption. There are now some nitrous timers—particularly on electronic nitrous controllers and nitrous-capable aftermarket engine management systems—that employ very sophisticated logic to estimate nitrous mass flow and predict time-to-empty.

WHY DO NITROUS TANKS REQUIRE A BLOW-OFF SAFETY VALVE ON THE MAIN BOTTLE CONTROL VALVE?

Pressures often exceed 1,000 psi in a nitrous system, which is why most nitrous systems are built using aircraft-quality braided-stainless Teflon core hoses. Higher temperatures—and especially thermal expansion in an overfilled bottle—are fully capable of pushing pressure even higher into a realm that could threaten the structural integrity of the tank, potentially causing a terrible explosion that destroys the vehicle and kills the driver. Apparently there have been only two nitrous explosions in history (neither of which injured anyone), mainly because federal law requires that nitrous tanks be equipped with a blow-off or pressure-relief safety valve that will vent the nitrous (usually all of it) if pressure should reach a threshold approaching the danger point. Tank explosions cannot occur unless someone has tampered with the safety valve, but it is not nearly as uncommon for the safety valve to let go and set loose the nitrous oxide in hot climates where the nitrous tank is solar-heated by direct sunlight. Nitrous tanks mounted in the passenger compartment of a vehicle must therefore have the safety valve vented outside the vehicle to protect the occupants from automotive nitrous, which is an inhalation anesthetic denatured to be an irritant.

WILL NITROUS DESTROY MY AUTOMATIC TRANSMISSION OR CLUTCH?

A very modest power boost should not damage a healthy clutch or transmission, particularly if the boost cuts out during shifts, and a bigger nitrous hit is fine if controlled and driven with finesse. It's the *shock loads* that eat manual clutches or torque converters and automatic clutches, so a soft-hitting or progressive nitrous system that improves power gradually is much safer than a hard-hitting gut-punch of a nitrous shot. If you are installing a substantial nitrous shot and plan to drive the vehicle like a maniac, you will want to beef up the automatic transmission or upgrade the manual clutch. In most cases the manual transmission is not the weakest link until you are adding a *ton* of power, though very hard driving with nitrous will almost definitely accelerate the wear.

WHY NOT JUST INJECT PURE OXYGEN INSTEAD OF NITROUS?

Pure oxygen injection sounds like a good idea in theory, but nitrous oxide is actually a better chemical supercharging agent in all respects (which I discuss in detail in Chapter 2). The gist of it is that the 6,000-degree fire chemistry of pure oxygen combustion is too radical for an internal-combustion engine. When it comes to air-enrichment with pure oxygen, every advantage goes to nitrous. Liquid nitrous oxide has

You have to put the nitrous solenoids somewhere, right?

combustion-cooling refrigeration properties that help to moderate the hot, fast combustion of oxygen-enriched air. Perhaps surprisingly, a tank of liquid nitrous contains more oxygen than a tank of compressed oxygen (and cryogenic liquid oxygen is not feasible for automotive use). Beyond that, nitrous oxide is safer, since it is basically inert until heated above 572 degrees F.

CAN NITROUS OXIDE CAUSE ME PHYSICAL HARM?

Yes. It could kill you by suffocation, cause significant freeze-burns, and get you high, or cause inhalation irritation to the extent that you lose control of the vehicle. A cloud of nitrous inside your vehicle could temporarily diminish visibility to the extent of being dangerous. That said, it is quite easy to inoculate yourself against any possibility of danger. All automotive nitrous tanks mounted inside a vehicle should be equipped with plumbing that vents nitrous outdoors if the overpressure safety disk blows out. If the nitrous tank does vent inside the vehicle, opening the windows is a fairly effective countermeasure. Obviously, you should never open the nitrous bottle valve when it is pointed toward your face or any other part of your body you care about. If you have a refill station of your own, you need to keep liquid nitrous off your skin and avoid breathing it in concentrated form (which will *not* be pleasant due to the sulfur denaturing agent).

WHEN SHOULD I CLOSE THE BOTTLE VALVE?

Close the bottle valve before removing the tank for refill or replacement, and any time the engine is shut off.

The first should be obvious, though it is possible to forget and start to disconnect a live nitrous tank—which could spray nitrous in your face. It is wise to get in the habit of closing the bottle valve every time you shut down the engine, mostly to make sure that you do not damage your engine if a leaky solenoid valve allows nitrous to bleed slowly into the intake manifold. Some poorly designed or installed nitrous kits will spray nitrous and fuel into the engine if the system is armed and you open the throttle wide when the engine is off. In either case, unintended release of nitrous into the intake when the engine is stopped could cause a serious backfire explosion upon restart (remove or disable the spark plugs and crank the engine to clear the fumes if you suspect this might have happened).

It is possible to fail-safe a nitrous system by installing an electrical bottle valve that automatically closes at shutdown (and perhaps purges the supply line). Alternately, you could install an audible alarm or warning light that activates when the engine shuts down if there's pressure in the nitrous line to remind you to check. You could design a warning system that closes a circuit to provide a cockpit alarm when the tank is open and the engine stopped—and even lights a low-power LED on the tank when the valve is open so you don't accidently try to R&R the tank when the valve is open. At least one nitrous vendor sells an ignition-delay device that by default forces the engine to crank any fumes out of the intake and cylinders before allowing the vehicle to start.

WHAT'S INVOLVED IN REFILLING THE NITROUS CYLINDER?

You need a large donor bottle that's oriented correctly for refilling. There are two methods of filling a nitrous cylinder, one of which involves a pump. Pumps speed the process and never require chilling the recipient bottle to get a complete refill. On the other hand, a refill station kit with pump costs as much as $800. The most commonly used DIY method uses gravity (or siphoning), because it is the cheapest and, in some respects, the easiest. Basically, you connect the donor bottle to the smaller bottle being refilled (positioned so that gas bubbles can easily escape from the recipient bottle as liquid flows in), open both valves, and wait 5 to 10 minutes while the nitrous liquid flows downhill from the donor bottle (or siphons downhill) into the recipient bottle—at which point you check the weight of the recipient bottle to see if it is full. Chilling the recipient bottle in a freezer will speed the process, as will making sure that the donor bottle is at a minimum of room temperature. Ad-hoc chilling can be accomplished during a refill by releasing some gas from the recipient bottle (usually requiring it to be inverted), causing the contents to self-cool as nitrous vaporizes inside the tank.

HOW DO I GET IT ON WITH A JUICED ENGINE?

The bottle valve must be open. The arming switch must be turned on. The engine should be operating under circumstances where it could freely accelerate without nitrous boost, and it is probably a good idea to have the wheels pointed straight ahead if the nitrous hits hard (potentially turning a rear-drive car sideways in a curve). At this point, putting the pedal to the metal at wide open throttle will

automatically trigger nitrous boost on most installations, though some may instead be triggered with a button on the shifter or steering wheel. In some cases a first stage of nitrous boost is automatically triggered by full throttle, with another stage triggered with a manual pushbutton. Some nitrous-capable aftermarket engine management systems and competition nitrous controllers can trigger multiple stages of increasing nitrous injection depending on a sophisticated set of configurable circumstances with the goal of delivering maximum acceleration without losing traction. Progressive nitrous systems are virtually always fully automated, but can be implemented to begin nitrous injection at unusually low rpm and potentially at part throttle.

WHAT ARE THE MOST LIKELY PROBLEMS I'LL ENCOUNTER?

- Rich mixture bog until supply line vapor has cleared
- Melted spark plugs from trying to push it with lean mixtures or wrong heat range plugs
- Fouled plugs from rich mixtures
- Detonation from too much ignition advance
- Detonation and combustion overheating from nitrous or fuel distribution problems, particularly with single-point wet nitrous systems on dry-manifold EFI engines
- Clutch slip from a hard-hitting nitrous system
- Fried auto-trans from a hard-hitting system that stays active through gear shifts
- Electrical problems from poor wiring techniques and materials, and other miscellaneous installation problems
- Tiny individual nitrous or fuel ports clog due to contamination not removed by inadequate (or non-existent!) filters
- Unpredictable performance due to temperature-based differential in nitrous mass flow
- You're shocked—*shocked*—at the long-term recurring cost of buying nitrous oxide

Nitrous micro-switches automatically trigger nitrous injection the moment you hit full throttle. *Nitrous Outlet*

Index

MOTORBOOKS WORKSHOP

The Best Tools for the Job.

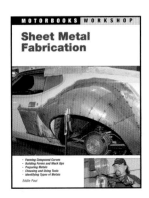
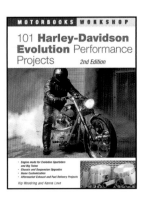

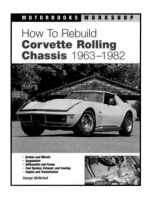
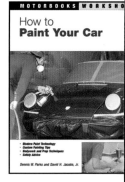

Other Great Books in this Series

How to Paint Your Car
136261AP • 978-0-7603-1583-5

How to Paint Flames
137414AP • 978-0-7603-1824-9

How to Master Airbrush
Painting Techniques
140458AP • 978-0-7603-2399-1

How to Repair Your Car
139920AP • 978-0-7603-2273-4

How to Diagnose
and Repair Automotive
Electrical Systems
138716AP • 978-0-7603-2099-0

Chevrolet Small-Block
V-8 ID Guide
122728AP • 978-0-7603-0175-3

How to Restore and
Customize Auto
Upholstery and Interiors
138661AP • 978-0-7603-2043-3

Sheet Metal
Fabrication
144207AP • 978-0-7603-2794-4

101 Performance Projects For Your
BMW 3 Series 1982–2000
143386AP • 978-0-7603-2695-4

Honda CRF Performance Handbook
140448AP • 978-0-7603-2409-7

Autocross Performance Handbook
144201AP • 978-0-7603-2788-3

Mazda Miata MX-5
Find It. Fix It. Trick It.
144205AP • 978-0-7603-2792-0

Four-Wheeler's Bible
135120AP • 978-0-7603-1056-4

How to Build a Hot Rod
135773AP • 978-0-7603-1304-6

How to Restore Your Collector Car
128080AP • 978-0-7603-0592-8

101 Projects for Your
Corvette 1984–1996
136314AP • 978-0-7603-1461-6

How to Rebuild Corvette Rolling
Chassis 1963–1982
144467AP • 978-0-7603-3014-2

How to Restore Your Motorcycle
130002AP • 978-0-7603-0681-9

101 Sportbike
Performance Projects
135742AP • 978-0-7603-1331-2

How to Restore and Maintain You
Vespa Motorscooter
128936AP • 978-0-7603-0623-9

How to Build a Pro Streetbike
140440AP • 978-0-7603-2450-9

101 Harley-Davidson Evolution
Performance Projects
139849AP • 978-0-7603-2085-3

101 Harley-Davidson Twin Cam
Performance Projects
136265AP • 978-0-7603-1639-9

Harley-Davidson Sportster
Performance Handbook,
3rd Edition
140293AP • 978-0-7603-2353-3

Motorcycle Electrical Systems
Troubleshooting and Repair
144121AP • 978-0-7603-2716-6

Visit www.motorbooks.com